D1714102

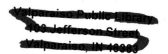

Men Who Batter

Men Who Batter

NANCY NASON-CLARK

AND

BARBARA FISHER-TOWNSEND

OXFORD
UNIVERSITY PRESS

OXFORD
UNIVERSITY PRESS

Oxford University Press is a department of the University of Oxford.
It furthers the University's objective of excellence in research,
scholarship, and education by publishing worldwide.

Oxford   New York
Auckland   Cape Town   Dar es Salaam   Hong Kong   Karachi
Kuala Lumpur   Madrid   Melbourne   Mexico City   Nairobi
New Delhi   Shanghai   Taipei   Toronto

With offices in
Argentina   Austria   Brazil   Chile   Czech Republic   France   Greece
Guatemala   Hungary   Italy   Japan   Poland   Portugal   Singapore
South Korea   Switzerland   Thailand   Turkey   Ukraine   Vietnam

Oxford is a registered trademark of Oxford University Press
in the UK and certain other countries.

Published in the United States of America by
Oxford University Press
198 Madison Avenue, New York, NY 10016

© Oxford University Press 2015

Library of Congress Cataloging-in-Publication Data
Nason-Clark, Nancy, 1956–
Men who batter / Nancy Nason-Clark and Barbara Fisher-Townsend.
   pages cm.—(Interpersonal violence)
Includes bibliographical references and index.
ISBN 978–0–19–935186–2 (alk. paper)
1. Abusive men.   2. Spousal abuse.   3. Intimate partner violence.
4. Church work with abusive men.   I. Fisher-Townsend, Barbara.   II. Title.
HV6626.N37 2015
362.82'92—dc23
2014016874

9 8 7 6 5 4 3 2 1
Printed in the United States of America
on acid-free paper

Dedicated to those who want to live differently tomorrow from how they do today and to those who walk alongside them on that journey

CONTENTS

You are about to read some amazing stories—stories of pain, of abandonment, of brutality, of neglect, and of cruelty. At times, you will wonder what makes someone treat someone else this way.

You will also read some amazing stories of strength in the face of tremendous obstacles. This might cause you to feel grateful for your own life circumstances or troubled that the playing field of our world is so uneven.

You will also read about the amazing number of people who walk alongside those who suffer the devastating consequences of violence. Here you will be challenged to see that it takes untold resources—fiscal and personnel—to respond with justice, compassion, and best practices in the aftermath of battery.

As you read our book, you will be confronted with the words *men who batter* used to describe their life experiences—such as stories of their childhoods, of their adolescent years, of becoming fathers at an early age, of drug and alcohol abuse, of being arrested and charged for domestic violence, of their experiences in prison, or of trying to get their lives back on track. You may find that their stories cause emotions to rise deep within you.

Our lives are also made up of stories. In fact, stories reach around the world. As children, we hear many stories that begin with "Once upon a time" and end with "And they lived happily ever after." Barbara Fisher-Townsend sometimes tells students her own story of growing up in an affluent home in Montreal with an alcoholic, abusive father and a mother who stayed with him for more than thirty years before she found the strength and resources to leave. Nancy Nason-Clark uses the RAVE (Religion and Violence E-learning) website to tell the Stained Glass Story of Domestic Violence, based on her many years of research into violence that strikes close to home.

We also have stories that arise out of the fieldwork for this book—the funny things we have witnessed in the years of doing the work, the sadness and angst we have felt at the end of a day of interviewing ten or more men who batter, exhilaration about the importance of the research that we have experienced after meeting a group of dedicated shelter workers, and the heart-wrenching stories of survivors related to the impact of violence on their children.

We have had awkward moments such as when a man in a focus group asked Nancy, "When was the last time you allowed your daughter to live on the street?" We had funny moments—and there were far too few of these—such as the time

Nancy was asked to stand inside the lines of a parking space to hold that space for one of the religious superstars who was speaking at a domestic violence conference and would only agree to arrive at the site moments before he was to be ushered onstage to speak. Another funny moment was when Barb was driving and Nancy was sitting in the passenger's seat with a "famous" DV speaker in the back, bringing him from the airport to a conference we had helped to organize. As we were cruising along the highway, he was complaining about how much travel he was doing, complaining about Barb's driving, and complaining about faith-based folk. He was writing some notes on the back of an envelope before his talk, a talk for which he had been paid a princely sum.

Many people made this research possible, including those who worked at the agencies where we collected data and those who ensured that the welcome mat was laid out when we arrived to conduct our fieldwork. Nancy would like to acknowledge with gratefulness the Louisville Institute for the Study of Protestantism and American Culture for its funding for the interviews with batterers and a grant from the Lilly Endowment that enabled us to explore the broader coordinated community response to domestic violence. Funding from the Social Sciences and Humanities Research Council, the Lawson Foundation, Status of Women Canada, a Fichter Award, a Constant Jacquet Award, and other smaller grants from various organizations, including the Muriel McQueen Fergusson Foundation, made the work reported in this book possible.

From Nancy: I have worked with a fantastic team of graduate students and colleagues over the years at the University of New Brunswick, including Lori Beaman, Catherine Holtmann, Christy Hoyt, Tracy McDonald, Charlotte McIntosh, Steve McMullin, Lois Mitchell, Lanette Ruff, Michelle Spencer-Arsenault, and Amanda Steeves. These are women and men who have played an important part in some phase of the research process or in the accounting of its funding. There are also many others to thank, colleagues who work elsewhere who have joined me on my academic journey through the years of this project: David Currie, Janet Jacobs, Otto Maduro, Mary Jo Neitz, Julie Owens, Irene Sevcik, Jim Spickard, Ken Swetland, and Kendra Yoder, to name but a few. On a personal note, I wish to acknowledge the tremendous support of Dr. David Clark, my life partner, a clinical psychologist and prolific scholar of anxiety disorders and depression who completed his own trade book, *The Mood Repair Toolkit*, as I was writing the last few chapters of *Men Who Batter*. Our two daughters—Natascha and Christina—offer me a richer, more fulfilled life than I ever thought possible, along with Jaron, Natascha's husband, who now seems like a son. Living a life full of peace and safety at home has always been a blessing for me, but I am even more grateful for it now than ever before.

From Barb: I have thoroughly enjoyed the experience of working alongside Nancy for so many years and in particular on this project. I wish to add my thanks to Nancy's to all of those people who were so supportive and helpful throughout our research process. I feel as if I have made some lifelong friends and valuable acquaintances. Having grown up in a home where violence and anger were present on a daily basis, I found this work especially meaningful. For more than forty years, I have had unwavering support and love from my husband, law professor David Townsend. Marrying him changed the course of my life in a positive way.

Together, we are grateful to Dana Bliss of Oxford University Press and to other staff who assisted in various roles, including Agnes Bannigan, Wendy Keebler, Simon Benjamin and N. Shyam Krishnan. We express our gratitude to the Series Editors, Claire Renzetti and Jeffrey L. Edleson, for including *Men Who Batter* in their Interpersonal Violence Series and for the anonymous reviewers who offered great support and helpful suggestions.

Men Who Batter

Introduction

Men who act abusively have their own stories to tell, journeys that often begin in childhood, ripen in their teenage years, and take them down paths they were hoping never to travel. *Men Who Batter* recounts the journey from the points of view of the men themselves.

The stories of the men and the snapshots of their journeys are based on many years of fieldwork. We focus primarily on personal interviews with fifty-five men connected to one batterer intervention group. Most of the men we interviewed had been incarcerated at some point for domestic violence, and we reinterviewed many every six months, four or five times. In essence, the book captures moments, memories, and details associated with the stories of men who batter told by the very men who have done so.

We explore the men's accounts of their lives within a broader framework of the agency through which they attended the batterer intervention groups and the regional coordinated community response to domestic violence, which includes criminal justice workers (e.g., probation, parole, judges) and those who staff shelters and work in advocacy. Based on interview data with this wide array of professionals, we are able to examine how one community, located in the state of Oregon, responds to men who batter.

HOW IT ALL BEGAN

Writing this book has been a journey for us, too—and often an emotional one. It began almost ten years ago, when I (Nancy Nason-Clark) applied for a research grant to study men who were abusive to their partners. For many years, I had been researching women whose lives had been affected by domestic violence and analyzing various components of the coordinated community response to abuse. I heard many women say, "If only he would seek help . . ." The assumption underlying this plea was that if a partner who acted abusively sought assistance and was accepted into an intervention program, he could and would change.

When the project began, Barbara Fisher-Townsend joined my research team as a doctoral student. Later she worked with me on a postdoctoral fellowship, and we have continued to collaborate ever since. For five years, we were totally immersed in the fieldwork—every six months, we traveled to the agency, observed group meetings, interviewed men individually and in focus-group settings, talked to workers, attended staff meetings, held focus groups or interviewed workers in community-based agencies, participated in activities of the broader domestic violence community, observed courtroom proceedings, and learned as much as we could about men who batter and those who seek to assist them (and their families) in the aftermath of violence.

We were not new to the study of domestic violence when we began this research project. For many years, Barb had taught courses in the criminal justice field, and my first project on child sexual assault had taken place almost twenty-five years ago. We knew a fair bit about intimate partner violence and abuse in the family setting when we designed the project. But we had never worked directly with men who had been abusive, and we had yet to hear their own stories—how their lives unfolded, the struggles they had endured, the broader context in which violence played a crucial part, and the journey of life in the aftermath of the abuse.

Like other social scientists researching abuse in the family setting, we knew of the statistics, the very high rates of violence that have been documented by large organizations such as the World Health Organization or the United Nations. Many governments also collect statistics on their own populations. In our 2010 book, *No Place for Abuse*, Catherine Clark Kroeger and I presented statistics from around the world that led to one overwhelming conclusion: violence against women in intimate relationships occurs in every country, and between one in three and one in four women at some time in their lives have been victims of it.

Data on domestic violence have been mounting; violence happens in all kinds of families and is no respecter of socioeconomic status or ethnic background or religious persuasion. We have been particularly interested in what happens when abuse strikes families that are very religious. In three different edited collections, we have sought to give voice to some of the issues surrounding abuse in families of deep faith.[1]

So while we were not strangers to researching family violence, we were relative newcomers to understanding the story of abuse from the perspective of the abuser. We understood that violence was not based on ethnic background, wealth or poverty, sexual orientation, education, occupation, or country of origin, although sometimes these factors were comorbid with the presence of abuse. We knew that children who were raised in homes that were abusive carried a greater possibility of future perpetration of violence or of victimization.

We had researched some of the factors to account for why Christian women stayed longer with violent partners. We knew that many religious leaders were ill informed about domestic violence and that, as a result, many women of faith were disappointed after they sought help from congregational sources.

Yet we believed that the journey of faith was an important component in understanding domestic violence for women who were religious. We knew that there were very few faith-based services for responding to domestic violence and that there was reluctance on the part of both sacred and secular workers to suggest one another as referral sources when violence struck families of faith.

We felt the broad skepticism among community-based workers in the domestic violence field toward faith-based agencies that wished to become part of any solution to domestic violence. We understood well that some religious people were very naive about rates of changed behavior related to those who had been abusive and sometimes dismissive of the rates of violence among families in congregational life.

We understood that religious people would sometimes use the Bible and religious language to justify the abuse they meted out to their intimate partners and/or their children. To our horror, we knew that religious women often used the Bible and religious language to justify their own personal suffering as victims of male violence. But we also knew that religion offered the language of healing, of hope, and of change.

We had read enough of the scholarly literature to understand that there were numerous intervention and treatment models for responding to batterers and that it was extremely difficult to assess the various programs' ability to help men change. We knew that collaboration between staff and between agencies offered increased potential for calling those who were violent to justice and to accountability.

But there were several things we did not know:

1. Whether the violated women who put their trust in programs that might help their husbands change had any reason for optimism.
2. Whether a faith-based agency could work well with other community-based agencies and professionals in helping men who were abusive.
3. Whether men in faith-based programs for batterers used religious language to talk about their violence and their experiences with intervention, justice, and accountability.
4. Whether men who battered would be willing to talk about their faith and other aspects of their lives.
5. Whether those workers who walked alongside the men who battered believed they were making any difference in the work they did.
6. Whether the men who were abusive would be willing to offer us a window into their life stories, over time, through many interviews.
7. Whether researching the stories of men who were abusive would alter our understanding of domestic violence and have an impact on us personally.

PREPARING FOR THE FIELDWORK

The planning phase for the research took many months, and during that time, we learned in particular the deep mistrust that some who work in advocacy have toward those who are interested in understanding the stories of men who batter. We also experienced again the skepticism that so many harbor toward people whose lives are informed, in part, by a faith perspective or by practices imbued with religious significance. That we were interested in men who batter and matters of faith seemed odd, misguided, or downright dangerous to some in the research field.

The research on which this book is based draws it data from three primary sources, supplemented by six additional research projects. These are outlined in the Methodology Appendices at the end of the book. We have chosen to place the stories of the fifty-five men we interviewed as the central core of the story we tell. Most of the men were interviewed many times over a four-year period, with intervals of six months between interviews. We held a further five focus groups (of between five and twenty men each). During the last five years, we have conducted a large number of interviews, and held an even larger number of conversations, with those who work with men who batter. The details of specific projects, including the interview guides, can also be found in the appendices.

Along with this rich and colorful portrayal of the journeys of abusive men, we bring twenty years of fieldwork with survivors and those who walk alongside them as they seek safety, healing, and wholeness for themselves and their children. Women who have been victimized by the men they love often hold out hope that if only their abusers could be held accountable and receive intervention, the violence would stop, and their own lives would improve dramatically as a result. This is especially true for women of deep religious faith.

Over the years, we have been interested in the way faith leaders understand domestic violence and respond to those families affected by it. One of us (Nancy) has carried out many studies that investigate the role of congregations and their leaders regarding abuse in families of faith, more recently focusing on how seminaries are responding to the challenge of equipping their students to assist both victims and perpetrators. One of us (Barb) has been immersed for many years in understanding the criminal justice response to violence against women.

While the main purpose of *Men Who Batter* is to highlight the stories of men, told from their personal points of view, this is countered by reality checks from their own case files and those professionals who have worked with them. Yet *Men Who Batter* is also a story of how professionals in the criminal justice system and those working in mandated batterer intervention programs (such as STOP, the faith-based, state-certified program where we met the men) understand their work and interpret its consequences. And finally, interspersed within these pages is another theme: finding religious faith or spiritual activity amid the chaos created by violence perpetrated at home.

Most chapters will begin with an opening narrative based on the story of one man, told over the course of many interviews, spanning several years. Using his own words as much as possible (presented in italics), the narrative will direct the reader to the subject matter of the chapter. Key features of the story will then be assessed against the backdrop of the other men who were interviewed and the other data we collected from case files, interviews, focus groups, and observations. Each chapter's emerging themes will be interpreted against the growing published literature on domestic violence, the response of the criminal justice system, and intervention programs. As we examine the challenges posed by the men's lives as they tell about them, there will be a brief commentary that seeks to ask how religious faith fits into the picture. Interestingly, most of the men whose lives we seek to describe talk freely—albeit intermittently—about God, faith, and their spiritual quests.

During the many years of working on this particular project, we have moved through stages of optimism and pessimism, times when the voices of survivors (within our minds) drowned out the voices of their abusers and many more times when the web of vulnerability seems to cover abuser and abused alike. We suspect our readers will also find themselves puzzled, disappointed, encouraged, surprised, and challenged as they sift through the various lenses to consider the stories of men who act abusively and those who attempt to hold them accountable.

It is a story of human vulnerability, of the pain and despair that abuse creates for everyone, of the long and arduous journey toward justice and all the hard work needed to enhance the possibility that accountability will be created within the life of a man who has battered (or batters) his intimate partner, his children, or other family members. By the end of the book, we hope readers will feel as if they know some of the men, understand some of their struggles, and appreciate some of their dreams and, like us, will be rooting for them to succeed. Abuse will only be eradicated when men who batter alter their thinking and their behavior.

WHAT IS ABUSE?

"I am not violent . . . but . . . ." These are often the first words spoken by a man who is being interviewed by an intake worker, a therapist, a police officer, or a researcher in connection with the violent behavior that has brought him into contact with either the criminal justice system or a program designed to overcome his controlling, abusive ways. At first blush, this seems like a naive attempt on the part of a man who batters to redirect the focus of the conversation away from his behavior to the treatment he has received at the hands of others, sometimes, but not always, including the woman he has hurt. For the most part, men who have acted abusively do not believe that they are violent men.

Throughout this book, we try to unpack this paradox. What do they have to tell us about their lives that might hold clues for those of us interested in understanding issues of violence that strike at home? How does a man who has been found guilty of domestic violence begin to narrate his own story of contact with the criminal justice system and the long shadow of the law that follows his life as a consequence?

Men who are violent compare themselves with other men. Most often, they do not compare themselves with men who treat women well—as equals—at home, at work, or in social contexts. They compare themselves with men who have been *more* violent than they have been. Their comparison group includes men who have served more time in prison, men who show no remorse for the harm they have caused, or men who do not care whether they ever reunite with their children. In large measure, they compare their own perceptions of the wrongs they have done and the harm they have caused by situating their attitudes, and, more important, their behavior and its motivation, against a backdrop of other men they have met at group, at work, in the bar, or in prison. Using this yardstick for measurement, they seem not so bad, or that is the conclusion they believe and communicate to others and to us.

It is interesting that in listening to the stories or reading the files of men who have acted abusively, there are regular references to "being a victim." Other researchers have also noted this: whether that means being a victim of his female partner's violence (Jennings and Murphy 2000), a victim of the system (Henning and Holdford 2006), a victim of his childhood (Tilley and Brackley 2005), or a victim of his addictions (Humphreys et al. 2005). Correspondingly, other researchers have argued that this kind of *victimization thinking* clouds the ability of many men ever to admit to any kind of control issues in their own lives.

At the beginning, most men are very surprised that they have been caught in the act of violence and resentful that their behavior toward an intimate partner or other family member has resulted in sanctions by the criminal justice system and a series of restrictions and costs for them in the years to follow. Resentment is a virus that grows in the lives of many of the men whose stories are about to unfold throughout this book.

Yet most men's inability to see themselves as violent at the beginning of their relationship with a batterer intervention program should not surprise us. Victims, too, have difficulty seeing themselves as battered women. Many years ago, we were presenting our research at a conference where we became acquainted with the work of Julie Owens, a nationally recognized trainer for shelter workers, herself a survivor whose husband served prison time for attempting to murder both her and her pastor father. She recounts calling a domestic violence shelter in Hawaii after hearing a radio advertisement for a support group for battered wives close to where she was living. She wanted to attend the group but was concerned that she did not qualify: "I am not a battered wife ... but my husband tried to kill me" (Owens 2011).

How one sees one's story, then, as a victim or as a perpetrator, is clouded by the group with which one makes comparisons. For the men in our study, it took many weeks of coming to group before they were willing even to entertain that they were, or had been, violent. This is despite the fact that almost all of them had been processed by the criminal justice system for the violence they had meted out to intimate partners or to other family members. They understood they had been caught in the act, but they could not see, at least in the early days of program attendance, that they were men who battered.

Defining abuse would seem to be straightforward, but it is not. Working with criminal justice, therapeutic, advocacy, and religious professionals in four locations (three in the United States, one in Canada), we developed an interactive website (www.theraveproject.com) that highlights several features related to the prevalence and severity of abuse and offers interactive resources and online training that might assist those who walk alongside families who are impacted by it. Readers interested in a fuller description can access the website, using the URL above, and click on the tab labeled "FAQs." This will take them to a drop-down menu of ten questions, including: "How common is abuse in intimate relationships?" "Why don't women leave men who abuse them?" "Why do men hurt the women they claim to love?" "How are children impacted?"

On the website, we define abuse as behavior that shatters dreams and causes pain. We note that sometimes abuse involves physical violence, such as hitting, kicking, or choking, and sometimes it involves name-calling or harsh words that are meant to hurt. Abuse can involve limiting or denying access to food, money, or other family resources. And sometimes abuse involves demands for sexual activity. But abuse always involves responses that are meant to control, shame, or humiliate another person through intimacy and shared experience. While women are its most common victims, at least in heterosexual relationships, both women and men can be victims, and sometimes both are. To be certain, peace and safety for all family members cannot exist when abuse is present.

HOW COMMON IS ABUSE?

The simple answer is that it depends. It depends on a variety of factors, including geographic location, culture, age group, and gender, to name a few. Between 2000 and 2005 in Canada, for example, 653,000 women reported being victims of spousal violence, with 26 percent of these women having been assaulted more than ten times. Statistics also show that younger age poses a higher risk, with women between the ages of fifteen and twenty-four reporting the highest one-year rates of spousal violence. Canada's Aboriginal women are also more likely to experience violence; in fact, they are three times more likely to be victims of spousal violence than non-Aboriginal women (Statistics Canada 2009a).

In the United States, the Centers for Disease Control and Prevention (CDC) report that nearly 5.3 million incidents of interpersonal violence occur each year among women ages eighteen and older, resulting in nearly 2 million injuries and 1,300 deaths nationwide every year. In 2000, intimate partner homicides accounted for 33.5 percent of the murders of women and 4 percent of the murders of men (Bureau of Justice Statistics 2007). On their website, the CDC report that among victims of intimate partner violence, about one in four women and one in seven men have experienced severe physical violence by an intimate partner (e.g., hit with a fist or something hard, beaten, slammed against something) at some point in their lifetime (see also Migliaccio 2002). This has led Howard Spivak, the director of violence prevention at the CDC, to state: "Intimate partner violence, rape, stalking—all of these forms of violence can create toxic stress on the body that is long-lasting and cumulative, and can negatively impact a person's health and well-being for the rest of their life" http://www.cdc.gov/violenceprevention/ nisvs/index.html.

So although "it depends," the numbers are alarmingly high worldwide. In fact, in every country of the world where data have been collected, the evidence is over-whelming: large numbers of women suffer physical violence from the men with whom they share intimacy and residence (Kroeger and Nason-Clark 2010).

UNDERSTANDING THE DYNAMICS OF ABUSE

Since the 1970s, the once very private problem of violence against women in the home has been recognized as a public issue (Dobash, Dobash, Cavanagh and Lewis 2000), and the literature on this issue has been growing. Population surveys to determine the prevalence of abuse have been conducted (Ellsberg et al. 2001; Straus and Kantor 1994), and narratives of victims/survivors have been examined (Kulkarni, Bell, and Rhodes 2012; Simmons et al. 2011). Other researchers have identified characteristics or developed typologies of abusive men (Dalton 2001; Panchanadeswaran et al. 2010) or examined the responses of the criminal justice system (Gondolf 2002; Ursel, Tutty, and LeMaistre 2008) or programs for male batterers (Gondolf 2002; Nason-Clark et al. 2003; Gerlock 2001).

Control is a central feature of abusive behavior. Abusive men attempt to control what happens at home and in the lives of their wives and children. They often feel a sense of entitlement to services and emotional support from the women they love. When they believe they are not getting what they deserve, they use power and con-trol to punish their partners or to achieve or maintain dominance. Sometimes men who act abusively were violated as children or watched their fathers hurt their moth-ers. Others suffer from low self-esteem or struggle with addictions.

Fear is the most common response of women to violence in their intimate rela-tionships. This fear sometimes takes the form of concern that the abuse could esca-late and fear of reprisal should the woman disclose her suffering to someone else. Economic dependence is a key factor for many victims, and other women cling to the promises uttered by an abuser shortly after his violent outburst, when he is tem-porarily remorseful for the havoc he has created.

Religious women are more likely than other victims of abuse to believe that they must stay in the marriage no matter what the cost; they also often minimize its impact on their children (Nason-Clark and Kroeger 2004). Conservative Protestant women sometimes believe that abuse is their personal "cross to bear" (Sevcik et al. forthcoming). Others lack support systems that would enable them to leave their abusive partners. For Aboriginal women in Canada, immigrant women, and especially African American women in the United States, the fear of incarceration of their partners deters them from calling 911 for help or fleeing a violent home. Faith traditions are sometimes guilty of encouraging women to return to relationships— even violent ones—after being offered advice that their own altered behavior will lead to a cessation of the abuse (Nason-Clark 2014).

Various theories about causes or conditions that lead to abuse have been identified (Brownridge and Halli 2001; Yllö 2005; Worden and Carlson 2005). From the perspective of a patriarchal framework, these causes generally fall under the rubric of "the social control of women" and "males maintaining dominance."

Bilodeau (1990, 48) states: "A man who exhibits violence verbally, psychologically, physically, sexually or financially toward his partner is not losing self-control; on the contrary, he is affirming his power, which he wants to preserve at all costs and which makes him neither monstrous nor sick. If he abuses his wife, it is because he has the privilege and the means to do so."

Loue (2001) argues that men's accounts of their violence differ depending on the audience, accounts that often consist of either outright denial or providing justification for the behavior. The deviance literature, historically, has referred to this as "techniques of neutralization," whereby those in conflict with the law may deny responsibility, deny injury, blame the victim, condemn the condemners, and/or appeal to higher loyalties (Sykes and Matza 1957). Ptacek (1996) examines the ways batterers perceive their violence, arguing that they cite loss of control and engage in victim blaming by claiming provocation. He further notes that abusive men argue that their wives failed to fulfil the "obligations of a good wife" (p. 106). Eighteen of the women in his research identified "preventing women from separating" as the motive for their partners' violence.

In our earlier research at a batterer intervention program in the state of Washington, we found that more than 20 percent of the men in the study admitted to the following behaviors in their relationships with their intimate partners: pushing, restraining, grabbing to prevent leaving, punching holes in walls, pounding/ slamming on a table, hitting with an open hand, slapping, shaking, gripping to prevent leaving, punching with a fist, throwing objects at or near their partners, blocking, raising their voices, destroying family property or vehicles, choking, kicking, and bumping (Nason-Clark et al. 2003).[2] These are behaviors that the men personally admitted to on the intake form. Other researchers have emphasized the tendency of men to minimize or deny their violence (Wood 2004; Dutton 1998; Pence and Paymar 1986), and some argue that batterer self-reports even grossly deny and minimize the reports of women who have been abused (Bograd 1988; Yllö 1988; Heckert and Gondolf 2000). Indeed, in that earlier file analysis, we found that most men rationalized, minimized, or legitimized their use of violence when providing the details of the incidents that resulted in them coming to the treatment program. Despite these explanations, the police reports found in the files indicated otherwise.

ABUSERS AND CHANGE

Some men who have acted abusively are determined to alter their violent ways and seek, with the support of the wider community, to change their behavior. Over the years of working in the area of domestic violence, we have interacted with clergy, therapists, advocates, and others who walk alongside families affected by abuse and who worked together with large numbers in our collaborative RAVE (Religion and Violence e-Learning) initiative. Additionally, we have met hundreds of men and women who do this work, through conferences, workshops, day seminars, and other forms of training in which we have been involved. Most of them know a few men who have changed, and that gives them hope in carrying on the work that they feel is important to do. The vast majority of abusers, it seems, according to what workers say in public contexts and over coffee and in question periods after training events, do not appear to leave their violent ways behind, at least over the longer haul.

Yet many abusive partners promise to change, and some even use religious language in an attempt to convince their wives, probation officers, pastors, or facilitators in a batterer intervention program that they are new men. Victims tell an important part of this story of change. They are the ones who are able to judge whether their partners are changing. Abusers' statements that give abuse victims cause for hope include "I understand why you were frightened of me." Abusers' statements that worry abuse victims include "I said I was sorry. What more do you want?" It is common for abusers to be apologetic after being abusive. But there are concrete ways to demonstrate change that involve more than saying "I'm sorry."[3]

SURVIVOR EMPHASIS ON TREATMENT/INTERVENTION

Batterer intervention is the process of confronting abusers who use power to coerce, control, and engender fear in their intimate partners. Intervention programs focus on ending the violence, and in order to do this, they must move men to the point of feeling empathy for the victims and accepting responsibility, in addition to becoming accountable, for their thoughts and actions.

With increasing frequency, the courts are referring men convicted of domestic abuse to intervention programs, thus indicating a level of confidence in their effectiveness (Bennett and Williams 2002). Such programs also offer hope for changed behavior in their abusers to the women victims who want the violence to stop but may not want to end the relationships (Horton and Williamson 1988; Timmins 1995).

Women who are survivors of intimate partner violence are looking for hope—hope that the violence will end and that they and their children can live peaceful family lives; they often also hope for reconciliation with their partners. They therefore place a great deal of trust in the ability of batterer intervention programs to effect change in their partners. Whether their confidence is ill placed or not is far from clear. What is clear is that as a society, we must do everything possible to make every home a safe home.

THE LEGACY OF RESEARCHING VIOLENCE IN FAMILIES OF FAITH

In a few short pages, it is not possible to condense more than twenty years of field-work and public engagement on domestic violence and religion. But it has had a deep impact on our understandings of the issues and the problems facing those who work in this area. We offer readers an overview of some of our studies and insights, with references for those who want to delve into the findings more fully.

- Based on survey data collected from Protestant clergy (n = 343; response rate 70 percent), we have documented that the majority of ministers are called on several times a year to respond to women who are being abused by their current husbands/partners, men who have acted abusively toward their wives/partners, or adults who are coping with issues of abuse from their past (Nason-Clark 1997; Kroeger and Nason-Clark 2010).
- Personal interviews with a sample of one hundred Protestant clergy explored the many ways clergy attempt to assist families where violence is present, offering assistance for both victims and perpetrators. While there was scant evidence that ministers dismissed victims' calls for help or minimized the need for safety for the women and their children, these religious leaders were not aware of the dynamics of abuse and were often manipulated by the abusers (Nason-Clark 2000; Nason-Clark 2001; Kroeger, Nason-Clark, and Fisher-Townsend 2008).
- Focus groups with women conducted in thirty congregations (n = 247) revealed that religious women suffering abuse who look to their pastors for help in its aftermath are often disappointed with the assistance they receive. They reported that their pastors had limited awareness and understanding of abuse, coupled with very little knowledge of local community-based resources to assist them. Moreover, their religious leaders seemed unable, or unwilling, to offer them help of an explicitly religious nature—the primary reason women sought their assistance in the first place (Nason-Clark 1998a; Nason-Clark and Kroeger 2004).
- Based on quantitative and qualitative data from clergy of many denominations (n = 550+), we have learned that there is great reluctance to refer abused women and other family members who seek the help of religious leaders to other professionals in the community or community-based agencies. Among those pastors who have little or no training, the reluctance to refer is greatest (Nason-Clark 1998b; Nason-Clark 2008).
- Fewer than one in ten pastors feel well equipped to respond to situations involving domestic violence (Kroeger and Nason-Clark 2001). Data collected at four seminaries from more than three hundred students reveal that seminarians also report both a lack of preparedness and some anxiety about their perceived inability to respond to families where violence is present (McMullin and Nason-Clark 2013).
- Church women offer one another an amazing social support network within their congregation or faith connections. Substantial numbers of church women have offered assistance to abused women they know; many

have provided in-kind or financial contributions to their communities'
battered women's shelters (Beaman-Hall and Nason-Clark 1997;
Beaman and Nason-Clark 1999; Nason-Clark 1995; Nason-Clark 2001;
Nason-Clark and Fisher-Townsend 2005).

- When clergy preach a message condemning family violence, discuss abuse
  in their premarital counseling, offer support, make referral suggestions,
  and give ongoing encouragement to women who have been battered, the
  evidence reveals that its impact is profound (Fisher-Townsend et al. 2008;
  Nason-Clark et al. 2011; Nason-Clark 2005).
- A small project involving ten church youth groups and their youth leaders
  in which data were collected on the help-seeking behavior of young
  men and women of faith revealed the important role of youth pastors in
  identifying and responding to issues of violence in the family and in dating
  relationships.[4]
- There is a tremendous need to build bridges between churches and
  community agencies on the issue of abuse. Mistrust between churches
  and transition houses, and other community-based resources continues,
  yet evidence reveals that initiatives to foster collaboration can be
  successful (Nason-Clark et al. 2013; Kroeger, Nason-Clark, and Fisher-
  Townsend 2008).

THEORETICAL FRAMING FOR UNDERSTANDING MEN
WHO BATTER

We situate our book on men who batter within five primary research conversations
that occur in the literature. As the book unfolds, it will become clearer how these
research areas, their findings and conclusions, and the ongoing controversies they
discuss and to which they contribute have affected our thinking. We build on the
work of many scholars in a variety of disciplines and are indebted to them for the
intellectual curiosity, the research skills, and the passion they bring to their work
and to their publications.

Criminal Justice Response to Intimate Partner Violence

Historically, the abuse of women by their intimate partners has been condoned
(e.g., "rule of thumb" law; see Lentz 1999), ignored, treated as a "private" issue,
and generally not taken seriously (Hirschel and Hutchison 2001; Epstein, Bell, and
Goodman 2003). While the women's movement of the 1960s and '70s was quite
successful in bringing this issue out from "behind closed doors" (Straus, Gelles, and
Steinmetz 1980) and into the "public" domain, attitudes of officials within the criminal justice system have not advanced sufficiently to ensure fair and equal treatment
of women victimized by intimate partner abuse (Erez and Belknap 1998; Stephens
and Sinden 2000). As Hirschel and Hutchison (1998, 2; cited in Hartman and
Belknap 2003) argue, "[Like the police], prosecutors have not traditionally been
overly zealous about pursuing cases against domestic violence offenders." Judicial
decision-making continues to rely on stereotypes based on patriarchal ideology

and on traditional notions of marriage, family, and femininity (Crocker 2005), and the best predictor of case outcome is still the extent to which the judge believes the woman was the instigator (Cassidy and Trafimow 2002). Additionally, Sheehy (1999) argues that women are not in a position of substantive equality in society and before the courts because they have not reached a state in which they are seen as equally credible and are certainly not equally free of violent assault.

For all these reasons, until about twenty years ago, the criminal justice responses to wife abuse, in both Canada and the United States, were wholly inadequate. However, within the last two decades, there have been positive signs of change, and some innovative programs are currently under way. As community interest in this serious and pervasive crime against women has grown and intervention programs have become more available (McFarlane et al. 2000), the responses of the criminal justice system in North America have improved.

The enormity of this crime has required various strategies of intervention by the criminal justice system in Canada and the United States, involving the police, prosecutors and their supportive infrastructure, the judicial system, and legislative bodies (Loue and Maschke 2001). New programs, policies, and procedures have been developed, yet some are not without controversy.

Police departments throughout North America have implemented programs of mandatory arrest for domestic violence. In the United States, by 2008, there were twenty-two states that mandated arrest in cases of intimate partner violence (National Institute of Justice 2008). In Canada, every jurisdiction now has pro-charging policies in place, whereby charges are brought in cases of spousal violence if there are reasonable and probable grounds to believe that abuse has taken place (Statistics Canada 2005). Pro-charging is meant to increase the number of charges brought, increase reporting of incidents of spousal abuse, reduce reoffending (Ad Hoc Federal-Provincial-Territorial Working Group 2003), give recognition to the seriousness of spousal abuse as a serious social problem, and work toward protecting individual victims (Brown 2000).

Research and discussion continue on the possibilities and problems related to mandatory arrest. Groundbreaking research by Sherman and Berk (1984) showed a decrease in recidivism when men were arrested. Other research has not been so definitive. While some researchers conclude that mandatory arrest may reduce subsequent violent behavior or may have no effect (Sherman and Smith 1992), others argue that it is effective only for those who have sufficient investment in the community so as to create embarrassment or discrediting (Thistlewaite, Wooldredge, and Gibbs 1998). There are also arguments that arrest does not work for men who are repeat offenders and that it may, in fact, increase the violence of certain men (Chalk and King 1998). This inconsistency in research results has led the National Academy of Sciences (Garner and Maxwell 2000; Maxwell, Garner, and Fagan 2002) to conclude that arrest in all misdemeanor cases will not on average produce a discernible effect on misdemeanor spouse assault. Alarmingly, recent research by Hirschel and Buzawa (2013) found that men who simply fled the scene of the crime were five times less likely to be arrested by the police, even though they were often involved in more serious cases of abuse, indicating a lack of commitment to mandatory arrest by police.

Another factor that affects arrest and its deterrent effect on recidivism is bringing charges. Ames and Dunham (2002) report on research they conducted in

Clinton County, New York. They note that the county district attorney's office was strongly pro-prosecution in domestic violence cases, yet only 100 to 150 prosecutions resulted from approximately 800 to 1,000 domestic incident reports filed yearly. Canadian numbers are somewhat more optimistic, based on UCR2[5] data reported by the Ad Hoc Federal-Provincial-Territorial Working Group Reviewing Spousal Abuse Policies and Legislation (2003). They found that charges were brought in 82 percent of spousal abuse incidents reported to police; in 13 percent of cases, police did not bring charges at the request of the victim; in 3 percent of cases, police used their own discretion, and charges were not brought. Aggressive prosecution policies have followed aggressive arrest policies, with no-drop prosecution policies becoming a trend (Hanna 1996; Buzawa and Buzawa 2003; Berliner 2003). However, research on no-drop prosecution indicates only limited support for the policy. Although Rebovich (1996) states that in a survey of large US jurisdictions, 66 percent of prosecutors' offices advised that they had a no-drop policy, Denham and Gillespie (1999) report that in Toronto, police are bringing more charges, but an equally increasing number of charges are being withdrawn in the prosecution phase. Reasons posited for this withdrawal include the notion that court professionals view domestic violence as a victimless crime because public order is not affected or because domestic violence victims and offenders are seen as "mutually combative" (Hartman and Belknap 2003). There is also often an assumption of reluctant or uncooperative victims guiding prosecutorial decision-making (Buzawa et al. 1992). Several other negative outcomes of no-drop prosecution policies have been identified, including reduced conviction rates, increased case backlogs, and increased victim dissatisfaction (Smith 2000). Additionally, no-drop policies are criticized as disempowering women who may seek to dismiss charges in order to pursue remedies regarded as more suitable to their circumstances (Davis, Smith, and Nickles 1998).

One unexpected consequence of mandatory arrest policies has been an increase in the number of females being arrested along with their partners. This may result from police being unable to determine a primary aggressor—in cases where there may be, for example, minor injuries to each party but no weapons or witnesses, where the victim is protecting the aggressor, or where police resent the call and arrest both parties (Ames and Dunham 2002; Hirschel and Buzawa 2002). For victim advocates, the primary concern regarding dual arrest is that the trauma of this event may be harmful to the female victims of abuse. This is also an issue for police officers, who are apprehensive that lack of discretion does lead to "dual arrest" even when one party's violence was self-defensive.

Therefore, while legal systems within both Canada and the United States no longer view spousal abuse as a "private matter" and respond much more effectively than in the past, there remain many deficiencies. As we tell the stories of individual men who batter, some of these deficiencies will come to light. So, too, will some of the frustrations of the criminal justice workers who work with them in structures that are less than ideal, where they experience little agency to make a difference.

While not all abusive actions lead to criminal justice consequences, the men we are studying and whose stories are told in this book have committed acts that have led them into contact with the criminal justice system, including the police, the courts, the judiciary, the prison system, and parole and probation services. Policies related to arrest, no-contact orders, and length of incarceration and the propensity of judges to refer men convicted of domestic violence to batterer intervention programs have an impact on the men and their journeys. To understand their stories in context, one must be aware of the broader criminal justice conversations that are taking place in the literature and among the professionals who work within the system.

Feminist Analyses of Violence against Women

Patriarchy and the gender inequality it creates have often been linked to violence against women. In her 1984 book *Feminism and Sexual Equality*, Zillah Eisenstein defines patriarchy as "the process of politically differentiating the female from the male, as woman from man. Patriarchy in this sense is the politics of transforming biological sex into politicized gender, which prioritizes the man while making the woman different (unequal), less than, or the 'other'" (90).

Early feminist theory focused primarily on the concept of patriarchy and the social institutions that help maintain it (MacKinnon 1989; Dworkin 1981). Continuing feminist analyses of violence against women center on the structure of relationships in a male-dominated culture, on power, and on gender. In patriarchal societies, both social structures and ideology support the dominance of men over women and rigidly defined gender roles (Dobash and Dobash 1979). The main factors, therefore, that contribute to violence against women include the historically male-dominated social structure and socialization practices that constrain and shape the lives of both men and women. Individual acts of violence are grouped within larger, structural relations through which male dominance is maintained. Violence against women is then one manifestation of a system of male dominance that has existed historically and across cultures; violence becomes a method by which to maintain social control and male power over women. The power relations found within a patriarchal society take many forms, from the sexual division of labor and the social organization of procreation to the internalized norms of femininity by which we live. According to Susan Schechter (1982, 238): "The challenge remains to see violent behavior as individually willed yet socially constructed." We continue to use the often-repeated phrase, *the personal is political*.

Intimate partner violence occurs within individuals' lives, but when discussing violence, we must carefully consider the issue of intersectionality wherein factors such as race, class, ethnicity, sexuality, and nationality are interwoven with the gendered power differentials found within patriarchy (Renzetti 2011; Sokoloff and Dupont 2005). Battered women can be subjected to many "microaggressions" in their lives based on issues of cultural diversity (Bograd 1999). The consequences of structural inequalities include issues of poverty, homelessness, (un-/under-) employment, lack of shelter space, and affordable housing, while internalized ideologies can result in certain women not being deemed "legitimate" victims, prejudicial court responses or those that have unintended consequences, and a notion of a culture of violence found within some societies. All of these factors, and others, contribute to an interlocking of aggressions against women. While our focus in this book centers on the stories of the men, the analysis of the harm they have caused has been influenced by developing feminist thought on violence against women.

Power and control are two central features in understanding the behavior of intimate partner violence. Without a doubt, it has been the early, and then sustained, analysis of patriarchy within feminism that has led to understanding men who batter as those who engage in individual acts that are socially constructed within a broader environment through which male dominance is celebrated and maintained. To look at the lives of men who have acted abusively without adequate attention to the broader feminist writing on violence against women would be ill advised and naive, to say the least.

The Importance of Understanding Lived Religion

For some time, sociologists of religion have been preoccupied with documenting and understanding what they believed would be the eventual demise of religion in the developed world. From this point of view, religious beliefs and commitments would have no foothold in the face of secular ideas of science, the human condition conceptualized by social scientists, and cultural pluralism. Other scholars of religion focused on ongoing human longings that might not be satisfied by the advancement of technology, modern medicine, and growing institutional complexity, and they argued that many men and women would continue to look to religion—and make choices about their involvement with it—based on personal perceptions of want and need. Theories of secularization and theories surrounding rational choice both find themselves impoverished (Ammerman 2014), and it is within that broader context of the failure of these two traditions to account for the social dynamics of religion in the midst of ordinary living that "lived religion" as a strategy and a perspective began to flourish.

We have been influenced by the impressive way in which this understanding of religion as it is lived out in the lives of very ordinary people can help us make sense of both choices and paradoxes at the individual level (why does John do what he does?) and at the level of social groups (why do so many Americans who attend church X, located in city Y, volunteer at organization Z?). From Courtney Bender's *Heaven's Kitchen: Living Religion at God's Love We Deliver* (2003) to Wendy Cadge's *Paging God: Religion in the Halls of Medicine* (2013), we see the power and potential of spiritual and religious traditions among those who walk alongside men and women whose bodies are failing them in the face of illness and death. Books such as Meredith McGuire's *Lived Religion: Faith and Practice in Everyday Life* (2008) and her earlier *Ritual Healing in Suburban America* (1988) help us to see how people think about the challenges they face daily, especially those challenges that are embodied. And there is Robert Orsi's *Thank You, St. Jude* (1996), a vivid portrayal of how religious people look to their faith traditions when they have exhausted their own intellectual and emotional resources and, as a consequence, place their trust in something that they cannot see but believe is present nonetheless. Another scholar, Marion Goldman, in *The American Soul Rush: Esalen and the Rise of Spiritual Privilege* (2012), documents the pull of notions associated with spiritual and personal growth, replete with diverse religious practices. The conceptual framework of lived religion permeates a cultural analysis such as Janet Jacobs's *Memorializing the Holocaust: Gender, Genocide and Collective Memory* (2010) and Mary Jo Neitz's (2000) fascinating analysis of changing sexualities and practices loosely connected to Wicca, as it does Nancy Tatom Ammerman's *Sacred Stories, Spiritual Tribes: Finding Religion in Everyday Life* (2014).

These authors, in particular, along with others within the "lived religion" tradition, have had an impact on the framing of our study and the way we have attempted
to communicate its results, the complexity of the individual stories and the emerging patterns revealed through the analysis. Several years ago, I (Nancy) was asked
to contribute a chapter to a book focused on methodology within this tradition
(Spickard, Landres, and McGuire, 2002). The title of my chapter, "From the Heart
of My Laptop," was meant to convey how my life work on abuse had affected me as
a scholar and a person. To be sure, there is a bidirectional link; studies of lived religion are willing to see and often even embrace that fuzzy line between researcher
and researched.

Lived religion abounds. One only has to observe ordinary people as they go about
their daily lives to see the importance of religious rituals, practices, and beliefs. We
speculate that lived religion can offer clues to why some men are violent and also
clues to how the journey is constructed after their violence has been named and
these men are suffering personally some of the consequences of the harm they have
caused others. As the stories of men unfold in the pages to follow, there will be many
examples of the influence of spiritual factors and religious practices.

Conceptualizing Violence in Families of Faith

In the early days of the transition house movement, perspectives informed by religious language or passion were regarded as part of the problem of abuse rather than
its solution (Brown and Bohn 1989). Yet others were arguing that a woman's personal
narrative and characteristics, including the importance of her religious faith, shape
her disclosure of abuse and the road she travels in her quest for wholeness (Clarke
1986; Fortune 1991; Halsey 1984; Fiorenza and Copeland 1994). There was evidence that community-based professionals experienced difficulty in responding to
the needs of highly religious women (Whipple 1987) and that religious leaders were
being confronted by the issue of abuse on a regular basis (Horton and Williamson
1988; Weaver 1993). Yet it appeared that few in the mainstream antiviolence movement were taking any notice.

When theologian Catherine Clark Kroeger and I first began to combine our
voices in print to argue that domestic violence was present but not being taken
seriously within contemporary Christianity (Kroeger and Nason-Clark 2001 and
2010; Nason-Clark and Kroeger 2004), there was substantial push-back in her professional contexts. She would speak about the shepherds neglecting their sheep (a
biblical reference taken from the Old Testament) and employ this narrative to draw
attention to the punishment in the next life that she believed would be leveled upon
clergy who neglected abused women and men in their congregations. Meanwhile,
I was collecting and analyzing sociological data that enabled me to speak with confidence and passion at seminaries and gatherings of clergy across North America
and around the world. My message was that there is a "holy hush" pervading religious organizations on the subject of abuse, and it trickles down to congregation
life (Nason-Clark 2000). I would argue that it is time to build bridges between "the
steeple and the shelter," time to "shatter the silence," by placing brochures in church
washrooms announcing that "Christian Love Should Not Hurt," time to talk about
domestic violence in premarital counseling, time to highlight healthy interpersonal

relationships in church youth groups, and time to preach messages from the pulpit that condemn any form of violence in the family.

The fragile relationship between feminism and conservative religious traditions has augmented the chasm between domestic violence shelters and local community churches, especially those that embrace an evangelical outlook, or Pentecostal worship styles. The impact for abused women in these traditions has meant that they are more likely to seek religious-only resources (pastors or "sisters in the faith") as they disclose their stories of pain and suffering. Moreover, they fear that looking to the transition house for refuge or community-based services might jeopardize their relationships in the church, especially with the pastor.

Women from these traditions are not abused at higher rates than others, but they are more vulnerable when they are abused. They are more likely to believe that divorce is wrong, or to be avoided at all costs, and to be especially optimistic that change is possible, aligning this with notions of religious conversion, altering an old life to a new one fashioned in likeness to Christ. In part, these vulnerabilities led us to develop training and resources available online for pastors, community-based professionals, and women themselves. Developed with a generous grant from the Lilly Endowment, these materials are available free of charge, and brochures, bulletin inserts, and posters can be downloaded and material contextualized to make them applicable to local congregations. Other resources, such as the Stained Glass Story of Abuse, video clips and podcasts, can be used within a congregational context or as part of the ongoing training of a ministry team or individual priest or pastor (for additional materials, click on the "Resources" tab at www.theraveproject.com).

Understanding the contested territory concerning violence in families of faith is a central piece of the bigger puzzle of conceptualizing how a faith-based agency—such as STOP, the one we are studying—and the men who engage in its programs make sense of the comorbidity of abusive acts and religious faith and practices. Moreover, strategies to harness any elements of a variety of faith traditions that can encourage violent-free living and respond with compassion, justice, and accountability in its aftermath need to be named, understood, and evaluated. Lived religion—how ordinary people bring spiritually infused practices into the weekly or yearly routine of daily life—might offer some "add-ons" that could prove useful in any attempt to understand why men who batter act the way they do and how those walking alongside them might assist them in the process of changing their thinking and behavior.

Looking inside the Mind of a Batterer

In early December 2012, I (Nancy) was invited to participate in a think tank sponsored by the organization Futures without Violence, formerly known as the Family Violence Prevention Fund. During a period of two days, we discussed many of the issues faced by batterer intervention programs across the United States. Programs such as Duluth or Emerge have been in existence for some time. Other programs, such as Caminar Latino or the Los Angeles–based Partner Abuse Program (GLBTQ) or the Fort Hood, Texas, Batterer's Intervention Prevention Program offer men's groups for specific constituencies of ethnic or sexual minorities or those who have served in the military. Some batterer intervention programs, such as Aid to Victims of Domestic Abuse in Houston, have been evaluated by large research initiatives like that launched by Edward Gondolf, and other programs have built in a system whereby they evaluate recidivism and other measures within their own agencies. But despite how long they have been in existence, the professionalism and the training of their staff, or even their commitment to follow recidivism rates in an attempt to become even more effective, there are problems that surface from time to time and other issues that never seem to go away.

As I listened to experts talk about their work and its challenges, I could not help but think, who knows what happens inside the mind of a batterer? Well, of course, a few authors have offered us their insights, based on their therapeutic experience or their role in developing, or running, programs for violent men. Lundy Bancroft is arguably the best known among this category for his book *Why Does He Do That? Inside the Minds of Angry and Controlling Men* (2003). Formerly a director of Emerge, the first program for batterers in the United States, Bancroft paints a picture of the perpetrator of violence against women, through his many years of working with abusive men as counselor, evaluator, and investigator. He addresses his analysis to women who have been victimized within their intimate relationships, noting that he wishes "to equip women with the ability to protect themselves, physically and psychologically, from angry and controlling men."

In *When Men Batter Women: New Insights into Ending Abusive Relationships*, Neil Jacobson and John Gottman (1998) intertwine scientific observation and interviews of severely violent couples, against the background of a control group of nonviolent couples who were dissatisfied with their marriages and other couples who reported that they were happy in their relationships. Dividing their batterer population into "cobras" and "pit bulls," Jacobson and Gottman help the reader to understand some of the basics and dynamics of battering, including a comparison of what they term "cobra" relationships with "pitbull" relationships. Using stories of both men and women from their research data as a means of describing the realities of abuse, they help battered women see the dangers inherent in staying in violent relationships and help men see the long-term consequences of their desire to control another person.

Others, such as Juan Carlos Areán (Areán and Davis 2007; Areán and Raines 2013), have focused more specifically on fathering after violence. Working now with the Latino community, he and other men have become committed to ensuring that men—who have been or are batterers—are offered the chance and the skills to (re)connect with their children. And then there are a small number of men, such as motivational speaker Jackson Katz, author of *The Macho Paradox: Why Some Men Hurt Women and How All Men Can Help* (2006); Rus Funk, executive direc-tor of MensWork: Eliminating Violence against Women and author of *Reaching Men: Strategies for Preventing Sexist Attitudes, Behaviors and Violence* (2006); and hockey player Theo Fleury—all of whom speak right into the hearts of audiences with their messages of moving beyond the macho male.

We believe that exploring the lives of men who are, or have been, abusive is a very important part of the work to reduce intimate partner violence in our culture. Featuring the men's stories, as told by the men themselves, is relatively uncharted waters in the social sciences. We are excited to bring to light the expansive data set we have collected during many years of field research. We hope to build on the work of others and in so doing make our own unique contribution.

ORGANIZATION OF THE BOOK

With our intellectual indebtedness named and our methodology outlined, we begin to tell the story of men who batter. First, we develop the background factors and begin to form an understanding of the abuse of the men in context by reflecting back to their childhoods (chapter 2), their teen years and early intimate relationships (chapter 3), and the downward vortex of living dangerously, exploring how their reckless behavior created chaos for others and the toll it took on the men themselves (chapter 4). Next, we focus on the stories of how men acted abusively, were caught in the act (chapter 5), and then began contact with the criminal justice system. Chapter 6 considers the various steps and stages of being charged and sentenced and then examines what takes place after sentencing: doing time and being monitored. The last chapters of the book are where our central focus is developed: the mandated attendance of men at a batterer intervention program, an agency we call STOP. In chapter 7, we look at the process of checking in at STOP group meetings and doing the work required to change thinking and behavior. Chapter 8 deals with the process of becoming—or refusing to become—accountable for one's actions. We conclude with chapter 9, in which we explore notions of hope or despair as we consider the journeys of men toward justice, accountability, and change—and the workers who walk alongside them. At the end of the book, we offer interested readers a series of appendices that outline the specific details of our methodology, the interview guides, our focus group questions, and other details related to the various research projects from which this book draws.

We trust that in the pages to follow, you—the reader—will become as engaged in these stories retold by us as we were in hearing them from the men themselves for the first time.

Childhood

Everyone's story begins in childhood. There is no escaping it. What happens in those early years sets the stage for what is to come. For most of the men we interviewed, childhood was not a carefree time of life. For many, there was instability. For some, there was poverty. For others, abuse was a threat or a reality—sometimes experienced, often observed. Isolation and loneliness were present. Some men talked of being bullied, while others did the bullying themselves. All of these factors could be considered risks, characteristics that might have a negative impact on the lives of children and thwart their healthy development and smooth transition to adulthood.

Not everything about anyone's childhood is negative, however. There are happy memories and stories involving laughter and fun. There are moments when life is good. Strength can be attained in difficult circumstances, and lessons are learned that have the potential to help when things are rough or when trials come. These are known as protective factors, and they can arise as a result of one's family but can also be related to the roles of other supportive adults, from school, from sports, from church, or within the broader neighborhood where one lives.

Not every man in our study had a difficult childhood. But the majority did. As we will see, some were in and out of foster homes, many saw firsthand the chaos, fear, and insecurity that accompany violence and addiction in the lives of their parents, and others were aware of the financial burdens they were causing for the adults around them—one more mouth to feed. Nevertheless, even in these circumstances, protective factors emerged. Sometimes other adults—say, a grandmother or a coach—filled in the gap and provided care and emotional support. Often, men spoke of learning lessons on the street or with friends. But many of these connections took them down roads that would have been best not to travel. In chapter 4, we consider in some detail the notion of living dangerously and its impact. But the seeds for living dangerously often begin in childhood. What is observed and experienced during the early years of one's life sets the stage for later periods. Childhood is the focus of this chapter. We asked the men to talk about their childhoods, and then we listened. In telling their stories—as they have been told to us—we challenge the reader to see and think about them in terms of risk and protective factors.

RISK-INTENSIVE CHILDHOOD EXPERIENCES

Jake Peters' earliest memories were linked to his placement in foster homes. For more than ten years of his life, he was in and then out of different families. *To tell you the truth, it was a very, very ugly experience. . . . I don't think the state really knows what goes on in there. I had firsthand experience—these people aren't your parents, you know. . . . I've seen kids get beat, I've been beaten myself. . . . I was in the system for a long time. I pretty much learned how to talk to the therapist and the staff members and pretty much work the system. . . . I had ten years of practice, a long time. Eventually, what really happened was the state told me my mother . . . that she needed to take me back.*

Dark cornrow braids framed his youthful African American facial features, and regular workouts at a local gym reflected Jake's newfound interest in a healthy, fit body. At twenty-eight, he had decided to make some new choices that would help him to reach personal goals. But it was not always so. For ten years, Jake was bumped from one foster home to another, having irregular contact with his dad. *Well, you know, my father wasn't really there. I mean, when he did come to visit me in those group homes and foster homes . . . I liked what he had to say, and I wanted to listen to him, you know, don't cry . . . don't let anyone put their hands on you, you don't ever start a fight you don't finish. . . . These early messages had a profound impact on Jake. I really wanted to connect with my father, so what he said I took to heart, for the most part.*

As a teen, when he was reunited with his mother, things did not go well, and Jake moved to live with his father. After a few months, he came back to his mother's house. And then he left again. In Jake's case, bouncing from one home to another, one location to another, and sometimes one state to another was out of his personal control. Thus, it was not surprising that when we first met him—in the early days of attending the program—we learned that he was longing for a period of stability in his life.

A year later, when we caught up with Jake again, he had found a stable job—as a bouncer at a local club—finished school, got a license and a car, and made some significant lifestyle changes, especially in how he related to women. By his own account, he tried to build a relationship with a woman before he slept with her, something very different from how things were in an earlier period of his life. He was now much healthier, had stopped drinking, and was about to finish his fifty-two weeks at STOP. He said he was on a new path. But there was a long road ahead.

He wanted to get established in a job that would bring him security and enjoyment. He wanted to find ways to relate to his parents, who had disappointed and hurt him in the past. He had a desire to learn how to be less shallow in his intimate relationships. He hoped that he had learned to put his drinking behavior behind him. All of these hopes and dreams amounted to a tall order. Only time would tell whether the therapeutic investments in his life and his contact with the STOP program would reap the rewards Jake claimed.

Risk factors for Jake:

- Instability.
- Abandonment/feeling unloved.

- Experience of abuse.
- Witnessing the abuse of others.

Instability includes factors such as low income, younger age, being unmarried or having multiple marriages, unemployment, less than a high school education, alcohol and/or drug abuse, previous criminal history, race, and residence location (Cavanaugh and Gelles 2005; Delsol, Margolin, and John 2003; Dalton 2001). The labor market has a lot to do with instability. Research has found that low-wage jobs serve as an impediment to young people's forming economically self-reliant families, that poor labor-market opportunities contribute to poor parenting conditions and related father absence, that disagreements over money are the strongest predictor of the dissolution of relationships, and that the lack of good jobs contributes to high rates of female-headed and welfare-receiving households (Woldoff and Cina 2007).

The next three factors are all related to "fragile families," defined as such because they most often consist of unmarried mothers and their children, who are at heightened risk for economic and social problems and family dissolution (Bembry 2011). Children living in a fragile family situation, where the disadvantages of young motherhood are often compounded by their partnering with men who have the least resources and have exhibited abusive behavior, are themselves at great risk for becoming abusive as they mature.

We have highlighted four risk factors in the childhood experience of Jake, although there are certainly many more. There was instability—moving from one place to another, never being part of the decision about when and where he would be moved, and yet feeling that he was part of the problem. Why else would he be moved? He felt that he had been abandoned by his mother and his father. Central to the way he told us his story was the notion that his mother was eventually required to resume her responsibility for him, and then, when that did not work out, his father took a turn. Moving from one foster home to another and then from one parent to another took a toll on his emotional well-being. He felt as if nobody wanted him. And very early in his life, he saw his own brother being abandoned in a bus station, as his mother, with Jake in tow, left the infant for someone else to find.

As a result, feelings of abandonment ran deep in Jake's experience, and this also took a toll on his early experiences of intimacy. He would be the one to abandon others, in order to protect himself from being abandoned. His relationships were shallow, and his needs were primary. When he was a child, there was really no one who took his needs to heart, Yes, there were workers who ensured that he had somewhere to live and food to eat, but Jake felt that there was no one watching out for him. Consequently, he felt unloved. In addition to having feelings of abandonment and instability, Jake witnessed and experienced violence in the places where he lived and from the people who were supposed to protect him and care for him. It is not surprising that Jake had little knowledge of what love was or how to receive it or give it.

Jake internalized one of the messages his father tried to give him when he was a child living in a foster environment: be strong; you can do it. The sporadic visits from his father and the advice his father dispensed during the minutes he spent with his young son formed a protective factor. As Jake told the story of his life, it appeared this message helped to carry him through. Now he longed for stability, and for the first time in his life, he was well positioned to take advantage of therapeutic supports and strategies for living differently from how he had in the past. We pick up his story again in a later chapter.

Clifford White, the oldest man we interviewed, was seventy-three. He had completed thirty months in prison more than a year before we met him and just completed the fifty-two-week batterer intervention program at STOP. We asked him to think back to his childhood and whether there were mostly positive memories or a lot of painful memories. *Painful, very painful. My mother was a drunk and a chaser, and I can't remember how many foster homes I lived in, a whole bunch of them.* We asked whether he had witnessed or experienced violence in his childhood home. *I didn't experience any personally, but I saw my dad knock a guy down a stairway, and I saw him slap my mom a few times. They would separate and get back together and separate and get back together and separate. She got run over by a car in L.A. 'cause she was drunk.* Cliff was raised by his grandmother, a very religious woman who lived in South Dakota. *She was the one who gave me discipline, taught me how to work, what work was all about.*

Like Jake, Cliff lived in foster homes for much of his early life. His childhood was characterized by fear, instability, and insecurity until his grandmother began to care for him. She embodied the protective factors he would take to adulthood: lessons of hard work and discipline. But her care was not able to override the legacy of two very out-of-control parents, whose lives were dominated by addiction and anger.

Risk factors for Cliff:

- Instability.
- Addiction in the life of his mother.
- Tragic death of his mother during his childhood.
- Addiction in the life of his father.
- Witnessing the abuse of others.

Each of these risk factors is problematic on its own, but when considered as a constellation, one can imagine how they increase personal vulnerability, which might lead to negative consequences in the life of a young man. In a synthesis of the literature on the intergenerational transmission of violence, Black, Sussman, and Unger (2010, 1027) argue that "witnessing interparental violence in childhood and early adolescence is associated with later experiences of intimate partner violence in teenage years, emerging adulthood, and adulthood." Relatedly, in a meta-analysis of the literature on the intergenerational transmission of violence, Stith et al. (2000) found that growing up in an abusive family is indeed positively related to intimate partner violence as adults. Social learning theory posits that within the socialization process—through observation, modeling, and reinforcement—children learn scripts for violent behavior, and they also learn that violence is an effective means of conflict resolution within the family (Bandura 1973). Add to that instability factors such as drug use, alcohol use, or other risk-taking activities (Gover 2004) and issues such as insecure attachment, school failure, poor problem-solving skills, peer rejection (Teague et al. 2008) or being a member of a fragile family (Högnäs and Carlson 2010), and the propensity for intimate partner violence increases.

According to Ehrensaft et al. (2003), experiences of parental rejection or abuse lead children to have problem-solving deficits—a risk factor. Yet "[m]altreated children are more prone to rejection by normative peers as a function of deficits in interpersonal functioning and thus are more likely to gravitate to an aggressive, deviant peer group" (741)—a risk factor. Those children with multiple risk factors do anticipate and attempt to avoid rejection within their interpersonal relationships (McCloskey and Stuewig 2001), but unfortunately, they are at risk of being victimized by peers (Holt, Buckley, and Whelan 2008)—another risk factor. The negative outcomes of living in a fragile family, often headed by a lone parent, include yet other identified risk factors, such as becoming a parent at a young age (Kelley, Thornberry, and Smith 1997) and dropping out of high school or school failure (Högnäs and Carlson 2010; Wolf et al. 2003).

Later in this chapter, we return to the issue of fragile families, which exhibit many of the risk factors we have listed above. Children living within fragile families, with on-again, off-again father figures and mothers stressed by their life contexts, may be insecurely attached to the primary caregivers in their lives. Lack of secure attachment between parent and child is a risk factor for later emotional and behavioral problems for the child (Edleson et al. 2007). When children experience neglect, emotional neglect, abandonment, and chaotic home environments with no safety or predictability—a complete lack of factors that we know are necessary for optimal child development—conduct disorders, PTSD, borderline personality, and other issues that are strongly linked to trauma may arise.

Also related to many of the factors listed above is the intergenerational transmission of family violence whereby violent parents beget violent children (Rosenbaum and Leisring 2003). This consistent link between exposure to violence in the family of origin and subsequent family violence (e.g., intimate partner violence and child abuse) in adulthood is also noted by Kerley et al. (2010). During primary socialization, we gradually come to believe in the values of our culture, internalizing its moral precepts and norms (Goldenberg 1997). Children who are exposed to violence are likely to internalize the norms of violence as constituting appropriate behavior in stressful situations. The narratives of many abusive men include issues of parental fighting and early problem drinking, which are identified as predictors of male perpetration of violence (Chen and White 2004; Delsol and Margolin 2004).

Clearly, the lack of normative childhood socialization has a negative impact on the lives of not only men who are perpetrators of abuse but also their significant others as victims. But even what may be considered normative in terms of male socialization is often based on shaming, which, according to Mejia (2005), can cultivate rage and violence as defensive behaviors.

Like Jake's, Cliff's early life was characterized by a host of risk factors. Both of his parents were alcoholics, his father had abandoned them during his childhood, his mother was killed while in a drunken state, and his earliest memories of his dad include acts of violence and aggression toward others. His grandmother became his protector, and she provided for him physically and emotionally. At her side, he witnessed the power of a faith community, the value of hard work, and the harsh consequences of discipline.

Cliff was an old man, Jake was a young man, but both experienced childhoods that were very difficult. And both went on to be abusive to women with whom they were in relationships beginning in their early twenties. In each case, the men began to model what they had observed. Later in this chapter, we talk about the longer-term consequences of witnessing or experiencing violence in one's childhood home. In Jake's case, the STOP intervention occurred shortly after he was found guilty of domestic violence. For Cliff, he spent a large portion of his life in prison, and it was not until he was well advanced in years that he began to learn another way to respond to the disappointments and frustrations of his life.

Many other men had little good to say about their childhoods. In fact, most of the men we interviewed reported that their childhoods were marked by trouble, poverty, and abuse. Biard [Buddy] Reed, a man in his mid-fifties, reflected: *My dad was an alcoholic. He died an alcoholic. . . . I didn't have a childhood. . . . My dad was very, very mean to me. . . . I got a lot of beatings.* Biard's story is featured in chapter 7. He was one of the very few men at STOP who was not plagued by drug and alcohol problems himself, and he was not required to attend classes as a result of a criminal justice order. He chose to come, and he chose to do the work that was required for change.

Not all of the men described their childhoods in the way that Jake, Cliff, and Biard did. Some men offered more of a mix of positive and negative memories based on their childhood experiences. Ben was one such man.

SOMEWHAT CHALLENGING CHILDHOOD EXPERIENCES

Ben Chamois characterized his childhood in a way that set him apart from those whose stories we have just told. He outlined many challenges, but his assessment of his childhood was not replete with negative language. Like many of the younger men we met at STOP, Ben was raised by a single-parent mother, and he was the middle of three children. His story involved the strength he drew from his mother's example of hard work, with which she herself was able to succeed amid difficult circumstances. She worked two jobs to support the family, and she attended college in the evenings. Ben said: *So I kinda grew up by myself, but I got really good at life. I learned how to get really good at life at a young age.*

Ben played baseball and prided himself on being the class clown. He mentioned that both he and his brother had anger problems while they were at school, fighting on the school playground and being a menace to the teachers. Yet he was never in trouble with the law before the incident that brought him to STOP, in which he ignored a no-contact order and arrived at his girlfriend's new apartment looking for some of his possessions. Ten months later, he was pulled over by the police for a minor motor vehicle violation (one taillight not working), and in the course of running a check on the car, the officers learned that there was a warrant out for him. He went to court, where he was fined and ordered to attend a batterer intervention program. He had been attending STOP for quite a while when we first met him, and he was about to graduate.

Even as he told us his story, it was clear how he was harnessing this negative experience for good. In fact, since he did not want to start a program in a new city where he had recently been transferred with his work, he drove almost six hours to attend STOP and did three group sessions in two days before driving back. At this rate, it was only a few more weeks before he was due to graduate from the program. *In a really roundabout way, I really appreciate it, you know. I think it's probably the best eighteen hundred dollars I have spent in a long time.* At our interview, Ben was very upbeat. He had a new house, a promotion at work, and a new girlfriend. When we asked him what he would like to be able to tell us in six months' time, he said that he would no longer be in this city but that we could call him directly. Since this was outside of the research protocols, we had no further contact with Ben.

Risk factors for Ben:

- Left often without parental supervision.
- Anger as a teen.
- Several bad relationships with intimates.

Protective factors for Ben:

- Mother's strong drive to succeed.
- Stable home life.
- Completed high school.
- Good employment.

Just as there are a plethora of risk factors that increase vulnerability related to intimate partner violence, so, too, there are protective factors that mitigate that risk. Teague et al. (2008) identify several factors that they believe either prevent or limit a propensity toward violence, including good problem-solving skills, supportive and caring parents, and a positive school climate. Social bonding through attachment to school and commitment to education are identified as protective factors by Payne, Gottfredson, and Gottfredson (2003), exemplified by the instrumental restraints of a commitment to education and the internalization of conventional norms and rules (Payne 2009). Several other factors that provide resilience against violence are identified by Tiet, Huizinga, and Byrnes (2010). These include more bonding to family and teachers, more involvement in extracurricular activities, lower levels of parental discord, fewer adverse life events, and less involvement with delinquent peers.

Resilience means having good outcomes despite the exposure to risk (Carlton et al. 2006; Masten 2001). Tiet and Huizinga (2002, 361) identify two constructs of the concept of resilience: adjustment (indicated by self-esteem, academic achievement, and psychosocial functioning) and low levels of antisocial behavior (indicated by the absence or low levels of drug use, delinquent behavior, and gang involvement).

A number of factors contribute to the resilience of children as they mature into adolescents and adults. Catalano et al. (2004) indicate that attachment and commitment to school are associated with a decrease in delinquent behaviors, including lower levels of substance use, gang membership, violence, academic problems, and sexual activity. Competent and positive parenting practices can also predict child competence, resilience, and change in child competence over time (Masten 1999). And of course, absence or low levels of adverse life events have been shown to predict better outcomes in children and adolescents (e.g., Tiet et al. 1998; Wiesner and Windle 2004).

A number of men described their childhood lives, like Ben's, as a mix of happy and painful memories. Often, the negative memories were associated with disrupted relationships with one or both parents or the presence of abuse in the home. In the lives of the men we interviewed, stability in childhood—or, at least their perception of stability—was an extremely important factor.

A small number of men characterized their childhoods in very positive terms. We turn to one example, the story of Drew.

A FAIRLY HAPPY CHILDHOOD

Drew Barley described his childhood as involving *a fairly happy home situation.* Shy and withdrawn by nature, Drew presented as a young man who would rather have attention directed toward someone other than himself. In this way, he was quite different from many of the men in group who liked the limelight. The backward-facing baseball cap redirected hair that otherwise would fall onto his face, obscuring his youthful features. His appearance suggested that he did not spend much time on how he looked: baggy jeans and an oversized T-shirt were his signature clothing items.

Drew was ordered by the courts to come to a batterer intervention program as a result of *a domestic disturbance with me and my wife.* Drew and Kate had been together for twelve years and married for eight; they shared two children, an infant daughter and an eight-year-old son. This was Drew's first contact with the criminal justice system, and as a result, his sentence included only mandatory group attendance, followed by contact with a probation officer. He lived temporarily away from his home (for less than three weeks) until his case came to court. At the point of our first interview, Drew had completed just ten weeks of the program, felt it was very useful for him, and was particularly drawn to the curriculum as presented at the various groups meetings of STOP.

Reflecting on his childhood, Drew talked about how his father drank a lot when he was younger. Then he mentioned his parents' divorce, although he was quick to add that *they both did what they could to take care of the kids no matter whatever problems they were having.* Later on, he talked at some length of his dad's involvement in his sports activities. Clearly, for Drew, the bonding that occurred around sports between son and father had an enormous impact, one that he wanted desperately to carry on with his own son, Andy. Having been a high school athlete himself, Drew took great pride in the relationship he had with his own son in carrying on the traditions he experienced with his own father. *I go to Friday groups. I used to be in Tuesday, but I coach my son's football team so they [STOP facilitators] let me switch.* Like his father before him, Drew coaches the teams on which his son plays. *My dad coached all my baseball and football teams and stuff like that until I got to junior high, It's fun, it's definitely a challenge.*

Unlike most of the other men in STOP, Drew was not battling long-standing alcohol or drug addictions, but he admitted that he had a drinking problem. *I didn't get assigned any alcohol treatment or nothing like that.... I didn't drink every day. When I did drink, I didn't really know when to quit.... I haven't had a drink or a beer or whatever since that incident ... so that's one of my agreements, but it is part of my probation, too ... yeah, it's part of my probation, plus it's an agreement between me and my wife, and she drank even less than me.*

Six months later, at our follow-up interview, Drew reported that *everything is going great.* He was halfway through the fifty-two-week intervention program, continuing with other therapeutic options (marriage counseling at another agency, plus private individual counseling for his wife), was still working at the same job, and was coaching his son's basketball team.

Several things about Drew's life set him apart from many of the men we interviewed:

- He was able to recall with some degree of enthusiasm his own childhood experiences.

- He did not have a history of trouble with the law.
- He had not lived dangerously for an extended period of time.
- He had been in a committed relationship for more than ten years and continued to have a strong bond with his children.
- He did not do drugs.
- His wife did not do drugs, nor did she drink to excess.
- Both Drew and his wife stopped drinking alcohol altogether after the incident that brought Drew into contact with STOP.

OTHER CRITICAL FACTORS IN CHILDHOOD

For some men, it was not life at home with their parents that caused them angst but life at school and with friends. Rudy Howes responded to our questions about childhood by discussing some of the very early challenges he faced at school. *I have been expelled from school since fifth grade. . . . I have been expelled since then because of fighting.* Rudy was an awkward child, wore glasses, was overweight, and grew up poor. He was made fun of at school, and he lashed out at others as a way to defend himself against their attacks. He was expelled on many occasions, so often that fifth grade was actually the highest grade he ever finished. When we met Rudy, he had almost completed his fifty-two weeks at STOP but was still attending classes (at no additional cost) until he was in a position to pay the money he owed.

Rudy had not been employed since his last jail term—serving time for an assault, coupled with a violation of the resultant postjail no-contact order. He had been living with his wife (against court orders) and his child, and when his parole officer arrived at the door, he was sent back to jail. Now he was living with his parents, doing odd jobs for them in exchange for pocket money, which he often used to buy cigarettes, cigars, or pot. *I have wasted a lot of money that I didn't have.*

His wife had been employed in the kitchen of a nursing home but had lost that job for repeated tardiness. She and the child lived on handouts from her grandmother, whose only source of income was her government-funded disability payments. Rudy spent much of his day taking résumés to various prospective employers, but with a recent assault charge and a fifth-grade education, there was little hope on the horizon.

Other men also had very difficult experiences at school. Scott Smythe lashed out at teachers. He spoke about his father being a drug addict since his early teen years. In his own life, he was arrested three times for assault before his thirteenth birthday. *Like I would be throwing desks at teachers, and I broke my principal's nose, and I threatened him with scissors, and lots of fights, lots of stuff like that. And it was all in grade school . . . then that's when I got expelled from school.*

A 2008 study by Teague et al. found that being suspended or expelled significantly increased the likelihood that a victim of physical abuse would commit a violent offense. Social bond theory (Hirschi 1969) emphasizes the need for attachment (to caregivers), commitment (to social institutions such as schools), involvement (in legitimate activities outside school), and belief (that these things are important) as resilience factors mitigating against delinquency and/or offending. Statistics Canada (2009b) reports that "individual-level risk factors related to rigorous parental monitoring, delinquent or criminal attitudes among peers, and low school attachment were strongly associated with violent delinquency."

Being bullied or bullying others was a central feature of many men's childhood narratives. When they were faced with disappointment or frustration, they used their fists. When they were made fun of, they used their fists. When life did not go the way they wanted, they used their fists. Aggressive behavior became the knee-jerk response to even minor situations causing anxiety or unhappiness. However, for some men, even thinking back to their childhoods was difficult, sometimes painful.

The World Health Organization (2002) defines bullying as intentional use of physical or psychological force or power, threatened or actual, against oneself, against another person, or against a group that results in or has a high likelihood of resulting in injury, death, psychological harm, maldevelopment, or deprivation. Bullying is identified as a marker for more serious violent behavior according to Nansel, Overpeck, and Haynie (2003). The term *bullying perpetrator* identifies someone who "chronically harasses someone else either physically or psychologically," and a *bully victim* is someone who "is being bullied or victimized when he or she is exposed, repeatedly and over time, to negative actions on the part of one or more other students" (Olweus 1993, 9).

Researchers posit that some youths who witness intimate partner violence may become highly sensitized or desensitized to detecting aggressive cues, either of which can make them more prone to bullying or becoming victimized by peers (Bauer et al. 2006; Voisin and Hong 2012). Youths who pick up excessively on aggressive cues in their interactions with other children may respond with more aggressive bullying behaviors to peers. Those who are overly desensitized to such cues can be at increased risk of being bullied or victimized (Bauer et al. 2006; Lundy and Grossman 2005).

THE PAIN OF THINKING BACK TO CHILDHOOD

For some men, thinking back to their childhoods brings back feelings and emotions they would rather forget. Perhaps it is too painful to label one's childhood as bad or difficult. As adult men, a few were able to identify with the challenges that their single-parent mothers must have experienced as they attempted to raise several children on their own. Others thought of alcoholic fathers and identified with their struggles. Some of the men spoke in terms that would suggest that they were giving their fathers some slack, in the same way that they hoped their own children would offer them slack when they thought back to their childhoods down the road.

We feature the story of Mike in chapter 7. He was an example of a man who decided he really wanted to change his life and do the work that was required to alter his thinking and his actions. When we asked him to reflect back upon his childhood, his upbringing, and his parents, he was somber. *Yeah, I guess I never knew I was doing it, but I am still addressing it. Internalizing . . . my emotions and feelings. I hate to admit it, but I guess that stemmed from my childhood, looking at who you are because of what you came from. In this situation, I just never, um, I have got a lot more problems than I ever knew that I did, um, a lot more that I need to address.*

We asked whether his childhood memories were pretty much happy or unhappy. *I try to be a pretty positive person, so I think maybe I suppressed a lot of that unhappy stuff. I prefer to think about the good times instead of the bad times. I never really deal with the bad times, the issues at hand. I just kind of ignore them, forget about them, and that doesn't really work.*

Thinking of the good times was certainly a strategy that some men, like Mike, were attempting to adopt. It was certainly a strategy that many men hoped their children would adopt as they reflected back to childhoods replete with unhappy memories, such as a father in prison, fighting in the home, or no-contact orders. Yet even as they spoke these words, some, like Mike, noted that it was not a successful way of coping with past difficulties. Like so many other things in life, it needed to be named, grieved, and then overcome. Suppressing it or ignoring it did not work. In Mike's case, as we show in chapter 7, once he began to change his life, treating his daughter well and being a good father were high on his priority list. He was determined to make amends, to be the father he never had, to make up for all those years when he was only thinking of himself—in religious language, he was determined to "reap the years the locusts had eaten."

FROM ONE GENERATION TO THE NEXT

For sure, among the men we interviewed were many very sad and disturbing stories of childhood. As we have shown, not all men had difficult upbringings, nor were they all poor. But many had a very rough start to life. Casiano Santiago was a man whose background affected how others saw him, and as a result, although he was never charged, he and his girlfriend were unable to keep their infant daughter. In fact, she was removed from their care almost as soon as she was born.

At eighteen, Casiano became a father. Days later, in the hospital, the Department of Human Services (DHS) took his newborn into foster care. Fourteen months later, we met Casiano for the first time. Wearing a baseball cap that was too small for his head, he was clean-shaven, with a baby face that suggested he was still in high school. But he had very grown-up troubles. Maureen, his girlfriend, was twenty. She grew up in a home that was by all standards dysfunctional. Her mother was a regular user of crystal meth, a woman Casiano describes as having a *criminal background*. She grew up poor, marginalized, and part of the DHS system.

Casiano was very confused about why his daughter was removed from them days after she was born. He wondered why she was placed in foster care. He had never been charged with any crime. He had contacted an attorney, who advised him to work hard and attend the groups in the hope of getting his daughter back someday. He was trying to do this.

Casiano's own parents split up when he was a teen. Casiano and his brother, together with their mother, went to live with their grandmother, who was alone and in failing health. The grandfather had been an alcoholic. His father was serving a prison sentence, and Casiano did not have contact with him for a very long time. At school, Casiano got in minor scuffles, was expelled, and then was suspended, after which he was placed in an alternative program. Eventually, he did not go to school any longer. A short time later he went to work for a man who was also a pastor, someone who offered him the first real break of his life.

We pick up Casiano's story again in chapter 9, when we consider more fully the role of the pastor of a very small church—a bivocational religious leader—who hired him as a carpenter's helper, believed in him, and offered him hope. With excitement, Casiano told us, *Right now, I'm making more money than I thought I would. It's amazing. I'm making like four hundred dollars a week, and at my last job, I was making like two hundred dollars, maybe, a week.* At that point, he was working for McDonald's. His wife was working at a car wash but had recently left because the other workers didn't treat her well.

We interviewed Casiano six months later. He was having supervised visits with his daughter. He and the baby's mother had graduated from the parenting class, and he was still working for the pastor's home improvement business. Casiano had almost completed his fifty-two weeks of the batterer intervention program. Yet he had no indication that his daughter would ever be returned to them. His attorney encouraged him to keep on trying to fulfill all the expectations of the program. He had an outstanding charge against him of burglary from before the child was born, but it had not yet come to court. He was picked up at the county fair. *I didn't even know what was going on.* He claimed he was innocent, but his legal counsel prepared him for the possibility that he would do *like fifteen days in jail.* These were matters that he discussed with his pastor-employer. *Oh, yeah, he knows. He's, like, "Well, at least you got a job when you get back."*

Casiano talked about his concerns for the future. *I am so like worried about stuff like my daughter, 'cause one time I got angry, and you know she's gone, and so now it's just like, it scares me to get angry....* Casiano and some other very young fathers had been identified as "at risk" parents. But they did not appear to have been told this, nor did they fully understand what was required of them to be reunited with their biological children. Casiano's girlfriend, too, had been so identified, with a mother who was an addict, and since her childhood, Maureen had been in the DHS system. All of this was tragic, and it was about to repeat itself in the life of his child.

CONNECTING WITH THEIR OWN CHILDREN

A consistent theme voiced by the men in the STOP program was the desire to keep connected to their children or, for those whose connections had been severed by others, including the state, to reconnect with their children. Connections were lost or strained when fathers were sent to prison. Connections were lost or strained when there was a restraining order or when the DHS removed children from the homes. Sometimes there was supervised visitation, but this was not always possible, or desirable, from the point of view of the child-welfare workers involved. Sometimes connections were severed by the mother. And once the children were older, sometimes it was the children themselves who wished for no contact.

To be sure, it was the men's violence, neglect, or addictions—and sometimes all three—that created the initial reason(s) for the separation of father from child. And it was often a continued pattern of violence, neglect, or addiction that meant that father and child require continued separation. In a few cases, it appears that men and women who were very young had their children removed by DHS from their care at the time of birth (while the mother and the infant were still in the hospital) as a result of having been identified as "at risk." Here it was the violence, neglect, or addictions of their parents—the grandparents—that separated father and mother from child. Marked poverty, inadequate housing, and a perceived inability to care for the child was probably an issue, too, but none of the men ever mentioned these factors directly.

For some men we interviewed, the desire to reconnect with their children occurred while they were in custody, when they had time to reflect on what was important in their lives and how they were planning to move forward after incarceration. From their cells, they often thought about how it would be different with their children. They were changing their attitudes and priorities. They were ready for a new start. But the men did not always take into account that reconnection with their children was not all about their wishes. To make connections would take not only initiative on their part but also willingness on the part of the children and often the children's mothers. Consequently, many men experienced roadblocks as they attempted to reconnect in their children's lives, but the desire for reconnection and a belief that it was possible often spurred them on to do the work required to change thinking and behavior.

Reaping the rewards of reconnection takes a long time, many years, and for some men, they never really materialize the way they were hoping they would. This comes as no surprise to someone looking at their lives from a distance. Some of the children did not want to reconnect with their fathers—fathers who had hurt them or had hurt their mothers or had shown little interest in their lives prior to a prison sentence. But for the men themselves, this was difficult to understand, and when its reality sank it, it was often accompanied with despair.

The hope of reestablishing relationships with their children often served as the motivating factor for doing the work that was required for changed thinking and changed behavior. Sometimes there was a mandate for batterer intervention group attendance placed on the father by child protection services before he could have contact with his child(ren). Many of the men we observed in groups had experienced this at some point in their lives. For others, though, their children were grown before the time for reconnection came. When this happened, the request for contact that came from the father often did not end the way the man was hoping. Sheldon Cramer's attempts at reconnecting with his three children offer an example.

A year after we met Sheldon for the first time, he had connected with his older daughter on MySpace. She had recently given birth to a daughter, and Sheldon was invited to see both his daughter and his grandchild. He told us that this made him very happy. He had found her online and asked to see her. She had granted his wish. This all occurred just before we met Sheldon. But two years later, in one of our interviews, he noted that he had not seen either his daughter or his granddaughter since. This saddened him. He had tried, but it seemed she did not want him to enter her life again. From his perspective, what more could he do? He had found her, and she wanted no ongoing contact with him. Sheldon also found his younger daughter online, and they had communicated using that medium, but no face-to-face meeting had occurred. With his son, he had no contact whatsoever. As he talked about this, Sheldon appeared resigned to the disappointing fact that his children did not want him to be part of their lives. For many other men, though, the story was less dramatic but disappointing nonetheless from their point of view. They had built up hopes that things would be great, that a wonderful reunion would occur, and that just as they had been thinking of their children, the children had been thinking of them.

There were some exceptions, of course. Bill, whose story we highlight in chapter 7, reconnected with his daughter after his prison sentence was completed, and she eventually came to live with him, leaving behind the family foster care that the state had arranged with her grandmother, Bill's mother. In his case, the girl's mother was not a viable option for care—she was still addicted to drugs and alcohol and continuing to live dangerously. As a result, she created no resistance for Bill's entrance back into his daughter's life.

CONCLUDING COMMENTS

For most of the men we interviewed, the groups we observed, and the case files we analyzed, the stories of men's adult abusive acts toward the women with whom they were in relationships were interwoven with their own stories of vulnerability that begin, many times, in childhood. In this chapter, we have considered some of the features of that vulnerability and how it is shaped by emotional, financial, and physical factors and challenges. The impact of an addicted parent or an abusive upbringing is a theme that emerges for some; others talk about feeling "left out," as if the good things in life were passing them by. On the other hand, a minority of them report happy childhoods, free from poverty, abuse, or life on the margins.

As we listened to the men talk about their lives, we understood that their early life experiences shaped the stories they told. For those workers who walked alongside them, they, too, saw the vulnerability of the men's childhood experiences. From their vantage point, the childhoods of men who batter are the training ground for adult abusive acts. The intergenerational transmission of violence—a consistent theme in the literature—can be observed clearly in the lives of the men who were part of our study. And yet there is evidence that change can occur. The patterns that are observed can be altered by intervention, and resiliency can begin to overtake the power of the vulnerabilities that men experienced as children. One of the strongest motivators to change was related to the lives of their own children. As we shall see in chapters 7 and 8, themes of fathering after violence are discussed in group and become part of the overall accountability plan. The importance of this message, we believe, and the reason men are so receptive to hear it, at least at STOP, relates back to their own painful childhood memories, which they are now facing within the group context. They say that they do not want to repeat for their own children what they themselves experienced at a young age.

Intimate Relationships

Between 2005 and 2009, we interviewed Pete Brown six times. We followed his story in and out of intimate relationships with various women. The first time we met him, he had recently been released from prison, where he was doing time for assaulting his elderly mother, a woman with Alzheimer's disease whom he was caring for in her own home. High on crystal meth and drunk on alcohol, he broke into her bedroom (which she had locked in fear), ripped the phone from the wall as she was talking to the police dispatcher, and threw it at her in a rage.

By his own account, Pete's desire for numerous sexual partners and variety in intimacy was something that had caused him a lot of trouble. Needless to say, it had brought a lot of trouble to the lives of countless women, too. As his story unfolded before us, we learned that Pete had been violent toward women for a long time. He was now in his forties, and his first altercation with a partner occurred when he was seventeen.

The first time I hit a woman, I was like seventeen, I think. She hit me when I was driving, and I backhanded her. I can still remember it. . . . I had a girlfriend named Michelle that woke up one morning and she had a bulging black eye. . . . I told her, say you got hit by a softball, to make up for my embarrassment or whatever you want to call it. And that was just the first time. After that, I was like slapping her and kicking her, you know, and so obviously, I have done violence with a woman.

Pete fast-forwarded to his first marriage. *And then with my ex-wife, sticking a gun between her eyes and behind her ear and dry-firing and her thinking she was going to die. I would say, this is violent. And today I haven't done that much since that incident back in 1995 except for my mother thing.*

For Pete, life revolved around drug use, excessive alcohol consumption, smoking cigarettes and marijuana, and sex. *I think of sex, I think of speed, I think of speed, I think of sex, and that is a very powerful thing, because sex is powerful, and with amphetamines it's a very powerful thing.* He grew up the youngest of six siblings, the only one of his family members to be addicted to drugs and alcohol and in trouble with the law. Pete was one of the few men we interviewed not to have children. He spoke at some length about his ex-wife and their lives together. From his account, Christine did not believe she was a battered woman. *I was putting a firearm to my significant other's head, dry-fired it twice, making her believe it was loaded. I have never hit her, but I tell you what, I sure wanted to hit her, I am telling you. The reason I say that is because we would be sitting around at Christmas or Thanksgiving dinner, and she goes, "That's one thing I can say about Peter, he's never hit me," and that used to piss me off, because what*

I did to her was much more horrendous than hitting her. It was physical and mental to the extreme, to the extreme, but she justified it in her head because I had never physically hit her.

Pete had been in classes for a few months. He spoke positively about the program, but his comments were more subdued than those of many of the other men. Pete was waiting to see how he felt after more classes and after his resolve to stay clean and sober had more time to be proved real. He talked about a new woman who came into his life after prison.

I have been going out on this, I guess you would call it a date—it's like I have known her for over three months, and we get along really well, and obviously she likes my company, and I haven't even kissed this woman, and I think, "Oh, God, this is so different." I am like, "Wow." When I was in prison, I told my counselor, you know, I would like to find me a date to be my friend and see what happens. The only relationships I have had, it's always been pretty quick to the sex situation. . . . I don't know how to act. It's embarrassing, I don't know how to act around a woman, to be polite and cordial and respectful at the same time, but boy, it's a whole new experience trying to be a woman's friend.

At forty-two, Pete oscillated between feeling sorry for himself and being thankful that he had no one other than himself to take care of. He talked about trying to stay positive, to be grateful that he had choices now—so different from life behind bars with no choice but to do what others told you to.

In six months, when we saw Pete again, we asked about the developing relationship with the woman he mentioned to us in our first interview. He confided that he was seeing two women, one who was a *friend with benefits,* meaning no commitment, no ongoing relationship, but friendship with sexual activity. *That's what she wanted—to have her cake and eat it, too.* There was an ex-boyfriend on the scene, too, so Pete said he held back, so to speak. *Now I am starting to see her again, and I am just taking it one day at a time 'cause I'm scared of having a relationship.* Pete's fear of a committed relationship came up in conversation each time we interviewed him. At our second interview, Pete was still living in a halfway house, a sheltered environment that helped to monitor and encourage his sobriety.

Six months later, two years after our initial interview, we interviewed Pete again. He had moved out of the sponsored environment and in with his girlfriend, a woman who worked as a cashier in a discount store. He spoke of the challenges of living with someone again and the paradox that when you are lonely, you want a partner, and when you have a partner, you want your space. The bicycle was gone; Pete now had a license and a truck, which he bought from his brother, who was working in another state. When Pete got frustrated in his relationship, he took a walk or a drive, some form of *time-out.*

The next autumn, we saw Pete again. He had now been with the same woman for almost two years—they gardened together, watched movies together, and even on occasion went to church together, something Pete had not done for a long time. He did not go back to the STOP program after he graduated. He was just glad to be done. But he said that he tried to practice many of the lessons he learned at STOP in his daily life. He was still clean and sober, but he had returned to smoking after many years free of cigarettes.

He spoke about his partner, who recently had surgery; her mother came from abroad to care for her daughter during this time. Pete was initially apprehensive about this. *I had this premeditated resentment about her being there, because I wanted to take care of her, but she did a really good job. Bless her heart! She is eighty-one years old. . . . . But her mother, the way that she expresses her love is through food. Her mom and me really got close 'cause she was here for eighteen days.*

Pete summed up his life at this point, in our fourth interview with him: *I get on my pity pot, and then my gratitude list goes to zero. Three or four years ago, after losing everything, going to prison, and I have a lot to be grateful for, and I just keep telling myself to do the next right thing.*

And what did this mean for Pete? *I catch myself. I can still be verbally abusive, and then I catch myself, and you can feel that voice that is rising. Linda says, "You are just a runner," and when there is an argument, I have to go. I learned that . . . that is when I lose my ability to be a human being. I have to flee the situation, because sticking around is just going to escalate the situation. She says, "You gotta run." I say, "I have to." That is my coping mechanism.*

One year later, the last time we met with Pete, he reflected back on his life with Linda. *I left that situation because I was going to break her fuckin' neck. She has power and control issues. I could have her arrested for her doing shit to me. I actually considered marrying this woman. That's all over and done. We talked about going to counseling but never did. She was very beautiful, but I have been away from her for a few months now. . . . I verbally abused her a great deal, but I would leave the house when I got angry, and I would leave for six days at a time.*

We asked Pete whether there were any new relationships on the horizon. *I have a gal that wants me to move in with her, but I don't want to jump into the frying pan.*

We had contact with Pete for a period of four years, through one focus group and five interviews. We listened to him talk about a relationship that was developing, became ongoing, involved living together, and almost resulted in marriage. We heard him speak of how it dissolved. During our years of contact, Pete's mother died, he had some brief encounters with his siblings, and he claimed several times that *life is too much of a struggle.* Pete's story offers a strong reminder that gains made can be easily lost, that success needs to be measured in small indices. However, it is noteworthy that despite his disappointment with Linda and their relationship woes, the police never had to be called to intervene. There was no physical violence, although there was marked verbal and emotional abuse. Had Pete not been through the STOP program, what might he have done to Linda? This is a question that is impossible to answer but sobering to consider.

These are some of the pieces of Pete's story as it was told to us:

- His first act of violence toward an intimate took place when he was seventeen.
- He exhibited severe cruelty toward his wife (dry-firing a weapon at her head).
- He exhibited severe cruelty toward his mother, who had Alzheimer's disease (physical and emotional abuse and neglect).
- He had several addictions, including drugs and alcohol and possibly a sex addiction.
- He was in many abusive relationships with women, during and after his completion of a fifty-two-week batterer intervention program.

Violence in adolescent romantic relationships is, quite alarmingly, common. The continuum of violence ranges from verbal or psychological abuse to rape and murder.[1] In their summary of several research studies related to violence in teen relationships, Mulford and Giordano (2008, 34) note that in the United States, approximately 10 percent of adolescents reported being victims of physical violence at the hands of romantic partners in 2006. The numbers were even higher for victimization through psychological violence, with between two and three out of ten teens reporting being victimized. Other researchers (Avery-Leaf et al. 1997) claim even higher rates related to physical and sexual abuse, estimating that between 30 and 41 percent of teens experience these types of violence in their dating relationships. In the younger age range of eleven to fourteen, 62 percent of respondents said they knew peers who had been verbally abused by dating partners (Liz Claiborne Inc. 2007). In Canada, more than half of teenage victims of violence between the ages of fourteen and seventeen were assaulted by close friends, acquaintances, or coworkers (Statistics Canada 2010).

Some researchers include psychological and emotional abuse in the definition of dating violence, while others include only physical violence. Two definitions help to clarify the issue:

Teen dating violence . . . is violence committed by a person who is in, wants to be in, or has been in a social relationship of a romantic or intimate nature with the victim. It occurs in both opposite- and same-sex relationships, between non-cohabiting and sometimes cohabiting partners. Dating violence which occurs between the ages of 11 and 14 is often referred to as "tween" dating violence. Teen dating violence includes physical, sexual, and emotional abuse.
(Violence against Women Online Resources 2010)

Teen dating violence and abuse is a pattern of destructive behaviors used to exert power and control over a dating partner.
(TeenDVMonth.org 2013)

Related to guns, in our viewing of more than one hundred cases in a specialized domestic violence court, almost every judgment included surrendering all firearms and firearms licenses to the police. Recent research by Vittes et al. (2013) found that women felt far safer when guns were removed expeditiously after violence. The risk of a woman involved in interpersonal violence being murdered by her abuser increases fivefold when there are weapons present in the home (Campbell et al. 2003).

According to the Uniform Crime Reporting Survey, in 2000, the top three most frequent offenses experienced by older adults from family members were common assault (54 percent), uttering threats (21 percent), and assault with a weapon or causing bodily harm (13 percent). Adult children and spouses accounted for almost three-quarters (71 percent) of those responsible for victimizations of older adults. Eighty percent of those accused of violently victimizing an older family member in 2000 were men.

Numerous researchers have discussed the complex relationship between substance abuse and abuse of women (e.g., Gondolf 1995; Brown et al. 1999;

Humphreys et al. 2005). High-risk men often present with correlated issues of substance abuse; in fact, the majority of men brought to the attention of the court for domestic violence issues have alcohol problems (Stuart 2005). A batterer's pattern of abuse, including economic control, sexual violence, and intimidation, often has little or no identifiable connection to his use of or dependence on alcohol.[2] Because many male batterers also abuse alcohol and other drugs, it's easy to conclude that these substances may cause domestic violence. The research notes that while they offer the batterer another excuse to evade responsibility for his behavior, they apparently do increase the severity and lethality of the violence.[3]

Risk factors associated with domestic violence include variables such as low income, younger age, being unmarried or having multiple marriages, unemployment, less than a high school education, alcohol and/or drug abuse, previous criminal history, race, and residence location. Other factors of interest include the number of children in the household and the wife as full-time homemaker (Yarbrough and Blanton 2000). Additionally, Faulkner et al. (1991) comment that men in intervention programs reported stress related to money, work, alcohol, settling arguments, and jealousy. Other characteristics of men in abusive relationships include elevated scores on instruments measuring sociopathy, narcissism and borderline behaviors, and depression (Tolman and Bennett 1990).

Michalski (2004) reports that exposure to violent networks does increase the likelihood of recidivistic violence. After men have perhaps served time in prison, have alienated their childhood families, and are barred from interaction with victims and children through no-contact orders that form part of their probation or parole, a big question for them is "Who can I turn to?" Avoiding the temptation to go back to the old ways, to seek our former friends and acquaintances, to visit old haunts, can be a great burden. Going back to the ways they know may be the easier track to take.

Men such as Pete are an enormous challenge for any program. Caught up in his own little world so completely, he had difficulty feeling empathy for others or caring about anyone's needs other than his own. Over time, he learned to take some responsibility for his actions, those that occurred in the past and those transpiring in the present. In what might be considered an act of responsibility, he left his relationship when he determined that there was a great possibility for danger, both for the partner and also, in Pete's way of thinking, for himself, since the STOP program had helped him to see that there was a great possibility of severe consequences for him. His leaving can certainly be interpreted as an act of self-preservation as much as an act of kindness toward the woman with whom he was cohabiting.

We turn from Pete's story of violence, which emerged in so many different relationships with significant women in his life, to Harry, a man of about the same age who had spent his entire adult life with the same woman.

Harry Cuomo had been married for almost twenty-three years to Angelina when he found himself handcuffed in his own home and led away by police. *The first and only time in my life I ever negatively touched her, I grabbed her by the hair on both sides of the head, and I got right in her face, and I said something. I cussed at her real bad, and I said give me the blankety-blank checkbook. That's exactly the words, except for the blankety-blank.*

For their entire married life, Harry and Angelina had experienced financial troubles, deep problems that they could not seem to resolve. Angelina's fear of Harry had risen to the point where a week before the event that landed him in jail, she had warned her teenage daughter, one of their four children, that she might need to seek refuge with her grandmother if the fighting between them got too intense. The plan was set: if Angelina told her daughter to go, she was to leave immediately and call 911 on her cell phone as she walked up the long driveway from their farm to the main road where the grandmother lived.

Harry was not a farmer, but his wife had inherited the farm from her family, and they raised sheep and goats there. He worked in one of the local mills in an attempt to keep everything afloat. Then he lost his mill job with a downturn in the economy. At this point, staying afloat was no longer possible.

His experience with the criminal justice system was very confusing for Harry. When asked, he did not seem to know if his case went to trial, how it was processed, or whether he was found guilty and of what charge. What he did know was that he went to road crew. In Harry's county, the sheriff's work crew was an alternative to incarceration, an option available to those sentenced for short periods of time or weekends. Those inmates who worked on road crew were allowed to return to their own residences at the end of each day. In a survey done by the National Crime Justice Reference Service in 1984, there were twenty-six states with some type of road crew, inmates were paid in twenty states at rates ranging from a few cents per hour to seventy-five dollars per month, and inmates had to meet standards for security that often meant excluding sex offenders and violent offenders.

Following his time on the road crew, Harry found his way to STOP. We asked whether his parole officer had made the suggestion, but Harry did not seem to think he had any experience with a parole officer or even what such a person did.

Harry loved the STOP program. When we first met him, he had been coming for almost two years, well beyond what he had been ordered to do. STOP offered him something that was critical at a time in his life when he was most vulnerable. When he left jail, he had nowhere to go. He couldn't return home, as there was a restraining order against him, and he didn't have any money that would enable him to live independently. At first, he stayed with a friend. After three weeks, he moved into a rooming house and lived there for eight months with two roommates. In that context, he met the woman he was now dating and to whom he had recently become engaged.

But we are moving a little too fast with the story, and we need to back up. Harry and his (second) wife, Angelina, met in church. She was a strong believer, and he was a new Christian. At the end of his first marriage, which had lasted only fourteen months, Harry had cried out to God to come into his life. He considered this a turning point, a time when he began to consider himself *saved*. Within a year, they were married. *And in short, she was a strong Christian ... she was also very much wanting to find a man and get married ... and I remember many times before we got married, going, "I don't want this."*

So why did Harry get married, despite his reservations? *I wasn't that strong of a person to really stand my ground. . . . I never forget the first time I went out to her farm to see her. I remember standing next to her; she was in bib overalls, in front of one of the fences, looking around at all this work. And I said, "God, am I glad that I don't live here!"*

The farm was run-down, there was far too much work to bring it back to where it had once been, and there were no resources to hire paid help. Not long into the marriage, Harry sought the help of a psychiatrist and began taking prescription drugs to ease the malaise he felt. He also sought the help of several pastors, none of whom he felt was very helpful. It is very possible that he was depressed, but he never called his despair by that name.

According to Harry, the first place he ever received the kind of support and assistance he felt he needed was STOP. That's what kept him coming and not wanting ever to terminate his relationship with the groups or the executive director, of whom he said, *I get so much from her [teaching].*

Harry's story can be summarized in four points:

- Low self-esteem characterized his life and led him to make choices— including his decision to marry Angelina—that he really did not wish to make.
- He had limited skills for coping with anxiety, interpersonal conflict, or anger.
- Prescription drugs helped to ease the malaise he felt.
- His passive-aggressive behavior turned violent at the point where he felt that the stress of his financial worries was outmatched by his strategies for dealing with his circumstances.

According to the often-cited Braden (1969), there are three key components of self-esteem: it is an essential human need that is vital for survival and normal, healthy development; it arises automatically from within based on a person's beliefs and consciousness; it occurs in conjunction with a person's thoughts, behaviors, feelings, and actions. Numerous researchers note the link between low self-esteem and poor choices, including aggressive and deviant behaviors (e.g., Cowan and Mills 2004; Donnellan et al. 2005). Certainly, Papadakaki et al. (2009) found a direct connection between low self-esteem and increased physical violence perpetration. Recent research has uncovered a link between insecure attachment along with borderline to mild intellectual disability and partner abuse (Buck et al. 2012; Weiss et al. 2011). Furthermore, 18.1 percent of the adult US population suffers from some form of anxiety disorder,[4] and within a twelve-month period, 6.1 percent of the adult population suffers from a major depressive disorder.[5]

Martin et al. (2001) found a significant association between financial hardship as a life stressor and physical abuse. When worries over money are added to other life stressors such as fighting between couples or perhaps even separation, there is increased likelihood that the tensions will result in violent behavior.

Harry was receptive to what STOP was attempting to do, and he quickly got with the program. Early on, he could see that he needed to acquire skills and that STOP was well positioned to help him acquire a tool kit for daily life. This is not to diminish in any way his angry, controlling behavior as it was directed at Angelina. But as Harry was able to develop a relationship with STOP facilitators and staff, he gained self-confidence, understood his passivity in context, and started doing the work that was required to change thinking and actions. An education-based program was just right for Harry, and the warmth and respect that the staff offered encouraged his own self-discovery and provided some strategies that he was able to employ to alter his circumstances.

Pete was without children, Harry had teenage children when the violence began, and now we turn to a man whose children began sustained involvement with the Department of Human Services (DHS) from a very early age.

Terry Ryder was thirty-eight years old when we first met him. As he described his relationship with his wife, the children they shared, and her parents, it appeared that there was a large web of extremely unhealthy ties among them. His wife's mother and father ran an escort business. Terry and their daughter were granted unsupervised access to their home on a regular basis when she was in her mid-teens, and soon after she was pregnant. For the next ten years of Terry's life, he was sometimes involved, but mostly uninvolved, with the lives of his children, his wife, and her parents.

I have a thirteen-year-old daughter and a ten-year-old son. My daughter I was not able to see from birth to eleven. I was only able to be around her for six months of her life. Her family, her mother's family, is pretty well-off; they kept her away from me.

He reflected on how he and his wife met. *The first time I met her—my daughter's mother—I was a body builder back then and in fairly good shape, a lot better than what I am now. At any rate, the first thing her mother done was grab my face and said I have got great bone structure and muscle definition, I would make cute babies. I was eighteen, she was sixteen, and her mom said, "Oh, you guys can have free rein of the house."*

They separated soon after the child was born. Terry moved to another state, and the child's mother *got into prostitution, drug dealing.* They had another child after a short reunion and then separated again. The children missed a lot of time at school and were eventually temporarily removed by the state.

When his daughter was in her early teens, Terry reconnected with her when he moved back to the area where she still lived with her mother. But they had a very rocky relationship. Eventually, DHS was involved again, and Terry *had a restraining order.* The girl's mother informed the authorities of his physical altercations with her—discipline for her disobedience, according to Terry.

Terry's attorney, who was a Christian, suggested that he might seek the services of STOP to help him become a better parent. When we first interviewed him, he had just started coming to classes.

Six months later, Terry said, *I have got a life and a new wife. I work full-time now. I come four times a week to get this over with.* His new wife was an undergraduate student, twenty-one years old, studying culinary arts. They met through Terry's roommate, her boss. *We have spent every single day together since then.*

Of the relationship he says, *we have a strong belief in God and so does she and I have changed how I look at the opposite sex. I have always been a good person, but the choices I have made was right time, wrong person. Now I look for someone who is like my mother.*

Several times during our second interview, he made reference to arguments or challenges. *I am a highly competitive individual, and so I challenge her.* Later he referred to a time when they went without speaking but said, *I didn't give her the normal salutation.*

Six months later, Terry did not accept our invitation to be interviewed again.

Here are some of the things we learned about Terry:

- He began fatherhood in his late teens but had little involvement in the life of his first child.
- A brief reunion with the mother resulted in a second child, followed by a longer period of separation.

- Involvement in the lives of his children began in a more sustained way in their preteen years, and at that point, he received a restraining order so that he could no longer have contact with his daughter.
- He married a woman fifteen years his junior, and his talk about that relationship was replete with warning signs of abusive behavior.

Terry was not mandated to come to STOP in the way many men are, but he was there at the encouragement of his lawyer so that there could be an eventual removal of the restraining order limiting his contact with his daughter. There was no indication in the two interviews we had with Terry that he had accepted any responsibility for his inappropriate actions toward his daughter. And there were plenty of warning signs in the second interview that his relationship with a new intimate partner had controlling and abusive features. It seems clear that Terry felt he had nothing to learn by his attendance at STOP; it was simply something to be endured.

The fourth man we introduce in this chapter on intimate relationships is Derek Knight, someone who presented as very low-functioning, who did not seem to fully understand himself or the world around him. As a child and a teen, Derek was bullied mercilessly, first by his brother, who was two years older, and then by other kids at school. He suffered from obsessive-compulsive disorder (OCD), manifested as a compulsion to clean things and keep items orderly. His brother would taunt him, putting ketchup and mustard on the door handle to his bedroom and messing up the order in which he had placed his clothes and toys. *I have an older brother, he's two years older, and every day he was just, like, he would harass me as many times as he could and beat on me, and all that good stuff, and he's been putting me down all my life. That's why I have a big issue with, like, self-esteem right now. It's like in my mind, he said, "You're stupid, you'll never amount to anything." 'Cause maybe my dad—I think he saw a lot of my dad hitting my mother.*

Eventually, Derek left school and got his GED. He was working at an assisted living facility for the elderly when he met a woman who was *kind of stalking me, you know, everywhere I went she would be there, she wanted to help me, and finally I got it into my thick skull that this girl likes me, you know, and so I started going over to her house and, you know, just hanging out. It was great. I liked her.*

Within a short period of time, they were married. When we met Derek, he was twenty-five, on three years' probation after spending ten days in jail, having been served with a no-contact order and a mandate to attend a batterer intervention program. The incident that brought him into contact with the criminal justice system involved an altercation with his wife over the remote control. *Well, my wife and I were watching TV one night, and she always got control of the remote control, and she was watching, like, I don't know, some female show, and I wanted to watch, like, the military channel.*

Disagreements over television viewing are not uncommon among couples, so what happened to involve the cops and the criminal justice system? *I don't know what happened, if I blacked out or not, but she said I was just, like, hitting her arms and her legs and her shins, and you know, the cops came that time. But she's threatening, I mean she has threatened to call the cops when I pulled the phone cord out of the wall. . . . I basically admitted to the cops about what I did, and I was jailed for ten days, and then the judge sentenced me to three years' probation, and I have to go to STOP classes and take my medication as prescribed.*

We asked if he had children. *Nope, no kids. I am still a kid myself, so it's hard to take care of just me, you know. . . . I feel like I have a twelve-year-old mind, but the rest of my body is growing.*

When we saw Derek for the second time, he was working in a warehouse assembling store furniture. He was still under the no-contact order, and his only support came from some neighbors, one an older woman he used to work for in senior home care. They went on walks. Another neighbor, an older man, coached him to be more assertive. Derek was still attending the STOP program.

Derek did not accept our invitation for a next interview.

The central features of Derek's story:

- He suffered from very low self-esteem rooted initially in his family of origin.
- He married the first woman with whom he had a romantic, intimate relationship.
- He had limited skills for coping with anxiety, interpersonal conflict, or anger.
- He had very limited aspirations for his life.

The final man we present in this chapter was one of the youngest men we interviewed, a twenty-two-year-old African American who had a four-year-old boy and another child on the way. Antwone Washington lived with his son's mother, a woman he had been married to for about a year. They lived with her parents. He worked as a car mechanic, and his wife was employed at a nursing home.

We asked how he found his way to the STOP program. *Me and my ex-girlfriend got in a big fight, and I ended up ripping the phone out of the wall, while apparently she was outside on the phone with the cops. So that's what got me here.*

We asked whether there was any physical altercation before she called the police. *No, we'd been fighting for a while, and I tried to park my truck on her car, and it didn't work so well. Collateral damage type thing, and when I went back to our apartment, I found all my stuff thrown about the place, my brand-new big-screen TV was tipped over and didn't work, and a bunch of other stuff of mine was broken or thrown about, and I lost my temper. I finally got everyone out of the apartment, and apparently she took the phone with her and she was on the phone with the Sheriff's Department, and I was rampaging through the house, and I grabbed the phone and ripped it out of the wall, and I was on my way to actually talk to a crisis counselor that I had talked to the night before, and when I got done talking to her and walked outside, they put me in cuffs and took me away.*

This incident occurred while Antwone was on probation. He had received an assault charge seven months after he got back from an overseas tour in Afghanistan. For this, he was put on eighteen months of probation. For the domestic assault charge, he spent forty-five days in jail and was ordered to enter a batterer intervention program.

Antwone had a really rough childhood. He enlisted in the National Guard during his junior year of high school when he was seventeen and began basic training that summer. After he graduated the next year, he was sent to Texas for training and then overseas. He left a girlfriend and an infant behind. He returned an emotionally wounded young man, filled with anger and without any skills for dealing with his feelings. Of his time in the Army, he said, *I'm paying hell for it.*

After two assault charges, one involving another male and one involving an ex-girlfriend, Antwone said he felt it was time to settle down and marry the mother of his little boy. *She's not a new girlfriend. I dated her back in high school, and we had a kid together in high school, so I just kind of decided it was really time to settle down and be a part of my son's life. . . . I knew how hard it was to grow up without a father, a real good father figure around, and I don't really want my son growing up the same way, so I should have waited a little longer before we got married and just got back together with her but not got married.*

We asked how long he had been married. *Almost a year now. We got our arguments and stuff that we have but nothing big, we kind of know our limits, and she knows that when I say I want to leave and go for a ride, she lets me, and I usually end up going and talking to my dad 'cause he can calm me down pretty good, so I'm gone a couple hours, and then I calm down, and we make up, and everything's good.* Antwone told us that there was another baby on the way and that his wife was in the hospital in case the baby was preterm. Her due date was seven weeks away. He did not mention that she was under the watchful eye of DHS with a high-risk pregnancy, but that was certainly possible given how their story unfolded.

When we first met Antwone, he had been married about a year and involved with the program for about the same length of time, although he had not yet completed very many classes. Living and working in another community, he found it hard to come to the program at STOP. He had little money and no transportation. But when he was told by his parole officer that his lack of consistent attendance would land him back in jail, Antwone found a way to come more often. He had several months of attendance before we met him. Six months later, he did not accept our invitation to be interviewed.

The central features of Antwone's story:

- His first child was born when he was still a teenager.
- He returned from a tour of duty with the Army full of anger.
- He had assault charges related to domestic violence involving an ex-girlfriend and assault of another male.
- He lived in an extended family context.

Antwone had very little money, very little freedom, and big-time problems. Despite his criminal record, he was able to obtain employment as a car mechanic, and his in-laws offered their home as a place for Antwone, their daughter, and their other children to live. He did not take the STOP program seriously in terms of consistent attendance and, as a result, was in a position where he could have his freedom curtailed and be sent back to jail for noncompliance.

FIVE STORIES, ONE MESSAGE

Pete, Harry, Terry, Derek, and Antwone were all men who had great difficulty dealing with life and with the women with whom their lives intertwined. But the reasons for this vary. There is not just a single story line of what a violent relationship looks like in the beginning. It is important, we believe, to see that their stories unfolded from contexts that were markedly different from one another. And yet there are certain similarities between them. In some ways, the two younger men, Antwone and Derek, offer a first chapter in the lives of other men whose stories we highlight later in the book. Antwone was a veteran of Afghanistan, had two assault charges, served a short time in jail, had a four-year-old child and a pregnant wife, and had not yet reached his twenty-third birthday. In part, his life was made meaningful by his wife, toward whom he claimed he was never abusive, and supportive in-laws, plus a job he enjoyed, even though the pay did not enable them to live independently of his wife's family. Derek was alone, without any support other than from two elderly neighbors who offered occasional acts of kindness toward him. He, too, was employed at a job he enjoyed. With a no-contact order in place vis-à-vis his wife, Derek spent a lot of time alone, master over the remote control of his television.

Pete and Terry, both middle-aged, were examples of men who began new lives with new women after their contact with the criminal justice system. We chose to highlight Pete and Terry, because Pete's story appeared to be much more hopeful in terms of a life free of violence than that of Terry, who within months of being married was exhibiting talk that raised concerns about his controlling beliefs and his abusive behavior.

Pete stands out as a man with an outstanding ability to be cruel, little insight into the harm he caused others, and little evidence of remorse. Yet even Pete was impacted by his contact with STOP. He completed the fifty-two-week intervention program and of his own volition left the latest of his many intimate relationships before he did grievous harm to his partner.

Four of the five men (all but Derek) had been involved in many intimate relationships and spoke without any prompting of the ease in which they entered into new relationships with women in their lives. A program such as STOP has the potential to assist such men in these new partnerships, with insights and strategies for coping with life's disappointments and frustrations. But to do so, the men must come to group, participate fully, do the work, and become accountable, issues that we discuss in the chapters ahead.

A LIFE SPIRALING OUT OF CONTROL

Stories of men who act abusively are replete with examples of failed relationships—beginning with their biological parents and siblings, foster parents, and temporary caregivers and followed by examples of early sexual intimacy and unwanted pregnancies. Many, like Terry and Antwone, begin parenthood early. They are not able to look after themselves, let alone take responsibility for a partner and a child. For many of those we interviewed—the men themselves and those who have worked with them—their early sexual experiences led to early parenthood and a life that was believed to be spiraling out of control. And control was exactly what they were attempting to regain—but in the ill-conceived, abusive, manipulative control over another human being, an intimate partner.

We had a very important revelation early on in our fieldwork. It was during a focus group session held early in the afternoon in one of the large rooms at the agency. About twenty-five men were present, a diverse group age-wise, with several ethnic and racial minorities represented. We asked what advice the men would give to a young man about to enter adulthood, based on their own life experiences. A few said what we might have expected, such as *stay out of trouble with the law, stay in school, listen to your elders,* and *never use violence.* But when one man said *use birth control,* several of the others nodded, said *uh-huh,* or shouted out something that suggested they agreed wholeheartedly with this man's comment. Later on, we asked other men about this, and it was clear that there was a general agreement that this was wise advice to a young man, advice many wished they had been given themselves.

At first, we did not understand the full impact of this. But over time, as we interviewed more men, held focus groups, and observed group meetings, we understood more fully the implications of early pregnancy on the life of a *man.* For sure, it has impact on a young woman's life—of that there is no doubt. But that has been recognized and researched for a long time, and social policies have been developed to try to deter both unwanted teenage pregnancies and the isolated single mom on welfare, from the vantage point of the mother or the child. All of this makes perfect sense, of course. But what has not received much attention at all is the impact on a young man. Many of the men we met began fatherhood very early. It was not something they chose, nor did they have much say in how the story unfolded after the women they impregnated found out about their pregnancies.

From the young man's perspective, at this point, his life was spiraling out of control. It was moving at breakneck speed in ways he never had imagined. It was going to change his life forever, and there was little he could do about it. Most of the men never considered that preventing pregnancy was their responsibility, nor did they even ask whether the woman (or women) with whom they were sleeping were taking some form of precaution against pregnancy. They were simply focused on the sex, pleasure for the moment, with little or no thought of tomorrow. But tomorrow came quickly, and they were catapulted into a reality for which they were in no way prepared. Antwone, featured earlier, joined the Army. Some dropped out of high school, such as Costenello, whose story we tell in chapter 7. Others curtailed their plans by dropping out of college. Some moved far away from the mothers in hopes that they could forget about how the pregnancies were developing. Others moved in with in-laws or had their girlfriends join their families. But as we heard the stories of the men, especially those who entered fatherhood before the age of twenty, it became clear that chaos entered their lives, too, there was little they felt they could do about it, and now they were bystanders in dramas for which they only held supporting roles.

Perhaps it is not surprising, then, that a substantial number of men felt that *they* were forced to grow up too early, robbed of their childhoods and their fun, and thrown into roles for which they were not ready. Regarded from this vantage point, the control and abuse they meted out to their partners were their inappropriate, inconsiderate, and damaging attempts to take control over their own lives, lives that they felt were spiraling out of control. In attempting to control someone else, with abusive acts and violent means, they were hoping to bring order into their own existence. This does not excuse their violent behavior. Rather, it is part of the explanation from the perspective of the men for why their lives unfolded in ways they never imagined possible.

Some men, as we saw in chapter 2, had observed and experienced a violent, controlling father. A few had observed and experienced a violent, controlling mother. Even fewer had experienced two parents who acted abusively. Many, on the other hand, had experienced one or both parents addicted to alcohol and/or drugs. And quite a few had lived in poverty at some point in their childhoods, often after having been abandoned by their fathers, by choice (through divorce or desertion) or by death. As we show in chapter 8, most men did not have family support (from their childhood homes) to call on when their own times of crisis came. But for those who did, the story often unfolded in a different way, as we reveal in the chapters to come.

CONCLUDING COMMENTS

The stories of the men who act abusively are replete with examples of failed relationships—beginning with their biological parents and siblings, foster parents and temporary caregivers, and followed by examples of early sexual intimacy and unwanted pregnancies in the lives of the women with whom they have been involved sexually. For many, they enter parenthood young, not really able to look after themselves let alone take on the responsibility of a partner and a child. From the perspective of those we have interviewed—the men themselves and those who have worked with them—their early sexual experiences led to early parenthood and a life that was believed to be spiraling out of control. And control is exactly what they attempted to exert over someone else—their intimate partners.

Living Dangerously

Danny Dorchester commanded attention when he entered the room. In his mid-thirties, shaved bald, standing more than six feet tall, and with a physique that suggested a commitment to working out, he was able to intimidate others. On one level, it seemed that intimidating others was something Danny really liked to do. We observed it in several contexts—the way he walked, looked at people, spoke in a group, and informally interacted with others. Yet his intimidation veneer was rather thin, and just below the surface, it was easy to see that all he really wanted was respect.

Within the first few minutes of our first meeting with Danny, he stated rather boldly: *I will start by saying that I do have a history of violence.*

His story had many chapters. *I grew up with five older sisters in a house of seven kids. . . . I had a terrible relationship with my mother. . . . My dad was my best friend, and my mother was an alcoholic. . . . My dad and I were really close 'cause I was the first boy. . . . I also had a younger brother that was three years younger than me.*

From Danny's perspective, his childhood was dominated by women who tried to control his life—five older sisters and an alcoholic mother he neither respected nor liked. He gravitated to his father, a man who owned and operated a successful small-town, business. His younger brother bore the brunt of Danny's childhood frustrations. *He was like a punching bag,* picked on frequently in Danny's attempts to gain self-worth.

The next chapter in Danny's life involved his teenage years and the beginning of his reckless lifestyle. *About sixteen, I started drinking really heavy. Worked for my dad, had all the opportunity in the world . . . it was just an outstanding opportunity, but I was too involved in chasing girls and fast cars and skipping school and partying—which is amazing that I did graduate. . . . I decided to move out when I was seventeen, and I never went back.*

His move out was prompted in large measure by his parents' unwillingness to allow his girlfriend to stay overnight. He got his own apartment and continued to work for his dad, and when he was not at work, he drank and partied as often and for as long as he could.

It didn't take long for Danny's addictions to begin to have a dramatic impact on his life. *You have to work exceptionally hard to hold things on track and live with that addiction, because it does impact your life. . . . I had several different girlfriends, and . . . I was probably very controlling in those relationships and really possessive, really jealous, you know. I didn't really understand how a relationship was supposed to work, because I didn't have a good role model.*

His childhood home had been marked by verbal, and sometimes physical, aggression. At times, he felt like the victim. *I had sisters, two of them in particular, that were pretty aggressive as far as picking on me.* At other times, he regarded his father as the victim. *Watching my mother be drunk and abuse my dad, like, verbally . . . and here was this lady that would torment him.*

For Danny, this led to one undeniable conclusion: *I just knew no matter what that I was never going to let a woman do that to me.* In Danny's mind, there was a direct link between his childhood experiences and his adult anger, his *zero tolerance for woman authority.* While his dad was Danny's *idol . . . unfortunately, I followed in my mother's footsteps.* His drinking would soon enslave him, as it did her.

The next phase in Danny's life began when he was in his early twenties, and his girlfriend found herself pregnant with their first child. He was drinking heavily, but with good credit and consistent employment, they were able to purchase a house. However, together they began a downward spiral involving alcohol, intermittent drug use, and then the regular use of crystal meth. For almost four years, Danny worked two jobs, drank regularly and excessively, used meth so he could keep on working despite the toll the alcohol was taking on his body and his mind, raced cars, and partied hard. His infant became a little boy, and the child's mother began to grow up, too.

Then Danny failed to come home one night. He returned later the next day, and there was an altercation: *she threw some cold water, and I put hands on her . . . throwing her in the pantry, knocking a bunch of stuff off the shelf.*

Marcie ran to the neighbors to call 911, and Danny entered into a long-standing relationship with law enforcement. He was mandated to attend a group. *I went through there for forty-eight weeks; it made me angry every time. It made me want to go home and raise hell with my partner. I went back to her, and we still beat the shit out of each other on a regular basis. I got nothing out of it other than satisfying the courts and getting them off my back finally after a year and a half.*

Shortly after an incident that threw them both into jail—since both admitted to the police that they had acted violently toward each other—Danny found himself living alone. *Anyhow, she separates, I started using methamphetamine [regularly]. . . . I could work around the clock . . . it was a miracle drug for me. It freed me from being trapped in this state of drunkenness. [Yet] I felt terrible . . . I had lost my family.*

Yet the sadness of what had been lost did not remain for long. Very soon, Danny began to *pick up all these hot girls, and they liked to do speed, and I was single, and it was just like really cool, and after about ten months of that, I met Judy . . . who is the victim in this case [for which] I ended up going to prison.*

For six years, Danny and Judy lived dangerously, a chaotic life that involved living only for and in the present. She had a child from a previous relationship who lived with them, he had a son who came on the weekends, and both of them moved in and out of jobs, persisted in their regular drug use, drank and partied as often as they could, and resided in a large ranch in the country. In Danny's words, *the addiction . . . it just, like, steals your soul.* Yet interlaced with the sense of regret was a longing for the days when living for the moment had not been so costly.

It was just we were so tied up in the addiction, after a while, it turns on a person where you get in your mind that you can't get up and do anything without it . . . and so we are in this state, we don't really want to use, but if you don't, you're actually sick, you know, you can't get going, your mind doesn't work. In my heart, I knew that we were in deep shit at this point. It's like, hey, both of us are a mess, we are trying to make this business go, we are not getting along, we are not making ends meet.

Over the six-year period with Judy, Danny was arrested on two occasions for domestic violence, family services twice removed Judy's daughter from the home, Danny entered in-patient drug rehab, his father died of cancer, and Judy did a home pregnancy test that came out positive. Referring to life at this time, he recalled: *I mean, that meth was just eating a hole in my head.* In short, things were completely out of control.

After rehab, many promises to each other, and hitting rock bottom, Danny obtained a long-haul trucking route for which there was a signing bonus, something he could use to pay off their mounting debts. From his mother's telephone (since theirs had been disconnected), he talked to his new employer about the start date for the job, less than seven days away. *I . . . went home and told [Judy] that I took this job, thinking that she was going to be happy. . . . Anyhow, I expected her to be happy and excited that something good was coming.*

But Judy was not happy. *Well, her response was, "Great, I'm pregnant, you're going to go off halfway across the United States and drive this truck and leave me here with all these animals to take care of, all this crap, that's so typical of you." And so I blew up.*

Within a matter of hours, Danny, in an inebriated state, caused a car accident (incidentally, a car owned by one of Judy's friends) that landed him and the other driver in the hospital. Danny was badly hurt, and the accident, and all the associated problems it created, threw them again into a spiral from which it was extremely difficult to recover.

After his release from the hospital, there was yet another altercation between Danny and Judy over his desire to begin smoking again; his lungs had been affected by the accident, and she was attempting to restrain him from leaving their home to buy cigarettes. She was scratched by his belt buckle as Danny grabbed her by the hair. *I am an abusive person. . . . I had my son there for the weekend. He ran out the door. He was afraid . . . he was ten at the time and called the cops.*

The next chapter of Danny's life began. His prison life got off to a bad start. *I have no idea how stuff works, I am new to prison, country boy, not really into all this, so I mean, I never really considered myself of the criminal nature. My crime is I'm an addict.* We tell Danny's prison story in chapter 6.

After prison, Danny took a step forward and contacted a halfway house called Second Chances. When we met him, he was living there, working through the NA twelve-step program, attending batterer intervention classes, and meeting with his parole officer on a regular basis. Without a license, he biked or walked where he needed to go and sometimes took the bus. No longer could he work in the trucking business, and as a felon, he was unable to obtain employment from either the state or federal government.

But ironically, this did not seem to depress him. On the other hand, the personal relationships that were important to him before incarceration had further crumbled as a result of his violence. His girlfriend was pregnant again and getting married to a buddy he knew well. His son—a young teen—was living at a youth center based on the boy's inappropriate and violent behavior at home and at school. These things caused Danny to feel sad.

After his release from prison, Danny developed a very good relationship with his probation officer. It was at this time that he became acquainted with STOP we were studying. The program, with its emphasis on compassion and hope, gave Danny reason for optimism.

No man that puts hands on a woman that's in his right mind is proud of that, under no circumstances. I don't care what your excuse, or if you are drunk, or sober, or what have you, there is still no excuse for it. For Danny, the faith–based nature of the intervention program meant that he could voice his misgivings about himself, his behavior, and his past without feel belittled or degraded.

Like many of the men we interviewed, Danny was keenly aware of the way staff interacted with the other men and himself in and out of group. For him, the importance of these interpersonal encounters was critical. Were they judgmental of the men in the program or condemning only of their violent acts? Were the therapeutic staff members understanding of how much many of the men had lost? Did they understand that in some cases, the men had also been violated, perhaps as children? Were they trying to work with them or simply fulfilling job requirements? Did they provide an environment filled with negativity and rules, or was there some flexibility with respect to how the program's goals could be achieved?

Once Danny assessed that his probation officer, the facilitators of the intervention group, and the director of the agency all had faith in him, he wanted to prove them right. He was motivated to complete the requirements, and this enabled him to set other goals, such as beginning community college. With a place to stay, an environment free of friends from the past, regular NA meetings, and twice-weekly group sessions, Danny was able to begin to curb the behavior that had ruined his own life and the lives of women he claimed to love.

At the close of our first interview, he remarked: *I was dying for thirty-four years, my life was hell from the time I was sixteen years old, and I come from good people, good quality . . . Minnesota folks that were married eight days short of fifty years when my dad died. . . . I have screwed up relationships that could have been wonderful.*

Six months later, we interviewed Danny again. He was still clean and sober, still living in the halfway house, still coming to group and beaming with the information that his first term of community college had yielded a 4.1 grade-point average.

We talked about some of the steps forward: attending classes and studying toward an associate's degree at the community college, ongoing accountability to those in NA, the batterer group, and the staff at Second Chances, where he continued to live. We talked about some of the steps backward: his return to smoking after three years without cigarettes, some of the tensions with his ex in terms of scheduling visits with their daughter, and the pull to date women who were neither drug- nor alcohol-free.

But best of all seemed to be a friendship he developed with a man who had graduated from the same intervention program. *There's a guy, and you guys probably remember [Bill, whose story is told in chapter 7], who has come through here. He's my number one dog, he's my best buddy, and I hang out at his place on weekends with my son and stuff, and . . . we celebrated his one year [of being clean and sober] this last Friday.*

Accountability, of course, means different things to different people, but for Danny, before he was willing to submit himself for accountability in an intervention group, he had to feel that the facilitators could *understand and feel compassion.* He also felt accountable to his friend Bill, to his probation officer, and to his son. He reconnected with his mother, who was a recovering alcoholic—clean for about four years. His brother, a speech therapist, had even made contact; *he's really strong in the Christian faith, and it's been kinda neat to be friends with him again.*

What did he like to do with his thirteen-year-old, now that he was able to focus, now that he was clean and sober, now that he was no longer doing time? *We do all kinds of stuff. He's a little trouper. I bought him a skateboard for Christmas. I ride my bike, and he takes his skateboard . . . we ride the bus to the mall . . . we shoot some hoops.* Parenting after violence begins one step at a time; it is something that needs to be learned by the men and monitored by trained professionals.

As far as relationships with women, *before it wasn't like that, I felt like I had to compete for my role, so to speak. . . . I was trying to do the American relationship thing, too, and right now, I am not trying to do that at all. I do not want any committed relationship . . . but I have been dating a couple of different ladies on a regular basis. One drinks and parties hard, and the other one is in recovery, so it's been kind of different, it's been kind of an interesting thing.* We asked how that could be helpful to him. He replied: *it's been a not good thing.*

When we returned six months later, Danny had been sent back to prison.

IS LIVING DANGEROUSLY A PATTERN?

Many of the men in groups and through our individual interviews talked about the centrality of drugs and alcohol in their lives, often from a rather early age.

Ned Curtis could be described as a scrapper, at least for most of his life. He had been in prison on many occasions, most recently for a ten-year period because of *manufacturing*, his fourth or fifth time for selling illegal substances. In prison, he connected with God, and since his release three years ago, he had been trying to live in a way that would keep him on the straight and narrow. Despite this, however, he had received a misdemeanor assault charge several months ago—for pushing an ex-girlfriend—which resulted in a mandated intervention group for domestic violence. That was how he found his way to STOP.

Ned lived and breathed the biking world: *I have been riding motorcycles for thirty-eight or thirty-nine years.* Intertwined throughout his life was contact with the law: *I was brought up in a really, really harsh environment.* From about the age of five, Ned had contact with the police, youth detention, jail time, and eventually prison. *I was very, very young, and I hung with older kids—they used to drop me down air-conditioning chutes in stores at night when they were closed, tie a rope around my waist. I did that for a long time, always getting in trouble. Took off with my grandfather's rifle from the services when I was like five, six, seven.*

How much time had he spent behind bars altogether? *In my whole life? I started my real time in 1968—I was probably about fifteen. . . . I know how to do jail, but I don't like it now. I'm going to be fifty-four. You know, I have missed a lot of my children growing up.*

The difficult and rough childhood he experienced could not be denied; neither could the difficult and rough childhood he offered his own kids. As a child, Ned was moved from city to city as his mother moved in and out of relationships with various men. She married his father, who was twenty-five, before her fifteenth birthday, had Ned at fifteen, and left when the relationship turned violent. In all, she married five times—twice to the same man. As a young boy, Ned did not think to call 911 when his mother endured abuse, precisely because the police were believed to cause trouble, not solve it.

It never took long for Ned to connect with older youths intent on breaking the law. As an adult, be began his longest prison sentence two weeks after his wife gave birth to their daughter, and they were divorced shortly after he completed his time. *We were divorced, she divorced me, and I was the one who had changed. She grew weary, and she just fell out of love, and this time I just let her go.*

Life in prison took its toll on his family. *I have a biological girl with her, and my stepson was very young when I hooked up with her. He is my son, too. And he is in jail right now, since he was, like, for the last two and a half to three years, he's been in jail for molesting my daughter when I was gone. . . . I should not have been dealing drugs. I should have been a father and a husband and all that, so all those years I went away, I left them to fend for themselves, and she sold one of my Harley-Davidsons, and just about everything else I owned to take care of her and the kids, and I was pretty mad about that for years. But God has been really good to me. I have got everything that I had back then, a hundred times better. A nicer motorcycle and nicer set of tools, whatever.*

At present, Ned was connected to a large Four Square church where he was a regular attender of Sunday services and midweek meetings. He loved the music and the many programs, and when needed, he was able to avail himself of the counsel of one of the many associate pastors, something he did shortly after his release from prison when he and his wife *were together for like ten, eleven, twelve months.* Was the pastor helpful? *He did his best, he listened a lot, he listened to a lot of venting. Now I am at a place where I have met a schoolteacher.*

Five months later, when we interviewed Ned again, the schoolteacher was gone, replaced by two women Ned was seeing: Sue, a mother with four difficult children, and Helen, who worked in his dentist's office. As he was describing these emerging relationships, Ned noted an altercation he had already had with Sue's teenage son and, by extension, the boy's father, a man not yet divorced from Sue. For Ned, new relationships brought enormous new challenges. These were issues Ned could, and did, discuss in the batterer intervention group. Here the facilitators and the other men tried to help him gain control over his emotions, challenged his erroneous ideation, and helped him see and live in the world in a different way from how he had in the past. But these challenges should never be underestimated. And there was very little evidence that Ned was putting into practice the lessons he was learning in group.

In each interview with Ned, punctuated by intervals of six months to a year, he talked about his grown children, of which he had several, by different women, spanning in age from twelve to thirty-five. He talked about wanting to reconnect with them, to tell his children that he had changed, to ask for their forgiveness. For some of his children, it had been ten years since Ned had face-to-face contact with them. He would like *to apologize to both my exes.* And with some marked sadness, he said: *She didn't give me the opportunity to see me change. My first ex says she doesn't want to hear [from me]. "I want Ned to go to prison." She wants to see my arms with no marks [no drug use] and that you are paying for what you have done by hard work. My second ex seems to think that I have gotten slicker six years later. I am not slicker, just six years older. . . . I hope that my kids will reconnect with me. It takes a long time for a scar to heal.*

From Ned's perspective, he had changed. The drug use had stopped, not a small feat for someone who was incarcerated six times for drug dealing. He had been clean and sober for some time. He had stayed connected with the STOP group, attending intermittently long after he completed his mandated fifty-two-week program. In fact, he said during our last interview, two years after our first one: *Here I am, still free, after knowing you girls for a while.* Since he was coming to the agency for our interview anyway, he decided to stop in and attend one of the groups. *I am happy I got the opportunity to come back today, and I have met staff and good people here. I met a guy who was at his first meeting here today, and he asked me for my phone number. I said, "Ask for my phone in six months."* This was Ned's way of telling the newcomer that he would have contact with him if that man did the work and stayed with the program. For someone who was thrown in and out of programs, Ned's completion of the work at STOP was noteworthy. However, so many years of living dangerously meant that it would probably never be possible for Ned to reconnect in a meaningful way with his children, to make peace, as he would like, with his two exes, who were both remarried, or to erase some of weight he bore for how his sons acted. The husband of one of his daughters was doing time, and his stepson was in prison for molesting his sister, Ned's daughter.

While Ned had some recognition of the harm he caused, he had limited insight into how unlikely it was that he could reconnect with the women to whom he was once married and the children born from those relationships. *I have no one to blame . . . I am responsible for my actions. There is nobody responsible for my actions other than I.* He longed to make peace with those he caused so much pain. But this did not seem possible. Speaking of one ex, Ned said: *She is so scarred. And I pray and pray and pray, and if she doesn't get some relief, I don't know what I will do. I don't hate her anymore. She is a wonderful mother. . . . She has a wonderful husband, I like the guy a lot, and he treats my kids good.*

Ned's religious connections helped him to cope with the disappointments of his life and to celebrate that he was no longer behind bars. *Six years free. Ride my bike, eat what I want.* These were some of the advantages of life outside the prison system. But then he said: *Once a batterer, always a batterer.* And in this context, he went on to tell of others with whom he had been in contact (friends or relatives) who had gone to prison for domestic violence.

He spoke very forthrightly about his involvement with his church, seeing his pastor, going to a home group, and getting to worship on Sundays. He mentioned that the pastor helped him after his release from prison. Ned noted that he had been a Christian for ten or eleven years, having converted when he was in prison.

As with Ned and Danny, years of addiction to alcohol and drugs took their toll on Pete's life, both mentally and physically. He presented as a man much older than his biological age of forty-two, yet he was trim in body type—reinforced by riding his ten-speed bike—and had a neat appearance. Impression management appeared to be extremely important to Pete. His talk was manipulative, and it became clear after a few minutes that flattery was another of his strategies. He moved from job to job, never very satisfied and easily bored. He appeared to have greater success in obtaining employment than in keeping it. At present, he worked for a manufacturing company, in the front office, serving customers.

Pete stated proudly that he had been clean and sober for twenty-six months. This was a tremendous feat for someone who lived to be high. *I loved methamphetamines a lot.* By his own account, Pete's desire for numerous sexual partners and variety in intimacy was also something that caused him no small amount of trouble, something we describe in chapter 3.

Working with men like Pete is an enormous challenge. Push too hard, and they become defensive. Fail to push hard enough, and they walk all over you. Even as he spoke about *being a know-it-all*, Pete saw the irony of his words. *'Cause I have this attitude like I know it all or something. Obviously, I don't, because I am back in the system again. That's what I can say about this STOP, that being treated as a human being that has made mistakes like every human being does is going to make a person more receptive to learn and pay attention.*

Arrested on at least twenty occasions, Pete served a prison sentence for assaulting his mother, an elderly woman with Alzheimer's whom he was supposed to be caring for in her own home. In fear, she locked her bedroom door to protect herself from an angry, drunken, and high Pete. He broke the door down, pulled the phone from the wall as she was calling 911, threw it at her, knocked her onto the bed, and stole some money from her purse. For these actions, he received a burglary charge, in addition to criminal mistreatment and assault.

His first arrest was for a DUI, and from there the charges escalated. The first time he hit an intimate partner, he was seventeen, and he assaulted several partners after her. *I always fall back on the alcohol and drug use. . . . I have always blamed alcohol for a lot of things. It's a good excuse. Today I finally recognize that alcohol is just a symptom, and Pete is the problem. Alcohol is removed out of my life now, and the drugs, but I think I am still messed up, it's just a little bit clearer, it is clearer, but . . . I am trying to grow up again and reprogram my thinking, and you know, it's harder being an adult. It is about being a responsible adult.*

TRAJECTORIES TOWARD VIOLENCE

Earlier in this chapter, we tell the stories of men who, often beginning in their teenage years, found themselves living dangerously. Here we address some of the many factors identified in the literature on interpersonal violence that, along with personal lifestyle pattern choices, place men on a trajectory toward violent behavior. We ask the broad question of what choices, experiences, and personal characteristics (demographics) lead men toward living dangerously. To answer that question, we begin this section with an examination of the personal characteristics (demographics) of men enrolled in batterer intervention programs and follow with discussion of the influence of socialization and support networks on personal choices, particularly those involving substance abuse and fatherhood. It appears that these issues are inextricably tied to feelings of powerlessness among the men (Ronel and Claridge 2003). Thus, personal choices often focus on the notion of taking back power, deciding one's own fate, being a man—often with unfortunate consequences.

Many research studies in the past twenty years have focused on specific demographic characteristics of men enrolled in batterer intervention programs, substance abuse issues, and lifestyle choices in relationships with intimate partners. Reported risk factors associated with domestic violence include younger age, less than a high school education, being unmarried or having multiple relationships, previous criminal history, lower household income, race, alcohol and/or drug abuse, and residence location (Cavanaugh and Gelles 2005; Delsol, Margolin, and John 2003; Dalton 2001; Daly, Power, and Gondolf 2001; Yarbrough and Blanton 2000; Hanson et al. 1996; Holtzworth-Munroe and Stuart 1994). Other factors of interest include the number of children in the household and the wife as full-time home-maker (Yarbrough and Blanton 2000); commencement of smoking before age six-teen (Easton, Weinberger, and George 2007), lack of health insurance, self-reported fair or poor health, and frequent mental distress (Vest et al. 2002). According to Statistics Canada (2005), spouses with children younger than fifteen in the house-hold were most likely to experience violence. Additionally, Faulkner et al. (1991) found that men in intervention programs reported stress related to money, work, alcohol, settling arguments, and jealousy. Other characteristics of men in abusive relationships include elevated scores on instruments measuring sociopathy, narcis-sism and borderline behaviors, and depression (Tolman and Bennett 1990). The majority of factors identified throughout the literature relate to stability, or lack thereof, in one's life.

Personal choices are also salient when looking at the trajectory toward violence. Lifestyle theory (Wooldredge 1998) focuses on "associations" and "exposure" that significantly correlate with victimization likelihoods. These associations and exposure do indeed influence people's choices about a range of behavioral patterns, including institutional patterns such as family styles, value orientations, and pat-terns of interpersonal and intergroup conduct (Hagstroem 1991). Jessor and Jessor (1997), in discussing "problem-behavior theory," argue that people who engage in risky lifestyles are also more predisposed to risky behaviors.

Taken together, personal characteristics and personal lifestyle choices have sig-nificant impact on whether or not one is on a trajectory of living dangerously.

DEMOGRAPHIC CHARACTERISTICS

In trying to understand why some men are interpersonally violent and others are not, it is important to examine personal characteristics. Who are these men who engage in violent behavior?

Edward Gondolf (2002) provides an inventory of the personal demographic characteristics of 840 men involved in four US intervention programs. More than half of the men were African American or Latino, and 80 percent were court-ordered into the programs. At the time of intake, almost half were between the ages of twenty-six and thirty-five, 20 percent were younger than twenty-six, more than half were not married, and 24 percent had less than a high school graduation. Of the 76 percent who were employed, two-thirds worked full-time and a similar number worked in blue-collar occupations. More than half of these men had been arrested for criminal offenses other than domestic violence. In a study of two programs in South Carolina, Dalton (2001) provided a picture of the "average" participant as a thirty-two-year-old man with a high school education and an annual income of just more than $21,000. In a Florida study of 404 men convicted of domestic vio-lence within a five-month period in 1997 who were attending a batterer interven-tion program, the average age was thirty-five, 25 percent had failed to complete high school, 72 percent were employed at the time of intake, and 47 percent reported working in an unskilled or semiskilled position (Feder and Forde 2003). Similar demographic characteristics are reported by DeMaris (1989) and Sherman and Berk (1984). Canadian data are comparable: the average age of 356 men in one study was thirty-five, average education was 11.9 years, 63 percent were married, and median income was $27,000 (Hanson and Wallace-Capretta 2000).

One stage of our research (Nason-Clark et al. 2003) involved an examination of the contents of closed files of 1,100 men who had been involved in a state-certified, faith-based batterer intervention program in the state of Washington who received court-ordered referrals. The demographics of men involved in that program differed slightly from those of men attending secular programs. Almost half (47.3 percent) of the men were married at the time the intake forms were completed, with a further 21.2 percent separated and 10.6 percent divorced; 21.0 percent were single. Men in the program ranged in age from fifteen to seventy-six, with 36.5 the mean age. The majority of men involved in the program were Caucasian (79.8 percent).

The men's educational attainment ranged from a fifth-grade education to twenty-two years of formal schooling; 33.3 percent reported twelve years of education, but a large number of men had received some postsecondary education (28.7 percent), and 16.2 percent indicated at least sixteen years of education. The majority (87.4 percent) were currently employed, with 28.4 percent reporting a skilled trade; a total of forty-eight men were employed in a professional occupation, twenty-three were police or security personnel, and eight were clergy. Of the men who were asked at intake about their criminal history, more than half (55.7 percent) reported that they had been incarcerated for criminal offenses.

Drawing on the characteristics found both in our own research and in the other studies cited, factors indicating a stable lifestyle are largely absent. Our research indicates that men often are currently in new relationships and have children from at least one previous relationship (often more) with whom they have little or no contact.

The importance of a stable lifestyle, built on a stable upbringing, was raised by a therapist in the agency where we conducted interviews, a man who both conducts intervention groups and sees clients on a personal basis. He related issues such as poor educational attainment, transient work, and emotional immaturity to the ability to grasp new concepts and work toward change: "For some men, they have the ability intellectually to grasp the concepts and to work with them in the present, and they are more amenable to change. I sometimes get guys who are illiterate. Both can change. There is sincerity among those who are rather limited; when they do see their emotions, they are very grateful. For a lot of men, they are in and out of jobs and in and out of relationships, and there is a lot of instability."

MEN WHO HAD NOT LIVED DANGEROUSLY

Not all of the men we interviewed had lived dangerously. Brett Turner grew up in a Pentecostal household with ample verbal abuse: *My father was very old school, authoritarian, not violent but loud, and my mom was loud, too. She's Italian, and I grew up in a very loud household, so a lot of that was kind of a change, meeting a lot more quieter people that aren't used to such loud interaction. But mostly happy.* Brett had not been in trouble with the law before. His downward vortex into domestic violence occurred after he returned from his tour of Iraq. *I was dealing with a lot of posttraumatic stress and drinking heavily, and I was very torn mentally at that time between what I felt was right and what I was doing. . . . And so that has been struggle and the struggle I had when I came back from the war. I am still in the Army.*

Brett had five children, three from his first marriage and two who belonged to his fiancée, children he now considered his. Even though his ex-wife and their children moved to the southern United States, he had contact with his children regularly by phone, and he had visitation during the holidays and summers. When we met Brett for the first time, he had been coming to STOP for about five months and had twenty classes under his belt.

Another example was Bobby Dorcas, a man who described his childhood as *good* and went on to explain: *I lost my father when I was about eleven years old, he was killed in a logging accident, so I grew up without a dad from that point forward, although I did have a male role model in my life, and he is . . . my stepfather now, and he came into the family when I was about fourteen and a half.*

When Bobby called his parents from jail after being arrested for domestic violence, *they were very supportive, and I spent my first thirty-five days at their house, because I wasn't allowed back at my home, and they just took really good care of me.* After that, his wife filed for divorce, and he was living back at the house he owned before he was married to her. His teenage daughter from his first marriage was living with him. A year later, when we meet him again, Bobby has completed his fifty-two weeks, is still employed, and has a new woman in his life. His daughter continues to live with him, and she is about to graduate from university. Bobby did not grow up in a home that was religious. Faith and spirituality were never been part of his life. *For me, it's mostly about trying to be a good person and treat people how you'd like to be treated.*

Bobby's family of origin provided assistance when crisis struck. This was also true for Skip, whose story we highlight in chapter 8. But these men, and a few others, were exceptions to the broader pattern of an upbringing that did not provide a basis for support throughout life. But in both of their lives—Bobby's and Skip's—frequent excessive drinking, intoxication, and partying, by themselves and their partners, created an environment where living dangerously was something they embraced as adults. In Bobby's case, it was in this context that he slapped his wife and she called the police.

When Bobby was sentenced, the judge told him that his mandated attendance at a batterer intervention program could offer him a new start. *I'd kind of made up my mind the judge had really tried to encourage me to not look at it as punishment and try to take the positive, what you could [take] from it, and so I came here with those thoughts in mind, and that's what I tried to do. . . . I've had the same job for twenty years, you know, I've raised four or five kids, or had a part in it, I'm a good dad, I have a lot of positive things about myself, and I know that, so I don't see [coming to group] as the end of the line.*

SOCIALIZATION, SUPPORT NETWORKS, AND LIFESTYLE CHOICES

Throughout life, humans experience ongoing processes of socialization, wherein we gradually come to believe in the values of a particular culture or group, internalizing its moral precepts and norms (Goldenberg 1997). Socialization begins within the family and/or caregiving situation and continues throughout our lives with peer relationships, school and work surroundings, religious involvement, and military service. The developmental course of intimate partner violence is mediated through all of these settings (Herrenkohl et al. 2007).

Childhood

"Homes should be places of love, comfort and support. Instead, for too many, it is a place of violence. It becomes a place where love and hate intermix and the price is devastated lives both for the batterer, the battered and always for the children" (Hope for Healing 2005). Rosenbaum and Leisring (2003) discuss the oft-mentioned intergenerational transmission of violence wherein violent parents beget violent children. Children internalize a culture of violence within the home. In one of our many interviews with the executive director of STOP, she noted: "[There is a] really high percentage of second-generation batterers, probably about 90 percent when you first ask about it. They all say they come from good homes, and then I ask how many people had experienced that, and it's just about everybody, and so these children are going to do this unless you do something really purposefully."

For violent men, the lack of normative childhood socialization has had a negative impact on not only their lives as perpetrators of abuse but also the lives of their significant others as victims. This lack of normative socialization was evident in the case of thirty-five-year old Jay Primer: *I was a heroin addict for many years, my mom died when I was eleven, and I raised myself on the streets of San Francisco, and I was a severe, severe drug addict.* Many other men described childhood homes replete with violence and substance-abuse issues that permeated their lives.

Overcoming and recovering from the impact of witnessing or experiencing abusive behavior during childhood is important to peaceful living. Conceptualizing the men and their stories as the STOP executive director once did, as "weeds rather than roses," might hold out a number of advantages for those who work with men who batter. Her comment was meant to reflect the fact that old patterns, beliefs, and behaviors must be discarded and new ones adopted through processes of resocialization that focus on healthier, more stable lifestyle choices.

Another STOP therapist agrees: "The most challenging thing I do has an awful lot to do with socialization, and connected with that is a man's ability to empathize and to feel. In [our state], there is a little different mentality about men . . . there is the rugged man, the pioneer. A lot of the men here talk about injustice [that] has been put upon them."

Indeed, Mejia (2005) stresses that during the preliminary phase of therapy with men experiencing trauma, the therapist needs to help the client redefine masculinity and resilience before the next phase, which deals with the experience and its legacies, can be addressed.

At STOP, staff members were keenly aware of the important role of early-childhood experiences. They encouraged the men to talk about some of their feelings of shame, disappointment, fear, and regret as they looked back and reflected on their own childhood experiences. The director and other facilitators believed that they opened up a conversation that might lead men to see the unhealthy and harmful ways they have interacted or failed to interact with their kids. As we observed groups and talked to the men individually or in focus-group settings, it was common for the men to want to bring their children into the conversation. As we note in a later chapter, improved or renewed relations with their children could be understood as part of the reinforcement for doing the work. To be sure, the men were rather naive in some of their expectations. Some thought that after many years of no contact or very limited contact, a generous number of gifts at Christmas or for a birthday would diminish or alter children's negative evaluation of them as fathers. Others seemed unaware of the impact that their absence and their violence had on their children. But for most, there was a deep sadness about both their own childhood experiences and the stories that their own children would tell about them.

Adolescence and Early Adulthood

Based on the theory of differential association, resocialization depends to a great extent on the types of networks in which individuals are immersed (Wright and Cullen 2004). Many of the men with whom we talked began their trajectories during their teen years, supported in their behavioral choices by peers who were making similar decisions. As one young man in his early twenties explained: *I have been a criminal most of my life, either on the streets or involved in gangs, so I didn't straighten my life up.* Certainly, those who interact with cultures that support deviant behavior will internalize deviant norms and values (Wright and Cullen 2004; Kaplan and Lin 2005). Choices of support networks are thus critical to becoming resocialized toward a healthy, violence-free style of life. The story of Casiano discussed in chapter 2 helps to illustrate just how much of a struggle this really creates in the life of a young man.

After Casiano's parents divorced, he went to live with his grandmother, a woman suffering poor health after many years of life with an alcoholic husband. Casiano had no contact with his father, who, by this time, apparently left the family because of physical altercations with his older brother. By the second time we met him, the father was in prison.

Reflecting back on the removal of their infant daughter from their care, Casiano said of the DHS: *Four days old—they took her from us. It's been a year and a half, and they still have not even said we are getting her back. It's like they picked up all of my dad's stuff. They read all of my dad's reports and said, "Oh, he's going to turn out just like his dad, so we might as well just take his daughter."*

One bright spot in Casiano's life was his employer, a carpenter who was also a pastor. In this man's small business—involving home renovations—Casiano worked as a painter and carpenter's assistant.

He said that for the first time, the future looked brighter than the past. On the job, he was learning new skills, which he hoped would eventually prepare him to attend community college and help to ensure financial stability for the rest of his life. His employer believed in him. He encouraged Casiano, gave him hope that if he kept going to classes, doing his job, and visiting with his daughter through the supervised visitation program, someday he might get her back. But Casiano worried. Would his daughter ever really get to know her real parents? Would she ever live with them? *I want her to know her parents and be with us, because we're not bad people.*

We asked Casiano if there was anything that he would like to ask us. *Do I seem like a bad guy?* He was so young, so vulnerable, and so unprepared to parent. His question was daunting.

ADULTHOOD

Friends can and do act as sources of informal social control to regulate behavior (Laub and Sampson 1993). They can also contribute to lifestyle stability through encouragement and example. In contrast, Michalski (2004) reports that exposure to violent networks does increase the likelihood of recidivistic violence. One man noted: *I seen some of my, quote, friends and they are doing the same old stuff.* Another man said that he kept being lured back to unhealthy choices, like a fish to a worm: *She really knows how to get me to nibble on that worm, she makes it bigger and bigger and bigger all the time. . . . So I try and disassociate that.*

Yet another man described how he went back to the familiar and relapsed into his old way of life: *And so I ran into my ex, . . . and I had been hearing a lot of stories about what she was doing, and I wanted, we wanted, to try to work it out. . . . So what happened was we started seeing each other again, and the next thing you know, I am back with her, and the next thing you know, I am relapsed. And it's back to the same old scenario, the same old thing, the drinking and the drugs and not doing the right things, and you know. This last time I relapsed—I was a cocaine user for a lot of years—well, I started using that methamphetamine they got all around here, and it just took me from who I was, it just took my soul, and I knew it, and things got bad between [my wife] and I again, and I woke up one morning, and I had nothing left, nothing. I was ready to go kill myself.*

These men all served time in prison for their crimes. When they got out with very little money, no jobs, and nowhere to live, where were they to find support? Such men often have alienated themselves from their childhood families. So family support is not possible, and they are barred from interaction with victims and children through no-contact orders that form part of their probation or parole. Big questions for them are "Who can I turn to?" and "Where can I go?" Avoiding the temptation to go back to the old ways, to seek out former friends and acquaintances, to visit old haunts, is a great burden.

James, Johnson, and Raghavan (2004) use the phrase "I couldn't go anywhere" to describe the social network context of violence and drug abuse. They argue that place of residence does influence one's social networks and exposure to drugs. The temptation is found in familiarity. Like fish to a worm, they are constantly drawn to the familiar, to a network that promotes living dangerously. One man described his efforts to resist returning to the familiar: *I had nowhere else to go. I could have gone out, I had places to go, but I knew I needed to get away from where I was at and the environment I was in. So I went to the mission.*

In the case of Danny, whose story we describe at the beginning of this chapter, the pull to live dangerously never really went away. And in fact, even when we saw him at the height of his success of achieving a 4.1 grade-point average for his first term at community college, he reported in his interview that he felt the pull of wanting to date women who he believed were living in ways that would lure him off his NA and AA abstinence goals. For him, the tug of war was between the friend he had met at STOP—who had graduated and was now living a life of sobriety, employed and in his own home, caring for a teenage daughter—and the life of partying and reckless abandon. Even before he relapsed and was sent back to prison, it became clear in interviews with us that his resolve to live clean and sober was wearing thin and the lure of the wild was getting stronger. These are the very real forces faced by men such as Danny. And these are the tugs of war that the army of professionals who walk alongside Danny and others like him must help them face. If there is to be any real hope for changed thinking and changed behavior—sustained over the longer term—diminishing the lure of living dangerously must be a central feature.

Comorbidity

Drug and alcohol abuse are key elements of the culture of living dangerously. Numerous researchers have discussed the complex relationship between substance abuse and abuse of women (e.g., Gondolf 1995; Brown et al. 1999; Galvani 2004; Humphreys et al. 2005), and several studies have associated alcohol use with elevated rates of marital violence (Cunradi, Caetano, and Schafer 2002; Fals-Stewart 2003). Research conducted by Amaro et al. (1990) showed an increased risk of intimate partner violence among women whose partners used either marijuana or cocaine. Relatedly, in looking at the impact of both drugs and alcohol, Tzamalouka et al. (2007) found in their Greek research that substance abuse was significantly associated with perpetrating physical and sexual violence against a partner. The numbers are alarming: spousal drunkenness and drug use were among the five most important variables distinguishing abused from nonabused women (Kantor and Straus 1989); 95 percent of perpetrators had used illicit drugs or alcohol during the day of the assault, and 45 percent had been intoxicated daily for the past month (Brookoff et al. 1997); and based on police data from nine states, Greenfield (1998) found that there was evidence of the perpetrator drinking in 28 percent of incidents of aggravated interpersonal violence, compared with 13 percent of incidents of intimidation against an intimate partner.

The majority of men in batterer intervention programs have alcohol problems (Stuart 2005). Usually, men with substance abuse problems have been required to seek treatment as a condition of probation or parole, and others have participated in self-help groups such Alcoholics Anonymous or Narcotics Anonymous past the bounds of their court order. Often, the narratives of these men include attributions of responsibility to their addictions. Rather than denying their violence, they believe that their violent behavior stems from their substance abuse (Cartier, Farabee, and Prendergast 2006). Research has shown, however, that this link is complex and that while alcohol and/or drugs serve as disinhibitors to normative behavior, they do not cause the violence (Willson et al. 2000; Rogers et al. 2003; Galvani 2004). While alcohol abuse was prevalent among the men we interviewed, the drug of choice for many was crystal methamphetamine, also known as speed or meth.

One man said, *I am a severe alcoholic, and I love methamphetamines on top of that.* Another man described his addictions quite vividly: *I have been all kinds of drinker; I have been a binge drinker, a daily drinker, maintenance drinker, workaholic function with a job while drinking, and just getting plowed every night.* Battling these addictions while simultaneously struggling to change their abusive behavior offers great challenges for these men. *'Cause once I had alcohol in me, my demeanor changed, it was not belligerent really until I really was forced into that situation.* Childhood and adolescent socialization often included exposure to drugs and alcohol within both the family context and friendship groups. Choices about drug and alcohol use were influenced by both exposure and association.

Many men talked about drugs and alcohol in their lives:

My mother was an alcoholic.

When we had big family gatherings, it wasn't uncommon to have a table this large full of whiskey and vodka bottles and tequila bottles and coolers full of beer, and you know, the younger guys, my uncles and older brothers and cousins, smoking joints.

It's just how I lived my life. It's all I knew, it's who I associated with, it's who I ran with, everybody I knew drank and used drugs, it's where I fit in.

My dad was an alcoholic; he died an alcoholic.

A man who had been in both AA and NA for many years discussed the origins of his path toward living dangerously: *I got in trouble with friends of mine for breaking into people's houses and taking their alcohol at a young age, thirteen or fourteen, and I was alcoholic even then.*

Many of the men were enrolled in drug and/or alcohol treatment programs concurrently with their interventions, and they spoke of working *one day at a time* with the support of their *higher power.* The presence of this belief in God "as you understand Him" is recognized as requisite in overcoming addictions. Larson and Larson (2003), in their review of research regarding spirituality's potential, found that "persons with active spiritual/religious involvement are at substantially reduced risk for substance abuse, addictions and suicide" (37). From this point of view, redemption and recovery are inextricably linked.

In seeking to change dangerous lifestyles into healthy lifestyles, men at STOP must overcome the trauma of very difficult childhood and adolescent years and develop new, appropriate networks of support. Their journeys are fraught with difficulties, with no easy fixes.

Fatherhood

I made my [child] promises many different times that I never lived up to.

The majority of the men we interviewed became fathers at a very early age. Research conducted by Wei, Loeber, and Stouthamer-Loeber (2002) indicates that by age nineteen, almost half of repeat serious delinquents have caused a pregnancy (46.7 percent), and 31.4 percent have fathered children. Among this group, rates of fatherhood are twice as high as for moderate or minor delinquents, and these more serious delinquents are more likely to father multiple children. Part of the culture of living dangerously involves having unsafe sex frequently and with multiple partners.

Over and over again, we heard men tell stories related to having children. Certain themes commonly surfaced: separation from their children, abandonment of their children, promises broken, responsibilities unmet, poor role modeling. These choices led men on trajectories toward living dangerously that had unavoidable impacts on their children. The stress and the guilt they felt as a result of poor parenting skills served to exacerbate unhealthy lifestyle choices, often increasing the risk of time in jail. One man told us about his loss: *I was trying to get my life in order enough to where I could petition the court for custody of my kids to get them away from their mother because she's still today still druggin' and drinking and not doing the right things, and April 1, I got a phone call after work, and my son was killed, my seven-year-old son.*

We asked another young man how long child protection authorities had been involved in his family, and he replied: *Oh, they have been involved for almost ten and a half years with the first daughter, the oldest, and our second daughter, we almost got her back, and then there was a relapse, and she was taken, and we decided to leave her because she is with her sister and her in my wife's mom's house, and so I got tired of playing back-and-forth games with my kids. I was in jail the last time, and now we are supposed to be getting this one back, the youngest. . . . I have never been upstate, but I have done about roughly a year on and off in county jail, in and out, in and out, all different times drug-related.*

LIVING DANGEROUSLY—FOREVER

At least one-third of the men we interviewed lived dangerously for an extended period of time, well beyond the days of their youth and early twenties. They were surrounded by others who drank to excess on a regular basis and used a variety of substances to ensure that they did not have to cope with the reality of life, the pain of the past or the present, or the boredom of routine. Dwight Fraser was one such man. His appearance set him apart from the other men we met in the first focus group we attended at STOP. His clothing was very dirty, as were his hands and finger-nails. He smelled of the woods and sweat, and his long, straggly ponytail suggested perhaps days without the benefit of a shower. He wore a plaid woolen shirt, jeans, and steel-toed work boots. Yet once he spoke, it was clear that Dwight had far more verbal skill and intellectual acumen than one might expect at first glance.

We learned later that Dwight wanted the other men to see him as a "working man." He made a very good wage in the woods and was very proud of his ability to keep on working despite the chaos in his personal life. Like a few of the men we met, Dwight was his family's *black sheep*. His two sisters were law-abiding, highly functional women who had families and professional jobs; Dwight would call them when he was depressed or drunk.

Dwight described his teenage self as *a wild kid*, and as we have followed his story during a period of four years, we would say there was little reason to believe that he had outgrown his propensity to live dangerously. During periods when he lived with his girlfriend, there were stormy encounters, and the police were called, some-times by Dwight and sometimes by the girlfriend, Denna. During periods when they lived separately and Dwight had roommates in his house, the police were sometimes called by Dwight because of the behavior of the roommates. Sometimes Denna called Dwight's drug and alcohol counselor to report on his lack of sobriety, and sometimes she texted him despite the no-contact order that *she* received in the aftermath of one violent episode. Contact with the police occurred frequently, not always for matters related to domestic violence.

After Dwight completed his fifty-two-week program at STOP, something that takes him more than two years to accomplish, he and his girlfriend began couples classes together. They attended regularly for about four months before deciding that this was not for them. In one of the couples classes we observed, we heard Denna say that they were both violent and that both of them abused alcohol and other substances.

In our last interview with Dwight, four years after our first interview, he speaks very disparagingly of his life, his future, his work, and the relationship with Denna. When we ask him about the way forward after his years of contact with STOP, Dwight says: *I'm not Buddha. I'm not Jesus, either. If somebody slaps me, I am going to slap them back, probably.* We ask him to summarize the most central features of his life in the last four months: *Banging my head against the wall, pretty much. It's been affecting my work, my physical being, my psyche. Depression—you can't think as well when you have these burdens to think about.*

For Dwight, as for many other men like him at STOP, living dangerously for so long meant that his world began to close in on him. His girlfriend's teenage son died from an overdose. He was without work for the first time in his life. His roommate recently was hospitalized for going on a heroin binge. With no friends apart from others who also lived dangerously and with a partner who lived the same way, there was little reason for Dwight to change. He was off probation, and he had completed his mandatory attendance at STOP. The one place that had been calling both him and his girlfriend to account for their behavior—the couples group at STOP—they decided was not for them. It was far too much work, Dwight concluded, for them to change their ways. As a result, from this vantage point, the future looked very bleak indeed.

Another, even more dramatic example was Kevin Grant, whom we met while he was on road crew for failing to fulfill the requirements of his probation. Married and divorced twice, Kevin had moved in and out of relationship with various women and their children and in and out of contact with law enforcement for his long-standing *career* (as he termed it) in the drug trade. His mother had been married six times, and many of the men in her life had been abusive. Kevin's own son was dating a stripper and had already been involved with the police. As Kevin described the web of connections among the women, children, and extended family members he had in his life, at present and in the recent past, most of the men had done time in prison, while the women and children lived in the shadows of the drug world and waited for their return. His current employment was selling hot dogs outside a hardware store six days a week, using the tips he received to buy movies. All of his energy seemed to be consumed by his angry, bitter outlook on life.

Sometimes men reported that the living dangerously part of their lives had come to an end. Vincent Perk was one such man. When we met Vincent, he was divorced from his ex, following the abusive altercation that had brought him into connection with the criminal justice system and then STOP. They had a middle-class life—owned a car dealership, had a nice house and a vacation home on the coast, and were parents of three children, two of whom his younger wife had brought into their marriage. *Little by little, alcohol got to be a problem for both of us and I guess led us down the wrong path, and as opposed to going home with our children after we closed up our business, three out of five nights, we would stop on our way home and have a beer. A beer turned into two beers, and three beers, and typically, it wasn't a problem, but looking back on it now, it was a huge influence on our life, but when you are in an addiction like that, you don't see what it's doing to you. You don't see what it's taking away from your kids and your family. So little by little, it became an issue for us. We started arguing at times, and the stress of running our own business and living together, working together, it just wore on the relationship.*

Vincent had been drinking heavily and daily since he was an early teen. Now he was approaching fifty, an uptight, angry, bitter, emotional man who was unwilling to see that he had caused harm to anyone. When we met him, Vincent had started going to AA and NA, groups that helped him to connect with the faith that was nurtured in his childhood. He had regular contact with his children, who were living with their mother and her new husband. At our next meeting with him, he was fighting for more contact with the children and keeping up with his sobriety and the support groups of AA. Vincent wanted the children to be under his authority, to obey the rules, to have law and order. He saw his ex as allowing them far too much freedom and far too many resources.

As we concluded our interview, he smiled and said: *It's not how many times you fall down that counts, it's how many times you get up.*

Vincent reconnected with his faith as his world started falling apart. He spoke of his first time coming to STOP: *Within fifteen minutes talking at the front desk there, I could tell that these people are here to help. The fact that it is faith-based, I've really had to dig deep and find my own spirituality to help through what I've been through the last five months. . . . I've always believed in God. I have two brothers that were preachers. There are seven kids in my family, and both the brothers that were preachers are no longer preachers, and they are both divorced, and they both have drinking problems and have been alcoholic.*

Vincent found the link between AA/NA, and religious principles interesting and comforting. While he was *forced to go to church* when he was younger and said prayers *with my kids at night,* he was not connected with a specific faith community, nor did he attend church. Yet the spiritual undertones of AA helped him to connect with its message. In his words, *part of the recovery is recognizing what you've done wrong in life and dealing with it. . . . Once you've recognized what you've done, you pick your head up and you carry on through life and take life one step at a time and continue.* He had learned to say the mantra of AA; whether he would have the resolve to live it, only time would tell.

CONCLUDING COMMENTS

In this chapter, we have been thinking about notions associated with living dangerously. Harnessing the stories of Danny, Ned, and Jake, we consider how living dangerously unfolds within the lives of the men we have studied—men who acted abusively and have wrought havoc in the lives of their partners and children. Living dangerously has taken its toll on their own lives, too, physically, psychologically, and in terms of life experiences, such as alcohol and substance abuse. We have considered the personal characteristics (demographics) of men enrolled in batterer intervention programs and the influence of socialization and support networks on personal choices involving substance abuse and fatherhood. These issues are inextricably tied to feelings of powerlessness among the men (Ronel and Claridge 2003)—powerlessness as children in troubled families; powerlessness as adolescents when they became fathers at very early ages; powerlessness in dealing with substance abuse; powerlessness in involvement with the criminal justice system in jail, on probation, or on parole; and powerlessness in dealing with child welfare authorities in trying to regain custody of children.

Caught in the Act and
Before the Courts

Full of self-confidence bordering on arrogance, Craig Winslow boasted about his leisure activities, his talents, the wealth he believed he was about to inherit, and the fancy life he hoped soon to be his in Hawaii or some other exotic location. Whether he was deluded or just a dreamer, Craig's first interview was punctuated by talk of grand schemes that involved money, snowboarding, and other aspects of what he considered to be the good life.

Big talk, however, would not change the reality of his current struggles. Craig's current life was dominated by the ramifications of his violence: contact with a probation officer, no contact with his three-year-old daughter, and an ensuing battle with the child's mother about custody arrangements.

Craig looked like any other twenty-something young white male who was deeply concerned about his appearance. His body was lean and fit, his head was shaved, and his all-black clothing gave off a message of strength and intimidation. Under this facade, there was a cauldron of anger that was boiling, steaming, and ready to erupt at almost any moment. And it did erupt the night he was taken into police custody after Marinda, his ex-girlfriend and the mother of his child, called 911.

At the time of the arrest, Craig and his ex-girlfriend were sharing an apartment with their daughter, although they were no longer in a relationship with each other. They dated other people, but neither of them brought new or potential partners to their apartment, fearing that it would upset Crystal, their little girl.

On the night of his arrest, Craig had come home late from work, as he often did. As a waiter at an upscale restaurant in town, he often worked past midnight. *I was working two jobs at the time, seven days a week. I was making a lot of money, and I've been doing that since the first year she was born. . . . So I was getting ready for bed, and Marinda wanted to get into an argument. And I didn't want to argue, not fight, and she was, like, "You need to leave," and I was, like, "I'm not going to leave; I'm going to sleep."*

Unwilling to negotiate about whether Craig could stay for the night, Marinda said, *"If you're not going to leave, I'll make you leave."* From the bathroom, Craig could hear Marinda calling the police, a five-second call that would change his life forever. His response was to *break the phone in half.*

Within a few minutes, Craig had interfered with a 911 call and threatened a police officer and was in the process of facing five charges including assault and a felony, since their daughter was present in the apartment, though sleeping, at the time of the violent ordeal. Outside the apartment, Craig was shouting at the police officers, trying to resist arrest, and causing such a scene that one officer took him to the station so that the other officer could respond more fully to Marinda. At the station, there was a further altercation with the police. As a result, Craig's jaw was broken, for which he required immediate surgery and the insertion of a titanium plate near his chin.

When we first met Craig, he had been coming to STOP for five weeks. Through a later focus group and in one batterer intervention group, we were able to observe his behavior. In each context, he presented as a know-it-all. He tried to outsmart the other men, asked questions that were meant to pull the facilitators into a debate, and attempted to challenge whatever the agenda was for the evening. Quickly, the other men decided they did not like him.

Craig was part of a rather small group of men we interviewed who were particularly resistant to change. His narcissism was coupled with an aura of intimidation. He wanted to be the center of attention, and his personal woes took precedence over everything else, including his little girl, from whom he was separated by a no-contact order. He declared that he would do whatever it took to regain custody of his daughter, but his actions betrayed his words. With a new girlfriend by his side, his ability to paint even his grim circumstances in a positive light was now in doubt; only time would show whether his resolve was as strong as his ego.

When we met Craig six months later, he spoke less of his child and more of the day when he would be free from all the obligations placed on him by the criminal justice system as a result of his violence. He had completed the STOP program, and since he was now on supervised probation, his new girlfriend could share his living space. He wanted to move away and be free of the past. When we returned six months after that, he could not be reached.

Central to Craig's story, as he told it, was the 911 call placed by his ex-girlfriend.

In this chapter, we unravel the stories of how men's abusive acts bring them onto the radar screen of community-based agencies and publicly funded services, including domestic violence or criminal courts. While chapter 4 examined the context of their lives, their choices, and their conduct, here we focus on what happens as their controlling and abusive behavior is made known to others. We also explore those men—few in number in our study—who do not come into contact with the criminal justice system and discuss how their stories and lives differ from those of the other men we have interviewed.

We turn from Craig's story to one that involves neighbors' calling for help.

Stu Wright found himself in handcuffs after some people who lived close by called the police. They witnessed him picking up his girlfriend and throwing her across the country lane after she had apparently slashed the tires on his truck. At the time, they were working out the finer details of their rather recent relationship dissolution.

And I was supposed to do a mental health evaluation after I got out of jail, but what happened was my girlfriend and me had an argument the night before, and the next morning she come back and was trying to slash my tires ... and I just picked her up and threw her across the road, and a passerby saw it and called the cops, and it was mean, and I ended up going to jail for domestic violence.

He was in custody initially for two days. But he returned to his property despite being told by the court not to, and that act of defiance landed him in jail for a further forty days. Like so many of the men, Stu did not like to be told what to do by anyone, including a judge or other workers in the criminal justice system.

By our fourth interview, Stu was able to tell us that he had graduated from the STOP program. He was still working six days a week in a manual labor job, and he had been clean and sober for almost four years, the length of time he had been in relationship with his current girlfriend.

As Stu told his story, it was very difficult for him to get beyond the unfairness of a neighbor butting into his life and creating consequences that might otherwise not have occurred. In some ways, Stu felt more resentment toward the neighbor than he did toward his ex-girlfriend who slashed his tires, and he felt very little disgust, or insight, at his own violent outburst. In his mind, she deserved what happened.

A different twist on being caught is when workers at a hospital report on the injuries of a victim to the police. This is how Costenello Ramrez's involvement with the criminal justice system began.

Costy had been a disc jockey at a local radio station since his community college days. Being a hard worker was very important to Costy, something he stressed to, and modeled for, his children. By our second interview, Costy had been laid off. With tears in his eyes, he tried to sound upbeat—saying that there were other jobs he could do—but underneath his warm smile, there was fear and apprehension.

Throughout their thirty-five-year marriage, Costy's wife, Milagros, had suffered bouts of poor health. She had epilepsy, and her medication, when she took it regularly, kept her stabilized. But Milagros did not like the way her medications affected her energy level and, as a result, often did not take them as prescribed. This frustrated and annoyed Costy. He talked about these frustrations as he contextualized the story surrounding the day of his arrest for domestic violence.

That day, I came home, and I have a list of her medications, and I went to see how she was doing on her medications. It was my fault, I hadn't looked for a couple of days, and I noticed it had been three days actually she hadn't taken them, and so we got into an argument. . . . I got so mad at her . . . I'm not mad at her, I'm mad at what she's done to herself, and I pushed her to get out of the way so I could go to the other room . . . and when I pushed her, she fell against the table, and since she only weighs eighty-two pounds, that's just what she weighed, it broke her rib. . . . When the rib broke, it punctured her lung, and there was three days there that we thought she was going to die.

Costy took his wife to the hospital. He told the story. Milagros told the story. Eventually, the police were sent to the house, and Costy found himself under arrest. He spent nineteen days in jail and received three years' probation, plus a court order to attend fifty-two weeks of domestic violence classes, as he calls them. With a no-contact order in place, Costenello was unable to get any information on his wife's state of health. He was not allowed third-party contact, so he was unable to receive information on her condition from his sons or grandchildren. Since he was accustomed to speaking with her at least fifteen times a day on the phone while at work, plus the time at home, Costy felt an incredible sense of loss.

Now he turned his frustration onto the court order and the program he was ordered to attend. Meanwhile, he wife was being cared for by her aging mother.

We reintroduce Costy's story in another chapter as we follow it over time. After several further interviews, we heard of the impacts of the STOP program on his life and his marriage. Two years later, Costy was back to working part-time at the radio station. His layoff was short-lived, and he was rehired rather quickly. At the end of our period of study, Costy and Milagros were still together, and the wider family unit, plus their church, had embraced them and the continuation of their marriage.

At this point, we have introduced the stories of three men—Craig, Stu, and Costy—and the varied ways in which their violence was "discovered" and they began their contact with the criminal justice system and the program where we were conducting our research. Craig's ex-girlfriend called 911, Stu's neighbors called the police, and hospital personnel informed the authorities that Costy, the husband of a woman who sought assistance in emergency and was admitted as a patient, had caused her injuries by his abusive behavior.

These three ways of alerting the police—the victim, neighbors, or a health-care worker—were raised often throughout our interviews. Sometimes, though, it was the couple's child who called for help, either by dialing 911 or by going to a neighbor's house and asking the neighbor to call. Sometimes it was a social worker at DHS who informed the police. And sometimes it was another relative, such as the mother or father of the victim, who made the initial call.

From our interviews, it appeared that the few cases where it was a child who called the police caused the men the most personal angst. Danny, whose story is highlighted in chapter 4, was one such man. It was his little boy who ran next-door and signaled the need for help. Biard, whom we meet in chapter 7, mentioned that his school-age daughter had been told by her mother to run up the lane to the next house if the shouting ever turned to violence and she was frightened for her own or her mother's safety. He, too, exhibited a great sense of sadness as he told this part of his narrative.

Other men, such as Costy, Stu, and Craig, exuded anger and frustration at others and the system that they felt worked against them.

In very few cases was the violence first disclosed to a religious leader. Some men, such as Felipe and Rob, whose stories are highlighted in chapter 9, went initially to religious leaders for counseling related to family life and were therefore on the radar screen of pastors and spiritual elders. Most, however, looked to religious leaders after the violence took place, in the aftermath of involvement with the criminal justice system or other agencies, such as DHS. It appeared that the removal of children from the home often prompted families of faith to look to their congregations' leaders for help. Perhaps they felt that support would be forthcoming and that their pastors would be willing and able to help them bring their children back home.

Since most of the men in our research were court-ordered to attend a batterer intervention program, there was an experience of being "caught in the act." And with very few exceptions, they could recount in some detail the context of that experience and how they believed the events unfolded. Two of the men who were not ordered by the criminal justice system to attend the program came initially because they indicated that they had been *mandated* by their partners in the aftermath of an abusive incident. In other words, they were offered an ultimatum by their wives: go and seek help, or the relationship is over. In one of these cases, the man stayed in the program for a short while, and in another case, the man continued long after the fifty-two weeks had come to an end. In the first case, the last information we had was that the couple was still together; in the latter case, they had divorced, and the man was in a new relationship.

While we never asked whether alcohol was involved at the time of the incident that led to the involvement of the police, many of the men reported that it was.

One man, for example, was so intoxicated that he damaged the inside of the police car after his arrest. Of his own admission, he had been drinking to excess since his teen years, but he had never been in trouble with the law before his first arrest after his wife placed a 911 call. Both men who had been wife-mandated to seek help reported that they were free from problems with alcohol, and there was no record in the files to indicate otherwise. In these two cases, however, the anger and controlling behavior were as severe and as frequent as those meted out by problem drinkers.

None of the men mentioned explicitly that the involvement of the police after a 911 call changed him or his behavior. But most offered examples in their narratives that would lead us to believe that it altered their lives in relationship to their partners, their children, and their extended networks. For some, this was the point where they had to reach out and ask for help of a financial nature from parents. Many men either lived for a period of time with older, often elderly, parents, and others received money from their parents that enabled them to obtain separate living quarters to abide by no-contact orders. Men often borrowed money from relatives during the early stages of no-contact orders, but the cost of maintaining two households was so prohibitive that they were forced to live either with relatives or with friends or roommates for a period of time. For men who had been living in houses they had purchased, this was humiliating. And the humiliation seemed to stoke the flames of their anger rather than strengthen their resolve to change their violent ways.

For some men, being caught in the act resulted from a call to the police without the consent of the victim. Trevor Jones was a man for whom religion and family life fit together like a hand and a glove. The two were inextricably linked. He found his way to STOP through a suggestion from his lawyer. At the time of our first interview, he was twenty-six, married, and the father of three children. He had been employed for six years with a printing company. Trevor was charged with an assault felony because his act of violence occurred in the presence of the children. There was an argument in the car concerning his extended family that escalated when his wife tried to prevent him from retrieving his wallet from a compartment between their front seats. He wanted to go play poker at the bar with his brother, and she did not want him to go. After he hit her in the arm, she went home to their duplex (next-door to his brother's home). At the time, her father was visiting with them. She told her father what had happened, and her father called the police, despite his daughter's pleas that he not do so. As a result, father and daughter no longer spoke to each other.

A restraining order was placed on Trevor, and it took several months before the case was settled in court. His wife appeared before the judge on four occasions to ask that the charges be dismissed. His lawyer suggested pleading guilty to a lesser charge of harassment, which he did, and Trevor was ordered to attend a batterer intervention program.

This was Trevor's first contact with the police. He was not addicted to alcohol or drugs. *I hardly ever drink, and I have never done drugs.* Trevor had little trouble feeling a part of the STOP program, and he connected extremely well to its curriculum. He would go home after each class and share with his wife new insights he had learned, and together they would discuss how their relationship could be enhanced. At another agency, they went to marriage counseling. They also sought help from their parish priest, who had married them, someone both of them respected. He supported them both during the period of their separation as a result of the no-contact order, and he continued to offer them encouragement for the steps they were both taking to change their ways of thinking and acting.

Trevor's brothers and sisters rallied around him, his wife, and their children in the aftermath of the incident that brought him into contact with the criminal justice system. During his period of no contact, in particular, they offered his wife and the kids the support they were missing from Trevor himself.

While he grew up poor for most of his childhood, Trevor reported that his early life was very happy. He had six siblings (another died as an infant), and his parents did what they could to provide free entertainment for the children on the weekends, such as going to the park and playing ball or swimming at the beach. He had been home-schooled by both parents, although his mother had a more active role in instructing the children. Since both parents did shift work, the children's lessons occurred at different times of the day.

Trevor mentioned how much he enjoyed his own children and the various activities in which he was engaged with them. He had no experience of living dangerously either in his teenage years or later in his twenties. His wife was a stay-at-home mother at the moment but was planning to go to university the next year, once the youngest child was a year old.

As a practicing Catholic, Trevor felt that going to mass with his family was important. The church was there for him in his time of need, and the priest was extremely helpful. Trevor credited the STOP program for helping to improve his relationship with his wife. He mentioned that he understood himself and his wife much better now, regarding both their past and their current struggles. He wanted to buy a house in the country eventually, something his brother was also hoping to do. Trevor had a strong family around him and a committed extended family. His parish church and the priest there offered support. He was employed, he owned a house, he had no prior record, there was no evidence of substance abuse in his life, and he was very hopeful about the future. He completed the program at STOP by the time we came back again, by doubling up and going to two classes a week.

For Trevor, religion and family went together. His brother and extended family network saw the church as part of their ongoing activities, and they attempted to live out its mandate to support and care for one another, especially in times of need. That was how Trevor would explain it. He lived next-door to his brother in duplexes they both owned, and their social lives were intertwined. (In fact, it was his insistence that he spend time with his brother that led him down the road to an abusive act.) He'd had regular employment and made wise economic choices that enabled him to own a home and support his family. While he liked to have a beer or two, he had never been a problem drinker. All of these behaviors were consistent with his family and religious network. He felt supported and ultimately accountable.

Like religion and family, the notions of support and accountability go together, too. Certainly, in the stories of the men we have followed, the impact of faith and the faith community can be seen most clearly when it permeated their family networks.

For others, notions of family living were disconnected from support that a pastor or a faith community might offer. Ted Sweet used to attend a church regularly back in the 1980s and reported that just a year or so earlier, he had started attending again. We asked if he found help there when he was at the low point of his life. He said no, that he did not seek help there for his troubles, but then he noted that he probably should have. Was there any reason he did not look to the congregation or the pastor for assistance, we asked? Ted said rather nonchalantly, *Oh, I don't know, I just didn't, probably just didn't feel worthy. You know, I probably felt just low.* For Ted, religion was disconnected from his family experience. Even now, he attended alone. He went to a mega-church where he could be anonymous. The flip side: no one was likely to hold him accountable.

Men in the STOP program were able to recount with many details the day someone called 911, calls that brought them into contact with the criminal justice system and eventually led them to STOP. We wish to highlight now three points from the stories of the men that give us confidence that issues of abuse have come onto the public radar screen, including agencies that are mandated to respond.

1. Certainty in Response

When a victim, a neighbor, or a family member calls 911, the call is taken seriously, the police come quickly, and charges are brought expeditiously; there is no question that once the call is made, there is a response. While it is clear from the literature that the certainty of response cannot be guaranteed across North America, the experience from our data is more optimistic. Almost any woman can be guaranteed, in the context where our research took place, that the police will come and that the violent behavior she reports will be considered to be a crime until shown otherwise. The gray area relates to whether charges will be brought, whether there will be dual charges, whether the prosecutor will follow through with the charges, and whether the perpetrator will be removed from contact with the victim.

2. Swiftness of Response

Swiftness of response relates to court organization. In those jurisdictions with specialized domestic violence courts or with judges who appreciate the need for swiftness, cases are handled more expeditiously. The specialized courts offer the structure to ensure that cases move through the system quickly and in a uniform manner. Judges who are well versed in the many issues around intimate partner violence are also able to recognize and address the context of each case and direct the responses of the criminal justice system to ensure that perpetrators face the full consequences of the law and that support for victims is not overlooked as these cases are adjudicated. While this advantages victims, it also produces an environment where there is support for the work of the district attorney's office, parole and probation, batterer intervention programs, and advocacy groups. Through our interviews with judges, it became clear that those who sought additional training were better equipped to ensure that the needs of both perpetrators and victims were taken into account in their courtrooms and in their judgments.

3. Coordinated Community Response

The interface between the court system and other facets of coordinated community response is critical. Some researchers such as Gondolf (2002) have highlighted the role of a coordinated community-based system of condemning violence in the family context and offering swift intervention in its aftermath. It is clear from our observations that judges do not always see that necessity, but it is also clear that when judges understand fully the impact of a coordinated community response, this enhances the impact of what they require of the perpetrator. For example, one of the judges in the jurisdiction of the STOP agency noted in his interview that he actually attended some of the events put on by the Domestic Violence Advocacy Council and that he had availed himself of specialized training given by STOP's director.

SPECIALIZED DOMESTIC VIOLENCE COURTS

While there was no specialized domestic violence court in the jurisdiction where we interviewed the men in our research, the local judge mentioned above indicated that he was very interested in the issue of violence in the family and thus ensured that perpetrators appeared in his court within several days of being arrested. He also followed through on their sentencing requirements by having them reappear on a regular basis or by tracking their progress through agents of the justice system. In his court, noncompliance with requirements had unpleasant consequences.

Specialized domestic violence courts, one of a variety of so-called problem-solving courts (Butts 2001),[1] have been established in recognition of the need for an intensive and coordinated approach to the pervasive problem of family violence and with the goal of creating a criminal justice system response to the issue of domestic violence that better addresses the needs of victims (Cook et al. 2004; Epstein 1999; Dawson and Dinovitzer 2001; Tsai 2000). Other general goals relate to improving the judicial response to the problem by coordinating criminal justice and social service agencies and holding defendants accountable (Gover and MacDonald 2003). To that end, there are several specific goals, including expeditious court processing, more appropriate sentencing, reducing case attrition prior to sentencing, and the provision of integrated services to victims (Denham and Gillespie 1999). In taking a social problem approach to crime, these courts serve a dual purpose: as agents of social control and of social change (Mirchandani 2005). The argument is that the technocratic approach to justice utilized by these courts mobilizes social control factors related to deterrence, those being effectiveness, certainty, and swiftness, in order to facilitate their goals of social change.

Key elements of the specialized court model are identified by Newmark et al. (2001, vii):

- A network of criminal justice and social service partner agencies that work together on making the model succeed.
- The specialized caseload of virtually all indicted domestic violence felonies in the jurisdiction and no other cases than domestic violence felonies.
- Trained and dedicated personnel from court, prosecution, offender intervention and treatment, probation, and victim service agencies.
- Vertical processing and standard practices to ensure consistency in case handling.

- Enhanced case information flow among partner agencies to improve judicial decision-making and partner agency operations.
- An emphasis on defendant monitoring and accountability.
- Enhanced protection for, and services to, victims.

In Canada, numerous cities now have established specialized domestic violence courts, including Calgary, Vancouver, Winnipeg, Moncton, Whitehorse, and Toronto. Some cities have only docket courts where perpetrators state their pleas. Those who plead not guilty are referred to criminal court, and those who plead guilty are quickly sentenced. Other cities have both docket courts and trial courts; those who plead guilty in these instances go to a specialized domestic violence trial court. A unique feature of these specialized courts is the precourt conferences that bring together the crown prosecutor, defense counsel, probation worker, agency liaison workers, victim advocates, and police officers, in order for them to exchange pertinent information before the case is heard.

In Ontario, the first domestic violence court was established in Toronto in 1996, and another followed soon thereafter in North York (Bradley 2002). The Woman Abuse Council of Toronto monitored judges' decisions and outcomes in these courts and reported on this project in 1999 (Bradley 2002). They found that specialized courts were better able to successfully prosecute domestic violence cases; had lower rates of withdrawals, dismissals, and peace bonds; had higher rates of guilty verdicts; and had higher rates of victims attending court. The great strength of specialized courts, according to Cook et al. (2004, E13), is that they "place the victim at the heart of the process." Women are better able to access the multiple and complementary options available to them. An alternative view is offered by Salvaggio (2002), who notes that critics believe public interests have tended to supersede the interests of victims and that the Ontario system does not adequately reflect the needs of women.

The Calgary response to domestic violence is noteworthy largely because of that city's organization, the HomeFront Society for the Prevention of Domestic Violence, which coordinates criminal justice and community responses and has developed protocols with fifty-two agencies, including hospitals, shelters, Aboriginal organizations, and child welfare agencies (Ad Hoc Federal-Provincial-Territorial Working Group 2003; Sevcik et al., forthcoming). This coordinated response accelerates resolution of cases, with 70 percent of all cases heard in the domestic violence court (Court 412) being resolved within a month from first appearance date (Van de Veen 2004). The most commonly occurring dispositions were offender treatment conditions (79 percent), alcohol or substance abuse assessment and treatment (52 percent), conditions requiring the offender to abstain completely from the use of alcohol (38 percent), and conditions prohibiting contact with the complainant (30 percent) (Van de Veen 2004, 84).

The advantages of a specialized domestic violence court are outlined by Helling (undated) in her overview of courts in Seattle, Sacramento, and Vancouver in Washington. These are increased accessibility for victims, specialized expertise of the criminal justice personnel, increased accountability of offenders, renewed commitment to solving problems and working together by criminal justice personnel, consistency in case handling, timely response, and sending a message to the community that the courts take domestic violence seriously. The Ad Hoc

Federal-Provincial-Territorial Working Group (2003) lists similar elements and adds "the provision of services that recognize the unique needs of spousal/partner abuse victims" (59). Helling also outlines the disadvantages of this type of system. She notes that putting "all the eggs in one basket" does not work if the court makes consistently bad decisions and women have nowhere else to turn. In addition, perceptions of bias favoring women may appear, the staff has greatly increased workloads, and there is a high burnout rate for all court personnel. These types of concerns are also reported by Newmark et al. (2001), who examined the specialized domestic violence court system in Kings County, New York. They note that these system agencies felt workload pressures caused by increased prosecutions, insufficient services for victims, and limited resources that serve batterers. Other features subject to criticism in the US context include peripherally related things such as the indeterminate effect of mandating batterer intervention programs as a condition of probation or sentencing and the questionable deterrent effect of alternative sanctions for domestic violence crimes such as enhanced monitoring and greater enforcement of severe penalties for violating orders of protection (Tsai 2000).

The Impact of Specialized Courts for Victims/Survivors

Women victims are extremely vulnerable regardless of the response of the criminal justice system because of risk possibilities. Just as they are at greater risk if prosecution is not pursued, they are also at greater risk if prosecution proceeds, because of their intimate connection with the perpetrator (Epstein, Bell, and Goodman 2003). There appears to be a reluctance to incarcerate men convicted of wife abuse, with between 30 and 50 percent of prison terms being thirty days or less (Prairie Research Associates 1994; Brown 2000). In another research study, magistrates given a series of hypothetical vignettes to react to were more likely to suggest prison when alcohol was involved or when the victim required medical attention (Gilchrist and Blissett 2002). Also, Hartman and Belknap (2003) note that the court officials in their research indicated that 17.1 percent of victims were threatened by defendants to coerce them not to testify. This real fear of retaliation felt by women was followed by problems getting time off from work, wanting to work things out with the batterer, pressure from his family or friends, previous bad experiences with the court, problems with child care, pressure from her family or friends, transportation problems, and fear of being arrested herself (Wolf et al. 2003).

Women face distinctive challenges in the courtroom, in part because the offender is known to them (and often loved by them) and also because criminal justice remedies often fail to offer protection and end the violence (Jordan 2004). For example, mandatory arrest and no-drop prosecution policies are indeed effective in curtailing the violence of some men, but for others, this response may increase their violence (Chalk and King 1998). According to Hoyle and Sanders (2000), many women do not seek criminal sanctions because they believe these are unlikely to help end the violence. They also believe that their "choices" within the criminal justice system are often coerced by the circumstances of their lives. Battered women are not a homogeneous group, and public policy could be better designed to accommodate the individual needs of victims.

Welcome to Specialized Domestic Violence Court

I (Barb) clearly recollect a visit to a court building in the northwestern United States where there were metal detectors at all doors and X-ray scans of all personal bags. Security personnel also were authorized to do a pat-down search of each person entering the building. But what stands out in my mind about that court entryway was a small plaque on the wall right beside the security area, placed there in memory of a young woman and her unborn daughter who were murdered by the woman's estranged partner as she entered the court building on her way to seek help from the criminal justice system. That image is engraved firmly in my mind. I think of the terror she must have felt as her assailant burst through the entryway, gun in hand, and shot her. I think of the chaos that must have ensued. It is an image that is representative, in the most extreme form, of the experiences of abuse and violence that women and children live through every day in North America—the terror and the chaos.

I made my way up to what was the family court area, where cases involving child custody, divorce, and so on, might normally be heard, although on the day I visited, each of the cases related in some way to abuse within the family. There was a court-appointed advocate to assist the plaintiffs with questions about the proceedings. She stood by the plaintiffs as they gave testimony and answered questions posed by the judge, who on this day was a woman. There were tales of abuse-related issues such as stalking, tapped telephones, and children not returned from visitation periods. The court session was only two hours long, and the disposition of most cases involved further appearances at later dates. As everyone was cleared from the courtroom, the judge looked down at me and asked what I was doing there with a notebook in my hand. I replied that I was a family violence researcher, taking notes, and she seemed quite interested and amenable to my presence, inviting me to come back again.

The experience of going to court was different in another city. I entered the criminal justice office building in the downtown area of a large city. There was no security check to get into the building. A sign on the bank of elevators directed me to the fourth floor for the specialized domestic violence court. As I exited the elevator into a very large open atrium, I noted a group of people assembled at the far end of the building. Walking toward this congregation of people, who I presumed were awaiting the start of the court day, I glanced around at the pleasant but sterile surroundings, a concrete structure with glass ceilings to allow light into the building. An attempt to soften the environment had been made with plants in large containers and sturdy wooden benches. I heard the hushed murmurs of many people speaking simultaneously. A young woman pulling a rolling case full of files, wearing a traditional black lawyer's robe for a court appearance, approached a casually dressed man and directed him to one side so that she could speak with him. For fifteen or twenty minutes, as I stood to the side and awaited the opening of the court, this young woman, who I began to assume was the court-specific public prosecutor, spoke with several men who were obviously defendants in the day's proceedings. As I waited, I had the opportunity to scan the court docket posted on the wall outside the courtroom door, which listed the order of proceedings for the day so that defendants knew when their cases would be called. It was a surprisingly long list, and the brief notes beside each defendant's name indicated that the vast majority of cases were new on this day. Approximately ten minutes before the start of court, the doors were opened to allow people to enter and take their places.

Large double doors led into the courtroom, the floors were carpeted in blue, the walls were brick interspersed with stripes of blue carpet, the ceiling was wood slats, and there were five long rows of wooden benches. The bench where the judge would sit was faced with the same blue carpet, and there was brick all along behind the bench and on both sides. In front of the judge and one tier lower on the bench were desks for the court reporter and the court clerk. These people entered the court ahead of the judge, and the clerk engaged in hushed conversation with various defense lawyers and prosecutors. The court reporter was ensuring that the recording equipment was in working order. Just below that station were two witness boxes, on the left and right sides of the bench. A sign in the front of the courtroom, accessible for all to see, read, "All microphones live, all conversations recorded." On the left side of the room was the prisoner's box, where defendants who had been held in the jail cells behind the door entered and were processed. A police officer stood by this box to ensure the safety and security of all those in the courtroom. When an interpreter was required, which was infrequent, he or she stood in front of the prisoner's box and translated for the court. Behind the "bar" that separated the bench from the rest of the room, there were tables on the left and right of the main aisle, with spaces for the prosecutors and the defense lawyers. In these very front rows of the courtroom, the defense lawyers were seated together waiting for their cases to be called. Occasionally, the lawyers quickly exited the courtroom purportedly to handle appearances in other courtrooms in the building. All of the lawyers, both defense and prosecution, seemed to pull large briefcases on wheels full of files.

In addition to the defendants waiting outside the courtroom were numerous other people waiting, and it was not until we all entered that who they were became more obvious. The defendants for the day were all directed to be seated on the left side of the courtroom, and most of them were surrounded by family members, friends, coworkers, clergy members, and others there to support them. On the right side of the courtroom were seated those who had been victimized by violence, always women, who often sat alone, with their heads down, looking very frightened and alone. A judge we interviewed who worked in specialized domestic violence court had also noted this tendency. This judge said that there was disappointment in the experiences of the courtroom when religious leaders or people of faith came, because they came in support of the perpetrators, while the victims sat alone, unassisted by anyone from a faith community. A judge from another jurisdiction also had mentioned this phenomenon. He, too, had misgivings about members of the clergy being involved, based on his experience. Sometimes a minister or other members of the faith community came with the men and spoke up in court, and, he said, "what they say makes me uncomfortable." What made him uncomfortable was that they commented on the fact that this was a really good guy, or they stated that the faith community did couples counseling and that "we will take care of this." A probation officer also described her experience working with a batterer and his minister. She mentioned that the minister kept telling the man to "just get a handle on it and turn to your wall." She said, "He had to go back to court two or three times, and every time, he got his minister in there to support him, and he was a rough one." Again, the women who have been victimized often sit alone, unassisted.

In this jurisdiction, there was a female court worker who moved among the women and spoke briefly with each of them. She stopped and sat down next to a woman if there appeared to be a need for explanations or a comforting touch. Her role was to provide support for these women as they moved through the criminal justice process. In addition, there was an Aboriginal court worker who was there to provide service to Aboriginal clients who had been victimized and a child advocate to speak on behalf of victimized children.

At a table at the back of the room, close to the main doors, were spaces for domestic violence court personnel, including a police officer who was available to swear in peace bonds and the victim/survivor advocates.

I later learned through conversation with various members of the court that every day before the court session began, each case was briefly discussed in a room behind the bench by all relevant members of the court team—lawyers for both sides, victim advocates, child advocates, court police officers, and others. This involved a run-through of any notable items in particular cases that should be highlighted when the case came before the judge.

As the judge entered the courtroom, we were asked to rise. Court was in session. Everyone sat down, and all conversations became muted. Beneath the surface, though, there was continual whispered discussion and movement at the defense lawyers' bench. Perhaps one would whisper to a colleague and then quickly exit the courtroom to take care of another appearance—there was coming and going this way throughout the morning—up and down, in and out, waiting for their brief appearance on behalf of their client.

On one particular day, there were twenty-eight cases on the morning docket. The judge was a male, the recorder and clerk were females, and there were two victim advocates in attendance. A review of several of the highlights of these cases tells the story of what happens on a typical morning in this domestic violence court. Since this was a docket court, those defendants who pleaded not guilty were assigned trial court dates—and even though they went to a specialized domestic violence trial court, the date was usually several months in the future. Those who pleaded guilty had their cases handled at the docket court level almost immediately. One practice of the docket court judges that was of particular note was the tendency, for each decided case, to repeat the same list of conditions to be met, including abstaining from drugs and alcohol, attendance at drug/alcohol counseling, surrendering all firearms, a fine of some amount, enrolling in a batterer treatment program, reporting to court as ordered, meeting regularly with the assigned probation officer (usually over a one-year period), having random urinalysis to ensure compliance with the no-drugs-or-alcohol order, and often complying with a peace bond or no-contact order. There appeared to be little variation in sentencing. Based on all of these conditions, it seemed that a coordinated community response approach was working in this city. And in fact, one of the local domestic violence advocates noted that there had been a good melding of agency response within this community: "We all have a professional lingo that is used to exclude other professions, so we developed common terms that we could agree on." Yet the rapid-fire listing of conditions by the judge in each case led me to question whether he was aware of how all of the agencies working to ensure that these conditions were met needed to be coordinated. After the defendant left the courtroom, how would all of this oversight take place? Which agencies needed to be brought into the court's decision?

Several of the defendants were in custody in a room to the side of the courtroom. As a prisoner's case was called, the police officer opened the door to the custodial cells and, in a loud voice, called for the defendant to appear. Into the courtroom came a man dressed in a bright orange jumpsuit, who stood behind a railing in the prisoner's dock, guarded by the police officer. What I noted immediately was that several of these men spent most of the time in the courtroom glaring at their victims. The phrase *if looks could kill* immediately came to mind. Even as they were answering questions posed by members of the court, they were focused on looking at the victim in an intimidating manner.

In one case, a man, well dressed and appearing to be in his fifties, was convicted of assault and threats for, while arguing over divorce conditions, grabbing his wife, throwing her, shaking her, and throwing a cup of hot coffee in her face. His twenty-two-year-old son tried to stop him, and he was also assaulted as well. The court was told that this man had no previous record. He was given a conditional discharge and probation for twelve months. His lawyer advised that he was in counseling currently and would also be in an anger management program, as there were other family issues related to the ongoing divorce. He would be starting this program in two weeks. The judge said that he wanted to make probation the same length of time as the anger management program. The defense lawyer explained that the program was for fifteen months and accepted that as a part of probation for his client—that it would end in fifteen months. The prosecutor agreed. The man was ordered to keep the peace, appear before the court when required, and stay in touch with his probation officer.

In a second case, the judge noted that this was the thirteenth appearance for this case. The lawyer read all the counts against the defendant, and he pleaded guilty to thirteen counts, while seven other charges were withdrawn. He made threatening calls to his ex-girlfriend about killing her current boyfriend; he made ten calls between midnight and four in the morning. He then threw a rock, breaking the windshield of her car, and threw a water bottle at another car. He broke his curfew and did not report to the constable when ordered. He harassed his ex-girlfriend, who was pregnant. He would phone at all hours of the day and night on her cell phone. He also phoned his ex's mother and her younger sister at all hours. He threatened to kill his ex-girlfriend with a gun. He also threw a coffee cup through the front window and caused three hundred dollars' worth of damage. The prosecutor noted that the accused had been in custody for sixty-six days, and, giving him double credit for time served, he was asking for time served and eighteen months' probation. The judge said, "He has got quite a record to be looking at that kind of arrangement. He has not complied with any arrangements that have been made. You will have to persuade me. A conditional sentence might be more appropriate." The girls involved in this case were fifteen and sixteen, and although they both wanted contact, the prosecutor was asking for no contact. Their mother did not want contact. The judge listed the terms—attending counseling for alcohol/drug abuse, domestic violence treatment, no intoxication and random testing, proof of attendance at programs, three restraining orders for no contact with the mother and other family members, and a DNA sample to be provided to the court. The judge ended by saying, "I don't have a lot of confidence in you. Your history gives me no reason for confidence. The only reason I am letting you out today is that it is your first time in adult court."

In many cases on that day, the defense lawyers requested new appearance dates for a variety of reasons, including that the defendant had other legal matters to be attended to besides the domestic violence charges, the lawyers were unprepared to represent their clients, delays were needed for defendants to seek legal advice, an interpreter was needed, the crown had just provided the disclosure and the defense lawyer requested time to read it and prepare, the defendant did not appear and a warrant was issued for his arrest, and family issues prevented an appearance. While the intention of every specialized domestic violence court is to have cases heard in an expedited manner, it is quite common for delays to happen. But when examining the cases of those who pleaded not guilty and were given trial dates months in the future, the delays in docket court were rather short, with two weeks the longest period of time.

According to a judge we interviewed in the northwestern United States, such delays were often welcomed by judges who did not have sufficient training in domestic violence. He believed, though, that the majority of cases appearing in specialized court were finalized within forty-five days. He maintained that in his court, 99 percent of those convicted of domestic abuse were mandated to attend a batterer intervention program, had no-contact orders imposed, were ordered to appear in court when summoned (with the court reviewing the case in 45, 60, 90 and 120 days), were placed on probation, and were required to successfully complete the intervention program. He told us that he said to each defendant, "I am very clear on those things. There is not any room for failure, and we absolutely expect you to succeed." He told us that he believed his job was to make it very clear that there were consequences and that the court would follow through. If, at the date of the first follow-up, the perpetrator had not complied, there would be no consequences; by the second follow-up, however, if there was still no compliance, then he would be sentenced to three to five days on a work crew, eight hours a day of physically work, and then, thirty days later, if he was still noncompliant, that sentence would grow to twenty days on a work crew. When men declared that they would not go to a batterer intervention program, they were sentenced to one year in jail. So the consequences were clear, and the follow-up was sure and swift.

Swiftness, certainty, and severity are the important elements of deterrence theory. This theory is based on the notion that if the punishment for the crime is swift, certain, and of proportionate severity, crime will be reduced; when there are specific punishments imposed, people will not reoffend (specific deterrence), and the members of the wider community will be deterred from offending if they believe they might get caught and punished (general deterrence). Stafford and Warr (1993) define specific deterrence as the "deterrent effect of direct experience with punishment and punishment avoidance" and general deterrence as the "deterrent effect of indirect experience with punishment and punishment avoidance."

By noon on the day of my visit, the roster of cases was coming to an end. The docket court would meet again the following day, as it did each weekday morning. I waited for the members of the public to leave the courtroom and then spent several minutes chatting with various court workers. The police officer at the back of the courtroom told me he had been doing this work for more than twenty-five and was a member of the specialized domestic violence response team. One of the victim advocates noted that it had been a "normal" caseload that day. As I entered the elevator to go to the ground floor, I noticed that my fellow occupant was one of the defense lawyers from the courtroom. When I mentioned that I had seen him in court, he made a very derisive comment about the role of victimized women in "causing" their abuse. Because of that comment, I left the courthouse in a state of reduced hope for change.

Doing Time and Being Monitored

After sentencing, many of the men we interviewed experienced confinement in a county or state prison facility. In this chapter, we consider their stories as they live behind bars as a result of their domestic violence or other illegal activities. For some of the men, there is a spiritual awakening that occurs during this period of their lives—a reconnection to a faith that was part of their childhood or adolescence. We also consider their postconfinement experiences as they continue to be monitored by parole or probation officers. Interwoven with the men's stories are the experiences of the criminal justice workers we have interviewed and our observations of court proceedings.

In her book *Prison Religion*, Winnifred Fallers Sullivan (2009) argues that enthusiasm for religion and enthusiasm for incarceration both flourish within the United States. A higher percentage of the population find themselves incarcerated than in any other country in the world. Citing US Department of Justice statistics, Sullivan (2009, 95) claims that more than 7 million people in the United States are either incarcerated or on parole or probation. Employing a variety of methodologies—ranging from survey data to ethnographic fieldwork—sociologists of religion have argued that the United States is a very religious country, in which people pray, attend worship services, and become members of congregations that they support financially and to which they volunteer their time. "Religious revival and law-and-order populism are not unique to the United States," Sullivan argues, "but the U.S. stands out in both respects" (2009, 4), especially as contrasted with secular Europe. Tracing the history of contemporary prisons to late-eighteenth-century England, Sullivan claims that notions of incarceration were promoted by Christians as a more humane form of punishment than the brutality of alternatives such as whipping, public humiliation, or hanging. As such, prisons were believed to be places where penitence and reform were not only possible but the consequences of confinement, appropriate instruction, work, and solitude.

Sullivan's research focuses, in part, on prisoners who participate in a faith-based prison reform initiative, one that she argues asks them to "reinvent themselves as free moral agents by using the tools of a populist and punitive theory of justice combined with various forms of vernacular Christianity" (2009, 9). Like so many other scholars, she is very skeptical of the effectiveness of faith-based social services, particularly in the absence of longitudinal data and the proliferation of self-serving, anecdotal information propagated by organizations dependent on voluntary contributions for their survival. Also like others, she argues that private agencies have greater discretion regarding their client base, that is, whom they admit to a program initially and whom they expel for a variety of reasons. As costs for incarceration increase and budgets for prisons stagnate or decrease, federal and state facilities find themselves serving more inmates but with fewer rehabilitation programs or educational resources.

Sullivan served as an expert witness at a trial centered on the constitutionality of permitting religious organizations to operate a prison-rehabilitation program in a state-run facility in Iowa. As a legal and religion scholar, she followed the lawsuit to examine the relationship between one specific form of religion, evangelical Protestantism, and one specific constituency of American citizens, those serving time in prison. Sullivan argues that for the most part, prisons welcome initiatives by faith-based service providers. She believes that family counseling, substance abuse programs, and prison rehabilitation are explicit initiatives that focus on the transformation of the self—something that aligns closely with conservative Protestant ideologies. Unlike the men we are studying who have come to the STOP program, those in the faith-based rehabilitation program at issue in the trial in Iowa are in a comprehensive prerelease program. However, as in STOP, the objectives of the program include teaching and mentoring to give men a sense of human dignity, self-worth, responsibility, and accountability, based on biblical principles. Within this model, change happens from the inside out. While STOP uses slightly different words and is linked far more closely to therapeutic and justice models adopted in secular, community-based agencies, it also fosters the belief that once men come to see themselves differently, they will walk the world in a different way. Here, too, there is the belief that change happens first on the inside, with how a man thinks or feels about himself and others. That the two—religion and incarceration—are linked conceptually should not surprise us. There is ample evidence in the stories the men shared of their lives in prison.

GETTING CONNECTED TO GOD IN PRISON: THE FIRST FEW DAYS OF CURTAILED FREEDOM

We interviewed Scott Smythe after he had been coming to STOP for eleven weeks. We learned that he met his current wife, Krista, just before he began jail time for assault on his ex. It was Krista's suggestion that he seek help at STOP after his time of incarceration had been completed.

Scott credited God and spiritual renewal for helping him to redirect his life and stay on the new course. By his own account, he didn't really like churches and *the browbeating you feel in them.* But he was definite that God *has done amazing things in my life. I mean, if it wasn't for the Lord, I don't think I would be sitting here right now. I would be upstate somewhere in one of the prisons. . . . The Lord has been changing me, and I don't really talk about it with many people.*

But he was very willing to talk to us about it.

Scott's spiritual renewal began soon after his incarceration. *I was in the county jail in one of the dorms, and I had never been in the dorms. Well, in the dorms, there's twenty-two guys all in the same room, and you are all in bunk beds. It's really hard, really, really hard, for a guy like me. I am a real quiet guy, and I don't like, I can't handle, all the noise. And I was in there, and one of the guys asked me if I want to go to a Bible study.*

Well, I figure Bible study meant we get to get out of the dorm and get away from every-body. He agreed to the idea.

Shortly thereafter, it was time to go. Scott went because he didn't want one of his dorm mates to think he was rude. *It's all about etiquette in jail, and so I went so I wasn't rude, but when I got done with the Bible study, it felt better, and it was just an uplifting thing 'cause they prayed for me and prayed for some of the hard times I was having, and it just felt better, and after that, I went to Bible study. We did one every night, and when I moved to different dorms, 'cause you get split up and different people around, I tried to keep a Bible study going the whole time, and that made my time easier.*

We were interested to know exactly how going to a Bible study made things eas-ier. *That was the first time I made it through a jail setting without going into the hole, without getting into a fight or without cussing at one of the guards and getting thrown in the hole or anything like that. It was a life-changing experience.*

But this was not Scott's first encounter with God or organized religion. His mother came from a Catholic background, but she was not a church attender. As a late teen, he had contact with a man who was very religious—someone who had picked Scott up when he was hitchhiking—and he went to church with that man. Scott claimed that God was chasing him throughout his teenage years and that he finally gave in to God. Scott saw the last time he was incarcerated as his surrender to God. Referring to his spiritual life, he said, *It's just me and His private little deal, so it's been a big thing in my life, I guess.*

We asked whether there was ever a religious leader or a pastor who was involved in his life. Scott mentioned the pastor who came to the jail and also his father's brother, a man who turned his life around when he was older and influenced others, such as Scott's father, after he had changed.

Later in our interview, Scott said that his faith had given him *a great degree of hope.*

We asked him to help us understand what this meant for him.

Um, I don't know, it's really, I don't think you could explain to somebody all the changes that I have seen happen in the last few years. It's too remarkable. Like, my dad was a drug addict from the time he was thirteen, and within the last few years, he has quit. And is clean and sober, and now he is taking care of himself, even. I mean, just the things that have changed around me and the way I—I don't know if it's because of Him, I just believe that it is. It's what drives me so much, I guess, 'cause it's amazing. There isn't very much at all that He hasn't changed completely, completely around for me, and that's about it. I don't know how else to say it.

Toward the end of one of our interviews with Scott, we asked him what advice he would give to a man who had acted abusively and been reluctant to come to a group like STOP. He was not mandated, so why should he come? *There is a better way, and I would try and cite a couple of examples that they have pointed out to me in class.* His advice covered many of the things he learned at STOP about tools and toolboxes, concluded with these words: *If you don't like this lifestyle, come with me. I'll help you. If you like the lifestyle, you are fooling yourself; you know, go ahead, go to prison.*

Scott reconnected with God in prison. It was not his first encounter with faith or with other believers. But something important transpired during his early days of incarceration. He saw that attending a Bible study group offered him something important that he needed. Initially, he went because another inmate invited him, and Scott could see that going to a group meant temporary respite from the noise of his bunk room and freedom to leave that space and the other men there. Once, at a Bible study group meeting, he felt the care and concern of the other men, and over time, Scott internalized a feeling of hope and the belief that he could change. He saw evidence of this in his own life, even in prison, and he held on to the notion that a changed life was possible even after his time of incarceration was over.

We never asked the men directly about whether they reconnected to God during their time in prison, but many of them volunteered this information as they talked about being incarcerated and the challenges of life behind bars. It quickly became apparent to us that other inmates were making suggestions to newly incarcerated men that they join a Bible study group or attend one of the religious services offered to men in prison.

GETTING CONNECTED TO GOD IN PRISON: FROM THE FIRST EXPERIENCE TO ANNOUNCING ONE'S FAITH TO OTHERS

We focus now on the first time someone inside prison connects a man to God directly, rather than as an invitation to the group experience. We do so through the eyes of Jay Primer. Jay was a man who had been angry at God for much of his life. What became critical for him in prison was that another inmate connected him to God and in so doing helped him to turn his life around, both on the inside and after he was released.

Jay had been a heroin addict for many years. His mom died when he was eleven. Life was difficult, and he basically felt as if he was on his own. *I raised myself on the streets of San Francisco.*

As a child and a teen, Jay was angry at God. *I was raised in the church, but ... after my mom died, I kind of got mad at God, because my aunts, being all of Christian background from way far back, Southern Baptist, you know, from Missouri, they told me God took her home. God took your mom home. Well, in a child's mind, I would never tell a child that, because it made me think, well, why did God come take my mom and He didn't come take Johnny's mom down the street, you know? And I was really angry with God for a long time.*

In jail, Jay reconnected with his religious past. He found God again.

I met this man, he was doing four life sentences, he had a tattoo on the side of his face, and he started talking to me about God. And I had a Bible, and I was kind of illiterate, you know, I hadn't picked up a Bible in years. And I was trying, and I didn't particularly like this Bible I had, and he was reading to me out of his Bible, and I said I want a Bible like that. . . . He said, [Jay], they are going to come back and take me back to prison, and when they do, I am going to throw it out here on the table, and it will be for you when I leave. It was a brand-new Bible ... I still have it, it's tattered, it's worn, but it's not from abuse, it's from use. And I started reading the Bible, and that's what I lived for ... it gave me a high no drug has ever given me.

Once Jay had experienced the personal benefits of religious practice in prison, he was quick to want to identify himself with God and his spiritual reconnection. He did this through having religious tattoos placed on his body. During our interview, Jay showed us his tattoos, which were meant to announce his newfound interest in a spiritual life. *This is one of my grandma's prayers. It says, "I can do all things through Christ." That was my grandma's favorite prayer, so I had that tattooed, and this one here, I put, "only God can judge me."*

The visual representations of his spiritual quest have two main purposes: to iden-tify to others that he has decided to join with other men in prison on a spiritual jour-ney and to serve as a personal reminder that he is a new person, a person committed to God and a renewed life, or a second chance, that God made possible.

The tattoos on Jay's forearms remind him of the importance of spiritual matters when the going gets tough. First, it is tough in prison. And later, it is tough on the outside. We discuss Jay's story more fully in chapter 9. One of his most difficult experiences after incarceration involved interacting with workers at the DHS. Of those trying times, he said: *I just keep looking down at my arms, I say prayers before I go in there, because those people, they are terrible, they are terrible, they are terrible, terrible people.* His passion flared at those in DHS, because they removed his child from their home, and Jay felt powerless to do anything that would turn these events around.

What is important to note here, however, is that Jay learned how to identify as a religious follower when he was in prison. He was always a religious *believer*, but in prison, he became a religious *follower*. The tattoos were one way to mark this shift in identification. They told the world that he had chosen to follow God and to accept God's mercy and offer of a second chance.

GETTING CONNECTED TO GOD IN PRISON: DOING RELIGION IN PRISON WITH OTHERS

Several men mentioned that one of the highlights of their weeks in prison was attending Bible study, a time when they could leave their cells, gather with other men, and feel that there was some light at the end of the dark tunnel in which they found themselves. Some mentioned a pastor or priest, a couple mentioned nuns, and more than a few noted the role of other inmates in drawing them to the study of the Bible, as we saw earlier in the story of Scott.

Most of the men enjoyed the upbeat music and the singing—something that many continued to enjoy as they attended large inter- or nondenominational churches in the area where we were conducting research. We attended a few of these facilities and interviewed the pastors when we were in the area to observe the services and the variety of programs that were offered on a weekly basis.

One local community church had several services on a Sunday morning and one on Saturday night, each of which drew more than a thousand people. The range of weekly services and programs was astounding: groups for those who were grieving the death of a loved one, divorce care groups, mornings out for young moms, grandmothers' exercise programs, men's Bible studies, overcomers groups, age-based activity and learning programs, and the list went on. We learned from many of the men at STOP that they attended, at least sporadically, groups such as these, particularly ones that focused on overcoming difficulties or getting together with other men. The upbeat music, led by a worship team, was also a big hit with the men. In fact, what they experienced at church after incarceration was very much like what they experienced on the inside when they attended religious services in prison. These faith communities tended to be weighted toward the practice of religion, rather than focused on specific beliefs. Religion, then, was what they *did* together, rather than a set of theological or ideological statements to which they adhered. What men learned in prison at these services was that God offered second chances, that you could learn to live differently, and that you felt better after you attended the upbeat worship and fellowship—lively music and the warmth of sharing your burdens with others. All of this offered hope, a theme that runs through many chapters of this book but features prominently in our conclusion. From this perspective, hope was rekindled in prison. Hope was something you felt. Hope was something you could put action to. As we will see, not all men were able to harness hope to their advantage, but for others, it became part of their mantra of living one day at a time.

GETTING CONNECTED TO GOD IN PRISON: DOING RELIGION ON YOUR OWN

For those who were sent to the *hole*, solitary confinement, the Bible was one of the few things they were allowed in their cells. As we saw in chapter 4, Danny's prison life got off to a bad start. *I have no idea how stuff works, I am new to prison, country boy, not really into all this, so I mean, I never really considered myself of the criminal nature. My crime is I'm an addict.*

He talked to the wrong person in the prison yard during his first few days there, and there was an altercation. When the guards yelled for him to submit and stop fighting, he did not. This landed Danny covered with pepper spray and then *put in the hole*, solitary confinement.

You get let out every other day for ten minutes on a dog leash, they escort you to a shower and lock you inside, and you have ten minutes to shower and shave, and then you are put back in your box, and you get six sheets of paper a week to write letters, and you get to know yourself really well in there, and that is what it took for me to finally just stop and really look at what was going on with me.

So what exactly did Danny think about in that cell, all by himself, day and night? *The choices I had made, most of my sisters are with God, with the faith, they are really religious, and they believe in Christ, and they have all been married, successful people with families, and also my little brother. I was kind of like the black sheep. So I started to look at this, at their lives, and my life, and how all this had came tumbling down, and I stopped trying to blame everybody else and started really taking a look at where I was responsible for some of this chaos, and I just made a decision in there.*

Amid the isolation, he read the Bible, divided it into sections that he would read each month. And while he was not a particularly religious man, he credited the turn in his life to the *conscious decision that I was done destroying myself; you know, God put me here for a reason.*

Danny's resolve lasted for several years after he was released from prison, while he was living under the watchful eye of others at a group facility, and then later as he was hired as that watchful eye over others. Once he was on his own, a few years farther down the road, after having begun to study at a local community college and engage with others socially, his resolve began to weaken, and as we have seen in chapter 4, the pull toward living dangerously overtook the decision he made in prison to change the course of his life.

GETTING CONNECTED TO GOD IN PRISON:
ACCOUNTABILITY FOR A LIFETIME

Ben Chamois found God, hope, an accountability program, and new goals for his life while he was in prison.

Ben spent more than five years in prison for assaulting his wife. At the time of his arrest,he was in his mid-twenties, having just come back from a tour of Korea with the Army. While he was away, his wife—the mother of his small child—began seeing someone else. Upon his return, they split up, and Ben went east to live temporarily with his father, a corrections officer. Four months later, he returned to the West Coast, and he and his wife decided to reunite. Shortly thereafter, he learned that his wife had had an affair with his recruiter. *I got upset, and my emotions . . . and I ended up hitting her twenty-five times, and so I was incarcerated for assault . . . a seventy-month stint.*

Ben found God in prison. *Well, you really don't have too much in there, and you kind of get made fun of in certain things you do in there, you know. My first year was straight hell and a lot of fighting. You got to fight, people are always testing you and stuff, and I actually got it for church [attendance], too. People made fun of you for going to church, but it just made me feel better, you know, there was something there, and I can't really explain it. And I was reading the Bible, and it was comforting me, and I was able to have my daughter come visit me there, and I was able to write her, and it was just like I would have trouble writing, and I would read the Bible.*

We asked him about his spiritual journey now, four months since he left prison. *The night we had group and my PO called me here and told me I could start visits with her, so it's been the past ninety days I got my own apartment, I got a good job, I can have my daughter back in my life. My life has been clean, hopefully, things are just going and going and going, and I gotta thank Him for all these miracles, because I write them down in my prayer book—I only got tools, I haven't got answers.*

For Ben, the most beneficial part of the batterer intervention program was the discussion about how the brain works, the effects of drugs and alcohol on the brain, and how it can rebuild. But what he liked most about STOP was the parenting classes: *I would have to say the parenting classes, definitely, it's awesome, awesome, awesome class.* He began telephone contact with his daughter, and six-hour visits would begin in a month's time.

Ben had a new girlfriend, who worked as a trauma nurse, and he had a job on an assembly line. He hoped to return to welding eventually, but he was very grateful for his well-paid employment. His parents divorced some time ago, and there was regret and sadness when he spoke of his mother. *She still chooses drugs over relationships.*

Ben was working hard to establish new friends and new connections. He attended a large Four Square church in town and went to an accountability group for ex-cons at another church nearby. He lived temporarily at Second Chances, a place for people who had just left prison, but he was able to leave after only two months because he had steady employment and had been able to save some money for the deposit on an apartment. For these things, he was very grateful. He also credited God for the new relationship in his life, a woman he met through one of his fellow inmate's sisters. Her husband had committed suicide two years before. Ben explained that he told her about his past, *showed her all my paperwork*, and had learned from her that it was best to reestablish his relationship with his daughter before he introduced the girl to her. All of this made sense to Ben—he suggested he would not have listened this way to women in his life before.

He spoke powerfully and enthusiastically about one of the programs he was enrolled in while in prison, which he calls Powder River. There he learned about the ripple effect[1] of all his actions. *That's the bottom line*, he said with great excitement. *You can hold yourself accountable all day for stuff, but unless you play the tape through and think of the ripple effect and how it hurts everybody,* it will not change your behavior.

He went on to explain how this program worked for him. *I had to do two affirmations before I left Powder River. One was that I was going to turn my anger against my addiction, which I have. And the next one was that I wasn't going to put my needs before anybody else's needs, especially my daughter's needs, again. And I learned everything about the ripple effect.*

Ben also explained how he used what he learned there as a way to evaluate his next steps. *I even did the ripple effect chart before I came and talked to you ladies. I think everything through now, and I think, I don't feel, I've gotta think it through. And it saved me, and it's helping me, and I use it really.*

I think that everybody should have to go through that program. I have been watching all my buddies. I tell you what, I have been going to these accountability meetings, and they are all going back to jail and prison, and they are not thinking, you know. They are just doing stupid stuff, and it's really sad. It hurts to see your friends go. And I think that could be me, and I think, no, that's not going to be me 'cause there's no way I would allow that to happen.

We asked Ben to help us understand some of the steps he had taken in his life to ensure that this would never happen to him. *I have a whole different class of friends [now]. My support group is through AA, and then my new girlfriend, her whole family, they just despise drugs. . . . And I just don't surround myself with those people anymore at all, I turn the other way. If someone is drinking or something, I will ask them nicely and with respect not to do that around me. I haven't seen no drugs since I have been out, but the alcohol, I have a few friends I have had to tell them, you know, when you are done and you want to respect me, don't come around me with that stuff. . . . I have probably made four good friends that I can call anytime. Matter of fact, one of them answers a hotline for NA now.*

Then he added a comment about the power of a supportive environment. *Every day, every day. I live a minute at a time. Absolutely, and I think that's something that you can't forget, and I have people reminding me all the time. Where have you been? Been in prison? But that's a reminder every day, so every day you don't take advantage of nothing, and you live day by day, definitely.*

Ben mentioned the Powder River Correctional Facility, opened in 1989, which provided selected minimum-security inmates with the opportunity to participate in residential alcohol and drug treatment, institution-based and/or community-based work programs, and transitional programming prior to their release. Inmates assigned to the facility were involved in residential alcohol and drug treatment and/or assigned to institution- or community-based work projects and transition programs offered there. It was a highly regimented program that included a daily routine of fourteen to sixteen hours of treatment, education, and transition classes in conjunction with institution- and/or community-based work.

GETTING CONNECTED TO GOD IN PRISON: RECLAIMING PAST RELIGIOUS INVOLVEMENT

Notions of a new start or a second chance were featured frequently, but indirectly, in the men's discourse as they discussed time in prison and tried to make sense of how they found themselves locked up, freedom curtailed, living a life that was spiraling out of control.

For many, it was a time to think back to what had been. For some, it was a time to plan ahead for the future. Costenello "Costy" Ramrez was intent on harnessing his past involvement in a church in an attempt never again to find himself in a situation like a county jail.

Costy grew up in a nominally Catholic household. His Mexican father was an alcoholic, and his mother was consumed by looking after her eight children. The household was loud and boisterous, and the father was very heavy-handed with the children and his wife. *There were very few times I've ever seen my dad hit my mom or anything like that, a lot of arguments, but my dad was overpowering, very overbearing . . . kept her away from anything other than raising the kids.* As a child, Costy had lots of friends. Yet *the friends could never come to the house. My father did not allow friends and people to come to the house, it just didn't happen. We didn't have friends come over and hang out and that kind of thing.*

I think that what I learned from my dad and my mom's life is that I didn't want that kind of [life] when I had my kids.

As a young person, Costy attended events at a local Pentecostal church. During his time in prison, he reconnected with God and his spiritual life. *I'll be honest with you, it brought me really close to God. . . . I didn't want to be a jailhouse Christian. . . . [Now] I read the Bible every day, I pray every day . . . I go to church every Sunday and go to Bible study every Wednesday. I go to men's groups. I mean, it is something that I should have done years and years ago, and didn't, but when I was in jail, I remember thinking to myself, I need God's help in this.*

For Costy, a jailhouse Christian was someone who looked to God when he was in trouble, and immediately upon his release, he returns to his old ways of doing things and forgets about God and spiritual renewal. From this point of view, jailhouse Christianity was akin to a "fire escape"; it lets a person escape hell's flames when he found himself in the heat. Costy believed that the difference between a jailhouse follower and the authentic variety was what happened when you no longer found yourself doing time. How did you act then? Did your identification with the faith and your religious activities continue?

Costy told us that he had prayed that God would help him to get out of the very difficult situation he found himself in at home, with a wife who was sick, had frequent seizures, and was greatly affected by her often uncontrolled epilepsy. *I really believe he answered my prayer kind of harsh*, he said of the way his life had unfolded in the aftermath of the violent episode with his wife.

Yet Costy never took full responsibility for what he did. The insight he gained—his personal resentment of his wife's physical and emotional challenges—translated only into helping Costy make sense of his actions. He showed no remorse, only a resignation that his life was not as grim as those of many of the other men in the STOP classes. He stopped his pot smoking but appeared to be addicted to pain killers—Oxycontin, which he was given by a physician to curb the pain in his shoulder. When we met Costy for our fourth interview, he was awaiting surgery. He spoke of the pain—not his abuse—as ruining his life. His wife was now caring for him. *She still has seizures. . . . She has been my rock for me, helped me through this whole thing and been there. And so that has been my whole life [since we last met], my arm.*

GETTING CONNECTED TO PROGRAMS, BUT NOT TO GOD, IN PRISON

Jared Morez spent time in the state penitentiary as a result of four successive DWIs. But he decided to turn himself around. He did not have a jailhouse conversion; in fact, he never spoke of his spiritual life in prison, but he decided to take advantage of the programs that were offered and to start to make some good choices for himself.

Well, I had DWIs. I had four DWIs, and that's what it took to get me going to prison. I did three flat off a three-and-a-half-year sentence. So I got my GED, I became a certified plumber and a certified drywaller while I was in there, so my time didn't go for nothing.

We mentioned to Jared that some men had told us that there were very few programs in prison and not many opportunities to learn new things. *That is someone who is thinking on the constant negative side. I mean, even in San Quentin, there is things for you to do unless you are just constantly getting involved in the gang violence and all the bad stuff. There's plenty of that in there; it's easy to go to the bad. The bigger challenge is to do good in there; just 'cause you're in there, you don't have to act like it, you know. I didn't.*

What helped him to make those wise choices when he was in prison? *Not having my family. I love my family, and I am not that kind of a person. I made stupid mistakes, and you know, anybody can change their mistakes. So I just pushed myself to do better while I was in there, make the best of it. And, like I said, I always love a challenge, and it's so easy to get into trouble, and it's just that easy. But to do good in a bad situation is a struggle in itself. . . . My mom always wanted me to graduate. And I wasn't going to do it out here in the free world.*

PROBATION AND PAROLE

According to a 2009 report by the Center for Court Innovation, there are now 208 confirmed domestic violence courts across the United States and more than 150 similar projects established internationally. As we noted earlier, these play an important role in responding quickly and effectively to abuse in intimate relationships. Another central ingredient in the response of the courts to battery involves probation monitoring. In fact, some researchers believe that probation officers are the most critical link between the criminal justice system and batterer interventions (Healey, Smith, and O'Sullivan 1998). A 2005 report from Statistics Canada points out that in four Canadian cities studied between 1997–98 and 2001–02, a sentence of probation was given to 72 percent of those convicted of spousal assault. Parole and probation officers serve to ensure that men who batter comply with all of the conditions of their probation. According to the National Portrait of Domestic Violence Courts (Center for Court Innovation 2009), 62 percent of the courts reported often or always ordering offenders to probation supervision. Courts that rated offender accountability as a central goal were especially likely to employ probation services.

On average, it was reported that offenders met with their probation officers twice a month. In specialized domestic violence courts, there is greater use of judicial monitoring of offenders postdisposition. A recent study of specialized domestic violence probation revealed that one thing that differentiated probation in these contexts from traditional probation was greater contact between probation services and abuse victims (Klein and Crowe 2007).

Mandated attendance at a batterer intervention/treatment program is most often associated with probation. Certainly, this was true with the men we interviewed and the many cases we witnessed in courts. Scott (2004) reports that in her study of a program that had close links with the domestic violence courts, men whose attendance at a treatment program was closely monitored by a probation officer were more likely to complete treatment.

A number of goals of probation for male batterers that tie this disposition to program goals have been elucidated by Mederos et al (1999, 10–11):

- Be intolerant about breaking the rules.
- Convey a message of disapproval about violent and abusive behavior.
- Monitor closely and unpredictably.
- Order the offender to attend specialized counseling.
- Demand consistent documentation from the batterer treatment program.
- Expect behavior change as a result of counseling.
- Develop rapport with the battered woman.
- Follow up on additional conditions of probation.
- Probation revocation/surrender

While we might have expected that the men would feel negatively about their interactions with their probation officers, we often found that this was not the case. They believed that the probation officers were somewhat flexible in monitoring the conditions required by their sentences. Of particular note was being offered a choice of which intervention program to attend, as voiced by three of the men we interviewed. Bill said, *I did fifteen months in prison, and part of my parole stipulation is I have to complete a program, a DV program, and so I was going to. I checked them all out, and I wanted to come to STOP, but they told me I had to go through what they call county mental health evaluation, and they referred me to another program, and I started going to that program, and I did about five weeks of it, and I told my PO I will go back to jail before I go back there, because it was just like being punished all over again every time I went in there, and I refused to do it. I says I won't do that one.*

Another man echoed that sentiment: *When I called my parole lady, I said if I can't get out of this program, you can take me right across the street and handcuff and put me right back in jail. . . . But some parole officers won't let people change. Why they let me I don't know. But I am sure glad they did.* Stu Wright voiced similar resistance: *I told my probation officer that if I had to do that program again that she might as well put me in county jail right now, because I refused to do it. I went through there forty-eight weeks; it made me angry every time.*

Generally, the process of interacting with probation officers was viewed quite positively, though endured with reluctance, among the men we interviewed, despite the fact that they were required to pay a monthly fee for this service. Brett Turner mused: *This time, you know, it's funny, I have a pretty good parole officer, I think, at least*

I enjoy his interactions. He seems to be very overworked, and since I don't give him any trouble, I see very little of him. So whenever I come in, he's, like, "Oh, let's just get you done and get you out the door," you know.

RELIGION IN THE PRISONS

In prison, personal safety is always a concern, and boredom is a constant issue. Men are separated from all of their significant others behind bars, and while visitation can and does occur, it is no substitute for regular contact with those you claim to love. In prison, life is just tough every day. Spiritual renewal offers men a way to see that there is life beyond the walls of the prison and that they are offered the choice of a "new start." There are rituals or practices that help to cement in the men's minds that there are others who will walk with them as they begin this new start.

Clifford, whom we introduced earlier, described it this way: *Anyway, I was in prison the very first time I went to church. They had this same guy I told you about that had been a prisoner, and he said come forward if you want to declare to Christ. And there was a black guy standing on one side of me and one on this side. I have a hard time telling this story. Anyway, I was all broke up and crying and all this, and both of these guys put their arms around me. And I thought to myself, here's me and here's these two black guys from the deep South, and I am a white man, and they are consoling me. I will never forget it. That really touched me, and I thought, boy, there is something to that.*

Inspiration, distraction, reprieve—whatever the motivation for picking up the Bible and/or attending Bible study groups, the result brought the men hope. Finding God or, more accurately, reconnecting with God in prison enabled the men to ritualize their new start, their resolve to live differently, first on the inside and then perhaps on the outside years later. Skeptics might believe that finding God while incarcerated is self-serving, but it is clear that for some men, it provided enduring support that continued to help them. These men who turned to faith in prison could have followed a different path—spending their time in the total institutional environment of prison learning how to become better criminals, rather than spending their time learning a framework for living. For many, their turn to faith served as a crisis-related resource mobilization (Ai and Park 2005) in order to cope with their prison circumstances. When they were released, their circumstances on the outside were also challenging and difficult on a daily basis. Many were able to harness the religious support they experienced and ritualized in prison for life after incarceration. According to Wilson (1997), it is the duty of law to remind people that it takes a lot of work to properly obey the law and to understand that self-control is part of an individual's responsibility to society, whether it is easy or not. From the perspective of the men we interviewed, friendship and faith in a hostile environment become one more interactive tool in the tool kit they are developing for life on the outside.

7

Checking in and Doing the Work

Bill Oakley was a forty-something, soft-spoken manual laborer who always held steady employment. He lived in several US locations, which might be interpreted as running from his problems. For many years of his life, that was exactly what he did—ran from problems and drank his sorrows and pain away. *I have had a problem with substance abuse in my life; there's a lot of alcoholism and drug addiction.*

Drugs and alcohol controlled Bill for many years. Under their influence, he got into trouble with the law. For a while, he would stop drinking whiskey and using cocaine, but before long, Bill would reconnect with old friends or coworkers and find himself sliding down the slippery slope to regular use and then despair. It was a downward spiral from which it did not seem he could escape.

He came into contact with STOP fifteen months after he was released from prison as a result of assaulting his wife. *I had domestic issue problems in my life many different times with my partner of thirteen years, and I ended up going to prison.*

Once his sentence was served, Bill was sent to a small community-based program for men who abused intimate partners. He did not connect well with the facilitators there and, in fact, claimed he would rather return to jail than complete the requirements of the program. In desperation, he sought the advice of his probation officer: *He was the first person who gave me any hope.* Based on conversations with him, Bill chose to attend the faith-based intervention program STOP, *because of my faith, [it was] faith-based, and I made the right choice.*

Bill found exactly what he needed: a program with a facilitation team who believed he could be a better man than he had been in the past. He found the approach helpful and the environment conducive to change. *I felt comfortable the first time I came here, and a lot of it has to do with the way [the facilitator] does class, you know. I have made some big changes in my life, though, since then.*

Bill couched the changes that have occurred in religious terms: *I realized I wasn't living my life the way God intended me to live my life, and when I came to that realization and that surrender, it's like God removed the blinders from me.... Everything I have learned from past treatments and all the years of going to NA and AA all made sense to me for the first time in my life, and I started being honest with people.... It's all in God's plan, that's all I can figure.*

So what were some of the steps that Bill had to take himself? *I give my life to the Lord every day.... It's been a blessing, the Lord has blessed me, and I am on the verge of getting custody of my daughter back ... by God's grace alone, because I know I could never have done it.*

We asked Bill what giving his life to God looked like. *It's by doing the next right thing, by being honest, by being accountable, by living on life's terms and doing the right thing rather than hiding in a bottle, which I did from the time I was fourteen years old.*

Through the program, learning life skills, and continued accountability, Bill lived each day through the lens that all he had gained could be quickly lost. But before he could become accountable, the subject of the next chapter, Bill had some hard work to do. *It's hard, every individual is different . . . nobody hands you anything, you have to work for it, and I am going to tell you something else. When you have led lives like most of these men led and I have led myself, it takes time. It doesn't happen overnight. You have to prove yourself. You have to show by your actions on a daily basis.*

Doing the work required was indeed a big struggle. *It's like the old cliché, you have to be sick and tired of being sick and tired. And until you get to that point, until you have made that decision on your own, you can't do it.*

At the end of our first interview with Bill, he was hoping to regain custody of his daughter. When we saw him the next time, he said, *I am single-daddying it, and life is good there.* His daughter was twelve years old. He had just started dating a woman, someone he had known for a long time. She was recently divorced and sharing custody of her two children with an ex-partner. This new relationship was a bit difficult for Bill's daughter to accept: *She doesn't like having to share her dad, you know.*

We asked what were some of the things he did for pleasure now. *We just hang out. We just hung out at my house Friday night and watched movies and had Chinese takeout, and what did we do on Saturday? Oh, Saturday she came with me, we went and painted my mom's boyfriend's mobile home for him. She came and helped me do that. And then yesterday, she had things to do. I teach Sunday school now. Yeah, so I did my Sunday school class, and then I had father-daughter day. We went in and went to a movie and stuff, and then we all went to a nice dinner out . . . fancy restaurant . . . and had a nice steak dinner.*

These activities were all very different from Bill's former life of living dangerously. *You know, I have a heck of a story, and there is healing. People can heal, and people do change their lives, you know, if you are willing to do it.* It is one thing to want to change, but it is quite another to do the work—day after day—that is required. And as we heard from Bill and others who decided to change their ways, there is a lot of very hard work to do.

In our later interviews with Bill, he talked about hope. *Hope is to me, it's like this is my thing on hope, helping other people every day. That gives hope.*

But it also led to sadness. Bill was helping Danny, whose story we discuss in chapter 4. He was inviting him to bring his son out on Sunday afternoons to his house and was keeping in contact by phone to offer him encouragement in his one-day-at-a-time approach to living differently from in the past. *Sad to say, he has started drinking again, and he is back in jail. DUI. I told him, too, a year before it happened. I said, well, it's going to get you eventually. I said, choices you make, these are your choices. I still support him as a friend and stuff. I have boundaries, he knows. He doesn't come to my house if he has been drinking, and I don't hang out with him if he's drinking. . . . You know . . . maybe he will get refocused again [in prison].*

In our last interview, it was clear that Bill wanted to talk more about the difficulties that Danny experienced. Of course, Bill was interested in Danny. But Danny's failures also challenged Bill and reminded him that he, too, is one day away from throwing all the hard work away. It was a very sobering thought.

He was doing really good. He has a problem, he doesn't like being alone, so he hooks up with the wrong women, you know, which a lot of guys do. . . . You gotta learn how to take care of yourself, that's one of the things I had to learn, I had to learn, which I've always been able to take care of myself, but I really had to learn and live my own life and learn how to, you know, you can't be co-dependent on other people, you have to be dependent on yourself, and then the good comes out of that.

We asked Bill what gave him the inner courage to keep going and just decide that against all odds, he was going to do all the hard work required of change. *Well, I was done, I was done. It was either suicide or get my life right, 'cause I wasn't going to keep on living like I was living anymore. Yeah, and the thing about it is, you have to be willing to sacrifice everything. If you want to, if you want to heal yourself, you got to put everybody away, and you have to do it alone, and you have to be strong.*

You can't keep hanging out with the same people and the same friends. I mean, if you have a problem with drugs and alcohol, and in my case, in my case, the way it worked with me, the drugs and alcohol, alcohol was the main problem. You got to find the root of the problem, and then you got to solve that problem, and everything else will follow. The domestic violence in my life all stemmed from alcohol. You know, I never had any legal problems with the police or the law in my life unless I was under the influence of alcohol. . . . I owe a lot of it to God, too. I am a firm believer that God helps those that help themselves.

For Bill, doing the work meant a number of things, behaviors that we discuss later in this chapter. These include putting away the old life, creating a new life, and actively ensuring that the things that weigh you down are removed altogether from your life or, at least, minimized as much as possible.

Scholars of religion refer to these as factors in the process of conversion. So do born-again Christians, those who take the language of the New Testament around new birth and make it a personal life decision. In Ephesians 4:22–24, we read: "You were taught, with regard to your former way of life, to put off your old self, which is being corrupted by its deceitful desires; to be made new in the attitude of your minds; and to put on the new self, created to be like God in true righteousness and holiness."

For Bill, this was a helpful way for him to construct the way forward: leave the past behind, create a new way of living, and keep away from those things and people that might cause you harm. In religious language, Bill had surrendered his life to God, repented of his sin, chosen to turn from his past and his evil ways, found forgiveness and peace of mind, and, in so doing, started a new life where he would attempt to flee from temptation.

How he was able to do this when so many others had failed was of great interest to us. So we explored with Bill a little bit more about his spiritual journey.

I have always been a firm believer in God. Yup. I accepted Christ when I was thirteen years old, but I lived by my own will. You know, I got led astray, and that's what happens, and I started drinking at a young age, and I started smoking weed at a young age, and I just progressed and progressed, and it became such a way of life for me, I didn't know any other way. That was just normal. It becomes a normality in your life, and you don't see the destruction it causes. And I don't know. I look back now and go, God, how did I waste so many years? Why did I?

We all have to go down certain roads to get to where we need to get to, and the sad thing about it is, most people don't get out of it, they can't figure it out.

But Bill figured it out, we told him. And we asked what had been a critical point in helping him to keep the one-day-at-a-time strategy and focus on the path forward? *I tried to, I quit, I tried to, I went through recovery, I mean rehab, several rehabs before, and there's all that information I learned over all those years. You know, when I came to the realization of this, I started, and I really surrendered to the fact that this was going to kill me, this was destroying my life. You have to come to complete surrender, and I swear I had such a spiritual awakening. It was like the blinders were taken, literally taken off me, and I saw everything clearly for the first time, and it all flowed into me, and it all made sense. . . . Well, living your life one day at a time is number one key, you know. . . . Tomorrow is a new day, each day is a new beginning. . . . And I am just maybe one of the lucky ones . . . well, I do believe God relieved me of this burden. In my heart, I truly believe that, with all honesty. . . . I had nothing left in me, and I had to get to that point in order to heal myself.*

We asked whether some other people helped him along the way. Here Bill was somber. *I keep my world real small. Yup, I like my world small . . . I am no social butterfly. I try to stay humble and grateful with everything I do. Humility is a great part of my healing, always remember, and I have to catch myself, and I do, and I remind myself to be humble.*

At the close of our second interview, his daughter had been back with him for more than a year.

Six months later, we saw Bill again. He had married the woman he was dating the last time we spoke with him, and he had bought a new house. His daughter was living with them, and Bill said, *Life is good.*

He spoke about his friend Danny. *He is drinking and running with the dope heads again. . . . He can call me anytime but only when he is sober. He gets in these dark moods, and he leaves me these messages. I don't have time for his negativity. He can't get away from that drinking.*

Then he reflected on his own life. *My life is good. I am at peace. Every day is a new day. No conflict in my life now or for the past several years. Say my prayers every day, in the morning and before I go to bed. I try to remain humble and gracious in everything that I do. I go to church. I am a religious man and go for their fellowship, but it all comes from yourself, and to be around like-minded people, you don't get it from going to church.*

We asked what advice Bill would give a man who did not want to attend a batterer intervention group and stop acting in abusive ways. *There is no advice that you can give him. Deal with it one day at a time. You have to deal with your inner demons, or you will never make peace with yourself. When you make peace with yourself, everything else falls into place. We all make mistakes. . . . So you need to make peace.*

We spoke about the future and the challenges. He wanted to go to court to gain full custody of his daughter with no visitation by the mother. Since the mother was still drinking and drugging heavily, Bill wanted to keep his daughter away from her. His new wife's ex was a drinker, and Bill wished that her children did not have to spend the weekends with him. He had worked so hard in his life to put drinking behind him, and yet it still had an impact on the lives of his family members.

Bill, his new wife, her daughter and son, and Bill's daughter were living together. He continued to work as a supervisor of maintenance. *I am the handy in handyman,* he once joked with us. At the time of our last interview, the blended family had been together for about six months.

He concluded our last interview, *You don't have to be looking over your shoulder if you are doing the right thing. . . . Life is good.*

Bill was like *many* other men in the program in that he:

- Had served time in prison.
- Was very reluctant to enter the program at the beginning.
- Had been addicted to drugs and/or alcohol.
- Had a no-contact order limiting interaction with his child.
- Wanted to gain full access to his child.

Bill was like *some* other men in the program in that he:

- Completed the fifty-two-week program in a timely manner and graduated from it.
- Wanted to be drug- and alcohol-free forever;
- Had regular employment for which he received sufficient money to support his family.
- Reported no particular financial worries.

But Bill's story was rather unique among the men we interviewed in that he clearly understood and could articulate what he needed to do to ensure that he never again fell back into the situation in which he found himself when his daughter was young. He was certainly not the only one doing the work, but for Bill, the empirical evidence was strong that he continued to do the work required to stay clean and sober and to use strategies other than violence in his interpersonal relationships. He knew that he would always be vulnerable to the influence of drugs and alcohol. He believed that his abusive behavior was linked to his drinking and use of other illegal substances, and there was no evidence in his life of any violent altercations when he was not drinking. Our interviews with Bill predated his relationship with a new partner and his reunification with his daughter. We followed his story in and out of a friendship with another man in the program, someone who had been sent back to prison. And even as Bill discussed his sadness about this situation, he appeared to use it to reinforce his own understanding of what he needed to keep doing to maintain the life he now enjoyed. Bill learned several lessons from his participation in the STOP program. His story makes it clear that doing the work that leads to change is the result of acquiring new knowledge, but perhaps far more important, it is the result of being treated with respect and then harnessing that to learn to treat yourself and others in a new way. In religious language, it is putting away the old self and putting on the new self, fashioned in likeness to God's design for life on earth.

Lessons Bill learned from STOP:

- Treat others as the group facilitators have treated you.
- You can only change yourself; you cannot change others.
- It is important to surround yourself with others who understand and share your new values and behaviors.
- Faith can be a resource that will assist as you resolve to change your life.
- The gains you make can be quickly lost if you stop doing the work.

We turn from Bill—a man who lived recklessly for many years and was ordered after his prison sentence to attend a batterer intervention group at STOP—to Buddy, a man who chose of his own volition to come to STOP in the hope that it would help to repair a very damaged relationship with his wife.

A CHOICE TO SEEK HELP

Not everyone who found his way to the STOP program was court-ordered to attend. A small number of men volunteered to come, although some described their situation as being *wife-mandated*. This meant that they received an ultimatum from their partners: go to a program and get help, or it's over between us. Buddy was one such man.

When we asked Buddy how he found his way to the STOP program, he replied that it was a result of his partner's suggestion. *OK, basically, I went through . . . a separation, and my wife had left a note for me to contact some different people for counseling, and so I looked into it deeper, and that is how I got hooked up with STOP. . . . I am not in a forced situation, I volunteered to come. . . . I am not an abusive person . . . but obviously, I wouldn't be here if I didn't need help.*

We spoke a bit about what it was like in the early days of coming to a group at STOP. *The first time I came and I walked into a group of men, it blew me away. I mean, I was so uncomfortable, didn't want to be there, and I didn't get that much out of the first class, because my focus was everybody else . . . and I thought, what am I doing here?*

Over time, Buddy became more comfortable with the group setting. In the group he attended, Buddy was the only man who was not court-ordered. He also had no prior issues with either drugs or alcohol. This made him feel better about himself and able to evaluate his situation as being not perhaps as dismal as he once thought. He found the content of the STOP program useful and became more confident of his ability to change some of his behaviors, especially the ways he was accustomed to responding when people disagreed with him.

Buddy drove a delivery van. When we met him, he was living on his own in his farmhouse, surrounded by a few animals and lots of acreage. He said he was very lonely. One of the few places where he socialized with others was at church. *I attend church, and I study, and I have a study group that I am going to. . . . You know, I continue with my faith.*

Coming to a faith-based agency made an enormous difference for Buddy. He probably would have been unwilling to come in the beginning if it hadn't been connected with his faith. When we asked him what he liked about the agency and its program, he said, *The courtesy and the way the system is handled.* But he wanted the program and the workers to be more explicitly religious. In fact, he criticized some of the advice he was given by group facilitators as an indication of a lack of faith, no doubt related to the fact that the agency was not opposed to divorce, something that he was desperately trying to avoid.

Buddy had a difficult childhood. His father, an alcoholic, treated him very poorly and was prone to severe punishment for wrongdoing. *I didn't have a childhood . . . my dad was very, very mean to me . . . I got a lot of beatings.* Life was also hard for his wife as a child. *But she had a rough childhood, too.*

We discussed the various things that led to Buddy's separation and his journey to STOP. *I am not really an angry person. I think that what happened is, I don't know if this is a gift or what, but I am one of them people that is right 99 percent of the time ... and I think that's where me and my wife, you know, she would say something, and she didn't like that I was right most of the time, she didn't like it at all. ... I didn't want to fight ... but I didn't want to be told something that I knew wasn't right, either, so I think that brought out anger in me.*

Over time, Buddy began to gain insight into his own behavior and the slow struggle it would be to change his way of thinking or acting. *But you know, anybody would hope that it would never happen again, and that is my plan, but there is no guarantees in life. ... I know how not to blow up ... I have learned to control my anger ... I am more relaxed now than I used to be.*

While Buddy was very positive about the intervention of the agency, he was extremely annoyed with the pastor of his church. He and his wife sought help at the church for the difficulties they were having in their marriage. *That was another thing that destroyed us. We went to the pastor and had him counsel us, and he is not a counselor, but he wanted to help. ... He took sides 100 percent and did nothing but pound me into the floor, and I disagreed with that. And he has no forgiveness, either. He hasn't forgiven ... I don't feel that my wife has, either, and without that, where do you go?*

Six months later, we interviewed Buddy again. He had finished the fifty-two-week program at STOP, but he kept coming for a while after he finished. He talked about some of the things he learned, some of the lessons he was trying to apply in his own life. *One of the things would definitely be the STOP, because a lot of times I think a lot of the problems in my marriage was that I would react too quickly and I wouldn't think about what I was doing or saying, and by the time it was over, I'd realize I'd made a mistake, and it was too late.*

He reflected on his involvement in his church and his involvement in the program. *That's one of the things I really liked about these counseling groups here, and they didn't judge. We had people in our classes that were Catholic, Christian, Seventh Day Adventist, they had Mormons ... and we didn't judge any of them. ... You are here to heal, you are not here to judge, and if there was more of that in this world, it would be a much better place to be, because you are being judged every day.*

During our second interview, Buddy was much more optimistic about the agency, reflecting both the fact that he had completed the program but also that he had participated in the hard work of change. He noted in particular that STOP *helps you to understand and be more aware of yourself and how your mind works, and ... reactions is a big one. How you react to other people and how you treat other people accordingly.*

Three years later, Buddy was able to come for another interview with us. *I am seeing somebody,* he said within minutes of seeing us. *I gave her a ring about two months ago, a friendship, promise ring sort of thing. I am not seeing anyone else, and I am waiting for her to decide.*

Buddy told us that life was still a struggle but that he had *stuck to the things here I learned pretty well. Still have a relationship with my ex that I divorced ... it has been a tough road.* Buddy wanted to have a relationship with his three adult children, but that was fraught with difficulties, especially with his daughter. He had some contact with his sons' children, and for that he was appreciative.

He summed up his involvement with STOP: *I was not mandated, my goal was to prove to my ex-wife that I was willing to put in effort in order to get back together. Even though it still failed, and we never did get back together, I gave up. [And then] she has been after me now for two years, and I am not interested anymore. So it is really sad. So now we are just friends.*

Buddy was a very difficult, very religious man. STOP provided him with the practical strategies to begin the process of change and the religious reasons it was important for him to do so. Without the religious credibility of the STOP staff, Buddy would have never agreed to begin doing the work that was required.

Three years later, there was evidence of change, evidence of the work he had been attempting to do. Buddy had consistent employment throughout his working career. He owned his own home, a farm, in the country, which at one point had belonged to his wife's family. He was never in trouble with the law. He had no alcohol or substance abuse issues. But he was a very controlling and abusive man nonetheless. Over the years, he had regular contact with religious leaders, but he did not always like their advice, especially since that pastoral input into their marriage suggested that Buddy needed to change.

Some of the lessons that Buddy took away from STOP were different from those men such as Bill, who had lived a life in which his addictions to drugs and alcohol consumed so much of his money and so much of his life and took him down roads he had hoped never to travel. But Buddy, too, had a lot of work to do if he was to change his way of seeing the world and how he was going to interact within it. Buddy also needed a new way to look at his life and a new way to interact with others, especially those who did not agree with him. To do so, he had to recognize his anger and his propensity to control others. And he had to want to change. Using the same religious language we used in reference to Bill, Buddy, too, needed to put away the old way of living and adopt a new way of thinking and acting. He learned the same lessons from STOP, but he applied them differently.

Lessons Buddy learned from STOP:

- Treat others as the group facilitators have treated you.
- You can only change yourself; you cannot change others.
- It is important to surround yourself with others who understand and share your new values and behaviors.
- Faith can be a resource that will assist as you resolve to change your life.
- The gains you make can be quickly lost if you stop doing the work.

For Buddy, letting go of his goal to be reunited with his wife was significant. That took a number of years for him to fully process and then release. He had to see that he could only change himself; he could not change his wife, nor could he control her choices. And neither could he control whether his adult children had contact with him or whether they encouraged their own children, his grandchildren, to have contact. He learned to be thankful when such interaction occurred with his sons and their children and to accept that his daughter wished otherwise. He was able to begin a new relationship and to learn that he needed to wait as his girlfriend decided on the future of that relationship. All of these new ways of interacting were part of what STOP offered to Buddy. This was difficult for him, to be sure, but, as with Bill, it would open new doors for new experiences, new employment, and new relationships that he would have never thought possible.

We have offered a detailed look at the lives of two men who attended the STOP program and decided that they would begin, and continue, the work that was required to bring change into their lives. Bill and Buddy are very different men. Yet each had very real struggles to overcome if they were to leave behind their abusive and controlling behavior. We see through their stories some of the impact that participation in STOP had on their lives, in the short term while they were still in group and over the longer haul as they attempted to put into practice what they had learned. We now consider how STOP was able to help in the process of change, and we begin looking at how the groups for men operate.

A BATTERER INTERVENTION GROUP MEETING

During our years of fieldwork, we observed a number of men's groups. During the early days of observation, our field notes are full of descriptive details about the men, their interactions with one another and with the group facilitators, and the process of group check-in. We were struck with the diversity of men in attendance, the similarity of their stories, the skill and patience of the facilitators, especially as it related to treating the men with respect and drawing out their participation, and the measured way comments and suggestions were made to individual men. Later in this chapter, we discuss the content of the curriculum. Notwithstanding the importance of what might be taught, what struck us as especially noteworthy were the strategy of inclusion for all and the pedagogy surrounding advice or reflective comments.

The Diversity of the Men: At seven o'clock on a Tuesday evening, the group began. There were sixteen men and one woman attending. The group was facilitated by the executive director of STOP, a woman. This is a snapshot of a typical meeting.

1. Man, 45-ish, wore a cap and a hoodie. He was living in a sheltered environment after his recent release from prison.
2. Man, 35-ish, looked Native American. He had recently completed "boot camp." The facilitator welcomed him back. In conversation, he frequently used religious language to explain his views or experiences.
3. Man, 73. He had recently completed his prison term. He spoke very freely of his Christian beliefs and the fact that he was a changed man.
4. Man, late 40s, dressed in black with a little ringlet emerging from under his ball cap, in ripped jeans but not as a fashion statement. He said very little.
5. Man, 45-ish, with a large tattoo of a knife on his arm. He had done time in prison and mentioned that he recited the serenity prayer daily.
6. Man, 35-ish. He was new to the group. His pastor had suggested that he come, so he agreed to attend ten sessions. His hands were dirty, as were his work boots, giving the appearance that he had just left a construction site.
7. Man, 30-ish, wore a black cap that he did not remove during the meeting. He spoke of his ex-wife, his new wife, and the challenges related to the relationship between his new wife and the children from his first marriage.
8. Man, early 20s, a very pleasant-looking African American soccer player, wearing brand-name clothing. He arrived late and made little eye contact with others.
9. Man, 35-ish, with a buzz cut. He recently completed his prison term and mentioned being grateful for a second chance. He was temporarily off work as a result of an injury.

10. Man, 35-ish, trim, in business-casual clothing. He said he had been coming to groups twice a week for six years. He offered sympathy to others when they reported difficulties.
11. Woman, mid-40s, wore a striped Oxford-type button-down shirt. She was a nurse, mentioned that she was a lesbian, and interacted little with the others.
12. Man, 30-ish. He arrived late, leaned against the counter, pulled his cap over his eyes, and promptly fell asleep. He mentioned working two jobs trying to support his family.
13. Man, 30-ish, wore a striped rugby shirt, very well groomed. He held his head up with one arm for the entire meeting. He acted as if he felt totally out of place.
14. Man, young Latino, with a manicured chin-strap beard, dressed in sports attire. He appeared agitated when another man dominated some of the conversation.
15. Man, 30-ish, with waist-length hair tucked up into his baseball cap, wore expensive-looking clothing, sneakers, and jewelry. He tended to dominate conversation.
16. Man, mid-50s, Native American, with a bandana on his head and a long ponytail. He slept most of the meeting and never spoke.
17. Man, 25-ish, with black ball cap on backward, a black T-shirt, and black shorts. He came in halfway through the meeting.

Group Interactions

Sometimes men brought friends or partners along to group. Others came with children who would go to the child care provided. In about half of the groups we observed, there was a girlfriend or a wife present. They were usually partners for whom there was a no-contact order, so meeting like this, at group, was the only time the couple could see each other.

This accounts, in part, for the very visible signs of physical affection between the men and the women who accompanied them to group. They would sit and hug, touch each other's hands or arms, lay a head on a shoulder, and sometimes kiss. After the group, there would be much kissing and hugging before they said a final good-bye. The facilitators did their best to give them some privacy, to make the partners welcome, but the behavior or words of the facilitators never detracted from the seriousness of the no-contact orders that made such public visitation necessary.

During almost every meeting that we observed, there was a man coming to group for the first time. He was never formally introduced. And he was free to tell as little, or as much, of his story as he wished during check-in. The facilitator always ensured that regardless of where the new man was sitting, check-in did not begin with him or near him, giving him ample opportunity to hear others before his turn came. Occasionally, a man would say "Pass" during check-in, but this was rare.

In most of the groups we observed, there were one or two men out of a total of fifteen or sixteen who were mild agitators. They would speak under their breath when a comment was made, or they would intentionally try to give the wrong answer to a question, or they would suggest that there was nothing new for them to learn. But for the most part, the interaction at groups was remarkably nonconfrontational—between men and between men and facilitators.

Sometimes men shared new insights during their check-ins. One example was a young man, in his early twenties, who had been asked by his parole officer to attend a victim impact workshop in a nearby city. This had a profound effect on him. He reported that the incident that brought him to STOP related to smashing a window when he was angry. The incident frightened his wife, and she called the police. The facilitator saw this as a teaching moment and interjected, "If a woman or a child sees you smash an object or a window, they see the potential that you could do that with their face." The man said that this was exactly what he had learned at the victim workshop, and he reported that this offered him a wonderful new insight, something that had never occurred to him before. We pick up more about his story a little later in the chapter.

Once in a while, men recognized one another from the county jail, but most often, they did not know anyone in the group before attending STOP. Since men could choose which group they attended each week, membership in every group varied week by week. Also, new men were joining the groups all the time. This meant that there were men at all stages of the process of insight, accountability, and change every time a group met. Men often shared their insights with others. For example, it was not uncommon for someone to note that his childhood had been *pretty awful.* Other men would nod or wince in support of such disclosures.

During one of the lunchtime groups, a new man said during check-in: *My wife committed adultery, and because I slapped her across the face, I am the one that got into trouble. If I had known that was against the law, I would have done something else.* To this, another man added: *I didn't know that what I did was against the law. If I had, I would have run around the block a couple of times.* A third man chimed in: *I unplugged the phone, and in this state, it is against the law to block your partner from calling 911. She called from a cell phone.* Another man piped up: *Why didn't you grab the cell phone?* This back-and-forth conversation then led a man we had observed in other groups as being a show-off to state: *You should have dealt with both phones!*

As this exchange was going on, most of the men were shaking their heads, not wanting to reinforce the man who wanted to antagonize the new man or to encourage any further development of the conversation. Men who had been coming for some time recognized both the vulnerability of the newcomer and his anger at having been ordered to come in the first place. The facilitator never entered the discussion at all. She waited until it was finished and simply turned to the next man whose turn it was to check in.

When it was his turn, the man who had earlier brought up the point about the usefulness of attending the victim impact workshop explained the context for his window smashing. His wife was home ill. He had promised to come home at lunchtime to prepare something for her to eat. He got very busy at work and was unable to keep his promise. Another man, a friend, had called her at home during the day and found out that she was ill. He insisted on coming over and bringing something that would make her feel better. She told him not to, but he came anyway. She let him in when he arrived with Gatorade and some homemade soup. When the husband got home, the wife said, "Perhaps God was looking out for me because I was sick." The gift of food from another man made the husband angry and jealous.

The other men in the group nodded in recognition. The husband had smashed a window but said that he didn't touch his wife. The other men felt that he showed great restraint. The man telling the story was a boxer, someone accustomed to hitting for sport or pleasure. The facilitator responded to the man and his story with these words: "This was not your finest moment." Nothing more was said. It was time to move on.

The first few meetings of a group set the stage for what was to follow for any individual man. He learned that the facilitators would never directly confront him in a way that made him feel more vulnerable than he already was, that the other men were struggling, too, with their pasts and the involvement of the criminal justice system in their lives, that what happened in group was serious business, and that it would be up to him, and him alone, to decide if he wanted to do the work required for real change. Otherwise, he could just endure the program.

It is very difficult to assess exactly how many men decide to "just endure" the classes or to stop coming altogether. Of the men who were part of our focus groups or personal interviews, very few came to only a small number of classes and then quit. What was more likely was for men to start out rather strong and then fade over time or to take a substantial length of time (say, two to three years) to complete the fifty-two-week program. Almost all of the men—and there were a few exceptions that we discuss at various points throughout the book—tried for at least a period of time to make some changes in their lives. But many got discouraged. There was too much work to do. Their progress was slow. They found it far too difficult to leave behind a life of living dangerously—drinking, drugging, and getting into trouble with the law. Their violence was meted out in this context, and the women in their lives often were also drinking heavily and using drugs. This is not to excuse or explain away the violence. It is simply to understand it in context. Not all of the men who attended the groups lived dangerously at any point in their lives, but the majority did. Very few of the men we interviewed had not struggled with addictions, although most of them were able to keep regular employment and support themselves and their families. They were not unaccustomed to having had some form of prior intervention in their lives, and it was in that context of having some group experiences in their past (not necessarily related to domestic violence) that they evaluated the STOP program so favorably.

Scott Smythe, for example, talked about how he was able to connect to the group, the facilitators, and the other men in it. *There was people there to say, hey, it's OK to make mistakes, it's how you deal with it now that counts. It helped. It helped knowing that I wasn't going to come in here and people were going to be going, "Oh, why did you do that" and "You're a bad person for doing that."*

The strategy of the STOP program was to build on any positive element in the life of a man who had found his way to the classes. By identifying changes in other men through the group process, the newcomer saw that change was possible. Other men spoke of their triumphs and their failures. Newcomers learned to expect both. But despite all this, there was a lot of resistance from the men, especially at the beginning.

We asked Scott what he would say to a man who did not want to come to group. He smiled. *I would just basically tell him that, "Hey, you know, there's a better way. Why don't you just come to class with me a couple of times and check it out, and you'll see it's made loads of difference in my life? Ask my wife, and ask my kids. But ultimately, it's up to you. If you don't like this lifestyle, come with me, I'll help you. If you like the lifestyle, you are fooling yourself, you know, go ahead, go to prison."*

For Scott, the positive effect of the group and the support of the facilitators helped him to quickly assess that he wanted to come. *My favorite is [the executive director], just because she's like a grandma to me, she's just so loving and caring, but all the group leaders are really good. They are really good at making you feel like a good person. They make you feel not so guilty. . . . We have self-esteem problems, you know, and feel bad about ourselves. We don't need somebody pointing out what we did wrong. We know that, we go over it all the time.*

We also observed this in groups where the facilitators were helping the men to see the larger picture, the context of their lives and the lives of others whom they had abused, frightened, and violated in a variety of ways. Some of the men themselves had been abused, frightened, and violated as children, teens, or adults. The facilitators allowed them to name their vulnerability and their pain, but they never allowed this to be used as an excuse for violating others.

Some men talked about their first meetings at another program. One man, seventy-three-year-old Clifford, had served many years in prison for his violence and said that he would rather be handcuffed and sent back to jail than go to one of the other programs in town every week for a year. What did he and others hate so much about the other programs? *Being cut down, demoralized, treated like you were dirt, put on a chair and having words hurled at you in the presence of so many others.*

There were a few men who found the process of checking in rather difficult. Jake was one such man. He was twenty-six years old, extremely shy, the father of two children, but living again in the household of his parents, a result of the no-contact order with his wife and no employment that would enable him to support himself.

We ask him to tell us about his experiences in group. *Occasionally, someone would talk to me and I will communicate with them for a little bit, but usually, I just sit there and kind of wait for the class to start, because I'm pretty shy, I'm kind of to myself, more of a person—I won't talk unless they talk to me, usually. . . . I try to be very polite . . . I was just afraid of talking over people.* Speaking of the process of checking in at the beginning of group meetings, he said: *Check-in was particularly hard for me because my life is pretty mundane.*

Since Jake was not involved in any faith community, we asked whether he found the faith-based aspect of the agency troubling at all. *They don't really push their beliefs on you too much, but they do bring it up a little bit for some of their lessons, which I find fine. It actually made sense, I think, that they made more of a nicer community, feel it more safe, free to communicate, because nobody is really going to judge you, and that's what's important to me, not being judged. Most of the time, it wasn't mentioned at all, very occasionally that they would bring up faith. Most of the time when faith was brought up, it was when somebody in the group brought it up themselves.*

Coming at the beginning was hard. But the men evaluated its impact rather quickly. When asked to speak about his early days of attending group, twenty-something Skater Borden said: *First thing is this place really works. It don't matter what edge you come with, what chip on the shoulder you have, where you are coming from. This place really works. Just give it the time, even if you go in there sitting with your arms crossed just like I was. It will get under your skin, it will get under the rage and the anger, and it will push it all out. And from my personal experiences, don't sweat the petty stuff. There is so much more to life than most of what I have heard, most people are coming in mandated to come to this program. They are from the same lot, drugs, alcohol, rage, violence, you know, a bad past, different things like that, out of the state prison system, out of the county jail system, and the things that got us there are not the things that we need to be doing in life. There is so much more to it, no matter how old we are, no matter how young we are . . . it doesn't matter when we start to learn that, whether, you know, it's at the end of our life or at the beginning, we still have so much more to take from this place.*

We have observed groups and listened as men talked about their experiences of group. Later in this chapter, we incorporate some of the things we learned from group facilitators, parole and probation officers, and others in the criminal justice system. But at this point, we want to highlight what we have heard the men themselves say and what we have observed ourselves in the groups:

1. All of those in attendance were treated with respect and dignity by the staff of the agency.
2. The mission of the group was clear: to help those who were abusive change their thinking and their behavior.
3. With very few exceptions, men did not want to attend a group like STOP.
4. Within a very short period of time, men determined that the facilitators were interested in helping them to improve their lives.
5. Staffers were knowledgeable, courteous, and flexible.
6. Hearing the stories of other men and their journeys over time was a very important part of the intervention process.
7. Incorporating a faith-based perspective added to the group (or therapeutic) experience for men who were religious and did not detract from the experience of men who were not.

Without exception, all of the men we interviewed felt that they had learned new insights and new information as a result of attending the STOP program. This was true for both those who decided to become engaged in doing the work and those who fought it at every turn, refusing to alter their ways, become accountable, or even admit their wrongdoing.

We turn now to consider what the men believed were some of the lessons they learned at group. As we have done throughout this book, we contextualize their observations and reports with their own stories of harm and vulnerability.

LESSONS LEARNED AT GROUP

Michael Clerk was a quiet-spoken man, age forty-one, who had been married for more than ten years to his second wife and was the father of four children from two marriages. He became disabled on the job seven years ago, and since he was out of work, the family had struggled to survive on his disability income. During our first interview with Mike, he kept his head down much of the time, huddled in his chair, wrapped in a heavy winter jacket on a moderate fall day. It became clear that he was hungry, and he appeared ashamed and withdrawn, not wanting to make eye contact.

Addictions were running his life as he self-medicated through the use of alcohol and street drugs to deal with the pain he suffered as a result of his work-related injuries. After his abuse became evident to one of his children's teachers, he was charged with and convicted of criminal mistreatment of his children. His wife also had an unstable lifestyle, and the four children were removed from the home.

During his time in jail, Mike had ample opportunity to consider the consequences of his behavior, and he was confronted there by his wife's new partner, also an inmate. An altercation between them put Mike "in the hole." Solitary confinement solidified his personal resolve to reunite with his family.

Once Mike got involved in coming to STOP, he began earnestly to seek change in his life. *I feel like I have gotten a lot more information, and I am here because I want to be here. I have a whole different frame of mind when I came here. . . . I feel like it was meant to be.*

The teaching methods at STOP seemed helpful to Mike and kept him coming back for more. *So far, since I have been coming here, we have sat down and watched a movie at one of them, and it was respect-based. We kind of go through the process of how your feelings and how your thoughts reflect on what your actions are, and what you do, and if you can make it so that your action changes. To me, I think that is a really good thing, because without it, a person really doesn't have the tools to change, and it is just what they need.*

The group environment was useful to Mike in several ways. Not only did it help his interpersonal skills, but listening to the stories of other men helped him to rethink his own positions on issues. *The helpful part of having a group right there is everybody has got a little piece of what is going on with you, something that you can identify with, and if they have a good something that works for dealing with that for them, then you can apply it to something else that works for you.*

Speaking of people who were new to group, he said: *The people that are new that come in, I see a lot of denial and trying to rationalize what they did and not really wanting to take accountability for their involvement in what's happened in their life—well, what I did was OK, or I did it for this reason. I see it now as making excuses, and why I can see that is I was kind of like that—what parts I play in that and what other people had done, why I did what I did. But now I can see it for what I did—it doesn't matter what everyone else did. I can now, instead of trying to rationalize and make excuses.*

We asked Mike whether there was anything else in the STOP program that we had not covered in our conversation that was helpful for him. *Yes, I think STOP kind of, they don't put you on the spot and say, OK, they are here to punish you. They are here to help you. And an atmosphere like that, to me, is going to even like jail, for instance. I am there to be punished, and I think, go ahead and punish me, I will take my punishment, but don't expect me to be receptive to it or enjoy it. I am not going to. But if someone helps me, then I am going to do everything I can to try and help myself.*

Although we never asked him to compare programs, Mike painted a picture for us to help us understand what it was like in the other program. This was important to him, and we listened intently to his story. *I always say, well, I went into this little room, and they put me into a little kid's kindergarten chair and sat me in the corner of that room, and there was two counselors there that stood on the other side of the room and had this big garbage can between them, and they would reach into this garbage can and pull out big jagged chunks of rocks, and they would hurl those across the room at me, and they would do this for two hours until I was black and blue and bloody, and they would say, "OK, you can go home now."*

He paused, and we nodded our heads for him to continue. *So I tucked my tail and walked out the door and said, "Well, see you next week when I have healed a little bit."*

I felt that they were doing just exactly what I was there for—they were saying they were addressing power and control and abuse, and they were doing that with those same tools that they were using against me, and you know, they were condemning what I did, and yet they were doing the same to me. They were abusing me just as I had been abusive in the past, so I don't think that's effective at all.

The way staff members interacted with the men in group enabled them to win over most of the men so that they were willing to keep coming to group, participating when called on, and picking up information and skills that would assist them with daily living. Within a short period of time, for most men, the staff had won their confidence and earned their respect. We believe that the majority of those in group were buying into at least the goals of the program. Sometimes it was the difficulties of their lives that kept them from regular attendance—work schedules, transportation, payment for groups, and issues of health. However, STOP staff went to great lengths to minimize the impact of these factors—they could pay later, there were many groups to choose from offered at different times and on different days, and the location was near public transportation. But it was only a minority of men who chose to do the work that was required of them, changing their ways of thinking and their ways of acting not for a day, or a week, or even for a month but for the long haul. Nevertheless, we believe that all the men learned some lessons. Their attendance at STOP was not in vain, nor was the enormous effort that staff expended to assist them in the process of doing the work that was required.

We outline below some of the lessons the men themselves told us they learned. The stories we have chosen here are all from men who had never submitted themselves to all the work that was required of them to change. And yet they, too, benefited a great deal from involvement in the program.

Lesson 1: You Need to Learn to Treat Women the Way You Want Women to Treat You

Zak Haggarty, a man who began practicing Buddhism when he was in prison and continued to practice while on parole, said of the group and its link to faith: *I thought I was going to come in here, and I was going to be not so much force-fed, but I was going to be handed readings with scriptures and Christian values and stuff like that, and it's not like that. They address it within their beliefs, but it pertains to everybody, to those who listen.*

He noted that one thing he learned through the group experience was that women are men's equals. In the past, he would have said, *I have women right here, and if they mess with me, [I will let them] know their place or whatever. Now I can say, you know, she is right by my side and not behind me. Does that make sense?*

Lesson 2: You Need to Practice Relating to Others the Way the Group Facilitators Treat You

Ted Clow, an angry Vietnam War veteran who severely neglected his elderly mother, found his way to STOP as a result of a mandate by the criminal justice system. He was found guilty of extreme neglect—a failure to feed, clean, and care for her physical needs, coupled with forced isolation and protracted impatience with her limitations—although physical abuse also occurred.

Speaking of the groups, he said: *You learn a tremendous amount. You're not learning their book by rote. You're learning their book by compassion and repetitive play.* Comparing his experience at another program, he said: *They treated you like a criminal over there, but here they treat you like a person who made a mistake.*

Lesson 3: Small Reminders Pay Big Dividends; Use the STOP Cards

Some of the men resented the money they had to pay to come to class, especially at the beginning. In Stuart Wright's case, it was thirty-five dollars per week. In our first interview, he said: *My personal feeling is that this course is just taking money from me, you know, I've already spent a fifteen-hundred-dollar fine. I spent many times in jail. I caused my own self to be in jail, and I understand all that, and then on top of that, I still have to pay to come to these classes, which has been over two years ago, and I haven't been in any trouble. I'm off probation in three months.*

We saw him again after six month. He was in a better position to reflect on what the STOP program helped him to accomplish. *This place never made me feel obligated, and they listen and teach out of the Bible and half out of what the state makes them do, and it is pretty cool.... They do not down me or belittle me or ... make you feel embarrassed.* He then referred to the "STOP cards". These were small cards that could be placed in one's pocket with the word STOP printed on a STOP sign. The card served as a reminder to employ the tools learned as part of the batterer intervention program. *I have hundreds of them, and I have used that in the heat of the moment.... It really works.... When I first started these classes, I was lost, lost, lost. Now I am starting to come back around. I threw away eighteen years of my life with my ex. I am starting to come back around, and this class has helped me with that.*

Lesson 3: Faith Can Be a Resource That Will Assist If You Decide to Change Your Life

Faith was part of the fabric of STOP, but it was very carefully interwoven into everything that happened rather than an add-on or an annoying distraction that appeared less than fully authentic. One could certainly have attended a number of meetings before putting together the fact that it was a faith-based agency or that the facilitators shared a common religious worldview. Not once did we hear men complain about the inclusion of spiritual material, although, as we have shown before, a few noted with dissatisfaction that religious factors were discussed less than they would have liked them to be.

From what we observed in the groups and heard from the men, faith was considered part of the tool kit that a person might employ as he lived his life, responding to circumstances that arose and making sense out of the important questions we all ask from time to time.

Jake Peters would advise other men who did not want to come to the program at STOP to *give it a chance. Grab that chair really, really hard, and you will find something that appeals to you.... I have seen a lot of men coming into the program and thinking you* were a bunch of man haters, you [women who are group facilitators] were scared, and so now you were going to do something to us. . . . Sit here. Come every day. Bring your body, and your mind will follow.

The faith-based nature of the program did not seem to matter to Jake, even though he was raised Christian. Yet, he said, *they treat you as a human being, and faith is involved. They don't push it on anybody, which I respect, but I also respect their religion, and there is some good stuff in it, you know, and they mush it in there with the, you know, therapeutic part of it, and it works really well.*

The fact that faith might be a resource in times of trial would not be news to those who reconnected with their spiritual traditions while in prison or those men whose religious beliefs and practices had followed them throughout their lives. But we think it is noteworthy that this message was part of what men who were not religious found in the program. The men never intimated that there was any pressure or even direct encouragement to accept faith; it was simply noted, like the other tools and strategies that were offered, that this might be helpful to some of them.

While these were certainly not the only lessons men learned, they were pervasive ones, noted by men who were doing the work and changing and also by those whose progress was very slow. Although the lessons learned were important, there were several other strategies at STOP, employed by facilitators and other staff members, that perhaps were more effective in drawing the men into the groups and encouraging their regular attendance and participation.

First, facilitators never did things to make the men lose face in front of their peer group. This was strategy number one. We observed many examples of this from attending groups. One man in his late fifties referred during check-in to his work as an engineer and then quickly added that he was not a *credentialed engineer*. The facilitator interrupted him to say, "We will consider you an engineer." In other words, "At STOP, we evaluate you in part by your aspirations: you hope to become an engineer." Given the opportunity to build men up in any of their nonviolent, nonillegal pursuits, the facilitators went to great lengths to do so.

Second, facilitators self-disclosed about some of their personal struggles. This was strategy number two. This occurred with some regularity at group. At a particular meeting, the content focused on the impact on the brain of different kinds of substances, such as heroin, cocaine, and other illegal drugs. Many of the men found this very helpful—the notion that their powers of reasoning and recall had been compromised as a result of persistent drug use. The facilitator was careful to close the discussion by including the impact of too much caffeine or too much smoking or too much work. At this point, the other facilitator confided that she drank too much coffee. It appeared that the purpose of this self-disclosure was to suggest that all of the men in the room and even the facilitators struggled with some form of addiction. The message was clear: everyone, without exception, had to deal with personal struggles and addictions. Recognizing the struggle was the first step. Dealing with personal struggles was described as a process, a long one, in which one needs to understand both the consequences of the addiction and strategies for overcoming it. The men were left with the thought that we are all in this together. No one mentioned that some addictions—such as workaholism—brought enormous financial rewards or that some addictions, such as Pepsi, were not illegal. Rather, the facilitators focused on the notion that everyone had to struggle—no one was exempt.

There were different strategies employed in group to get the men connected to one another and, most important, to the material that was being discussed. One was the use of videos. One evening, the facilitators showed a video depicting a violent altercation after a marital dispute. The story had a number of features—the man was drinking to excess, the woman had endured a bad childhood, the couple had bills that were mounting—so that there were a variety of ways the men could connect themselves to the story revealed on the screen.

It never took very long for men to volunteer comments. At least a few men each time would spell out for the others what a video was trying to accomplish. They usually did this framed by some self-disclosure. For example, the first man to speak after one video said that he, too, had experience with alcohol abuse. He went on at some length to say that you couldn't make a person change; that person had to be ready. Another man framed his response to the video with regard to his fourteen-year-old daughter's request for a cell phone and his new wife's refusal to take equal responsibility in saying no to this child of his from an earlier marriage.

Several men in group would not speak out unless spoken to. One facilitator did not call on all of the men to respond to the video, but when she did call on someone when there was a lull in the conversation, there appeared to be no hesitancy to make a comment. After observing many groups, we noticed that if a man did not want to respond when called on, he would say "Pass" or "Nothing to add," and the facilitator would then offer an excuse for him, such as "I guess Bill is too tired tonight."

Some men in interviews confided that they were frustrated by the slow pace of movement through the curriculum on any given evening. There were several reasons for this, including the fact that men were at different stages of entering and completing the program, so that newcomers and veterans alike were present at any group. But perhaps more important, the facilitators most often regarded diversions by an individual man as teaching moments for the entire group and as a way of hooking the individual man into the dynamics of the group and what STOP was trying to achieve. It appeared that this strategy was very successful for the most part.

Sometimes at group meetings, there were moments of great emotion and even tenderness expressed from one man to another. An example of this occurred when one man, in response to a video, shared about his own father having told him never to call again. He also heard these words from his own sons. Another man leaned over and patted him on the arm and said, "I am sorry, buddy." That man, we learned later, was a group mentor.

UNDERSTANDING THE ROLE OF RELIGION AT STOP

Religion offers a language and a strategy for change: leave the past behind and begin anew, repent, turn from evil, and embrace God, and practice loving kindness toward others. Some Christians believe in the concept of a new birth, a change in perspective that is accompanied by a new way of thinking, forgiveness for a past lived in selfishness, and hope for a future lived in submission to God and God's commandments. Sociologist Nancy Tatom Ammerman (2014) talks about Golden Rule Christianity, the belief that you should treat others as you would like to be treated. She argues that there is widespread agreement in America that this is how one ought to act.

All of the staff members at STOP endorsed a religious worldview that was Christian in orientation, and they espoused a philosophy consistent with notions of evil deeds, repentance, forgiveness, and changed behavior. But they were not naive. They were grounded in an empirical reality and understood that change has to be measured in small indices, that what one says is not necessarily indicative of what one does, and that leaving behind a life where one has lived dangerously, abused alcohol and drugs, and acted violently toward others does not happen often. They worked within a paradigm that had both secular and sacred undertones. They were well educated in psychological and social-work models of behavior, and they understood family systems and addictions. They were not easily fooled. But neither were they cynical. They displayed—we might say exuded—a very interesting and impressive blend of social-work training, evidence-based skepticism, and Christian compassion. From the perspective of the men, though, there were three main components: knowledge, respect, and hope. But these three gems were loosely connected to the elements we identified above. These elements could be observed in the groups and were discussed by the men, although they were not named as such. We identify them below as operating principles.

Principle 1: Take Men's Talk of Religion Seriously, and Then Harness It to Help Them Change

Jay Primer sprinkled religious language and examples of religious behavior throughout our interview. He indicated that he watched religious programming at home and read his Bible on a regular basis. In fact, he noted that when a verse was mentioned in group, he would write down the reference and later look it up in his Bible at home. *I always come in with my binder and write myself down things that I want to look through in the Bible, what verse she was talking about.*

The staff and facilitators never questioned men's use of religious language to explain their lives or their circumstances, nor did they question a man's resolve to live differently after an experience of spiritual awakening. Sometimes these religious experiences occurred when they were incarcerated, but sometimes they did not. The spiritual awakening was always related to some form of prior relationship with God, a pastor, a priest, a church elder, a religious congregation, or other people of faith. In other words, these experiences did not occur in isolation from a broader context where religion was, or had been, important as an identity marker or pattern of rituals or lived experience of faith. Essentially, what happened was that beliefs and actions of a religious nature that had once been held and perhaps had once been important were resurrected at a time of deep personal anguish.

Staff at STOP and group facilitators in particular acted as if the spiritual quest might be one additional resource that could help a very vulnerable man accept responsibility for his wrongdoing and change his erroneous thinking and behavior. Unlike some of the workers within the criminal justice or advocacy system, they never said things such as "You don't appear to be acting like a Christian." They never pointed out the chasm between the religious belief system that men claimed as their own and the acts of violence that they had committed against their partners, parents, or children.

In part, this was a reflection of two very different underlying assumptions: (1) that everyone acts in ways that are inconsistent with his or her belief system and (2) that religion calls people to change their behavior. Many, if not most, of the men we interviewed mentioned that the staff members were nonjudgmental. We never asked them about this directly, nor did we probe in any way specifically about their feelings concerning group facilitators or other agency staff. But this was important to the men, and so they talked about it. This was very important to the staff, too, although we did not understand its impact fully until we had been in the field for many years. And workers in other venues, such as the criminal justice system and domestic violence advocacy, almost always mentioned positively—and with admiration—the way staff at STOP treated perpetrators.

Principle 2: Teach Life Lessons within a Positive, Affirming Environment That Recognizes, and Is Recognized by, the State but Submits Ultimately to the Authority of God

The programs at STOP were indeed recognized by the state, and the workers had professional credentials and were well versed in social-scientific understandings of domestic violence, family relationships, and personal failures. Their education and their professional competence to perform the work they did were important to them and critical for the recognition they received from the criminal justice system, domestic violence advocacy, and child protection services. However, the staff members at STOP also believed that they were in submission to a higher authority: God, and God's word revealed in the Bible. Later we discuss how these workers understood the link between their religious lives and their professional competence. They blended the sacred and the spiritual in the work they did and how they did it.

One of the few men we interviewed who was not ordered by the criminal justice system to attend STOP was twenty-four-year old Jake. Within moments of our meeting him, he was telling us about his experiences with another program in town. *They didn't encourage treatment too much . . . pessimistic attitude. . . . It was like you were guilty. It seems like everybody was in the doghouse when you went.*

While he was not ordered by the court to attend STOP, Jake was not unfamiliar with the criminal justice system. He did time in prison for drug-related offenses. It was while he was in prison that he decided to turn his life around, try to get his son back, and say goodbye to the lifestyle he was living. *Because it's really easy to change once you get in there and you got that time to you and yourself with you and your God, but at the same time you still got to deal with the consequences after the fact. So that's basically where I'm back now.*

Jake grew up in California, an young African American person who was a born athlete. Things at home with his stepfather were difficult, and life for his mom was hard. *I am going to say that he wasn't a real positive dude. So basically my family was the street and my buddies . . . we got away with a lot of things.* Then tragedy struck. His younger brother was killed in a car crash when he was fifteen. At that point, Jake was a student in a community college and playing football and *having babies by the wrong woman.* His brother's death sent his mother back to church and Jake to another state, where he was living totally on his own and beginning his downward slide into trouble with the law.

Jake was the only man we interviewed who talked about STOP in the same way as one might talk about a church. *You kinda feel like a congregation when you go to a STOP meeting, because you know they allow everybody to speak their piece and to check in, and it's just a real positive attitude. You know, it's like a congregation is the best way I can explain it. You know, but it's a learning environment as well. So. You know, that's just like church.*

Harnessing men's religious beliefs and practices to help them change their violent ways was something that STOP staffers considered extremely important in their work. And they were uniquely positioned to be able to do this, given the blend of training and personal religious practices of the staff. It is extremely interesting, however, to consider how the men themselves interpreted the blend of information that they received and the strategy and compassion with which it was communicated. The underlying message for the men, although no one named it directly, was that we all must submit to God, and we all must submit to the law of the land.

Principle 3: Process Supersedes Content

From the first time we attended one of the staff meetings, we were told that the most important things that happened at STOP were related to factors other than the content of the curriculum. They were not disparaging the instructional materials they used, not at all. To be sure, they were continually revising and adding new insights into what was offered to the men within the context of their group meetings. And they were appropriately proud of this. But it was never the content of their instructional materials that facilitators and the executive director considered to be their raison d'être. All staff members were clear: they treated people differently here.

At first, we were inclined to dismiss the importance of this viewpoint. However, once we began focus groups and interviews, it became obvious that the men themselves believed this to be true. There was something about the way all the staff at STOP treated them that made an impact. This was even true for the man who was most critical of the program, Costenello Ramrez. His criticism was focused on his assessment that the program was not faith-based enough and that there was a lack of structure to the content of group meetings.

I'm just expecting more tying it in with Christianity or the scripture or whatever it is, and I haven't seen it. And don't get me wrong, I don't think that it is a bad thing that they do. I'm just a little surprised that it's not as organized as I thought it would be.

Just four months in, Costy had a lot more classes to get under his belt before graduation. And yet his frustration was evident. *I don't feel that sometimes they come in with a lesson plan, they just come in and they kind of have an idea of what they want to talk about, but then they lose control of the class, or they don't bring it back to where we were. There have been times we start on something and then it goes off to everyone talking, and the class never ended.... Some of it, to be honest with you, it does nothing for me.*

Yet despite his evaluation, he learned some new insights. *I think that what came to me that night, I didn't know I had that resentment inside of me, but through the class, kind of hearing what they had to say, and we started talking about resentment, it just hit me, like someone hit me in the head with a hammer. . . . I never even thought about what it was, why I was so mad at her. . . . I was watching her die in front of me because she had given up on herself, and I think that night, that's what did it . . . she was eighty-two pounds, she was turning gray, and she just wasn't taking her medication.*

Like most of the men in the program, Costy did not want to be told what to do. He preferred to tell others, to be the one in charge. He grew up under very strong domination in his childhood home and, perhaps as a result, chafed under authority. Costenello was one of eight kids, a middle child, whose Mexican father was an alcoholic, while his mother spent most of her time raising children, supported, in part, by welfare. His father was *definitely heavy-handed, talked down to my mom, kept her away from anything other than raising the kids.*

When Costy was younger, he attended youth services at a local Pentecostal church, but by his own admission, *I never took it seriously.* During his time in jail, he reconnected with God and his spiritual life. Over the time we followed his story, through four interviews, he was very involved in a local interdenominational church, attended regularly, went to a men's group and other midweek events, and enjoyed the social connections that his faith community offered. Of his spiritual life, he said: *I read the Bible every day, I pray every day, I look forward to taking my grandson to church.*

One example of coordination between the staffs at various agencies working with the men in the STOP program involved Costy. Three months after he began the program, he was scheduled to have neck surgery. At this point, there was a no-contact order with his wife, and he was living in a very small studio apartment. His wife contacted him because she was concerned about what was going to happen to him when he was discharged from the hospital. On a previous occasion, when he had surgery of a similar nature, he was bedridden for a period of almost two weeks. Costy told his wife that he could not have contact with her and that he had no control over what would take place, but he gave her the name of his probation officer. Costy's wife called the probation officer to ask for special permission to look after him post-surgery. The probation officer contacted STOP and the group facilitators to see how Costy was progressing with the program, and a determination was made by the probation officer that supervised contact could take place.

Six months later, when we interviewed Costy again, he was almost finished with the program but was planning to begin couples classes at STOP with his wife. Six months after that, when we interviewed him, he was quite pleased with those classes. He felt that he was learning how to communicate and listen to his wife and that together they were doing much better as a couple. We interviewed him five times. His story remained consistent, that there was only one event where there was a physical altercation, the time he took his wife to emergency. His interaction at STOP helped him to see that he and his wife were engaged in behavior that was tearing them apart. He gained insight into the *why* of the event (pushing his wife into a table, which resulted in a broken rib for her) that triggered the police to arrest him after the hospital called to report what had occurred. But he never fully accepted responsibility for what he did without bringing up her medical state (epilepsy) and her inattentiveness to her medication regime. They had been together thirty-five years. STOP helped him to see how he could be a better person and how their marital relationship could be enhanced. But STOP was never able to help Costy see that he was a violent man.

It appeared that both partners felt they needed each other, both understood how they contributed to the problems they were experiencing, and STOP was willing to work with them both. The mandates of the criminal justice system were met, the STOP batterer program was completed, and for the period of time we followed Costy's story, there was not another abusive episode. He was always more critical of the batterer groups than of the couples group, and he claimed an affinity to the other men in the couples group where the focus was clearly more on interactive features of the relationship and how both partners could be more intentional about enhancing it. He never believed that he alone was the problem, only a part of the problem. The content of the domestic violence curriculum and overcoming power and control never won him over. He never took full responsibility for what happened. But interestingly, he felt called on to change some factors in his life, and for that he was willing to become accountable. He submitted to the philosophy of the couples class and found it very helpful. He resisted the notion that he alone was to blame. He preferred to consider it a family or couple problem that required a solution involving both him and his wife.

Costenello had never lived as dangerously as some. And his life was characterized by several important stability factors—advanced education; regular, consistent employment; married for thirty-five years; two children with whom he had always been in a relationship; and for some of his life, a faith community that really mattered to him. However, his childhood had been marked by abuse and his adult life by substances to dull the pain (marijuana and OxyContin). His prior connection with the police was limited to a charge of possession of marijuana.

He spoke of what he learned in group: *I have learned respect for myself first of all, and for everybody around me, and I think I am working on that. . . . I would just like to be a better person all around, and if this is what it took to make this happen, I am more than happy and glad that God put me in this position. You know, because that's what I want to do. I have spent a lot of time, a lot of years of my life, being not a bad guy, but it's just about me and me and me and me, and everybody else, you know, was with me, but it was all about me, and I am just about me. I am learning there's more than about me.*

From Costy's point of view, the classes should be more controlled, the conversation kept on topic, and the men challenged to listen more and say less. But Costenello's goal was not the same as the program's: to keep all of the men coming week after week after week until they completed the entire fifty-two-week program. The STOP program tried to enable all the men to have a chance to speak. But some men only wanted to be heard themselves. They had no time for the voices of others, even others in similar situations to the ones in which they found themselves.

Principle 4: Modeling Your Religious Values Pays High Dividends

The final principle we wish to identify at this point relates to the acts of compassion of the staff toward the men and women who come to their agency.

Arguably, the biggest challenge for staff at STOP was to get the men to come to the program, week after week, when it was convenient and when it was not. Of course, attendance did not ensure that the men would buy into the program's goals or even begin to do the work required for change. But without consistent attendance, these loftier goals would never be met. The executive director understood this challenge well. She gave considerable thought to the agency's location, its physical surroundings, access to public transportation, and many other factors that we identify and discuss more fully in the next chapter. Yet she and her staff believed that they had a responsibility to do everything within their power to help the men want to come. One of the ways they fulfilled this self-imposed mandate was through modeling their religious values. At first, this was not apparent to us. There were so many other things to see and attempt to understand. But once we caught the significance of the modeling of values linked to their faith perspective, we could see it at every turn. It permeated the agency. But, like breath, it was taken for granted by those who felt called to work there. No staff member ever mentioned it directly, but some of the men did, and we observed it, too.

One of Antwone Washington's earliest experiences of coming to the class was in the buildup to the Christmas season. He told a story of the generosity of the workers at STOP. *It kind of shocked me, because I came in, and about twenty minutes after class started, they took everybody in the classroom and took them into a conference room over there and gave them a bag in a room full of toys to get their kids' stuff for Christmas. So it was kind of cool. That hooked me right there that they do stuff like that.*

There were lots of acts of kindness that were offered on a regular basis—coffee in the room where group was held, pizza and pop on evenings when men would graduate, popcorn to be popped for someone who needed a snack, cold water and cups for those who were thirsty, fresh flowers and nice surroundings for those needing a minute of peace and serenity, and an excellent program of child care if the men needed to bring their kids during class time.

It was a fine line walked by office staff, the executive director, and group facilitators—they were providing an intervention service, not offering food and clothing to the hungry or discouraged, although many of those who sought help at STOP were in need of these items. But these acts of kindness—going over and beyond—were an important part of what the men saw and believed to be true of the workers. They cared. They went out of their way to be friendly, courteous, helpful, and supportive. But they were not pushovers. They were doing serious work, they were professionally trained, and there were severe consequences if the men did not comply with court orders to attend the group meetings.

FROM THE PERSPECTIVE OF THE FACILITATORS

During our years of fieldwork, we attended many staff meetings and interviewed all the facilitators, some many times. At first, some of the staff members were more uncomfortable with our presence than the clients were. But in time, this changed, and all of the staff appeared interested in what we were doing and engaged in friendly conversation with us before and after meetings, in the main office, or in the hallways.

At the beginning, we asked a lot of questions about what it meant to be a faith-based agency. This seemed to be a relatively difficult question for staffers to answer. It was not that they were resistant to us asking about it. They seemed not really to know what to say. We found this rather surprising.

At our very first staff meeting, a year before our fieldwork began in earnest, we asked the question outright. One worker said, "Working in a faith-based agency allows me the freedom to integrate psychological principles with biblical principles and use those and be able to share scripture and have time for prayer, depending on the situation."

Another worker, who led women's support groups, said, "We have a very brief devotional and then end in a short prayer, and we often talk about how the topics may filter through a belief system." We later learned that this was a woman who at one point had come to STOP herself in search of healing and wholeness and had, in the intervening years, gone back to university and obtained qualifications that would enable her to be hired by the agency. She continued, "I've always given women the ability to respond to whether the information is helpful. I certainly would not want to use scripture in a way that abuses women, so I try to always check in with them and make sure that I am presenting it in a way that is helpful and not hurtful."

At this point in the conversation, the executive director jumped in. She said that the agency drew its inspiration from the book of Proverbs. "We want to give some information to equip people how to live, to be understanding and just in everything they do, so we have an assumption here that the scriptures shed light on successful choices, ways to make choices for successful living." She nodded towards the wall, pointed to the poster depicting a wheel, and moved into a discussion of how the wheel for understanding abuse was always being updated based on new information and new insights that came to her or one of the staffers.

The message to us early on was that STOP was evolving, learning, responsive to the academic and therapeutic communities, but clearly rooted in a scriptural foundation. As we looked around the room, we saw some posters and other displays on the walls that supported this contention. This was a learning environment, it was caring, it was up-to-date, and it was not trying to hide—or to advance—its biblical base.

We steered the conversation at the staff meeting toward a discussion of the role of faith in the lives of men who have been abusive. The executive director said, "Oftentimes, when people get into a great deal of trouble, they become very faith-based themselves, very religious, and I think the driving fear is that there is legitimacy to their experience of that." This was a point that we did not really understand at first. The staff felt that men needed to be affirmed in their claims of spiritual experiences. While other workers in the criminal justice or advocacy systems were prone to make light of these awakenings, staff at STOP listened to the men and attempted to harness the men's spiritual proclivities as one more tool in their tool kit for the journey ahead.

The discussion at staff meetings often turned to how workers at STOP treated the men better. This was their favorite way to illustrate the faith-based nature of their work. Try as we might, they did not want to focus on the curriculum or the content. They were faith-based, from their perspective, because of their attitude toward and treatment of those who sought help there. Period. In the words of the executive director, "One of the things that I think they would say is that we treat them like responsible adults. . . . We assume that they are people who try to make their way in the world, and if possible for a very legitimate adult reason, they might be late. If they are late, they don't get in trouble—in terms of like you would do with a child. There are consequences, of course—if you are more than fifteen minutes late, it is recorded. . . . Like an adult, if you are late on your taxes, they are going to fine you, and it's not because they are mad at you, it's because there are consequences. So they have consequences, but they don't get into trouble."

Staff members noted that most of their clients had a lot of experiences of being disrespected. So when they were treated with respect, they noticed. And when they were treated disrespectfully in any context—including, of course, other batterer intervention programs—it fed the hidden anger in them, and they shut down and couldn't receive the information that would give them the opportunity to change their lives.

In essence, STOP staffers felt that what they did was fairly similar in terms of content to other batterer intervention programs but that *how* they did it set them apart from others. The *how* piece was connected in part to the incorporation of a faith perspective, but it was also in very large measure a strategy for seeing the men as consumers of a service they were providing—a service that had the potential to change their lives and the lives of their children and partners. As a result, the staff and the executive director at STOP wanted to do everything within their power to help the men to want to come, to listen and participate when they were present, and to add all of the things they were learning to a tool kit that would assist them to make better—nonviolent, noncontrolling—choices in the future.

We often heard the executive director say either to the staff or in group to the men, "You can only star in your own movie." In other words, the only actions you could control were your own. And when you tried to be the star of someone else's movie, things could go horribly wrong.

In our early meetings with the staff, we were focused on trying to understand the content of the program, its curriculum, and its goals. But as we observed the groups, talked to the men, interviewed the staff, and participated further, we realized that the content or the curriculum played a secondary role to the broad imperative to keep the men coming, to listen to their stories, to follow their progress, to answer their questions, and to give them some insight into their behavior and some tactics to change it. What was most central was how the men were viewed, respected, and considered as co-participants in a strategy to change their thinking and their lives. If this could be successful, even measured by very small indices, the lives of those they had harmed, frightened or otherwise affected negatively would also be changed in very significant ways. Often we heard staffers say, "I do it for the children."

We learned that prayers were sometimes said in groups, but we never observed this. We learned that the facilitators sometimes used religious stories or religious language to make a point, offer an illustration, or encourage the men. We observed this from time to time in the groups, although it was never overpowering so as to ostracize men who were not explicitly Christian or religiously inclined from another faith-background. But when men who were religious used their religion to justify or excuse the abuse, the facilitators responded with passion and challenged them directly, employing the language of their faith traditions. They did it in such a way that there was no question that this agency believed that God condemned violence in the family and that they were partners with God in helping people to change and leave violence and abusive behavior in the past. There was no doubt that they were passionate about this. Religious excuses or justifications for abuse would not be tolerated.

From staffers, we learned that they wanted to encourage men to incorporate their faith as part of their journey toward accountability, healing, and change. We did not observe this often in the group setting, although in our interviews, men often reported that this happened in their own lives. It was part of the process for religious men who were doing the work. Because the facilitators were prone to take seriously the religious talk of the men, the men who talked this way were reinforced for attempting to incorporate their faith into their daily lives.

Contrary to what some members of her staff had said earlier in a meeting, the executive director noted that many men "come here with expectations that we are going to butt heads with them. And we are not sparring off, squaring off, challenging you at every point." As a result, she said, "they do calm down." The executive director believed that she was firm with the men, but she saw herself "kinda like their grandmother or their mother." We noted that many of the men saw her this way, too.

She offered an illustration. "It would be like a teenager who doesn't want to make their bed. We would just keep saying, 'You've got to make your bed.' And they'll say, 'Nobody in the world makes their bed.' 'Probably not, but you will make yours.' 'Only a bitch would make me make the bed.' 'Well, you have got to make yours.' So what is helpful to them is that we try to disarm. . . . The common denominator in the men we have . . . is immaturity. I would say that this is the common piece—not in all areas of their lives—some of them in all areas of their life." This prompted us to ask about her fears or concerns for her own safety. "They are far more frightened of me than I would ever be of them. . . . They know that we are the last stop for them, and some of them don't mind going to jail that much—most of them would rather not.

We ask about the demographics of their clientele. The age range of the men in group was from late teens to late seventies. Most of the men were in relationships, but many were no longer in relationships with the women with whom their violence brought them into contact with the criminal justice system. Most of them had children, and in most cases, the children were present in the homes when the abuse occurred. We learned that over time at the agency, more and more of the men in groups were court-ordered to be there. This was the power of word-of-mouth success, although this assessment is our own; the staff never intimated this.

But word-of-mouth success, from clients, from parole officers, and even from some judges, came with a cost: the other programs and their staffs barely tolerated STOP's existence. During one of our many interviews with the executive director, we learned that there was a huge bias against the treatment of batterers in the state where the STOP agency operates. Rather, it was an intervention state, and she said, "And here we are treating in the middle of this." In STOP's local area, there was a strong domestic violence council and a very strong domestic violence advocacy agency. We learned that from the beginning, that agency's directors were always supportive of the executive director of STOP but that their board was not always favorable toward the faith-based nature of the STOP program or the faith-based inclinations of its director.

Some of the facilitators at STOP had actually worked in explicitly religious ministries earlier in their careers. An example was a man we will call Joshua. He was trained in pastoral counseling and was also a licensed marriage and family counselor. He had worked at STOP for many years, leading groups and providing individual counseling. Years before, he was an instructor at a Bible college and worked in pastoral ministry.

We asked him how other pastors regarded his role at STOP. "There is a guardedness from pastors. Sometimes it raises red flags. There has been a change in myself and in the ecclesiastical community over the years, and they are now coming to grips with abuse. They are more aware of it now and out of their denial. . . . The more conservative Christian communities are more reluctant. Their patriarchal structures have been conducive to that."

As other therapists at STOP did, he mentioned that women of faith stayed longer in violent relationships than other abused women. And he said that men of faith "recognize the disparity between what they believe and what they do. If court-mandated, they have resistance, and there are walls, but normally the walls come down, and then the men are softer and more receptive to what we are teaching here."

He talked about the pressures on men and in particular the idea in the state where he was working of celebrating "the rugged man, the pioneer." As a result, he said, many men talked about the injustice "put upon them." He then compared his facilitation work (in the groups) with his private practice at STOP. "For a lot of men, they are in and out of jobs, and in and out of relationships, and there is a lot of instability."

When he was asked why some secular agencies did not like to deal with religious people, he laughed and said, "They don't like to deal with religious people, of course not. Particularly the rural evangelical Protestants, who are closed and resistant to people speaking in their lives. It's a control issue. Some are dangerous with the Word, using the Bible to justify things that the Word never says." He noted that some of the participating agencies in the domestic violence council were displeased with what STOP did. Yet, he said, "for the men, we hold them accountable, and yet we believe they can change. We believe in them. Others don't always believe in them."

FROM THE PERSPECTIVE OF THE ADVOCACY COMMUNITY

Workers new to domestic violence advocacy in the geographic area where STOP was located said in interviews that they were surprised by how batterer intervention services and the faith community could work together. For many, this was their first experience of collaborating with people of faith in the pursuit of a social justice goal. Once they started cooperating with staff at STOP, it was easy for them to see the link, and they appreciated the perspective that STOP brought to the collaborative table. As a younger woman, rather new to working in domestic violence, said, "Faith is a big part of a lot of people's lives, and even though they are abusers or in a family setting like that, that faith is still something that they believe in and can learn from."

Almost always, the initial barriers to cooperation between the secular community-based domestic violence agencies and the faith-based STOP agency were mediated through personal connections, first and foremost with the agency directors but also through their many and varied staffs. Over time, workers in the community-based agencies met women whose partners had been in the STOP program or families who had been part of one of STOP's parenting classes. These connections with clients or families of clients reinforced the positive assessment of the STOP agency.

It is important to note that these connections were not social connections, born out of living in a smaller city in a rather rural state. Instead, they were the result of the executive director of STOP and her staff making connections with the broader domestic violence advocacy community. It was the result of intentionality, although no personnel at STOP named it as such. The executive director attended with regularity the monthly domestic violence advocacy community meetings, as did several of her staffers, although, of course, at any one meeting, there might be only one or two STOP staffers present among the fifteen to twenty assembled workers.

It was clear that the executive director of STOP, in particular, was a community team player. Others in the domestic violence advocacy community and within the criminal justice community (which have limited connections with each other) saw her in this way. In our conversations with them, they offered several examples of how she would give a workshop, volunteer for a committee, or host a small event at the STOP premises. They saw her at work, and they liked what they saw. They heard her speak, and they found her arguments for including the religious community as part of the solution in the aftermath of domestic violence persuasive. By and large, many of these criminal justice and domestic violence advocacy workers did not have positive interactions with churches or their leaders in their day-to-day work, although some of them were people of faith themselves. But with STOP, they were very impressed with the talk and the walk—in other words, what they heard STOP staffers say about their work and what they observed in the lives of their clients. One of the workers noted that when she worked for legal services, she would sometimes receive referrals from STOP, and she found this impressive.

What was slightly more controversial—though less so these days than ten years ago—was the notion of keeping families where there had been violence connected and in communication, especially for the sake of the children. In the words of one domestic violence advocacy worker, "Keeping the family together is something that they try to do . . . . Agencies seem to think that they have to be split apart . . . . I think a lot of faith-based people go there because they don't feel like they are going to have to make a choice between the family or, you know . . ."

Later in the conversation, this same worker said, "I think that they are more than just Christian people providing a service. . . . They created their title [the name of the agency] to let people know right up front that there was going to be Christian content in their form of intervention, but they are not exclusive to Christians, as I understand it, or to any particular part of the Christian tradition."

Some of the secular workers noted that they had seen curricular materials from STOP, presumably when the executive director had made a presentation. But such material also might have been shared by a client who had found it helpful. Those who had viewed STOP materials noted that it had content that not only was directly related to the values of Christianity but also made specific references to the belief system. This never drew further comment, either praise or criticism.

We found interesting the degree to which shelter staff members and their directors understood the need for explicit religious materials for victims and perpetrators of domestic violence who themselves were people of deep religious faith. In large measure, they framed it as an issue of cultural competence and spoke of it in much the same way as they talked about the need for specific services for Spanish-speaking women. In fact, the executive director of the large women's agency noted that STOP had developed their services, in part, to respond to what Christian women who were survivors had said to them: "I think also what they found out when they talked to Christian women was their biggest interest was in trying to find a way to make men change their behavior. . . . They shifted their services more toward the batterer intervention services, because that, you know, was what they heard."

We had learned this, too. STOP had been growing dramatically in the area of batterer intervention, to the point where at the end of our fieldwork, they were seeing two hundred or more men a week in groups. While the impression of many of the community-based workers that we met in focus groups or interviews was that many of the men at STOP were self-referred, we did not find this to be true. It appeared that in its early years of operation, more were self-referred, but during our fieldwork years, there were far more mandated men than those who came without a court order. In fact, there were very few men in the groups we observed, the interviews and focus groups we held, or the presentations we gave at the later stages of our work who were not there by a criminal justice mandate or by order of the DHS (for the eventual return of their children from foster care).

We were interested to hear how community-based workers made sense of the success of STOP. It was their opinion that they had a "similar philosophical foundation" to other batterer intervention programs. But then they noted that "connecting with somebody's religious beliefs works really well for STOP." One worker went on to explain that the faith community could become "a little support group," where "somebody is checking in on them, pastor is checking in on them, you know, other guys in some prayer group are checking in on them." We develop this notion of accountability much more deeply in the next chapter but note here that it was a widely held belief among workers in community-based services that STOP had some distinct advantages because many of its clientele were linked to religious congregations.

In one of our focus groups, a very experienced domestic violence advocate put it this way: "People are watching that are in the community, which is not true necessarily, of course, for these other people unless they have a probation officer, but that probation officer is not the same as a community of people who care about you."

The potential impact of the watchful eye of a caring community was significant. And that community might be mobilized out of care for the man who had acted abusively, but it could also be mobilized to ensure that there was safe visitation for the children or mobilized primarily out of safety concerns for the mother and her children. Regardless of the motivating factors, the impact was that for men who are religious or connected by way of their partners and/or children to religious congregations, there was an added monitoring community. It assisted with accountability, as we show in chapter 8, but its main advantage might be that it helped to ensure buy-in, at least in the early stages, to the STOP program.

Another factor mentioned by a few of the advocates and criminal justice workers was the fact that STOP "tends to hire people who are actually therapists . . . people who are actually qualified as a marriage and family counseling person, or something like that, whereas the people who do the interventions in other programs may not necessarily have those kinds of degrees." While we never assessed the qualifications of workers in other programs, it is true that at STOP, the workers were highly qualified licensed marital and family therapists and licensed and graduate trained social workers and in at least one case also had pastoral qualifications.

We interviewed most of the workers at STOP. Several of the women therapists had been in abusive situations earlier in their lives. One worker said, "My mother was the abusive person, and so knowing that it was not a male problem but an abusive person problem helped me to have an open mind to both women and men."

We asked about the role of the church or their own congregation in terms of an understanding of the work they did. Here we encountered some unexpected connections. A middle-aged woman therapist said, "My church provided [help] while

I was dealing with my issues over the marriage [and eventual divorce as a result of abuse] that prompted me to go back to graduate school and get training. There were people who were incredibly damaging because of their ignorance—they just did not understand."

By and large, workers at STOP were more cautious, or humble, about how other workers in the community viewed their services: "I have never heard of the people in mental health advocating for our program. We do have a reputation at the county jail as being a program that is recommended by those guys. . . . I also have heard there are pastors and people in the community who do not like STOP."

But there was no such modesty about the experience of working at STOP. The same woman said, "I work in the most incredible place on earth. It really is the most wonderful place to work." We asked her to help us to understand this more fully. "I think it is about the people that have been hired here. . . . When new people come on board, it is kind of like, where does the executive director find these people?"

We asked whether there had ever been times when clients were uncomfortable with the notion of a faith-based service. "While I was in graduate school, I worked [in the performing arts], and I had a lot of friends in the lesbian and gay community, and I get referrals from them, and I have had several lesbian women coming in over the years, and it was becoming an issue for them." What was becoming an issue was the fact that there were not any batterer intervention groups for women. As a result, women who were or had been abusive were allowed to enter one of the male groups. By the end of our fieldwork at the agency, there was a woman-only group. For sure, many women who were not lesbians might be interested in attending a batterer intervention group, but the issue of opening attendance to women was initially raised by lesbians through their therapists, who brought it to the attention of other staff members and the executive director.

We asked whether there were any ways in which the abuse or the journey toward healing was different for men who were religious compared with men who were not. Workers had quite a lot to say about this. One offered, "I see men who are religious or having a faith base. Their wives put up with a lot more crap before they did something about it. And so what you hear sometimes is that he kind of took advantage of her commitment because of her faith, and he utilizes that to keep her from leaving."

She continued to describe some of the specific needs of these religious men when they were in group, where "we also do find that they require a spiritual or biblical basis." She gave an example and noted that because she often co-facilitated with a male who understood the Greek of the original biblical texts, that facilitator was able to "combat something out of context" when it was raised by one of the very religious men. Would this be around issues of submission, we asked? "Yes, that would be a big one, or a lot of time just what leadership means. We try to put a whole new flavor on what leadership means. And the other one is when trying to get her not to divorce him or leave him using the Bible."

At the close of our interview with this facilitator, who also saw abused women as part of her therapeutic practice, we asked if there was any hope that men who had been abusive would change their violent ways. "Definitely, there is hope," was her reply. "I would not be doing this if there was no hope." She wanted us to know that compared with her former work with sex offenders, there was some hope in working with batterers. "I definitely think there is hope—maybe not for every single person. We see guys who are definitely changed men. We have a guy about to graduate on Tuesday night. He is astounded at how different he is. [Other] wives are hungry for the things he is learning." She concluded, "A lot of the healing comes from the process, not specifically the curriculum."

We agreed. The process was critical, and the atmosphere that was created in the agency—an interesting blend of the utmost respect for the clients and the work of changing their attitudes and behaviors and a passionate condemnation of the violence they have meted out to others.

HOW THERAPISTS AT STOP THINK ABOUT
THE ROLE OF RELIGION

We were interested to know how therapists thought about the relationship between their work and faith and the degree to which this was discussed among them. One of the younger males, who had recently completed his MSW and was doing practicum hours toward licensure, said, "Each therapist has their own style. Probably some of that is driven by their own beliefs and values and their own experiences with faith."

We asked whether there were any staff member who would be explicit about not having a faith perspective. "If there are, I don't know of any," was his reply. He continued, "It is important, though, to have some sort of a faith perspective that they have utilized in their own life, and they use that in such a way to promote changes in a client." Then he qualified his response: "It is not done with heavy overtones, so people can reach out one-to-one and get it at their own speed, and there are clients that never bring the faith issue up, and in those cases, from my own experience, I don't ever bring it up, either. But there might be examples of meditation or meditation and prayer. How does that relieve stress? How would that be useful to you? Have you ever considered that? There might be other circumstances where a client has a very dominated faith-based language and faith-based belief system, and in those cases, we don't hold them back, either. It is an opportunity to teach, to learn, opportunity for changing—the road is there for either type of client. That is how I view things, and that is my experience."

Many of the workers wanted to respond to what they believed were the very important words of this therapist regarding affirming spirituality in the men with whom they worked. A middle-aged woman who worked mainly with children said, "I was a preacher's child. So that is a very integral part of my journey, because I grew up with this faith. I had been through several marriages. I kept failing, but that didn't coincide with what my belief system was, so I had to work it out." She went on to explain that this was how STOP operated, helping people to work out how their lives and their faith coexisted. She said, "You can never err on the side of grace, so when I come across people in my role here at the agency, you can offer them grace, remind them of all that grace in our faith."

As we observed in groups and heard the men say, the workers linked their own narratives into the help they provided to others. In so doing, they did not set themselves apart from those they were seeking to help. They offered the message "We have been helped by others, and we in turn can help you."

FROM THE PERSPECTIVE OF THE CRIMINAL JUSTICE SYSTEM

In our focus group with probation officers, we learned that they regularly referred clients to STOP and regularly offered STOP as a suggestion to clients who had been ordered by the court to attend a batterer intervention program. Moreover, these workers were in regular e-mail contact with the workers at STOP to ensure client compliance. As the parole and probation officers discussed the program at STOP, they seemed most impressed that it was not a "cookie-cutter treatment approach. They respect the individual, and they give out a lot of respect." To be sure, it was not easy to respect someone or to treat someone with respect who had been engaged in horrendous acts of violence toward others, especially an intimate partner or a child.

The probation and parole officers were also of the opinion that men who were involved with religious congregations, by and large, had more invested in change, "a lot more of their act together," to use the words of one man. One younger male parole officer added, "They are probably not using drugs really heavily and have some kind of a family that brought them to there in the first place. A lot of the people that we have that go one time or don't go at all are just out on the streets, using drugs every day." It was the view of the criminal justice focus group that STOP had lower rates of noncompletion than other programs, but we were never in a position to assess if this was true.

When we spoke to one of the judges who carried a significant portion of the domestic violence cases in his court, he replied, "It is a special interest of mine, and I take it seriously." We learned that he mandated 100 percent of his domestic violence cases into treatment, after sending them to the local mental health facility for evaluation, particularly related to specific mental health issues and drug and alcohol dependencies.

He spoke of being "a fan" of the STOP program. He had spoken to the executive director and had been present at some of her speaking engagements. "I really like what I hear. I have talked to defendants who have been in the program, and I like what I hear. I really like the idea of using a person's faith as a base for treatment. It is a good hook."

As we discuss in chapter 5, this judge noted that within seven days of a domestic violence offense, someone was in his court. "Whenever someone is arrested within one of my cities, they call me within seventy-two hours, usually twenty-four, and I set the bail amount. Most of the time, they cannot post, and even if they do post, I will try to get them in within a week. . . . I put a no-contact order in place, but I know that realistically, it is just an order, and they can violate that. They are less likely to violate once we have had a face-to-face."

He spoke very knowledgably about domestic violence and what was available in the local community. He read all the assessment reports of the mental health agency on the men who appeared before him, and he preferred that the assessments be conducted by one agency that was not the treating agency. Throughout the conversation, the judge mentioned by name various people within the domestic violence community whom we had met through interviews or at the domestic violence council. He talked about a conversation with the executive director of the women's domestic violence advocacy center about changes that might be best for more successful buy-in to batterer intervention. We spoke briefly about intervention services in the lives of men who acted abusively. He said, "I can't even say whether treatment in general is effective except that we have very little recidivism."

CONCLUDING COMMENTS

From the moment a man called the STOP program to inquire about the batterer intervention program until he had completed the fifty-two-week series of classes and even beyond, the office staff and the facilitators treated him as a valued consumer of a service they were attempting to provide. They offered an interesting blend of competence and compassion. Their knowledge and professional credentials were acquired from advanced education and relevant clinical experience that was positively evaluated by the state and certified by the appropriate boards. Their compassion was linked to the various spiritual traditions within contemporary Christianity that used the scriptures as a call for social justice and a guidebook for living well.

At STOP, men were invited to begin a process of changing their attitudes and their actions. Staff members treated the men with respect, self-disclosed about their own struggles, and offered strategies and information that would equip them for living differently from how they had in the past. This was very hard work, and few had the internal resources and the external support that enabled them not only to begin the process of change but also to continue to do the work required over a sustained period of time.

Faith, beliefs, spiritual practices, and connection to a religious congregation were all part of the many resources that those at STOP believed could help a man to live life in a new way. Using the language of the spirit and modeling compassion and respect, facilitators at STOP helped men to understand that abuse was not part of God's design for healthy family living. For those men who had adopted specific religious traditions, the STOP program helped them to draw strength from their faith practices, strength that could assist them on the journey toward healing, wholeness, responsibility, and ultimately accountability and changed behavior.

8

Accountability

Interpersonally warm and comfortable with conversation, Skip Moore told us about his life working in maintenance and grounds care on a large university campus, a job he had held for almost twenty years. Skip grew up in a middle-class home; his father was a nuclear scientist at a large state university, and his mom toured in the performing arts. As a result of extensive childhood travel and social capital that was acquired from his parents, Skip was more adept than many of his peers at articulating his views, particularly in writing.

This explained how Skip found his way to STOP. He had been court-ordered to attend a batterer intervention program, and together with his parole officer, he chose one of the other options in the local area. But things did not go well there. The facilitators chided him for failing to take personal responsibility for assignment completion, thinking that the letters of empathy and responsibility he submitted to them were written by someone else. *I was accused of having a ghost writer on my second letter, so that was my exit interview.*

He refused to go back. The facilitators underestimated his ability and lacked knowledge of his family background. They concluded that he was cheating, having someone else do his work. As a result, he changed programs.

Unlike those of many others, Skip's memories of his youth were predominantly pleasant. He lived abroad on three separate occasions when his father was on sabbatical, and as a consequence, Skip's world was much larger than those of many of the other men we interviewed.

Yet underneath the surface, there was anger. As a teenager, Skip got into minor scuffles at school. At home, his sister had some health problems, and when Skip felt deprived of the attention he sought, he would act up. By thirteen, he was drinking to excess, and as a young teen, he was involved in several breaking-and-entering events in an attempt to sustain his drinking habit. By the time he was twenty, he was addicted to alcohol. *I have been all kinds of drinker, I have been a binge drinker, a daily drinker, maintenance drinker, workaholic functioning with a job while drinking, and just getting plowed every night and making it to work in the mornings.*

Once Skip became a father, he tried to reduce his drinking. *I think I got more responsible when I had children.* Yet both Skip and his ex-wife did lots of drugs and consumed large quantities of alcohol. They were both on a downward spiral, which led Skip to do things he never believed he would do. His relationship with his children—now grown—had remained positive. But when they were younger, they frequently sought respite with their grandparents when things got heated at home. Now, many years later, through AA and other therapeutic supports, Skip had remained clean and sober for an extended period of time. He attributed the changes in his life to spiritual renewal. *I depend on God.*

By the time we met Skip, he had a new partner and a new attitude. He credited the batterer intervention program for helping him *own* what he had done. While the past might be behind him, it cast a long shadow.

SKIP'S STORY AND NOTIONS OF ACCOUNTABILITY

Accountability is the key. In Skip's case, one program failed to assist him on the road to accountability, and another one seemed to succeed, at least for a time. What can we learn from his story? How long would Skip keep accountable? And when his mandated attendance at the program ended, then what?

In this chapter, we focus on the issue of accountability. What is the nature of accountability in the life of a man who has acted abusively? When and how does it begin? And what set of circumstances or intervention strategies help to foster its development? Are there any lessons we can learn from men in batterer programs that might offer us clues to enhanced personal accountability for past actions and a resolve not to repeat abusive behavior?

Skip entered the STOP program with great reluctance. Having one bad experience under his belt, he was skeptical and bitter and, of course, resentful about having been ordered to attend such a group in the first place. At first, he was unable (and certainly unwilling) to comprehend the pain he had caused by his abusive actions toward his partner and their children.

We discussed what it was like when men first entered a batterer intervention program. *There's a time when you can't differentiate the true from the false.* For Skip and others, the early days of group attendance set the tone for whether or not the men would buy into the program and develop a nonconfrontational relationship with the facilitators. How they also saw other men in group was important, too. When men first started group, they talked quite a bit about *being a victim.* Our observations were confirmed by Skip and others. *Yeah, so being the victim, I think, is one thing maybe you hear a lot.*

For men found guilty by the criminal justice system of victimizing an intimate partner, this personal account of victimization may be a little difficult to understand. Yet when they first enter any program—and especially a mandated one—most of the men are defensive, unsure what to expect, angered at having been ordered to come, feeling sorry for themselves, and a long way from developing empathy for those they have hurt.

At the STOP program, Skip felt there was less talk of forced separation, court orders, restraining orders, and other demands of the criminal justice system. Here there was more emphasis on learning—how to act in caring ways, how to alter your behavior, how to think before you act, how to change your way of thinking.

Yet many men are not ready for this type of intervention until they have been forced by the criminal justice system to understand fully the consequences of what they have done to others, the harm they have caused. Skip had a difficult experience in his first encounter with a batterers group. He hated to go, he resented the money it cost, he felt condemned, and he felt that nothing he said or did was understood as being good enough. In essence, Skip claimed that he felt trapped in a room with facilitators he neither respected nor trusted.

This set the stage for his receptivity to STOP. For Skip and also for others, this program was like a breath of fresh air. He was challenged to try to understand his life, his actions, and his past. Why did he behave the way he did? What caused him to resort to violence? There were so many questions to be answered or at least addressed. And then he would be invited to begin a process of change.

Once there, it didn't take long for Skip to begin to see things in a new way. *My life has already improved, you know. . . . Like I said, I never thought that I would strike a woman. . . . So, like, with me, the whole relationship with Margie before we got married, and there was the honeymoon and the courting and just all the excitement . . . then responsibility for the kids. . . . Me reacting the way I did . . . it was a process that was building up, because I was angry, and I would wreck a door, hit a window, break a stereo, something like that, and I always thought, well, at least I am just breaking things. . . . But somewhere along the line, I crossed over, and it was just, like, I don't give a crap.*

At this point, things began to unravel in Skip's life in a big way. At the time, he felt he was out of control. But through his participation in an intervention group, he realized that control was exactly what he was attempting to establish. *And I didn't care that law enforcement was involved or whatever the consequences were. It didn't matter, because right at that particular time, I was just out of it. They say out of control, but the group facilitator says no, you weren't out of control, you were in control because you were trying to control the situation.*

At the close of our first interview with Skip, he mused about his new life and new situation. The message was upbeat. His firm handshake and smile offered reinforcement.

We learned several things at this point in Skip's story. In some ways, he was very much like the other men in the program. In some ways, he was very different. His story also gave us a glimpse into the working of the agency and the staff who facilitated the groups.

Skip was very much *like* other men in the program in that he was:

- Resistant to having been ordered to attend a batterer intervention program.
- Feeling that no one was interested in his life or his personal story.
- Believing that his life was out of control.
- Angry at the intervention of the criminal justice system in his life.
- Able to establish a new intimate relationship after the termination of the relationship that brought him into contact with the law.
- Feeling a sense of remorse for how things had turned out.

He was *unlike* many of the other men because he was:

- Able to articulate his views clearly, orally and in writing.
- Employed, consistently for many years in a good job.
- Financially stable.
- Well connected to a social network and supported by his family of origin.
- Maintaining ongoing positive relations with his adult children.
- Willing to learn how to think and act differently.

Early on in his interaction with STOP, Skip was able to learn some new skills, to challenge some of his erroneous thinking, and to begin to apply to his own life a new way of responding to an intimate partner. He could see the value of group attendance and was being rewarded personally for having adopted some of the program's content.

We could also see through Skip's eyes some of what made the agency work:

- Personal connection with the facilitator.
- Time spent at intake and at group to learn Skip's story.
- The agency's belief in the role of education and new skill acquisition.
- Positive effect for Skip of coming to group each week, which created a buy-in for him to the facilitators, the curriculum, and the other men in group.

To be sure, Skip's life should also be understood from a broader perspective. Like other men, he had learned cultural messages of what it meant to be a man, the value of standing strong, being individualistic, looking out for number one. He had learned that you get what you demand and that you can use force when things do not go your way at home. From his perspective, he did what he wanted until he was stopped—that is, until the criminal justice system cast the long arm of the law. Skip felt entitled to a good life, had caring, generous parents, and lived many of the privileges of an upper-middle-class teenage background. He was controlling, impatient, and demanding, even by his own account. He felt he deserved to be heard when he spoke and to be treated well. And he felt that when he was not treated the way he felt he ought to be by Margie, his wife, he could use force to reinforce his wishes. He never felt or acted this way at work. He did so at home, because, at least in the beginning, there was no one stopping him.

Clearly, there were societal, cultural, familial, and even religious factors that influenced how Skip saw the world. The importance of his family dynamics, including the influence of social class, should not be underestimated. In part, Skip was aided in escaping the consequences of his actions for a longer period of time than many of the men in our study by a high-functioning family of origin. Well-off, generous parents stepped in to fill a financial or emotional gap in Skip's life when he was called to task by others—his partner, his employer, or, later on, the police. He also had a religious grandmother, and from her, he learned that faith was a resource you could call on when the going got tough. But, as with so many abusive men we interviewed, the pull of entitlement and the erroneous belief that his needs were all that mattered kept Skip behaving in ways that brought pain and angst to those who loved him and whom he claimed to love in return. How Skip was able to harness some of these cultural, familial, and religious resources later on his road to accountability we will develop in the pages to come.

Almost five months later, we interviewed Skip again. His upbeat attitude remained. *I gave my fiancée an engagement ring . . . we picked a date.* He started to reminisce. *I knew her before I married my ex-wife.* Then he moved on to the present. *We went and saw a finance person yesterday, sort of to talk about retirement, financial planning.* Skip wanted us to know that these proactive strategies of advice seeking were the result of his new way of doing things. This was not how he acted in his first marriage. He wanted us to understand that he had grown as a person, that he had incorporated some of the principles he learned in group.

Then he gave us an update on his one-day-at-a-time journey. *Three years and two months, a little bit more*, he said with a broad smile. But the struggle—the real struggle—continued.

Skip had finished his fifty-two-week program, but he missed it.

As several others did, Skip came intermittently to group for a short period of time after his "graduation." In other words, he came even when he did not have to. Through observing the impact of what he had learned in group, and what he chose to implement, the new skills he was acquiring became valuable to him. Rarely did staff members mention the fact that some men continued to attend group long after their mandated presence was no longer required. However, we found it noteworthy. Several men mentioned this within the context of their interviews, but it was not until later on in our data collection that we came to understand the real impact of this decision on their part. We believe it was part of the process of accountability, part of some men's initiative to take seriously the wrong they had done and the new way they wanted to live. There was no guarantee, of course, that they would be successful in their attempts or that their resolve would sustain them over the longer haul. But even so, it was evidence of effort and an internal accountability system beyond that generated by either the criminal justice mandate or therapeutic alliances.

LIFE AFTER THE STOP GROUP

What are some of the pieces of the puzzle to understand Skip's altered thinking and altered behavior? From his point of view, there were two main pieces: personal motivation and accountability.

His buy-in to the program began at the point where he realized that there was something at STOP that transcended a punishment model for what he had done wrong. Once he entertained the notion that he had something to *gain* from group attendance, he got with the program. He observed that its content was educational in nature and that the facilitators were helpful, and he gained insight into other men's resentment and lack of therapeutic progress.

His personal motivation was named. *I mean, every time I was here, I was here to learn.* While Skip never talked about himself as a consumer, the STOP program treated him as if he had a choice. This deliberate strategy on the part of the executive director of the program was critical to its ability to keep men coming to the program week after week. Later in this chapter, we outline how this unfolds.

For Skip, once he was motivated to change, accountability became part of the process to help him achieve *his* goal of change. In this way, both the STOP groups and Skip harnessed some of the strategies and language of twelve-step programs such as AA and NA. A private-practice counselor (someone Skip sought out on his own) helped to keep him on track. *I have a therapist, and he was asking me, "Well, what do you do with Margie when you guys have some disagreement or something?"* Skip's response: *I am trying.... I work on it, but usually, it's let a sleeping dog lie ... but sometimes you gotta wake the sleeping dog up and talk to it.... The TV is worse than heroin.* And Skip would know from experience.

Talking is hard work—even for someone who is comfortable with words. Group intervention, psychotherapy, church, and family living were all encouraging Skip to speak. So what helped him to change? The criminal justice system, the batterer intervention group, AA, the reconnection with his faith, the support of his childhood family, a new relationship, his kids, and the ongoing support of a private therapist were all central pieces in supporting Skip's motivation to change, one day at a time. Also important were others with whom he had regular contact, such as his coworkers and supervisor and a religious congregation.

For Skip and many others, the coordinated community response was critical. In his case, it was loosely coordinated. His probation officer was aware of Skip's commitment to the faith-based batterer intervention program and was very supportive of the goals and outcomes of that program. Meetings with the probation officer reinforced the gains Skip was making in group. Regular updates from the batterer intervention group facilitator to the probation officer meant that there was a seamless flow of information between the group's leadership and the criminal justice system. It is important to highlight here that these informal interactions help to ensure that the gains toward increased accountability that a batterer accepts for himself are reinforced by the institutions with which he has continued contact. But the role of friends and family is also critical.

Skip's parents and children noticed small changes in his life and encouraged him in his hard work to stay clean, sober, and nonabusive. As Skip made gains in his own life, he was able to share those in contexts where he could encourage others, such as AA meetings and through group check-in at the batterer intervention program.

Reconnecting with the faith of his grandmother, which he made his own during a short period of his adolescence, enabled Skip to have another language for his new start. Regular attendance at a church reinforced this new beginning. While he never became particularly active, he said, *I get to service on Sunday.* He often went alone, since his partner had bimonthly weekend custody of her daughter, and mother and daughter would go elsewhere.

Skip was able to stay focused on the goals others helped him to claim as his own. It was hard work. It was ongoing. Gains made can be so easily lost. Ultimately, Skip was accountable to himself, to those who assisted him along the way, and to a loosely coordinated community response team that believed violence had no place in family life.

THE DYNAMICS OF A BATTERER INTERVENTION PROGRAM

Batterer intervention groups differ, the personnel differs, the curriculum differs, and so does the tone. Some groups focus more on punishment, on what you did that was wrong. From the point of view of Skip and other men in his cohort, the faith-based group he attended focused on helping them to change who they were and what they did. It offered insight.

This was in stark contrast, said Skip and others, to other groups' focus on the choice to abuse, *choosing to abuse.* We felt his skepticism. Not surprisingly, most of the men resisted this. They felt, *No, I don't have a choice; I am backed into a corner.*

Skip's tone changed *Well, you are not backed into a corner. And there is no excuse for physical abuse, mental abuse.* These were points he had learned since coming to a group that sought to teach him, respect him, and ultimately change his beliefs. For many men in group, there is the interface between drugs and alcohol and domestic violence. *I think it's a component. . . . I don't believe at all that it's the reason for it, it's just the fuel on the fire . . . it's the beliefs . . . what your belief system is. . . . I believe you . . . change your belief system and other things change along the way.*

While we never asked about other programs they had attended, many men, like Skip, wanted to compare STOP and other groups in the local area. Articulating how the programs were different was not difficult for the men; they simply offered a story or two of their own, as we saw with Pete in chapter 7. Most often, their stories revolved around personal issues of humiliation or shame. As they saw it, while their violence was condemned at STOP, the facilitators went to great lengths in an attempt to understand them as people, their struggles and short-comings but also their hopes and dreams. And the response of Skip and others? *I look forward to coming here, whereas the other one was just dread, I just dreaded the other one.*

As an example, Skip talked about how during the baseball playoffs, he made sure that he arrived for group *a little bit early.* Group facilitators would turn on the TV thirty minutes before group started so that the men could gather and look at sports. For those living in a shelter or without TV, this became a highlight of their week. And it worked for the facilitators, too, because the men arrived early. This act paid big dividends. The men felt respected and in turn respected the group facilitator.

THE DYNAMICS OF THE STOP PROGRAM

The STOP program was organized with the notion of consumer choice as an important element. It treated the men as if they made a choice. It operated as if the program was in a competitive environment, competing for consumers. That did not diminish in any way the content of the program, the competence of the staff to provide it, or the severity of the consequences of noncompliance. But it did impact the environment in several important ways.

Since STOP believed that the men made a choice and treated them accordingly, and the men themselves believed that they made a choice, their court-ordered attendance felt cloaked in the language of choice. It was true, of course, that the men did not need to attend the STOP program, but they did need to attend one of the groups in the local area. But what does talking about choice and treating the men as clients or consumers actually mean?

The space, or physical location, where STOP group meetings were held was very pleasant. It was roomy, filled with natural light, appropriately furnished, and very clean. It was decorated appropriately, with soothing colors on the walls and furnishings to match. For individual appointments, such as the initial intake, the waiting area was large enough to accommodate several people, with comfortable chairs, artwork on the walls, and up-to-date magazines. There was also a vending machine that sold snack food and drinks.

There was ample privacy in the main waiting area to talk to the administrator about payment. Her office was next to the waiting room, with a sliding glass window to enable direct contact with those who were seated there or standing at the window's opening. When the window was open, there was no barrier between the men and the office staff. There was an atmosphere of warmth but also of profession-alism. It set the tone and encouraged client compliance.

The office administrator, who by the end of our fieldwork was sometimes also assisting as a group facilitator, created a very positive, friendly environment as clients entered. Her affirmation of individual clients might include questions about their children, a recent sickness or injury, or employment. It almost always included calling them by name and making small talk about the day—the weather, the season of the year, or local news. It was commonplace for clients to go to greet the administrator before making their way to the group room, even when there was no reason other than a brief chat compelling them to do so.

The STOP offices were on the second floor of a professional building in a very nice area of the city. There was free parking available and bus service within a short walk. The outside of the building was indistinguishable from that of other office buildings in the area that house physicians, accountants, and insurance brokers. Respect for those who came was paramount, but permeating the space was also respect for the serious nature of the intervention that took place within the offices. It was clear that the agency believed its work was serious and very important—you could sense it even in the waiting room.

The meeting room where the STOP groups were held was well equipped, with a large board meeting table and swiveling high-back chairs around it, and the room itself had other seating away from the table and closer to the bank of windows for those who wished for a bit of distance from the facilitators. There was a whiteboard, a TV and DVD player mounted on the wall, appropriate charts and information around the room and in brochures, and, in one corner, a coffee machine, a small fridge, a microwave oven, a popcorn maker, and a counter area.

About fifteen minutes before group began, the TV was turned on to the sports channel so that those who arrived early could catch up on the latest scores or replays. STOP would rather reward those who came early rather than penalize those who came late. For this reason, doors were not locked when the group began, so those who arrived a few minutes late could slip in without undue attention, although the chairs near the door were often taken, and latecomers had to climb over several other men to find a seat.

When a man was scheduled to graduate from the program, there was pizza at that last class so that all the men had a chance to celebrate his accomplishment. Given that there were new men added to each of the classes on a regular basis, this meant that some men who were fairly new to the program observed this rite of passage of the seasoned veteran.

The blended nature of the groups offered a chance for men who were participating for many weeks to be able to gauge their individual progress. Sometimes men challenged each other in group, but more often, the angry, resentful newcomer offered the veteran evidence of his own journey toward accountability and change.

The mandated STOP intervention groups were state-certified and ran for fifty-two weeks. There were normally two facilitators (often one male and one female), and group meetings ran for at least ninety minutes. As we noted in chapter 7, they began with a check-in time, when all participants were asked to state their first names and to offer something in the way of an update of their lives or circumstances. The program was very child-friendly.

This could be observed in the number of examples that referred to children as part of the oral presentation of the curriculum, the way staff remembered the names (and other details) of the children related to the men, the desire of staff to see men improve their parenting skills, and also the provision of child care on site. Enhancing the lives of children who had witnessed (or experienced) abuse was high on the priority list of the agency. A lot of staff time in meetings was devoted to discussing ways to have positive impact on the children. They attempted to be creative but realistic. All of the therapeutic staff knew how fragile the relationship was between the men and their children. Yet they saw that improved relationships with their children could be the carrot that kept the men who were fathers coming to group. We saw that, too.

Flexibility, within boundaries and carefully monitored, was another strategy of the program we studied. There was some flexibility with regard to the payment plan (in terms of exactly when the money was received and closely linked to ability to pay), but there was also some flexibility related to attendance at group. For example, the men could "double up" and attend two groups in a week, when their paid work was going through a slack time or they were between jobs. Also, the men could alter which group they attended in order to accommodate their changing work schedules. Sometimes they even received credit for classes attended elsewhere. If a man needed to leave a few minutes early or arrived a few minutes late, again, there was some flexibility. However, all of this was carefully monitored to protect against abuses or manipulation. But it gave an extremely positive message to the men: we are working with you.

The STOP groups were part of much larger agency that offered private counseling to women, men, and couples and held parenting classes and worked directly with children and teens. Its focus was clearly related to both individuals and families, recognizing that not all families are healthy. Many of the offerings of the agency involved abuse in intimate partner relationships or within the family context, but its services were not exclusively linked to domestic violence. During our years of study, the agency underwent a name change to more accurately reflect its focus and mandate on issues broader than domestic violence alone.

Financial stability was a central part of the agency's story. Because of this, STOP's programs and services were able to engage in longer-term planning without undue concern for financial solvency. In large part, this was a reflection of those responsible for its creation, development, and present direction. It remained under the leadership of one of its founders, who was a member of an influential family in the region. The family had business acumen and substantial wealth. Mediated through the agency director, at least in part, there was a strong social justice imperative and a long history of social activism and therapeutic engagement. The network of support offered—financial and otherwise—should not be underestimated.

Interpersonal warmth and professional curiosity were woven in an interesting blend into the life and demeanor of the executive director. She was well trained, read voraciously, and attended conferences regularly. Almost every time she returned from a training venue, new concepts and ideas were introduced to the staff (and intervention groups) and then evaluated informally for impact. It would be a mistake to overlook how effective the executive director was in setting the tone of the agency, for both staff and clients.

There was a remarkable degree of attachment of the staff to the agency, its mission, and the executive director. Staff needs were considered, a priority was given to flexible working arrangements, and there was no hint of any degree of dissatisfaction with the agency's mandate or current direction. At times, however, it seemed that this apparent devotion might stifle healthy debate or the ongoing professional autonomy and development of those not in leadership. But individual interaction with staff never suggested that this was the case, nor did informal behavior that we observed over many years.

Since staff members were encouraged to share their own life experiences, including stories of vulnerability, a blending of problems and potential solutions permeated the conversations among staffers and sometimes even between the facilitators and the men attending groups. Accountability, then, in a general sense, permeated the agency from the top down. It excluded no one. While staff members were very respectful of the agency director, everyone in the agency took some responsibility for ensuring that others were held accountable. It was commonplace for staff members to ask about the needs of one another, particularly related to overwork, time off, eating healthy, or exercise.

Staffers at the agency were trained mostly in social work, with many holding graduate degrees and professional licensure in the field of social work; others were credentialed as licensed mental health counselors. They represented a variety of faith perspectives and attended various local congregations for worship. They varied in terms of level of involvement in, or leadership of, church activities.

Staff turnover was low, particularly as contrasted with other similar agencies where we obtained data. This led to a high degree of solidarity among the staff and a thorough knowledge of local programs and resources. It also enhanced referrals from staff within the criminal justice system as positive working relations stood the test of time. On the other hand, swift action was taken when staff members failed to perform their work duties or appeared to be in personal noncompliance with the direction of the agency or its management. There was little evidence of staff cynicism or lack of respect toward clients or the work. Such would simply not be tolerated. During our time of research, one staff member was hired and then dismissed after about one year of work for behavior that was regarded as not complying with the agency's overall direction.

The agency director was involved in working within a coordinated community context. This included a commitment to attend the local domestic violence advocacy council, to show support for the women's shelter and its associated programs, and to ensure that there were intermittent updates of the work of the agency with the directors of other initiatives in the local area. She was regarded as competent, successful, and a team player. While her personal faith and affluence were known throughout the community, that did not seem to draw either criticism or praise. The results of the agency's work and the director's personal commitment—and skill—in working with families in crisis were what mattered most to others in the broader domestic violence community.

Noncompliance among the men within the program swiftly led to agency contact with parole or probation. But what happened next was unfortunate. It appeared that staff within the criminal justice system had such large caseloads that they were not always able to follow up on these leads in an expeditious manner. Yet eventually, client noncompliance led to consequences. This was an integral part of any coordinated community response to domestic violence.

Given the size of the agency, in terms of staff resources and clients, it was not surprising that they had links to the local state university and other smaller private colleges. The placement of student interns in the agency is one example of collaboration with the university. This supportive link with higher education no doubt was a factor in the agency director's willingness for us to engage in a research project at that location, one that involved site visits twice a year for a number of years.

The reputation of the agency within the criminal justice, therapeutic, and advocacy community was solid. While some did not personally endorse the faith-added approach, there was no sense that their work was compromised by religious persuasion, nor was there any evidence that the agency was proselytizing clients or pushing a faith-based agenda or reluctant to accept clients from a variety of faiths (or no expressed beliefs). Perhaps surprisingly, the men were more critical of the agency's reluctance to talk about matters spiritual than they were likely to suggest that matters of faith were pushed. Several very religious men were quite annoyed that the agency did not express more openly a faith-based perspective. Yet other men referred to how well group facilitators were able to call religious men to accountability, particularly by refusing to accept their attempts at justifying abuse using the language of the scriptures or their faith traditions.

The success of the agency in numerical terms alone was a matter of some discussion (and speculation) within the local community. The number of men who attended weekly groups could go as high as two hundred. Our informal conversations with professionals in other jurisdictions of the country (at conferences or other venues) suggested that this numerical success must be a result of selection bias—that is, working with men accused of, or charged with, less serious violence. But this explanation was simply not true, and no one locally ever suggested that the program drew or catered to less serious offenders.

Over time, the two other state-certified batter intervention programs in the local area were in serious numerical crisis. One closed, and it appeared that the other might not be economically viable over the longer term. As the program we were studying gained in reputation both within the broader criminal justice community and among the men who were its graduates, this further weakened the remaining alternative. This was not a cause for any celebration among the agency staff, though. In reality, the STOP program needed other alternatives in the area as a point of comparison. Men who were disillusioned with other programs became their best word-of-mouth support. This was especially instrumental when men new to the program complained about having been mandated to come; other men simply challenged them with a reality check of the other available options.

There were three major challenges to the program under study in terms of its long-term viability and continued numerical success. First was the question of leadership succession. This was a critical issue. The executive director would soon need an exit strategy, at least in terms of her full-time work hours with the agency. At present, there was an attempt to respond to her heavy schedule by frequent vacations, for rest and renewal. But at some point, this plan of overwork followed by rest, would become untenable, especially as she advanced in years. While there might be staff members being groomed for the position, there was no clear successor—in terms of vision, competence, or resource network. Second, there was an overdependence of the staff on the leadership. The degree to which this has been cultivated is not clear. But under dynamic leadership and exponential growth, there was little time given to developing autonomy among the staff or decentralized authority for operations or planning. The low staff turnover suggested that those workers who had served in the agency for so many years were either pleased with their work environment or had few other choices for employment. Yet the evidence certainly weighed in favor of work satisfaction. They liked what they did, they felt supported at the agency, and they reported no worries about the agency's ability to thrive well in the future. Thus, unlike so many others who worked in smaller counseling agencies or within the advocacy or batter intervention movement, they did not appear to be distracted by financial worries or the possibility of closure. Finally, with limited paperwork kept in the official files, there was little documentation to assess progress or recidivism within the criminal justice system or even evidence of change in the lives of men who had participated in or graduated from the program. Certainly, the executive director recognized this problem, but with so many demands on her time and talents, there had not been the resolve to redirect her own or staff time to collect follow-up data other than consulting the local papers for arrests of men who had once been in the STOP program.

ACCOUNTABILITY IN CONTEXT

It is hardly a new or surprising observation to state that accountability is a major key to working with men who have acted abusively with their intimate partners. Researchers over the last twenty-five years have either hinted at the importance of accountability or been stymied in how to encourage it or sustain it with those with whom they worked. There are several factors to consider in any discussion of accountability. We begin by looking at the local regional context of the agency under study and then move more broadly to talk about cultural and societal factors in a more general sense. We close with a brief discussion of the role of religion.

Criminal justice workers—those in parole and probation, policing, and the courts—see the value of batterer intervention group attendance as increasing the possibility that a man who has been abusive in the past will stop being abusive in the future. It is a way to ensure that his behavior keeps on being monitored, part of a series of checks and balances between the criminal justice system and intervention services. A man who has been mandated to attend a batterer intervention program must continue until the mandated number of sessions (weeks of intervention) is completed. In the West Coast state where we were interviewing, that number of weeks was fifty-two.

We learned about the philosophy of the agency from several sources, including interviews with staff and clients and focus groups and interviews with other professionals working in the domestic violence, religious, or criminal justice community. Their stories and experiences of working with STOP were remarkably similar.

The executive director of the agency made it clear that they drew their inspiration from the scriptures. She pointed to the book of Proverbs and the injunction to give information to people about how to live, how to be understanding, and how to be just in everything they did. She explained that at the agency, there was an assumption that the scriptures shed light on successful choices, on ways to make choices for successful living. "There is a pragmatic assumption," she said in one of our many interviews, "that if you do things one way, you are more likely to be successful than if you do things another way."

She claimed that at STOP, the strategy of working with the men was pragmatic rather than dogmatic. Over time, through observations and listening, we learned what this really meant: it was a way to differentiate the faith-based program from the other options available in the local area, which were much more regimented in terms of structure, curriculum, and strategy. The dogmatism surrounding some of the other programs—dogmatism that led some workers in the criminal justice system and the advocacy movement to criticize them—was linked in part to what was perceived as their strident feminism and inflexibility regarding how the model of work with abusive men was implemented within their program.

We spoke to one of these directors, who reported that her program followed curriculum established by others and that those in the program did not have either capacity for or interest in deviating from the model they had chosen to implement. They were employees of an agency, hired to do a job, trained and committed to working with men who were abusive. She spoke of being frustrated with the clients and with the criminal justice system. She did not speak disparagingly of the faith-based program, something one might have expected.

The faith-based agency director, on the other hand, was much more like an entrepreneur, often availing herself of new information, through training opportunities, conferences, or reading, committed to improving the intervention that she and her staff were providing, and desirous of meeting the needs of her clients, the abusive men. She was not shy or reticent to point this out. In her mind, this differentiated her program from what others were doing, locally and in other parts of the country.

The executive director of STOP was not limited by financial constraints personally, nor was the agency. This is not to speak disparagingly about the other programs but rather to draw attention to the fact that the executive director of the faith-based agency was herself developing an emerging curriculum, based on her own notions of best practices gleaned from her exposure to other professionals and the literature. The experts she would discuss at staff meetings or in individual interviews with us were rarely those who approached the issue from a perspective of faith. Rather, she was harnessing the research or the perspective of others within her own blend of faith, social-work practice, and intervention experience.

Frequently, in staff meetings and informal conversations, she made mention of the fact that they were trying new things within their programs or that she had been exposed to new ideas and was eager to share them with others. Rarely did staff introduce new ideas at staff meetings, but on the odd occasion when they did, it was met with enthusiasm by her and others.

STOP had a very pragmatic approach to the problem of working with abusive men, but it was not really steeped in any one model of intervention services. Yet it was informed by feminism, social work, social justice, and family therapy. The program certainly took the notion of power and control seriously, understood its roots as being linked to patriarchy and childhood experiences of powerlessness and abandonment. It framed abuse as a social justice issue and understood women and children as its primary victims. Yet it clung firmly to the notion that change was possible—even if it was not probable—among men (and women, too) who had behaved badly and abused their partners, their children, and/or other family members. The agency's workers understood well that this belief put them at odds with other workers in the community and within the domestic violence movement generally. But this did not deter them; it simply strengthened their resolve.

From the agency director's perspective, the men were the consumers, and she had a responsibility to sell the service of batterer intervention to them. Selling a service, from this vantage point, means that the agency must offer something that the men want. For sure, this had implications for the agency's philosophy and the way the workers intervened in the lives of the men. It had implications for the way the agency treated men who were unable to pay, who might need to arrive a bit late or leave a bit early, who might wish to double up on groups so that they could attend more than one in a week where their work was slow and miss a group in a week when they were working overtime.

Once we grasped the importance of this message to the agency and its work, we could see it everywhere: the physical location, the furnishings and ambience of the offices, the flowers and magazines, the coffee and food, the equipment, and the way office staff, facilitators, and even the executive director responded directly to the men. The men were valued as people, the problems they experienced and to which they contributed were seen as serious, families and relationships were important, and, most critically, it was never too late for change.

The casual yet professional look and feel of the surroundings did not detract from the seriousness of the business that was done. Men were not allowed to treat workers or one another with disrespect. They were not permitted to interrupt one another or to mutter comments under their breath or to disengage during group. There were monitors for security purposes and sufficient other staffers around should there be a need for additional assistance.

During the five-year period when we were collecting data at two different intervals each year, we observed a large number of groups and an even larger number of interactions between staff and clients. We were struck with how consistent the delivery of service was, how well the men and the staff members treated one another, and yet how often men were called to account for themselves or how often they chose to call out one another.

In conversations with the administrative staff, who were tasked with collecting the fees, sending out the bills, answering the phones, and interacting weekly with the clients, we learned that they were often the ones to encourage the men to keep on coming to group and to pay what they were able to for the intervention services they received.

"Clients see therapists at a reduced rate for abuse issues in their lives," remarked one of the office staff. "When I first talk with a client when we are setting up an appointment, they say, 'Oh, there is no way, I just got a job,' so I say, 'We would rather you came.'" Our interviews with office staff were peppered with comments of "we" relating to the agency. It was their view that together they were part of the intervention team, and accordingly, they took a great deal of pride in ensuring that the services that were offered to clients were first-rate.

From the perspective of the administrative staff, transportation and finances were the major impediments faced by the men who were either mandated or encouraged to come. Accordingly, they sought to do everything within their power to make it easier for them, to take away any excuses the men might have to stop or interrupt their attendance.

Many men had either lost their licenses or were no longer able to afford a reliable vehicle. Given the agency's excellent location, men whose cars were not working could ride a bike or take the bus to the agency. In our interviews with men, transportation was sometimes mentioned, particularly by those attempting to reclaim autonomy and mobility after incarceration or loss of driving privileges. Sometimes they would show us their bikes or talk about the advantages of their increased physical exercise.

Loss of self-esteem in the aftermath of criminal justice processing of men's violence was something the agency recognized and was attempting to remedy with small steps that could, in the words of the agency director "help men to walk the world in a different way."

During one of the many staff meetings we attended, the executive director was summing up her recent interaction with an expert in "fathering after violence." It was typical for her to give an update on her training opportunities or informal interactions. While such sharing was part of helping the staff keep up-to-date with what others in the field were doing, it was also a way of reaffirming the importance of their work and how the agency was perceived in the broader community. The expert's words to her were offered with pride. "You respect them," is what he said, and to the executive director, these words were like gold in her hands.

As she so often did in these contexts, the executive director went on to tell the staff a homespun story as a way of reaffirming the mission of the agency and its work. "God is a Jewish grandmother showing pictures around heaven, and that is how I am with my boys. They have made courageous efforts, and I am so proud of them. Shame and humiliation are so near the surface, it takes a lot of courage" to face up to the violence."

We hardly ever heard the executive director use discouraging words in staff meetings. She was rallying the troops, coaching, training, and setting an example. In private meetings with her, her mood was sometimes more subdued, but even then, year after year, time after time, she was almost always upbeat. When pushed by questions or comments, she was realistic about the slow rate of change, the small indices that had to be used to calculate such change, and the very real setbacks that occurred. She was well aware of the dangers, the cynicism of others, and the manipulation of many with whom she worked. But she was doggedly determined that change could and did happen and that she was going to do everything within her power to make change possible. "For the children," she would say. And for the men themselves.

Many of the programs highlighted in the literature or in brochures or reported in professional journals or books involve the fact that the real consumers are the women who have been abused. The batterer groups are held with the men, but the facilitators or the therapeutic staff regard the abused as their real clients.

A very good example of this is Lundy Bancroft's 2003 book, *Why Does He Do That? Inside the Minds of Angry and Controlling Men*. In his introduction, he states:

> I consider the woman that my client has mistreated to be the person I am primarily serving . . . my goal is to give her emotional support, help her learn about counseling and legal services that exist for her in her community (usually for free), and help her get her mind untangled from the knot that her abusive partner has tied. I can make it more difficult for him to manipulate her, and

I may be able to warn her of underhanded maneuvers that he is planning or of escalation that I'm observing. As long as I stay focused on the woman and her children as those who are most deserving and in need of my assistance, I can almost always make a positive contribution, whether or not my abusive client decides to seriously face his own problem. (xxi)

In the STOP program, this was not the way it was articulated to the staff, to the men, to the women they violated, or even to the broader domestic violence community. The men who acted abusively were the clients, first and foremost. Those men have hurt, violated, controlled, and abused their intimate partners, other family members, and their children. There was utmost concern for the safety of the women and children and safeguards in place to ensure that their emotional and physical health were the top priority, but the consumers, the ones who were primarily being served, were the abusers.

This may seem like a small point, like splitting hairs, but it is not. Its ramifications are huge, and it sets the STOP program apart from others. Some may wish to dismiss outright this perspective, and at first blush, this is understandable. But what STOP did, and was very successful in doing, was to place the accountability for the abusive behavior squarely on the abuser's shoulders and then to place itself accountable for attempting to call him to account. From STOP's vantage point, the agency failed if it was unable to call him to account or to engage him in a deeper process of accountability.

In doing so, they supported the woman who had been violated and the children who had either witnessed or experienced the violence, but other services they offered responded directly to these family members. The batterer intervention groups were for the men, and those at STOP believed that their success could only be measured by whether or not they were able to help men change their violent ways.

Accordingly, it mattered to the staff that the men were treated well, that their progress was affirmed, that they learned skills and strategies for coping with life, their controlling behavior, and their anger. It mattered that they established or reestablished relationships with their children. We would often hear staff members say, "We do it for the children." But when pushed to explain themselves further, they would admit that learning to father after violence was a long road, with many bumps and significant challenges.

There were great attempts to encourage staff to help men deal with their shame and humiliation and lots of reminders to staff that this took a lot of courage on the part of the men with whom they worked. The message here was that the work of therapists and group facilitators was difficult, but so, too, was the work they were calling the men to do.

During one staff meeting, one student intern related the story of a family with whom she was working in which the husband was charged for chasing his wife down the street while she was running and screaming and holding their small child. He was coming behind them with a butcher knife. He never caught up with them, and when the mother slowed down, he slowed down in response. We learned that this incident had developed over his wife's unwillingness to give him sufficient money to buy her a Valentine's Day card. Apparently, she had reason to believe that he might use the money for gambling. Now, eighteen months later and after regular contact between the husband and the STOP program, the mother, described as courageous and wonderful, was at a point where she was willing to let her young child have a supervised visit with the father.

The student intern had been coaching both the father and the child separately and was now reporting to staff on their first supervised visit. She had indicated to the dad that he should not approach the child but should let the child approach him. The staff members all became very excited when they heard the student intern report that the child exclaimed to her father, "Chase me, Daddy, chase me!" They interpreted this as some level of deep resolution to the frightening and violent incident that took place more than a year ago where the father was indeed chasing the child and the mother. Apparently, the dad brought a Mother's Day card to the visit and placed his hand over the child's hand to help her sign the card, extolling the virtues of the mother who had washed her clothes, cared for her, fed her, and in every way cared for her while the father was absent. This, too, created great excitement among the staff, who saw this act as highly symbolic of the failed Valentine card exchange.

In response to the story told by the student intern, the executive director explained that other programs did not let men "give." To give to their family's life was hope-giving for the men. "What he did was horrible to that baby," she continued, "but he is now ready to give back." She praised the student intern for her intervention.

Another worker commented that this was redemption. Then the student intern said, "He asked me about hope. How am I the holder of hope? My heart breaks every single day, but God has called me to do this. God has called me to help her daddy."

To this, the executive director replied, "We are one beggar telling another beggar where to find food. If I can do it, you can do it, too!"

At this point, several workers chimed in about hope and value and the fact that they drew hope from the healing in their own lives. Summing up, the executive director said, "One thing that gets someone fired from here would be unkindness. We can be frustrated, yes. But unkindness is intolerable. Some of these folks [the men] invite you to be unkind. But the men soften over time. The intakes are the most rocky."

Another worker, an older social worker, said, "It's the office administrator's job to tame the wild beast." A younger worker smiled and said, "Beauty and the beast," referring to the fairy tale but also a nod to the fact that the administrative staff member was a very attractive woman.

Again, the executive director chimed in: "We are not here to fight with anyone. The worst thing we could do is not to let them come. Everyone makes sense of their story in context. We listen to their story in context. . . . The road to self-respect is accountability. Self-respect comes when they say, 'This is not a good thing!'" She noted that her response to a man who was telling his story of violence might be "This wasn't your finest moment. . . . I understand that your intent was to be heard." Then she turned to us in the meeting and said, "These men grew up as weeds, not as cultivated roses."

We then asked directly about accountability. "Accountability is beyond the walls of the agency," the executive director replied. "Our paradigm is to work with the men to build an internal accountability system, and then we model accountability ourselves. An accountability system would really be a focus where you have learned to do reflections rather than offering sanctions."

The conversation drifted to therapist accountability and self-care so that they would be prepared for the work and not overwhelmed by it.

CHALLENGES TO THERAPEUTIC NOTIONS OF ACCOUNTABILITY

One of the complicated issues facing STOP staff and others in the criminal justice system involved no-contact orders. At one level, this is always a challenge for a coordinated community response to domestic violence. But in the state where this agency was located, battery between partners was considered a felony if children were present. If an abused woman breaks the no-contact order, her children can be taken by social services and placed in foster care, and she is only reunited with her children after she gives reassurance that she will no longer have contact with her abusive partner. Such reassurance must be given in the context of counseling.

This created a particular challenge for STOP staff and their collaborations with colleagues in parole and probation. So how is this resolved? In this local community, the agency director worked together with the staff of parole and probation to ensure that no-contact orders were taken seriously and upheld and yet that over time, there could be a lifting of the order by a parole or probation officer in a case where a woman came to group with a man and some level of supervised visitation occurred there. In those cases, we were told, the director of probation services and the agency director share legal responsibility for lifting the no-contact order.

According to the agency director, this was a specific example of how the philosophy underpinning STOP's services met the challenges of criminal justice processing of domestic violence cases. It showed how two workers—one based in a therapeutic environment, one based in criminal justice service—worked together to assist men who had shown themselves to be accountable for their violence, doing the work required of intervention, and where there was strong victim support for a continued relationship.

While there was nothing explicitly faith-based about the desire of the therapeutic agency to forge links with workers in the criminal justice system, it was linked to the faith-based considerations from the agency director's point of view: "Our worldview has to do with [the notion that] people can change, families are important, women are fully functioning adults just like men, and you have to fully respect what the woman wants to do with her life."

From this vantage point, the faith-inspired perspective of the agency director motivated her to challenge what she believed were impediments within the criminal justice system and the broader secular community to notions that women should leave their abusive partners forever and limit as much as possible relations between their children and the fathers who have treated them badly. She contended that there was a bias in the broader alliance against Christians being involved in domestic violence intervention. Yet she claimed that the work the agency had done over many years had helped it to gain credibility. "It was only through giving time, being there, getting training, and sharing whatever we learn, over time, that there was a confidence built in our expertise in knowing about these things, and then our rearrest record is very good."

This confidence in the staff, and especially in the executive director of STOP, was clear in the broader community as we interviewed those in the criminal justice system, including parole and probation officers, judges, and advocates of the women's shelter. We consider the relationship between the shelter and the agency later in the chapter, but first, we turn to consider the relationship between the agency and the workers within the criminal justice system.

In our focus group with parole and probation officers, we tried to understand what some of their reservations might have been concerning a faith-based agency working with batterers. For some, this was hard to articulate. Others felt that the workers might be naive, lacking in knowledge or skill, easily manipulated by the men. We asked what exactly the executive director had done or said that began to dispel their reservations. Again, this was hard for workers to pinpoint, but it was clear that they expected religious rhetoric to pepper her conversations, that she would be lacking in "real" understanding of the issues, and that she would be "taken in" by the manipulative efforts of the abusive men.

We also asked them about the frequency of their referrals to STOP and what factors they took into account when deciding what program to suggest to a particular abusive man. Interestingly, one of the workers said that she did not send any man she considered to be high on sociopathy to STOP, for fear that he would contaminate what was going on within the program. Another worker noted that one of the other programs in town did more regular urine testing and that he would send some of his clients there instead. We asked him how often he referred men to the STOP program. "I would say once or twice a week, up to six times a week," he replied.

We asked several questions in the focus group that encouraged the parole and probation officers to discuss what they thought about the faith-based program. They noted that the courts only approved of three programs in the local area and that the faith-based program was one of the approved programs. One worker mentioned the use of Bible passages, and another referred to its brochures. As the discussion progressed, a younger parole officer remarked that he did not think that the services "really hinged on the Christian part of it." Then the discussion turned to what STOP does well.

"I don't know that they are unique, but what I appreciate about STOP is that it's not a punitive approach, nor is it a condescending approach to the offenders—so these workers at STOP have done some pretty courageous things, and the problem I had with some other agencies is that they can get into the punitive approach, and I think that what I like about STOP is that they convey the attitude that each person is an individual, it's not a cookie-cutter treatment approach, they respect the individual, and they give out a lot of respect, which makes our job a lot easier than if we send a client to another program and all they do is tear the guy down—it doesn't help us at all."

When the focus group discussed accountability issues, the criminal justice workers were unanimous that the faith-based approach might have some distinct advantages. The younger male worker started off the conversation. "I think that anybody who is involved with a priest or a pastor is going to have a lot more of their act together, probably a lot more to lose in life than some of these other guys that we run into." A supervisor chimed in: "It does make sense, because right there, the men are saying that they are willing to communicate or listen to an authority figure. I mean, I would assume that they are going to if they are involved with the church."

From the perception of the criminal justice workers with whom we spoke—probation, parole, and the courts—STOP had better program completion rates than other agencies. Also, they believed that speed in accessing the service made a difference. "The faster that you can get them into the program," said one of the older female parole officers, "the greater their success."

At one point in the focus group, conversation turned to some of the challenges facing churches and religious leaders when domestic violence strikes families of faith. Workers had quite a lot to say about their experiences working with local clergy, experiences that were not nearly as positive as those involving the faith-based agency. All of the workers had examples to share of religious leaders who sided with the abusive men, gave poor advice, and failed to take seriously the safety and security issues of the victims. One worker summed it up by saying, "I don't know if safety would be [a religious leader's] primary concern or if the spirituality of the people would be the primary need."

From the perspective of one of the judges working in the court system in the region, STOP was a program that he admired: "I am a fan. I have heard the executive director talk, and I really like what I hear. I have talked to defendants who have been in the program, and I like what I hear. I really like the idea of using a person's faith as a base for the treatment. It is a good hook."

We found it impressive that the judge had taken such an interest in what intervention services were available in the local region and was able to speak with such knowledge about the various programs. When probed during one of our interviews, he said, domestic violence "is a special interest of mine, and I take it seriously. I can give cases special attention. I am able to read over each and every evaluation for a domestic violence offense. . . . I read them over, from police, from court clerk, that someone seems to be violating an order, and I get them in within a week or so.

While we have interviewed judges in other locations about their domestic violence work, it was the intense interest of this middle-aged man to work in a coordinated community response that captured our attention. We learned that he occasionally attended other domestic violence events in the area and sometimes met with staff or directors of various agencies. We were particularly intrigued to hear of his reflection on the role of faith in the life of a batterer or the role of faith on the road toward accountability and change. "If they [at STOP] have gotten somebody who is a person of faith, they have gotten an institutional basis for dialogue with the person, which I think is a real challenge. Treatment, possibly the majority of domestic violence treatment, is that the provider and the client are coming from two very different worlds."

The judge went on to describe how he had thought that a man needed to be a Christian to attend STOP, and then he learned that this was not true. What impressed him most was the way they treated the clients. "They come from a basis of, look, we are not saying you are an evil, worthless person. You don't have to stand up and say, 'I am dirt.' We think you need some help on ways to have a healthy relationship, and we are going to help you become the best husband or partner that you can be. I like that."

The judge, who tried many of the cases in the local area, reported how challenging it is from his vantage point to assess whether there is any hope for change. "The problem from where I sit is that I can only see so much—what's in my courtroom and what the windows show me. I spend a lot of time talking with people to try to find out as much as possible from the defendant and from the victim—try and find out what is going on. On darker days, I think no. But on brighter days, I think, yes, this guy has really started to see things properly." He went on to explain why the problem was so very difficult to change. "If you grow up and your dad beats on mama every night, how are you going to know differently? Even with no contact, they have to pay support. If the victim comes in and asks for a waiver of no contact, we would set a hearing."

Trying to support the victim is very difficult. From the perspective of the bench, one is in a no-win situation with the survivor. "Dealing with the victims is much more difficult. They have not done anything wrong, and they are looking at you and saying, 'You are ruining my life, keeping me from the one I love, kids from their father, why are you torturing me?' I don't like playing God, and I feel like sometimes that is what I am doing." The judge tried to explain to victims that he was trying to protect them, but he often felt that his words fell flat. "I have victims that hate my guts. Those women are prime candidates that if it happens again, I am not reporting it."

RELATIONSHIP BETWEEN THE WOMEN'S SHELTER AND THE FAITH-BASED AGENCY

The relationship between the director of the large women's shelter and STOP's executive director went back many years, predating the early days of the faith-based agency. They met first when the shelter director was working as a domestic violence advocate in a rural area, and the woman who would eventually start STOP was asked by a group of local churches to offer a workshop. It was in this rural context— watching the role of the churches and seeing the support they sometimes offered victims—that the advocate was challenged to rethink her position on whether churches could be part of a broader community-based solution to violence in intimate relationships.

After the faith-based agency was formed, the advocate was hired as executive director of the very large women's shelter in the city. Once STOP was up and running, it became, she said, "the centerpiece for my interaction with the religious community. Through the years, I have worked with them in, you know, different capacities, from different ways."

Other domestic violence advocates with whom we spoke also mentioned the role of the agency in the broader community. "I am not personally a religious person, so I am speaking basically from the fringe, but from what I have heard is that a lot of it [their teaching] . . . is how they sort of bring people in, they sort of can show people what the readings [from the Bible] say and why what they are doing [being violent] might not be the most appropriate. And keeping the family together is something that they try to do. . . . [Domestic violence] agencies seem to think that they have to be split apart."

The challenges for collaboration between agencies where one espouses a faith-based mission and the other is secular should not be underestimated. In fact, over the years, we have interviewed many shelter workers in various locations in the United States and internationally about their reservations concerning working with religious leaders on issues related to domestic violence. There are many roadblocks, and there is a pervasive view among many in the secular community that churches and their leaders have little to offer either victims or abusers in the aftermath of domestic violence. In fact, churches and their leaders are usually considered by shelters and their staffs to be part of the problem rather than part of any solution.

At the faith-based agency, there was explicit use of religious resources, although our direct observation is that it occurs less frequently than those who work in other agencies believe to be the case. The director of the women's shelter said, "I have seen . . . their materials and stuff, it definitely has Christian [content], I mean, not just values but specifically, you know, Bible verses or whatever, so that it is very specifically directed to that belief system." Brochures and posters sometimes referred to scripture verses, and there was no hesitation on the part of facilitators in harnessing the Bible during their group sessions or referring to passages in staff meetings. But based on our observations over many years, it would be an exaggeration to say that this occurred frequently. We sat in on many groups where there was no explicit reference to anything that could be considered directly spiritual or religious in nature. On the other hand, there was overwhelming evidence of a caring attitude toward the men, something the agency believed was an explicit outgrowth of its faith-based orientation.

Shelter staff believed that STOP, with its faith-based emphasis, was making very important inroads in helping abused women who were religious. Here the domestic violence advocates observed what our research has shown: one of the most significant preoccupations of religious abused women was their goal to see their husbands or partners change. In the words of one advocate, "What they found out when they talked to Christian women was their biggest interest was in trying to find a way to make men change their behavior. That was what they wanted. They didn't want to have to flee their home, live in a strange place, try to get their own job. . . . They shifted their services more toward the batterer intervention services, because that, you know, was what they heard [abused women say they wanted]."

There was the perception among the advocates that the faith-based agency had more self-referrals than court-ordered cases, but that was not true according to the case files we read, the men we interviewed, or the experiences of the staff in the agency. But it was pervasive in the community—not that STOP had an easier workload or that it held men less accountable but that it had more men who were motivated to change because it had higher rates of self-referrals.

Interestingly, it was the opinion of the advocates that the training level of the faith-based agency staff far exceeded that of those who worked in the other intervention programs in the local area. They noted, and we confirmed, that the staff members at STOP were mostly trained at the postgraduate level, with MSW degrees. However, some were licensed mental health counselors with undergraduate degrees.

One of the probation officers in the city reported that she had twenty-one clients who were part of a batterer group at STOP during the last couple of years. In particular, she noted that the agency also had services for victims and services for children, something that made their work with the men even more impressive to her. During a focus group with probation officers, we learned that there had initially been some skepticism about a new faith-based agency in town, but that had dissipated as workers had very positive experiences in working with the staff. In part, this was mediated by the professionalism, expertise, and personal warmth of the agency's executive director. Almost without exception, secular workers in probation and parole told us that they had some initial reservations about what a faith-based agency's workers might be like but that these negative expectations were later found to be not true.

OBSERVATIONS FROM THE FIELD

Early on, it became apparent to us that it was very difficult to assess whether men were accepting personal responsibility for their violence despite rather heroic efforts on the part of the criminal justice system and therapeutic interventions to assist them in doing so. In chapter 7, we noted that most of the men in the early stages of group attendance—and in our first contacts with them in focus groups or personal interviews—reported that *I am not violent.* As we argued earlier, in large measure, the men used as their frame of reference for this statement someone whose violence was greater than their own. They also blamed, or explained, the abusive acts as a response to something that happened to them. In this way, they attempted to situate responsibility for the violence on shoulders other than their own.

We highlighted the story of Pete, who remarked how hard it was to be an adult, to take responsibility, to act responsibly, and to do so on a regular, ongoing basis. There is ample evidence throughout our fieldwork of how hard it was for the men to do the work. Staying clean and sober took effort, there were setbacks, and the consequences of failed attempts should not be underestimated. So, too, with learning to think and act in nonabusive ways; to relinquish the desire, need, or behavior of control; and to do this on a regular, ongoing basis—when life was going well and especially when it was not.

Becoming accountable for one's actions—whether to a parole or probation officer, to a therapist, to the facilitator (and other men) in group, to a judge, to a priest or pastor, to an intimate partner, to one's kids, to one's broader family network, and ultimately to oneself—takes motivation, skill, and assistance. How many men who have acted abusively are able to do this?

There is the snapshot approach through which to answer this question and the video camera, or longitudinal, response. As we interviewed and reinterviewed Skip over several years, our personal assessment of his progress in becoming accountable changed. During the first two years of contact with him—punctuated by six- to eight-month intervals—it appeared that he was well on the road to doing the work required of changed thinking and behavior. We had observed that he was willing to challenge other men less engaged with the STOP group, had become aware of his own vulnerabilities, and added skills and knowledge of how better to respond to disappointment, frustration, and relationships in his own life. He was following through with consistent group attendance and meeting regularly with both his parole officer and a private-practice therapist.

In our fifth meeting with Skip, almost a year after he was engaged to a new partner and several months after he was married to her, his interview was punctuated with more disparaging talk of the relationship. He appeared to focus much less on his journey, the air of excitement about the new relationship had passed, and he seemed resigned to the fact that things might not be as good as he had hoped. When we returned to the agency six months later—now several years since Skip had been in the program—it was the first time he did not accept our invitation to be reinterviewed. A further six months later, on our last visit to the agency, we were able to interview him again. He had experienced some health problems, he was considering an early retirement, and his hopes and dreams had shrunk a little. His plan for the year ahead was summarized as *Stay married. See the kids. Maybe my step-daughter will have a baby.*

OTHER EXAMPLES OF INCREASED ACCOUNTABILITY

Another man who showed early evidence of enhanced personal accountability was Jake, a young African American man, who, at twenty-eight, decided to make some new choices. Jake grew up in a turbulent family situation. As a result, he entered the foster care system early, shortly after his mother attempted to abandon his seven-year-old brother in a bus station. We asked what advice he would give to a man who was ordered to come to STOP but didn't want to. *I was that guy. I didn't want to be here. I was angry.* So what advice would he give? *Give it a chance. Put your hands, and tuck them, under your seat. Grab that chair really, really hard, and you will find something that appeals to you. . . . I have seen a lot of men coming into the program and thinking you were a bunch of man haters, you were scared, and so now you were going to do something to us. I have seen them change, so that is what gets my attention. . . . Sit there. Come every day. Bring your body, and your mind will follow.*

Jake eventually followed the advice he now would give to others. He came. He sat. He learned. And he began to see changes in his own life. Those lifestyle changes included how he related to women. *Actually, I go out on dates now. Talk to the person first and get to know them. It was always donkey backwards before. Now I actually date.* Jake's concept of *donkey backwards* referred to the notion of sexual intimacy as a first step in relationship building, rather than a result of friendship and commitment. By his own account, he was learning a different way to experience life.

In our last interview with Jake—which occurred six months after he finished the program—he was finding himself referring other men to the STOP program. The initial buy-in took some time, for in total, it took Jake almost three years to complete the fifty-two-week mandated program. But once he could observe changes in his own life and reap the benefits of those changes, such as obtaining full-time employment for the first time in his life, he was swift to comply with the program. It was at this point that he became accountable to a group of people who wanted to keep him on a journey of change.

A very different example of increased accountability came from a young man who, when we first met him, presented as almost incapable of conversation with adults. When Skater first walked into the room where we conducted interviews, he refused to maintain eye contact, sniffled constantly, and appeared uncomfortable in his own skin. By our fourth interview—in a span of almost two years—Skater was a new man. The ear plugs were gone. He was engaged in the conversation, not just answering questions but participating fully. Gone were the signs of consistent drug use. He still wore the baggy pants and the oversized T-shirt, but his countenance had been altered.

Skater arrived at the intervention program as a result of assaulting his father, but this was not his first involvement with the police or domestic violence. *I have been a criminal most of my life, either on the streets or involved in gangs.* The child welfare department had been working with his children for the last ten years, temporarily removing two of his three children from the home. One year later, Skater had a new place to live, and his daughter had been returned to them. *I went from straight gang-ster to stay-at-home mom. It's the old joke; it keeps me out of trouble.*

Soon he would no longer be under the watchful eye of the state, and Skater con-fided that this was a *little nerve-wracking.* Why? *Well, ever since, you know, even before I turned eighteen years old, I was in trouble with the law, and in trouble with this, and in trouble with, you know, all these organizations and everything else. So I always had somebody there, whether it was drug and alcohol treatment, whether it was a probation officer, a parole officer, whether it was cops, whether it was a prison guard ... somebody there pulling my strings ... and now all the strings are going to be cut, and I am going to be left to my own devices, and it's real scary to think OK, now I am going to have to use everything that I learned.*

For Skater, accountability meant acting like an adult. Where alcohol or drugs once numbed the pain, Skater was forced now to deal with current problems and past troubles head-on. He had some health issues that surfaced as a result of his past addictions. He still had no employment. And at this point, he was caring full-time for a two-year-old, his youngest. This was a lot of responsibility for someone who had dodged personal accountability most of his life. *I am clean and sober, and I am a family man and just gotta keep going forward with that. . . . No matter what stresses went on throughout the day, once my daughter is in my lap and watching TV with me and in that peaceful moment with her thumb in her mouth, it's just like nothing matters. Nobody else's crap going on throughout the day that got even close to under my skin, it doesn't matter. All that matters is keeping her around and doing the next right thing.*

Skater kept up intermittent contact with the STOP program long after he gradu-ated. He and his wife took parenting classes as a couple, and his wife had contact with a support group. By our third interview with him, Skater was able to reflect more about the group itself. *First thing is, this place really works. It don't matter what edge you come with, what chip on the shoulder you have, where you are coming from. This place really works. Just give it time, even if you go in there with your arms crossed just like I was. . . . Most people are coming in mandated to come ... from the same lot, drugs, alco-hol, rage, violence, you know, a bad past ... out of the state prison system, out of the county jail system, and the things that got us there are not the things that we need to be doing in life. There is so much more to it, no matter how old we are, no matter how young we are.*

One year after we met Skater, he was volunteering at the local church, running one of the cameras for the televised service. Transported to and from the worship center by the foster parents of one of his children, Skater and his wife felt welcomed by the community and supported in their efforts to change their lives. His wife had a promotion at work—in a fast-food restaurant—and things were looking up.

Another year later—almost two years after our first contact—life was continu-ing to improve. Skater had been working for more than six months, and routines appeared to be in place. *I am staying out of trouble. Almost off of all of probation for the first time in my whole life. Few months away from finishing everything. Basically, learning how to live life family-oriented and raise a child. Living life one day at a time and praying to God that I get another day.*

For Jake, Skater, Skip, and many other men we met at STOP, accountabil-ity for their past and planning for their future became part of what the program helped them to achieve. Whether this could be sustained over the life course was impossible to know. But we have followed them for several years, and there is reason to be hopeful that some men who have been abusive can change, will accept a degree of accountability to others in the criminal justice and therapeutic communities, follow through on intervention services, and then internalize that accountability as part of the way forward with their lives.

We have chosen to highlight three stories from men whose lives and circumstances were very different. Skip was older; Jake and Skater were both in their twenties. Skip was more affluent and reported a healthy and rather happy childhood. Jake was African American. Skater was a father whose children had been in and out of foster care. Skater and Jake grew up in environments that would be described as chaotic. Skip and Skater were married; Jake moved in and out of relationships. All three were ordered by the court to attend the batterer intervention program. All of them had been under the watchful eye of the criminal justice system for a protracted period of time. All of them had been dangerous and committed terrible acts of violence toward those with whom they were in relationships. All of them believed they were given a second chance by STOP, taught how to understand their own behavior, and challenged to change it. What united them was that each of them chose to become accountable in the aftermath of intervention services for domestic violence, and each made some rather significant changes in their lives, changes that were recognized by others.

But there are countless other examples of men where this was not so. The most dramatic examples of failed accountability were those men who simply refused to believe they had ever done anything wrong, despite police reports and their own case files documenting their violence.

Ted Clow was one such man. He fumed over the need to become accountable for his violent actions, *the whole concept of taking responsibility for what you did. I didn't do anything, all they wanted me to do was lie and say that I'm sorry I did it. I didn't do anything.* These words of Ted came during our second interview with him as he was describing his desire to be treated well by others. Ted, a war veteran and approaching age sixty, wanted to rant about how poorly he had been treated by another program in town. *They treated you like a criminal.* He was never able to move past his resentment toward others. By our third visit to the agency, Ted had suffered a heart attack and died.

Kevin Grant was another example. From the moment he introduced himself to us in a focus group, it was clear that he was one angry, bitter man. He made no attempt to hide his resentment toward his ex-girlfriend, whom he blamed for all his current troubles. And he blamed an ex-wife for all his troubles before that. He harbored resentment toward those who worked for the criminal justice system, blaming them for all the hoops he had to jump through. And there was also resentment also toward other law-abiding citizens, whose ease of life and lifestyle he envied. To sum it up, Kevin was all about anger, bitterness, envy, and resentment. Not surprisingly, Kevin situated his story in terms of the harm others had caused him.

Our contact with Kevin was limited to one focus group and one interview, at which time he had been coming to group for about four weeks. Since Kevin did not comply with earlier court orders, he got his probation revoked—*the judge says I didn't even try*—and he was then mandated to live and work for 180 days in a supervised facility and to show up each day for road crew. When we returned six months later, Kevin was back in jail.

We have been attempting to show how the concept of accountability is understood by those who work with men who batter and examples of how the men themselves become, or fail to become, accountable for their actions and altered in their behavior. We now turn our discussion to how religious faith fits into the picture.

RELIGIOUS FAITH AND NOTIONS OF ACCOUNTABILITY

I just know that . . . you move closer to God, God moves closer to you, and more will be revealed. This was how Skip saw the link between his spiritual life and the ongoing struggle to be clean, sober, and nonviolent. At first glance, there appeared to be an army of professionals attempting to keep Skip on the journey toward justice, healing, and accountability. Some of these women and men had their own personal faith, some were in faith-enriched work environments, and others were rather skeptical that religion had anything of therapeutic importance to offer a man like Skip.

As he learned more about the web of interconnections in his own life through the batterer intervention program, Skip tried out his newfound knowledge on others with whom he was in contact. For example, Skip learned not to blame his violence on alcohol use. This he then mentioned to his NA/AA sponsor, the person who was assisting him with staying clean and sober. *I mentioned to my sponsor that a lot of times when I got violent, I wasn't on alcohol or anything, but he said, "Well, you probably had it in your bloodstream."* This explanation seemed to satisfy Skip's desire to understand his own actions, but in reality, we would argue that it was evidence of an explanatory tug of war among the various therapeutic modalities in Skip's life. While working in an interdisciplinary roundtable context enhanced efficiency, referrals, and accountability, each group of workers had its own turf, so to speak. And with that turf came a series of explanations for why things happen. For example, drug and alcohol counselors thought differently about domestic violence and its link to alcohol from domestic violence advocates or facilitators in a batterer intervention program. One consequence, then, of the men interacting with a large number of staffers from different agencies and models of intervention was negotiating the language, explanation, and culture of behavior to be altered and the change process itself.

Like Skip, most of the men we interviewed felt comfortable talking about their own spiritual quest, usually without any form of prompting on our part. The issue was spontaneously raised in response to other issues. When it was not raised by the men themselves, we asked about their faith. Even in these contexts, there appeared to be no reluctance to discuss personal spirituality, regardless of whether the men were connected to a specific faith community or whether they embraced no particular religious tradition at all. The men often spoke of various Christian religious traditions (e.g., Roman Catholic, nondenominational) with which they had been in contact.

For those men who had been incarcerated, some connected with their faith during their stays in prison. But in almost all cases, they were reconnecting with a faith that had been nurtured much earlier in their lives, rather than adopting a totally new frame of reference. In this way, it was a specific form of religious conversion—at the point of crisis, looking for pieces from one's past that might assist one on the road to wholeness. Analysis of the data among the men reveals no particular pattern for which men experienced the reawakening of their spiritual lives after judicial sentencing to prison. Catholics, Pentecostals, and Methodists alike reported these experiences. For Danny, whose story is highlighted in chapter 4, it was his placement in solitary confinement that led to his request for a Bible to read. As we noted in chapter 7, for Bill, it was the prison chaplain. And for Scott, it was attending Bible study in jail that led him to see that involvement with faith gave him hope for the future. In each case, however, there were three essential elements: (1) The reconnection with faith brought warmth to a cold reality about their lives and circumstances and offered a new language, the language of the spirit, to conceptualize the way forward. It offered words for a new start, turning away from the past, and embracing a new beginning. (2) The reconnection with one's spiritual life brought hope that tomorrow could be a better day. This fueled motivation to change and an eventual willingness to become accountable, not just as a mandated criminal justice response to the wrong that had been committed but a decision to begin to do the work of altering how one thinks and how one acts. And (3) the reawakening of a past connection to faith brought charity, a community of people—religious by choice and/or tradition—that embraced the language of change, the hope of a better tomorrow, and random acts of kindness toward those who had stumbled.

STOP combined these three elements in interesting ways, although never named as such. Each of the workers was a person of faith, but it would be inaccurate to conclude that they shared a religious world perspective. They did not. What they shared was a religious language, cultivated from a variety of traditions, for a new start. Staffers spoke of that new start in different ways, to one another and to the men. This language spilled over in conversation with other workers from the criminal justice perspective and within the advocacy community. It was clear to us that throughout the domestic violence community in the local area, professionals understood that STOP spoke and acted the language of faith, maintained hope for change, and went to great lengths to offer charity (in terms of kindness and assistance) to men who had acted abusively.

However, the STOP agency and staff were steeped in reality. They were not unfamiliar with the culture of violence, the abysmally low rates of long-term dramatic change, nor were they unwilling to accept the evidence of clients who gave up hope and stopped doing the work. But, as with many parole and probation workers, judges, and clergy, hope kept them doing their work, despite countless examples where hope had failed, recidivism had occurred, and change had to be calculated in small-measurement indices.

NOTIONS OF ACCOUNTABILITY AND THE STAFF AT STOP

The executive director of the agency chose her staff carefully. It was clear that many of the administrative workers had been clients at some point and that the director had helped them to get their lives in order, which often included going back to school for more training. We talked to several for whom this was the case. Other staff members had shared her vision from the early days, although one of the cofounders of the agency was no longer working there. While we were conducting our fieldwork, two workers left, one of whom was terminated for not treating the men with respect and the other for an apparent unwillingness to accept the agency's philosophy. In both of these cases, swift action by the executive director ensured compliance with the mission and strategy of the program. While there was never any hint of disgruntlement among the staff, the degree to which everyone seemed to accept without challenge all the policies and procedures was noteworthy. Even staff meetings—of which we attended quite a number—were devoid of differing points of view, surprising for a highly trained group of professionals working together.

At the most basic level, workers at the agency were held accountable to endorse the mission wholeheartedly. It appeared to be the executive director alone who charted the strategic planning of STOP. There was no evidence that others challenged her, but there was no evidence that a potential challenge would be tolerated if it occurred. She was a visionary with the skills and personal resources to bring her vision to reality.

On many occasions, we talked with the agency director and the staff about whether they thought that faith made a difference in the lives of men who had been abusive. One staffer responded, "I don't know if their faith, I don't know the degree to which that matters, but the truth is that we do treat people differently." This was the mantra of the agency. They believed that they were working according to Christian principles in how they interacted with the men, and that alone made a difference.

To support this position, the executive director told of a man who was one of the first participants in STOP groups: "He said to me the other day, 'I changed because you cared about me. Somehow I really sense that the people here took the time to know me and understand me.' . . . Some of the fellows here come in not real likable, and I really believe that most of the people here . . . really care about these fellows . . . and it is real, and it is true, and I do think that is huge in some of their lives."

This was about the only time that we heard the executive director compare her program with others in the local area that she felt treated the men disrespectfully. "Where in the other programs, a lot of the guys have said they are treated disrespectfully, that is what they are used to, that just feeds the hidden anger in them so that they shut down and can't receive the information that will give them the opportunity to change their lives. . . . They can do disrespect better than we can. They are good at it."

We probed with questions related to faith and the work they did at the agency with staff members in individual interviews. The issue of accountability was often raised in this context. Joshua was a highly trained group facilitator who co-led several groups each week. He had worked as a pastor, had two graduate degrees, and had worked as an educator. It was his perception that there were some small differences involving men of faith in the groups. "By golly, the base values and morality, the sense of accountability and responsibility to do something greater than oneself. They recognize the disparity between what they believe and what they do. If court-mandated, they have resistance, and there are walls, but normally, the walls come down, and then the men are softer and more receptive to what we are teaching here." We asked whether battery looks different when the abuser is a man of faith. "I can't say there is a difference in how violence is meted out," he said, "but Christian women stay longer." This is certainly true within our research, which we have been collecting for the last twenty years; women of faith are more hopeful that change can and will happen and show greater reluctance to leave their abusive partners, temporarily or forever.

We asked Joshua to talk about hope and change. "I totally believe there is hope," he said, "but I don't believe a woman ought to keep herself in a situation where domestic violence is happening. In the Christian community, there are a lot who stay and keep working at it. I say, 'Get out!' Safety is number one. But faith makes a huge amount of difference. What I often try to see happen is for them to have internal motivation to change where a man says he wants to change even if she never comes back."

At STOP, it was difficult to assess just how many men who participated in its programs were in stable relationships with stable jobs, both factors that the literature notes are important features of greater program completion. In our case-file analysis at another faith-based agency in the state of Washington, we analyzed data from more than 1,100 closed case files. As we discussed earlier, it appears that the men in the faith-based programs may have more life-stability characteristics working in their favor. They are more likely to be currently married, to be employed at least some of the time, to have some contact with their children, and to have completed high school. They do not appear to differ in terms of many family-background characteristics or the presenting problems surrounding their current life circumstances. That is, they are as likely to have witnessed or experienced violence in their childhood homes (perhaps more likely), to have drug and alcohol addiction issues, and to have committed very severe acts of violence against a current or former partner. In chapter 2, we compare these data to those reported by Edward Gondolf, a researcher who has been studying batterer intervention programs for a long time; as we show earlier, men who attended the faith-based program we studied in Washington reported more life-stability factors than those reported by Gondolf.

It is also true that there may be more motivation to change for some men in faith-based programs because of the role of spirituality and the presence of religious resources either in their own lives or within the lives of those they have harmed. Yet trying to dissect the power and potential of this religious factor is not straightforward.

We asked individual workers to talk about the role of faith in their work with clients. An older male therapist replied: "It's pretty rare for me to do hard-core religious work in therapy, like praying or reading the scripture. Sometimes the man or the woman will say, 'This [a religious factor] has helped me to overcome,' and then we will talk about it. Some of the participating agencies are very displeased with what we do. . . . For the men, we hold them accountable, and yet we believe they can change. We believe in them; others don't always believe in them."

An intake worker at the STOP agency said that it was initially not very common for the men to talk about faith, and then after a number of sessions, "it comes out in subtle ways." It was more common for the men to talk about childhood experiences and how they were raised. From his perspective, many of the men did "a period of doing life without faith. . . . A lot of people I see are just beginning to embrace their faith again."

In many ways, what we observed within the STOP program was a receptivity to faith and its importance in a person's life. In our five years of going to the program, we never witnessed in a group or heard in an interview or a focus group that a faith-based agenda was being pushed, even from clients who claimed that they did not endorse a personal faith. However, we heard from a few men that there was not sufficient talk about faith—in other words, that the faith messages were too subtle.

The workers at the agency were very forthcoming about their own experiences. Several of the women had been in abusive relationships in the past, had undergone therapy as part of their healing, and then entered university or graduate school as a way to reclaim their lives and plan for a brighter economic future. Some had been engaged in a private practice before the agency was begun and mentioned that the timing of the agency's opening corresponded to their own work plans. One middle-aged therapist said, "It was a perfect fit, and so this is how it came to be that I am here. God put it in my heart."

Most of the workers felt that the agency had an excellent reputation among criminal justice staff and former clients. They also felt that there were pastors and people in the community who did not like the work of STOP. Interestingly, all of the pastors with whom we spoke in the local area were supportive of the work of STOP, though perhaps not as enthusiastically as the secular workers. This is a very interesting and perhaps unexpected finding, until we probe its significance a bit further.

The STOP program was able to intervene, and was recognized for intervening, in the lives of very difficult people. Judges, the courts, and probation and parole services all recognized both the competence and the spiritual integrity of the workers and the intervention services they provided. Perhaps this is a little difficult for religious leaders to swallow. At a time when the status of religious leaders is declining in both secular and sacred contexts, to see the role of faith-informed credentialed laypeople being recognized by the community as experts in bringing faith-informed help to very troubled people may be challenging. For faith leaders to refer clients to STOP, they had to realize that the circumstances surrounding the needs of the men or women who initially came to them for help were too great for them to respond to alone. This may have been hard to do, especially since a central part of STOP's identity in the community was linked to the fact that it was a faith-based service offering very troubled people hope for changed lives.

In earlier research on clergy, I (Nancy) found that referrals from clergy to other sources of help (therapists, social work agencies, lawyers) were least likely among those clergy who reported that they knew little about domestic violence and most likely among those who indicated that they had been exposed to training in domestic violence. In *The Battered Wife: How Christians Confront Domestic Violence* (Nason-Clark 1997), I explore in depth clergy knowledge of, and experience with, families affected by abuse. A dramatic pattern among the clergy we interviewed from many different denominational backgrounds was that they resisted referring those who came to them for help. And where referrals were needed most—among those pastors and priests with the least information about abuse—they were least likely to occur.

In *No Place for Abuse* (Kroeger and Nason-Clark 2010), Catherine Clark Kroeger and I offer a sustained argument for why religious leaders need to take this issue seriously, and we provide spiritual and practical resources to assist clergy in understanding the dynamics of abuse and the process for working together with others in the community in a collaborative fashion. At STOP, working together with local agencies was something they did extremely well.

One of the graduate-trained therapists talked about how her personal self-disclosures and her links to the community offered her opportunities to highlight her work in other contexts, thereby increasing referrals to the agency as well. She went on to explain that several of these clients were neither abused nor abusive but were coming to her for individual counseling. She said that a question sometimes asked was "Do I have to be abused or abusive to people to come here?"

We asked her to reflect on what she felt was most helpful to clients and what she saw the agency offering them. Without taking a breath, she said, "Like, when we have guys graduate, they say, 'You really cared about me.'" Then we focused more specifically on men of faith. Not unlike other workers, she noted the fact that religious women were more tolerant of the abuse and stayed longer. "I see men who are religious or having a faith base. Their wives put up with a lot more crap before they did something about it, and so what you hear [from the women who have been abused] sometimes is that he kind of took advantage of her commitment because of her faith, and he utilizes that to keep her from leaving."

From the agency's perspective, accountability was a process developed with the men who attended the batterer intervention groups. For accountability to take hold, the men needed to begin to take account of what they did in the past, understand the harm they caused to others and themselves, and learn ways to recognize and challenge their erroneous beliefs and behaviors and to adopt new strategies and responses for dealing with life and intimate relationships.

The STOP agency brochure stated:

[I]n our intervention with men who have issues in the areas of anger, power and control, we focus on the men's personal accountability in recognizing and owning these advantages, beliefs and behaviors, not on their partner's actions. The "anguish of this accountability" can be very difficult.... [O]ur experience and the vast body of literature and research available around these issues, indicate that if the men don't recognize the advantages they have as men and take responsibility for their behavior, the treatment prognosis for them and their relationship is poor. Therefore, our emphasis on accountability before empathizing with men in treatment is intention. . . . To summarize, when working with the men's groups we intentionally start with accountability for their behaviors and then move toward empathizing.

According to the executive director, who also led batterer intervention groups, "the road to self–respect is accountability. Self-respect comes when they say this is not a good thing." The agency literature emphasized this perspective, stating: "you can take responsibility for your attitudes and actions and be accountable to learn kinder, safe, respectful beliefs and behaviors and you will be on your way to self-respect and better relationships." In one of our interviews, the director emphasized the role of the entire domestic violence community in ensuring what she identified as different components of accountability: "Accountability is beyond the walls of the agency. Our paradigm is to work with the men to build an internal accountability system, and then we model accountability ourselves. An accountability system would really be a focus where you have learned to do reflections rather than offering sanctions. . . . Accountability with sanctions makes people liars. But self-accountability is essential. And self-respect is essential, both to make better choices."

From the perspective of a coordinated community response, accountability is a series of checks and balances to ensure that the safety of the victim and the children is a top priority, that violence between intimates is challenged by the strong arm of the law, that court orders are upheld, and that resources are available for all the family members who are impacted when violence strikes at home, including the very people who have perpetrated that violence. Accountability can include urine testing and no-contact orders, but it may also involve supervised visitation and support groups for victims. In the local jurisdiction where we were collecting data, it almost always involved mandated attendance at a batterer intervention group and follow-up by parole or probation services.

A REALITY CHECK FROM THE LITERATURE

In the domestic violence literature, the term *accountability* generally refers to personal and professional monitoring of the person who has acted abusively. It includes monitoring strategies from a variety of professionals. It also includes the journey toward greater ownership for the wrong that has been committed. A central ingredient in batterer intervention work involves helping the offender to take responsibility for past actions and to develop empathy for the victim. Some, but not all, batterer intervention programs require that men in the program write a letter of empathy (told from the point of view of the woman who was victimized) and a letter of responsibility (written from the point of view of the man who was the perpetrator).

In our analysis of case files from another faith-based batterer intervention program (not STOP), where these letters were part of the requirement for graduation, we learned that almost two-thirds of the men completed the fifty-two-week state-certified program. Among those men who were court-ordered to attend the program, completion rates varied. That is, when a judge ordered a man to attend, he had about a 60 percent likelihood of completing the program as he had been ordered to do. For those cases where men of faith had religious leaders who also encouraged attendance, the rates increased to almost 80 percent. To be sure, for men of religious conviction and practice, the added piece of accountability—to a pastor, a priest or another religious leader—was noteworthy. At STOP, such a file analysis was not possible given the scant information that was kept on each man.

ACCOUNTABILITY FROM A CHRISTIAN PERSPECTIVE

Accountability is a word that is often used in Christian religious circles. It has a long history. In the New Testament, there are many references to the fact that what is done in secret is known to God and will be revealed at some future time. The Christian scriptures teach that all people will be held accountable for what they have done wrong (sins of commission) and what they have failed to do (sins of omission). That is why corporate prayers in many Christian traditions (Anglican, for example) ask for forgiveness for both types of personal failure.

The Pauline epistles broaden the concept of accountability to suggest that what occurs on earth is viewed, at least metaphorically, by a "great cloud of witnesses." The apostle Paul uses this as a way to contextualize how he thinks about the "marathon race" of life, a picture that his first-century audience would understand well. He—and, by extension, we—is on the track, and all around others are watching. Who are these people, and what do they see? That is what creates the accountability—the audience and the implications of what they see. By this, we are built up, encouraged, or shamed. It is not unlike the concept of looking-glass self, developed long ago by social theorist Charles Cooley. Essentially, Cooley argued that we use others as a looking glass in the development of the self. And we make interpretations based on what we think they see, on the cues set before us. Consequently, we feel pride or shame as we interpret others' responses to who we are and what we do.

For Pauline passages in the New Testament, this cloud of people who have gone on before are watching him, encouraging him, shouting and cheering, as he completes the race. This is meant as encouragement for keeping on and not stopping the race prematurely, but it is also a deterrent for acting in ways that would be against God's law or would bring shame to the cause of Christ. It is a powerful religious image and has the potential to be harnessed in ways that might enhance accountability for people connected to their faith traditions.

Early in 2013, I (Nancy) accepted an invitation to be a guest lecturer in the doctor of ministry program at Gordon-Conwell Seminary's Charlotte, North Carolina, campus. My task was to help pastors understand some of the dynamics of abuse and how they might work with others in a collaborative community response. One of the students, a male pastor in his mid-fifties, asked me to offer a personal example of accountability as a way to illustrate further how they could help others to "keep account." I explained that the goal of accountability is to internalize the voices of others as a way to shape, encourage, and correct one's own behavior. I said that in my life, the cloud of witnesses might include my parents (now deceased), those who taught me when I was young, my mentors or advisers through university, my colleagues around the world, my closest friends, and my husband of thirty-five years, a clinical psychologist and depression researcher.

For a man who has been found guilty by the criminal justice system of violence against an intimate partner and who is now a felon because the abuse occurred in the presence of his children, whom might this group include? His cloud of witnesses would certainly include probation or parole services, the police, and a judge, but it might also include the person who collects the urine sample, the children's social worker, the facilitators at the domestic violence group, and other men in group involved in the long and arduous process of learning to behave differently from how they have in the past. For some, it will include other family members, friends, or coworkers, and for many religious men, it includes a pastor, a priest or another religious leader and a congregation of people who worship together. Harnessing the potential of this spiritual resource is an extremely important part of calling those who claim to be religious to account for their lives and behavior.

Cook (2006), writing from a restorative justice perspective, uses the term *accountability dynamics* to refer not only to becoming accountable within the criminal justice system and to society, taking active responsibility, but also to obligations toward those who have been victimized directly and indirectly, performing remorse. Central to this notion of taking active responsibility, then, are the steps of admitting involvement in the offense, expressing remorse, and accepting collectively articulated resolutions.

Accountability is a process inferring action rather than just intention. In order to launch the necessary continuum of actions, there must be a constellation of interwoven responses that lead to the ultimate goal of becoming accountable for perpetrating violence within the family context. These responses begin within the criminal justice system and continue through the batterer intervention program and through involvement in other programs at community-based agencies. According to Jory, Anderson, and Greer (1997), accountability relies on challenging the abuser's sense of entitlement and getting him to rethink the meaning of respect at every stage of the intervention process.

Entitlement is a very important part of understanding why violent men act the way they do. Lundy Bancroft, in his book *Why Does He Do That?* (2003), sees entitlement as a key feature in understanding the mind of an angry and controlling man. Psychologists Neil Jacobson and John Gottman (1998) use the images of cobras and pit bulls to identify two categories of men who use violence when they do not receive the personal space, peace and quiet, attention, and/or gratification they demand of their partners. In an earlier chapter, we develop at some length the question of why, some of the factors that can help us understand what goes on inside the mind of an abuser. It is important to point out that accountability is unlikely to occur until a man's belief about entitlement has been challenged. Where entitlement flourishes, the fruit of accountability is unlikely to grow.

ACCOUNTABILITY AND THE CRIMINAL JUSTICE SYSTEM

Accountability is understood by the criminal justice system as something that involves the police, the courts, the prisons, and parole and probation services. Ensuring that the law takes seriously the crime of domestic violence has been slow in coming and is in part the result of much pioneering work by feminists, researchers, and those who work in the various professions linked to the law. Our colleague Linda Neilson, a lawyer and family violence researcher, has been collaborating with the judiciary for many years, helping judges and attorneys understand the full extent of the impact of domestic violence on children. Her 2009 book, *Domestic Violence and Family Law in Canada: A Handbook for Judges,* is now being used by criminal justice workers in various countries around the globe as a window into how cases have been adjudicated and the impact of these decisions. Central to her argument is that scant thought has been given to the full impact on children in the decisions that are rendered. Neilson argues that a failure in one part of the legal system affects other parts, and as a result, real people fall through the cracks.

Like the judge we interviewed in Oregon, whose comments were echoed by other judges in two additional jurisdictions, judges often find themselves in situations where the legal options available seem no match for the complexity of the problems they see. Many of the "solutions," such as incarceration or no-contact orders, bring even more hardship for the women who have been violated. Understanding this no-win situation is the easy part; responding with best practices is what is difficult. To be sure, it is a challenge even to conceive of what a best practice would be. During the last twenty years, in particular, several strategies have been developed and employed, some with greater success than others.

The enormity of the crime of family violence has required various strategies of intervention by the criminal justice system in Canada and the United States, involving police, prosecutors and their supportive infrastructure, and the judicial system and legislative bodies (Loue and Maschke 2001). Within each of these constituent groups, the need for accountability has helped shape policies and procedures. Responses include mandatory arrest (Dobash and Dobash 2000; Finn et al. 2004), dual arrest (Hirschel and Buzawa 2002), protection orders (Burgess-Proctor 2003), probation (Ames and Dunham 2002), mandating offender treatment programs (Saunders and Hamill 2003), no-drop prosecution and the incarceration of offenders (Ventura and Davis 2005), liaison with social services agencies (Ad Hoc Federal-Provincial-Territorial Working Group 2003), and development of specialized domestic violence courts (Denham and Gillespie 1999; Bradley 2002). With all of these responses, it is indisputable that the criminal justice system now recognizes the necessity of dealing with domestic violence cases in a more serious and concerted manner, ultimately with a view to the goals of offender accountability and victim safety.

Management of the various responses within a coordinated community response has been recognized as crucial to increased accountability. According to a report of the government of British Columbia (Critical Components Project Team 2008, 32), "[l]ack of coordination, from the local level to senior levels of government, has negative repercussions for women's safety, offender accountability, policy and program accountability, and system costs."

Recently, many perpetrators are being adjudicated within specialized domestic violence courts, one of a variety of so-called problem-solving courts (Butts 2001). These courts have been established in recognition of the need for an intensive and coordinated approach to the pervasive problem of family violence and with the goal of creating a criminal justice system response to the issue of domestic violence that better addresses the needs of victims (Cook et al. 2004; Vallely et al. 2005). Other general goals relate to improving the judicial response to the problem by coordinated criminal justice and social service agencies and holding defendants accountable (Gover and MacDonald 2003). In taking a social problem approach to crime, these courts serve a dual purpose, as agents of social control and agents of social change (Mirchandani 2005).

Where specialized courts have not been available, their goals may be attainable when judges have a specific interest in domestic violence. As we noted earlier in this chapter, one of the judges we interviewed took a special interest in cases of domestic violence, and even though he was not working in a specialized domestic violence court, he ensured that the cases of domestic violence were seen expeditiously. Another judge mentioned to us that one of the chief advantages of a specialized court was the speed with which a domestic violence case was processed. Timeliness of the criminal justice response, along with follow-up of cases, does help to increase offender accountability from an external point of view. This judge went on to say that when someone is arrested, he is called certainly within seventy-two hours but most often within twenty-four hours. He believed that perpetrators were less likely to violate any court orders once they had a "face-to-face." It was during this face-to-face meeting that he could "plant the seed of worry."

These sentiments are echoed by another judge working in a specialized domestic violence court, who said: "I am very clear, on those things there is not any room for failure, and we absolutely expect you to succeed. . . . There is a clear difference between a judge who sentences someone and says you will complete [batterer intervention] and never looks at the case again. [I say,] you are going to be on probation, I am going to have a review at 45, 60, 90, 120 days. . . . [The] linchpin of any good [domestic violence] court is that there is very strict screening with three basics: (1) specialization so that everyone involved has the dream, (2) fast track, and (3) intensive follow-up."

The requirement of batterer intervention program attendance is the most common disposition in the criminal justice response to domestic violence. These programs have become a key element of the programmatic intervention agenda of the criminal justice system. They developed in response to public acknowledgment of wife abuse as a serious social issue, in addition to increased political and legal reaction (Mankowski, Haaken, and Silvergleid 2002). As programs evolved, debates developed (Davis and Taylor 1999; Bennett and Piet 1999) about how these programs effectively and efficiently fit into the overall response to violence against women. One of the most widely debated issues is accountability, as this is often identified in intervention programs as a key theme, yet within most programs, there are no resources to assess how this is actually demonstrated (Bennett and Williams 2002).

In a Canadian court decision, Mr. Justice Douglas Lambert highlighted the societal imperative of accountability that needs to be addressed through the justice system:

> I want to say particularly in this case that society has a deep interest in this kind of conduct. It is not a private matter between parties to the relationship nor a matter that goes away if there is forgiveness within a relationship. This kind of conduct endangers and imperils society. In addition the guardians of the social interest, the people involved in social work and the police who are called out and into these situations, must have the protection of the law and the understanding that these offences will not be ignored by society. . . . Other people are at risk. Children are at risk and the neighbours are at risk.
>
> (cited in Critical Components Project Team 2008, 19)

In order to ensure accountability of perpetrators within the justice system, three things are necessary: appropriate and consistent sanctions, effective enforcement orders, and a coordinated response (Aldarondo 2012). Numerous programs and policies related to consistent sanctions have been implemented in the past twenty years, with mixed results (Sloan et al. 2013).

In the United States and Canada, essentially all jurisdictions now mandate arrest in cases of intimate partner violence. In Canada, every jurisdiction has pro-charging policies in place, whereby charges are brought in cases of spousal violence if there are reasonable and probable grounds to believe that abuse has taken place (Statistics Canada 2005). After conducting a rigorous multisite analysis of records from five police arrest studies, Sherman, Schmidt, and Rogan (1992) disputed the lack of effect. Rather, they argued, arrest consistently had a modest deterrent effect on perpetrators. This inconsistency in the results of mandatory arrest is also highlighted in the work of Simpson et al. (2006).

Arrest and charging policies seek to achieve both general and specific deterrence, and deterrence theory does inform studies of arrest and intimate partner violence (Williams 2005). Whatever the deterrent outcomes may be, they are, of course, based on the police actually following through with the arrest. Considering that the critical components of effective deterrence theory include swiftness, severity, and certainty, when one or more of these elements are missing, the deterrent effect is greatly reduced.

Mandating attendance at therapeutic treatment programs for men who have been charged with and/or convicted of wife abuse (Gondolf, Heckert, and Kimmel 2002; Hamel 2012) has also been an important and consistent response of the criminal justice system. As with mandatory arrest, however, there is little agreement on the effectiveness of such programs. Researchers have identified numerous variables that contribute to attrition and/or recidivism, including demographic characteristics, attitudinal and personal variables, and levels of motivation (Gondolf 2000; Day et al. 2009; Coulter and VandeWeerd 2009). Another frequent response of the justice system to the problem of domestic violence is the issuance of protective orders for victims in the form of no-contact orders, civil protection orders, and Criminal Code peace bonds (judicial recognizance orders) (Burgess-Proctor 2003; Johnson, Lunn, and Stein 2003). Since the purpose of this type of order is to protect victims and their households from further harm, it is essential that these types of orders are taken seriously both by the perpetrator of violence and by the police and agents of the criminal justice system in terms of enforcement. Yet Sherman, Schmidt, and Rogan (1992, 238) refer to protective orders in the United States as "a hoax on the victims, a promise to protect them that will not be kept." The limitations of protection orders identified by Finn and Colson (1998) include widespread lack of enforcement and related uncertainty about enforcement by both police and judges. These issues are further exacerbated by victim reluctance. One Oregon judge told us about women coming to his courtroom extremely angry that they were unable to have contact with their partners. They noted that not only had they suffered violence, but they also now had no one to parent with, they often had reduced income because of dual-household expenses, and they loved their partners and wanted to be with them. This judge remained adamant that there was to be no contact for at least a year because of the possibilities of further and perhaps more lethal violence. The assumption behind a coordinated community approach is that it will produce more effective results than isolated and unsystematic interventions (Post et al. 2010). Uekert (2003) details two necessary elements for this coordinated response: (1) key stakeholders must actively participate, and (2) the stakeholders must reach consensus on the most appropriate response to domestic violence in their communities.

COORDINATED COMMUNITY RESPONSE

The varied policies and procedures found within a coordinated community response all contribute to ensuring accountability. Gondolf (2004) argues that program effectiveness is substantially dependent on the intervention system of which it is a part. Some researchers believe that probation officers are the most critical link between the criminal justice system and batterer interventions (Healey, Smith, and O'Sullivan 1998). Mandated attendance at a batterer intervention or treatment program is most often associated with probation. Several of the goals of probation for batterers identified by Mederos, Gamache, and Pence (1999, 10–11) are related specifically to accountability: monitoring closely and unpredictably, demanding consistent documentation from the treatment program, and expecting behavior change. According to the group of probation and parole officers with whom we spoke, the follow-up process in terms of program completion and accountability is critical. The monthly meetings held between offenders and their probation or parole officers help to ensure accountability simply by confirming that everything is on track in terms of employment, housing, no-contact with victims, abstinence from drugs and alcohol, and so on. But perpetrators are also held accountable through sanctions if they are in violation—every time—and this group reports that about 20 to 25 percent of cases do violate terms of probation or parole.

According to Heath (1998), another common form of collaboration involves informal meetings between probation officers and community service providers that are meant to enhance communication and cooperation. We witnessed and participated in this type of informal meeting numerous times during the course of our research, in scheduled informal meetings, luncheon presentations, coffee breaks, and shared meals. People representing different components of the coordinated community response gather to share ideas, to discuss issues and problems, and sometimes to debrief (or practice self-care) from very difficult workloads.

Within intervention programs, regardless of curricular strategies, a key goal is moving perpetrators of violence toward becoming accountable for their actions. During the early stages of therapeutic intervention, many men attempt to maintain a normative identity (Henning and Holdford 2006) by offering socially desirable responses, impression management, and, perhaps, self-deception. To begin the journey toward change, however, it is necessary that men acknowledge their violence. Unfortunately, many men never reach that stage of acknowledgment. Their emotional residue of anger, shame, denial, minimization, and attributions of blame is so deeply entrenched and they have dedicated so much effort to mitigating culpability that they remain unable to develop a new behavioral paradigm based on relational equality and respect. Men who do not become accountable during the course of their programs, who continue to blame others for their circumstances, have little prospect for change in their behavior. Becoming accountable for one's actions—whether to a parole or probation officer, to a therapist, to the facilitator (and other men) in an intervention group, to a judge, to a priest or pastor, to an intimate partner, to one's kids, to one's broader family network, and ultimately to oneself—takes motivation, skill, and assistance.

ACCOUNTABILITY AS DEFINED BY OTHER BATTERER INTERVENTION PROGRAMS

According to David Adams (updated from 2003), there are now more than fifteen hundred batterer intervention programs in the United States and more than two hundred in Canada. With those numbers, there is a multiplicity of intervention models, each utilizing a variety of methods that integrate ideas from different sources in order to understand and intervene to effect change. Yet regardless of orientation and despite the eclectic mix of methods found in most intervention systems, there are important core items integrated into the majority of programs that are considered central for success in batterer intervention. These include the priority of victim safety, a focus on the behavior of men who have acted abusively, recognition of the impact of abuse on family and community, and certainly taking responsibility for abusive actions.

The Duluth curriculum, developed in the early 1980s by the Domestic Abuse Intervention program of Duluth, Minnesota, focuses on "power and control" and emphasizes critical thinking skills around a variety of themes, including nonviolence, nonthreatening behavior, respect, support and trust, honesty and accountability, sexual respect, partnership, and negotiation and fairness. This model takes the blame off the victim and places accountability for abuse on the offender.

The well-known dual-phase EMERGE program, in Massachusetts, combines awareness of abusive behaviors with cognitive restructuring. EMERGE teaches that participants must take full responsibility for their behavior, understand that abuse is a choice, understand and validate the harm their actions have caused to others, adopt new ways of communicating, respect the opinions and wishes of others, identify and change attitudes that lead to abuse, and be able to identify red flags for abusive behaviors. Each of these teachings contributes to those who have acted abusively taking accountability for their actions. Once abusers take accountability within the first eight weeks, they are then allowed to move on to the next twenty-six-week phase of the program which focuses on education and cognitive-behavioral therapy.

Within the Colorado based AMEND (Abusive Men Exploring New Directions) program, group leaders are seen as "moral guides," taking a firm stand against violence and confronting the client's behavior as unacceptable and illegal. Establishing accountability and building client skills are identified as goals of this program through emphasis on identification and awareness of the problem; taking responsibility for the abuse; enhancing self-esteem; building anger management, developing appropriate conflict resolution, communication, and stress-management skills; and remaining chemical-free.

In Northern California, the Manalive violence program was developed in response to women's experience of violence within particular ethnic groups and the need for it to stop. The mission of this program is to help men stop the violence and to recruit successful graduates to become community violence prevention and restoration activists within their own cultures, particularly Spanish and Cantonese groups. There are three major principles identified by this program: (1) men's violence against women is learned behavior that can be unlearned, (2) men must be accountable for their violence, and (3) community beliefs that support and encourage men's violent behaviors must be changed to end abuse.

Michael Stosny has developed a different approach to dealing with batterers in his Compassion Workshop. This twelve-week program uses a variety of teaching methods based on the theory that abuse is a result of a failure of compassion for oneself and others. The HEALS technique is the core of this workshop—Healing, Explain to yourself, Apply self-compassion, Love yourself, Solve. After learning compassion for themselves, men are encouraged to extend that compassion and be accountable to others.

All of the groups mentioned take accountability seriously, although some do not mention it by name. Some batterer intervention programs have deliberate strategies for attempting to create and foster accountability both between the men in groups and their facilitators and between the programs and the broader institutions and agencies, such as the criminal justice system, which may monitor the abusive behavior. Almost all the programs have ways to assess victim safety. The executive director of STOP referred regularly to many of these programs. We never heard her speak disparagingly about any of them, although she often mentioned positively the work of Stosny and the EMERGE and AMEND programs. While STOP's notions of accountability were certainly akin in many ways to those of other programs, STOP had some unique features, and, we would argue, these were in no small way linked to both the faith-enriched environment of the agency and some of the faith-based principles on which their work had been established. In the last several years, we have had opportunities to meet the directors of many batterer intervention programs—at workshops, conferences, or roundtable discussions. Like the executive director of STOP, they, too, were deeply committed to the work they did and to a coordinated community response. Most, however, did not consider the role of faith or religion to be something that might be considered a source of strength (i.e., an asset) in the journey of a man who was abusive to an intimate partner or other family members. The collective wisdom here was that religious ideology was part of the problem surrounding domestic violence, not generally part of the solution. As for many therapists and other first responders, working with highly religious people was something they would rather not be called on to do (Whipple 1987). To be sure, men and women of deep religious commitment can be unwilling to listen to a secular adviser, preferring instead to submit to a religious worldview mediated through a pastor, a priest or another spiritual leader. They can be prone to challenge alternative explanations of events or even to accept that there are multiple ways to understand a situation or a problem. For these very reasons, a faith-based agency might have some additional capital for working with highly religious people. However, our experience with and exposure to two other faith-based agencies (besides STOP) suggest that this might not always be so. The link between STOP and the broader community-based services was a critical feature of its implementation plan; this was not the case in the other two agencies, in different jurisdictions, although the executive directors of both wished it could be.

Within most intervention groups, there is a strategy of "deliberate accountability" (Dignan et al. 2007). Not only are the group leaders constantly assessing accountability, but the men also assess and scrutinize one another's narrative and performance during the course of each group session. They attempt to hold one another accountable, because they know the power of denial. They can easily recognize the difference between those who continue to blame others for their behavior and those who have learned to become accountable.

What have we learned about accountability in the life of a man who has been abusive? To be accountable is to be answerable for one's behavior. It is synonymous with responsibility (DeRuyter 2002) and occurs when a person is able to influence a situation or has power to change it. It involves owning what one has done and charting a way forward. It includes submitting oneself to the checks and balances imposed by others and eventually internalizing those very goals for oneself. It is very hard work, and the road to accountability and changed behavior is long and arduous. It does not happen often in the life of someone who has been found guilty by the criminal justice system of battering an intimate partner.

Batterer intervention programs recognize the necessity of accepting responsibility for one's abusive behavior as an important step in the intervention or treatment process: "Violent and abusive men must begin by admitting that they have in fact perpetrated acts of violence for which they are responsible and are to be held accountable" (Dobash, Dobash, Cavanagh and Lewis 2000, 62). The first step in acknowledging responsibility is to face the feelings of shame, guilt, and embarrassment that will accompany the process and "take an honest look" at the abuse (Jenkins 1990). From a peacemaking perspective, offenders must willingly and actively participate in their own healing, and that might include both traditional treatment programs and publicly taking responsibility and becoming accountable for their actions. Accountability and change are intertwined: without becoming accountable, there will be no change.

Staff at the STOP program understood the importance of accountability in the life of a man who acted abusively. So, too, did the workers in the criminal justice system with whom they collaborated. As did the advocates at the women's shelter. There was no disagreement on this point. Becoming accountable is key.

Where there were differences was in the strategies and plans, carrots and sticks, for achieving accountability. The STOP program—and those men who were successful within it—stressed the necessity of doing the work necessary for change—acting on one's beliefs, practicing different behavioral techniques, making sure to get to classes, or asking for and offering appropriate support. The actualization of the work meant numerous things, such as participating in therapy to overcome alcohol and/or drug addiction, attending to social interactions to ensure appropriate responses, seeking additional professional help as necessary, and providing support and setting examples for children. Many men firmly believed that while they learned a great deal in the groups, it was only through personal effort that their lives would improve. Motivation was thus a central ingredient (Scott 2004) to becoming accountable. At STOP, the executive director and her staff believed that treating the abusive men as consumers of their services would increase the men's motivation. There was some evidence that this strategy was working.

From the perspective of the men, personal motivation to change was linked with an ongoing or possible relationship with their children. Throughout our interviews, many men discussed the impact of their previous behaviors and choices on their children. Their children's trauma, their children's broken dreams, and the apprehension of their children by social service agencies all appeared to be at the forefront of the men's thinking about accountability.

Notwithstanding the dreams of some men, the reality of those researching abusive men and parenting reveals otherwise.

Edleson and Williams (2007, 11) state that "what little information does exist on the parenting of men who batter reveals that they are likely to parent differently than other fathers." Among other factors, they report that men who batter often use their children as a strategy to affect the children's mother.

Accountability is not a solo sport; it is achieved through a broad community that for an abuser may include the criminal justice system, court orders, prison workers, probation and parole services, and a host of other workers helping to create monitoring structures in his life. Families can and do offer support, encouragement, and (sometimes) forgiveness. But many men have burned the bridges to both their families of origin and the families they helped to create as adults. For those who do not currently have these ties, their burdens are heavier, and their pain becomes evident as they struggle to speak of these lost connections and their hope for renewed healthy family living.

This much-needed hope is another necessary motivator. Hope signals a warrant for action, that action process forming the core of accountability. It helps to provide the *why* for behavior. For men who have acted abusively, hope is not based on a hoped-for thing but rather on a state of affairs, that being the prospect of tomorrow being a better day, leading to the outcome of change. Becoming accountable is very much linked to hope. Without hope for a changed future, why bother? Hopelessness inhibits action. The nurturing of hope as an action process in men who have acted abusively is a key to changing their behavior. It is the carrot dangling in their vision, and they can keep moving forward because of rays of hope that come both from within themselves and from those with whom they interact.

Throughout each man's journey toward changed thinking and behavior, the need for accountability is highlighted. The criminal justice system—through its development of coordinated community response models—has embedded accountability into virtually all policies and procedures. Therapeutic staffers in intervention programs record each man's journey toward accountability as he moves through the required program sessions. Also important is that men in treatment programs hold one another accountable for doing the work necessary to change. For some men, movement along the accountability continuum is minimal. For others, there is no movement. But for those who do find the strength to make the journey, to become accountable for their decisions and actions, men such as Skip, Jake, and Skater, the results indicate evidence of changed thinking and changed behavior.

As we close this chapter, there are still many unanswered questions. Yet we can argue with confidence that the very best chances of changed thinking and changed actions in the life of someone who has been abusive result from a coordinated community response that combines criminal justice responses that are swift and monitored, batterer intervention services for which there is a seamless flow of information, bidirectional accountability, and an enhanced understanding of the men who come to the groups. For men connected to religious leaders and faith communities, by persuasion or relationship, even a tenuous one, an important element in their journey toward accountability involves faith and practices connected to a religious tradition.

CONCLUDING COMMENTS

It would be hard to imagine anyone involved in domestic violence work who did not appreciate the importance of helping those who have been violent accept responsibility for the harm they have done and to become accountable for their future actions. For those who approach the work from a criminal justice perspective—as a judge, probation officer, member of a police force, prison guard, or attorney—the rules of law and the implementation of the policies and procedures of a given jurisdiction are paramount. For those who approach the work with social-science or therapeutic training, engaging abusive men to cooperate or collaborate in the process of change is central. For a community-based effective intervention to occur, the various participants around the collaborative community table must appreciate and welcome the multidisciplinary input and respect the various roles represented. Religious leaders—and others working from a faith-enriched or faith-based perspective—have often been excluded from the response team when violence strikes either families of faith or women connected to church communities.

This chapter on accountability challenges such a notion. It offers a needed corrective to those who regard religion as only part of the problem—rather than part of the solution—to violence in the family context. The language of faith can be harnessed to help a religious man become accountable for his violence and to chart a new way forward, one that leaves behind his controlling and abusive actions. Viewed as part of a community-based response to violence, religious leaders, congregations, faith-based agencies, and faith-enriched workers have the potential to speak the language of hope and of faith but also the language of guilt and remorse, of sin and evil. As such, they may be one part of the puzzle for helping an abusive religious man change his violent ways. Like any responder, a faith-enriched worker or a faith-based agency must be evaluated: the philosophy underpinning the work, the training and competence to provide it, and the connections to the criminal justice system and advocacy groups, including shelters. No agency that responds to those affected by domestic violence should ever work as an island unto itself. It, too, must be accountable, even as it helps those who have been or are abusive to stop their violent and controlling behaviors. The lives of Skip, Jake, and Skater have been highlighted in this chapter to illustrate what accountability looks like in the lives of real men—men who have been abusive, processed by the criminal justice system, and court-ordered to attend a batterer intervention program. We see the role of social and cultural factors, family and individual characteristics, and the impact of intervening agencies such as the criminal justice system, therapeutic and intervention agencies, and religious congregations and spiritual leaders. Their stories offer us clues for understanding the process and the challenge of change.

When we are asked by religious leaders or others in the helping professions whether we see any hope for change in the lives of men who have been controlling and abusive, our response is crafted around notions of accountability. In fact, it is hard to conceive of anything more critical in the life of a batterer than helping him to account for what he has done and putting structures and strategies in place to hold him to continue to account for his actions.

9

Hope or Despair?

Our concluding chapter addresses the question of hope or despair. Is there any evidence that men's journey toward justice and accountability is successful? We challenge the reader to consider this question by reflecting carefully on the lives of the many men we have followed in our study and whose stories are documented in this book.

George Forthwright was in his mid-fifties, stood more than six feet tall, and was intimidating. He had two graduate degrees and a secure, well-paying job as chief financial officer at a small lumber company. George found himself in jail for the first time in his life after the police were called by his teenage daughter during a dispute with his wife over unpaid bills. He had exploded in anger at Grace and *slapped her a couple of times.* Part of the sentencing he received was mandated attendance at a batterer intervention group.

As the story unfolded, this was not George's first exposure to STOP or his first violent outburst. Seven years earlier, he had found his way to the agency on his own. *I have anger issues I've had for a long time, not just with my wife, necessarily, with anyone in general.*

George grew up in Southern California, raised by his mother, maternal grandmother, and two older sisters (one of whom was from an earlier marriage of his mother). His father died when he was five, and following this, his mother had a short failed marriage that was abusive and at least one boyfriend whom George did not like. *So my father figures were typically my coaches, and coaches back in those days were pretty strict, abusive.* At this point in our first interview, his voice trailed off as he was reminded of various men who treated him poorly.

As a young man, George played football, basketball, and baseball, and through his school years, he became close to a coach who introduced him to evangelical Christianity. He went to university on a sports scholarship, and from there, he launched his career in financial management. When the company he worked for suffered during the recession of the late 1990s, he was laid off. George then bought a restaurant business, and from his perspective, this was when his life began its downward slide. He had not taken into account how this new venture would affect his wife and family. A full-time homemaker, Grace was uncomfortable with the business and resentful of what it required of her and George. With two teenagers in high school, three toddlers, and a restaurant, tensions began to build, and financial obligations began to mount. George's drinking increased the arguments with Grace, a nondrinker, whom he described as a *fine Christian.*

When we met George, he was finding it really difficult to get another job—he had interviews and on one occasion was even offered a job, but a background check revealed his conviction, and the job offer was rescinded. He was particularly bitter about the fact that twenty-five years of professional experience seemed to count for nothing when one had recently spent time in jail. *I put my character up against anybody. I'm not a loser, I'm a winner, and I'm very upset about that. But this is the result of government doing. . . . I didn't need to be thrown in jail like I was, you know, I could have easily gone into counseling. . . . Yet they saw fit to separate us and to put us through a lot of unnecessary additional expense.*

George remained committed to his church, where he attended worship services and a weekly group for men. In jail, he connected with the chaplain, with whom he formed a supportive relationship. At STOP, he was financially unable to come to more than one session a week, given his outstanding court costs and regular payments to his probation officer. His bitterness came out again: *So there's a cottage industry that goes along with this, and as a result, people are making money off this program.*

Resentment was a common theme throughout George's interviews. He hinted at being resentful that his wife chose full-time care of the children and the household over paid employment, then resentful that she was uncomfortable throwing herself into the restaurant business, resentful about the consequences of his violence toward her, and resentful of his mother and sisters during his early years.

Yet despite all the bitterness, George spoke very positively about the program and its impact on him. *I've really gotten a lot better. I used to be pretty angry. Up to and even before I had my incident, I was very angry and against everybody in the whole world. I was very unhappy, and, you know, that's gone away in layers, and the things that could easily, would easily, set me off, I am really finding that they don't anymore. That I actually, I can identify them and, you know, say, let go all that. . . . You know, I have had a lot of blessings, and that's been one of them . . . just my ability to have a little more loving heart, be a little more open to people.*

During our last interview with George, we learned that he and his wife had joined the couples group at STOP and that his faith, which was reawakened during his short jail term, remained strong. He credited his church and the facilitators of the batterer intervention program for helping him through the difficult times and influencing him for good. From a criminal justice perspective, he had completed what was required of him, and there had been no further contact with law enforcement. From a therapeutic perspective, George and Grace were working together to make their relationship stronger. They had strong connections with their church and the pastor, and they continued to be involved with their children and their wider family network. There were accountability measures in place and no evidence of any further physically abusive behavior.

But was George a changed man? He was bitter and resentful and took minimal responsibility for the havoc he brought on his family and himself. He tended to blame circumstances and others for his violent outbursts, but he acknowledged that he had a part to play—something that the STOP program helped him to do. He was far more comfortable in the couples group, where there was an emphasis on working together as a couple to solve the problems faced in the family context and beyond.

In this chapter, we think about themes related to hope and despair as they intersect with the lives of individual men, such as George, with whom we had contact over the several years of this research. These themes—hope and despair—also had an impact on the workers who were there to walk alongside them. In George's life, there were certainly elements of hope, but there were also elements of despair. They were commingled. And the same was true of the lives of many of the men we introduced in earlier chapters or highlight in the pages to come.

Over time, hope was sometimes replaced by despair. This seemed true as we listened to the stories the men told us of their lives and circumstances. It also seemed true as we listened to workers in the criminal justice system, the advocacy community, therapeutic agencies, and religious organizations. The story of a particular man could exhibit several reasons for hope concerning changed thinking and changed behavior. As we followed that man every six months for a period of years, we saw the progress, heard his accounts of success and of new ways of acting, and believed, with him, that there was indeed evidence of altered thinking and changed behavior. And then, in another six months, that hope could be dashed. Perhaps he was back in prison, or he was back to drinking to excess and using drugs, or he was speaking in a way that made it clear he had no intention of keeping on doing the work required for change. Hope and despair were themes also facing those who did the work, who needed to motivate themselves and their clients or congregants for the hard work of change and the exacting cost of accountability.

Hope could be found in George's story, as could resilience in the face of an economic downturn or looming fiscal realities. But there was ample room for caution. George never accepted fully his responsibility for the abusive acts he committed, nor did he believe that he needed to change his way of thinking about his wife or their relationship. Like many other men, he was far more comfortable accepting *some* of the responsibility, *some* of the time. These were messages inherent in couples counseling, and George appeared to be willing and even enthusiastic about the progress *they* were making in this context.

After George completed the fifty-two-week groups for overcoming power and control, the facilitators assessed that he would be a good candidate for the couples program. For a protracted period of time, he and his wife kept going to group, and in our interviews with him, we would hear his positive reviews of the experience. While the curriculum did not differ dramatically from that of the batterer intervention groups, the strategy did. In this context, both husband *and* wife learned how each of them contributed to the malaise of family life, and both learned how to alter their thinking and behavior. Attendance was not court-ordered, and the group experience itself was more upbeat. Whether that would be the case without the men first experiencing the STOP groups was hard to say. In some ways, it was not dissimilar from the experience of men coming to STOP after they had attended another group. The comparison was striking. It was certainly to the men's liking. From the men's reports and those of group facilitators, it was clear that the women also enjoyed going to the couples group and benefited from it. But, we repeat, it was not a substitute for the batterer intervention groups; it was a supplement after successful completion of the mandated classes.

Within the domestic violence intervention community, couples groups are regarded by many with a degree of suspicion. Even discussing the topic can be considered somewhat controversial. This is especially true among those who work in advocacy organizations or transition houses, where the primary focus is, and has to be, on ensuring safety for women and their children. From the standpoint of these workers, bringing couples together compromises issues of safety and empowerment for the woman and thwarts the journey toward justice and accountability for the offender. Yet there is an undeniable reality: many women do not want to terminate their relationships, temporarily or forever, with the men who have been abusive toward them.

Couples conflict groups are utilized for couples who are hoping and planning to stay together in relationships. Following separate interviews with an agency therapist related to suitability assessment and safety protocols, the probation or parole officer of the court-adjudicated batterer is consulted and has the final decision of whether any particular couple (where the man has a court order) may participate in a couples group. Part of the pregroup interview process involves careful screening to ensure that no other complicating factors within the relationship are likely to compromise the efficacy of the program. A recent research study by Todahl et al. (2012) details, through narrative analysis, the experiences of couples enrolled in a multi-couple treatment program. No participants in their study reported being harmed as a result of the involvement in the couples group. A bonus for some—those ordered to live apart as a result of a conviction of domestic violence—was their ability to reunite in group and work together toward a common goal, especially a reunification plan.

We turn from the story of George and Grace to that of a young Latino couple, Felipe and Chiara Domez. Felipe and Chiara began to look for help when the DHS took their little girl from their home and placed her in foster care. In the tailspin that followed, Chiara received information about the faith-based program for families involved with domestic violence from her DHS worker. She acted on the referral suggestion right away.

Adamant that they were not guilty of child abuse but clear that they had been involved in domestic violence as a couple, Felipe and Chiara were on a mission to get their child back. They were young, still in their twenties. They were vulnerable, as working-poor Latinos in a region of the United States that was not very diverse ethnically. They were very, very scared.

Simultaneously with their involvement in the intervention program and personal counseling at STOP, Chiara sought help from her pastor for their personal troubles. Felipe accompanied her to pastoral counseling and received church-based information and training related to the family. During our first interview, Felipe talked about the help they were getting. *When we talk about how we want to raise our kid and what our goals are for her, it makes us really have to think about it . . . to look at myself and not want my child to grow up the way I have, or having to go through a dv like me and my wife went through. So I guess that's what it's been doing for me is opening my eyes to myself.*

What was childhood like for Felipe? His father was a serious alcoholic who made extra money as a pool shark. The four children were scared of him, especially when he would come home drunk and with money and then begin to argue with his wife. At school in the rural South, Felipe learned early that *if you aren't one of the bullies, then you are one of the ones getting bullied.* In response, Felipe had a *history of constant fighting.* He even pursued it as a sport. He had an athletic body and *the attitude, I guess, as a fighter.*

Felipe did not choose to tell us that he had already done time in prison until our second interview, although we learned of this earlier from his case file. He had received four DWIs and spent time in the state penitentiary as a result. There he learned some new skills, got his GED, and became certified as a plumber and a dry-waller, work that had kept him employed since his release. He met Chiara one year after his release. She was sitting in the food court of a shopping mall with some of her girlfriends, and he and his buddies walked by a couple of times. He was capti-vated by her looks and her smile. She found him cute. They exchanged cell numbers. Before too long, they were married and had a child.

Like many men in the batterer group, Felipe drank to excess. *You know, alcohol is a downer, it just ruins everybody's life pretty much, so I am not invisible to it. And it's got its hands on me, and obviously, it came back to bite me in the rear end. . . . I am not untouchable.* At this point, Felipe was talking about the incident that caused Chiara to call the police. They had been arguing, Chiara slapped him, and he fought back harder. She wanted their story on file. This prompted law enforcement to contact DHS, which did a home visit and took the child on the suspicion of child abuse. No charges were ever brought. This prompted action on the part of the Domezes. *So me and my wife decided we are going to try to satisfy DHS, enroll ourselves, get help for what happened way back then and just continue this course of bettering ourselves. . . . So I am here mainly to try to get my daughter back. We know nobody hurt our child, but they don't, so they want us to attend these classes.*

At our first interview, Felipe spoke very enthusiastically about gaining insight into his own behavior, his past, and his relationship with his wife. But he remained focused on his primary goal: the return of his little girl to their home. He spoke of change and of God. *I don't think anybody can really change without him. That's my belief . . . you know, do whatever works for you, but definitely look at yourself for a minute 'cause if you don't, then you will never really know who you are.*

As for many people, crisis brought them closer to their spiritual side. *I have always believed in God, but I never believed in it wholeheartedly, and now I believe a little bit more stronger. I have never been a crier, and when this happened with my daugh-ter, I prayed to God, and I just busted out in tears, so I definitely feel there is somebody listening to me.* Felipe's contact with religious matters was very interesting. Raised Catholic by a father who practiced his faith and a mother who was rather indiffer-ent to hers, he found comfort from his Christian background even though he never embraced it fully. *I don't like to play two-faced, but I like the words, I like the words from the Bible, and that is what the pastor preaches to me, so I love to hear it. . . . And the book that we study on the secret to family happiness and everything that's in there, the Bible backs up, so I believe it.*

In groups, Felipe said, the facilitator did *a really good job with trying not to offend people that don't believe in God. She will quote a scripture from the Bible every now and then, but she won't push God on anybody. . . . She has it memorized, and that is about it. I think it's just enough so that it won't scare somebody away that doesn't believe or make them mad or upset.* He thought for a moment and then concluded: *If you can have backup, it might as well be God.*

We talked about the various things Felipe had learned in counseling or in group. *I have been through different classes. I have a pretty big tool belt now. And it's getting bigger, so I have quite a bit of tools now that strengthens me inside. I have to tell you, now I feel pretty much untouchable as far as the stresses from life.*

From Felipe's point of view, the intervention helped him remain violence-free through the very stressful period of their daughter in foster care. He joked: *I am telling you, if my brothers, or someone, has a problem, I could probably repair it for them right there on the phone. . . . I have learned a lot, and with the stress that me and my wife are going through right now, I think without the tools that I have, I would have crumbled a long time ago. . . . I got plenty of tools on me right now.*

His easygoing manner, his smile and good looks, and his self-confidence all worked in Felipe's favor. Yet it was this very confidence, bordering on a boastful attitude, that gave some cause for concern. Felipe admitted that he could get angry pretty easily, *one of those short fuses,* as he called it. *But with all the help I am getting and all the people in my life, all of a sudden, I think I am able to address things easier and keep it calm instead of boiling. I am warm.*

With an army of people attempting to give them support, Felipe and Chiara were staying the course. Felipe was in a drug rehabilitation program, he was in a batterer intervention group, they were in parenting class, both were having individual psychotherapy, Chiara met regularly with the DHS worker, and they both met weekly with their pastor.

The supervised visitation took place at church; one of the elders of the congregation brought the Domezes' daughter from the foster family to them at church. After the service, the elder returned her to the foster home. They saw her on two other occasions each week, bringing the total number of hours of weekly visitation to four. We asked Felipe to help us understand the goal of the elder in helping them. *He's a really supportive guy as far as us getting the help we need. . . . He wants us to get as much as we can so that we can be the happy family that the book is talking about.* The elder came to the Domezes' home each week and met with the facilitator of the parenting program and with the social worker at DHS. He was certainly committed to a community response to Felipe's and Chiara's problems.

Six months later, we interviewed Felipe again. The child had been returned to her mother on the condition that she and Felipe lived apart. They complied with this DHS order, but it was causing financial strain. He was allowed to see their daughter in supervised contexts but not at Chiara's place of residence. Felipe was living with his parents. It simply was not possible for them financially to have two separate living spaces. Yet they needed to fulfill the DHS no-contact order between Felipe and his child. So his parents let him move back home. *I love my parents, I love my parents. They are great. They are very supportive of everything I do, everything I am going through. They know how far I have came since I have been to prison, and they know how many successes that I have had since I have been out, so I am on a constant uprise, even though some people try to bring me down.*

When we saw Felipe six months after that, he was still attending classes, still working at the same job, and hoping that soon the family would be reunited. Using the AA mantra of "one day at a time," Felipe noted that if he stayed the course and fulfilled all the obligations, it would happen, he just needed to be patient. *One day at a time is that tool belt that I am adding together.*

One year later (more than two years since we had first interviewed him), we learned that Felipe had gone back to drinking and that Chiara had taken their child and gone back to Texas. The couple were seeking a divorce.

The story of Felipe and Chiara was a reminder of how critical the expanded time framework of our study proved to be. At the one-year point, there was reason for optimism, and that was even true at eighteen months. But by two years, the fiscal realities, coupled with the complications of living apart from each other and for

Felipe living back with his parents, had taken their toll. Apparently, the cost was too great, and the wait was too long. An army of professional workers—representing the criminal justice system, child welfare, therapeutic agencies, advocacy and religious organizations—were attempting to provide support, emotional encouragement, accountability, justice, and assistance in charting the way forward. It would be hard to imagine how any man or any couple could have been offered more supportive services than Chiara and Felipe were. Yet it was not enough to keep them together as a family unit after two years. But it was successful, very successful, in keeping all the family members safe. While there was no indication that the police were ever called again by Chiara within the time limits of our research, the pull of excessive drinking and his submission to its pull were not matched by the support and hope for change offered to Felipe by a variety of programs and people. The story offers a reality check. Even an extremely well-planned and carefully executed coordinated community response is no guarantee that change will occur in the life of a man who has been abusive, even if for some sustained period of time, he is cooperating with the plan and working toward that change in his thinking and in his behavior. Without a doubt, cases such as Felipe's, filled with so much hope at the beginning and exhibiting such a fine level of coordination among criminal justice, therapeutic, family, and religious networks, cause a fairly sizable number of people—linked both professionally and personally to the case—some level of despair in their aftermath. They try to focus on the safety of the mothers and children, but there is no denying a level of hopelessness for workers that sets in regarding men who batter and who are unwilling or unable to give up their excessive drinking or drug abuse. We take up that theme of worker's hopes and dreams later in this chapter.

The longitudinal nature of our study was critical in that it allowed us to look at changes during a significant period of time in both the thinking and the behavior of men who had acted abusively. At times, we were pleased to hear of real progress in men's lives; other times, we were discouraged as we began to hear the phrases we had heard in earlier interviews, *she makes me do it* or *she pushes my buttons*. Like those who worked with the men who acted abusively, we were rooting for change in men's beliefs and behavior, but we were grounded in a reality that reveals that change does not take root very often or for very long.

In the two cases we have described in this chapter so far—George and Felipe—there was a strong link to their community of faith and to that community's leadership. Both men were very positive about the involvement of the clergy in their lives and the good that resulted from these pastoral efforts. In George's case, this appeared to have been reinforced, or reestablished, during his brief time in jail, but for Felipe, the connection of his wife to their church was a source of enormous support for her and the family unit. In fact, the leadership played a remarkable role in offering the Domezes comfort, accountability, instruction, empathy, and very practical support. For both men, religious engagement was not new, although for George, it took on a new significance during his brief incarceration. Jailhouse religion, as it is sometimes known, was discussed more fully in chapter 6, but one of our key findings should be repeated here. Men were reconnecting in jail with a faith and religious behavior that predated their offenses. It was something to which they were returning or that was being reawakened in their lives. At their low point or time of need, they saw religion and religious practices as important again.

We turn from these two families and their positive assessment of a religious leader's intervention to a man who was extremely religious and was never satisfied with the help of his pastor or church family in dealing with the troubles he faced in the family context.

When we first met Rob Mellor he had switched careers and changed marriage partners. He was in his late thirties and had just recently begun to work for the public school system, teaching science to students in junior high and high school. This followed many years of work in sales, where he was required to travel across the country and be away from home. Currently, Rob lived under the same roof as his seven children in a blended family situation. In the aftermath of a violent incident, Rob sought assistance at STOP because his wife, Brenda, was unwilling to allow him to return to the family home unless he agreed to go to classes. *Personally, I think that she is the abusive one. . . . I wanted her to get into the program, but she was unwilling, and at the time, she wouldn't let me back in the house unless I agreed to go through this, so it was, like, "OK, fine. I will do anything to get back into the house."*

Brenda was a physiotherapist and had learned of STOP through her church friends, on what Rob refers to as the *Christian grapevine.* When we first met Rob, he had been attending classes for about nine weeks. He wanted us to know that he was not like other men in the program, those who had been court-ordered to come. No judge told him to come. He didn't have a parole officer. He was at STOP because his wife was unreasonable. She called 911. She wouldn't come for help. She was the problem. And to add injury to misery, she had been talking about their marriage, telling things *that weren't exactly true,* to friends and others in the congregation.

You might say Rob endured the group meetings at STOP. *No big deal, I guess. . . . I always think I am better than everybody else in the sense that, OK, Joseph can handle seven years in prison for something he didn't do, I can handle this ninety days. If Peter can be crucified upside-down, OK, I can do this.* These were references to biblical characters, and he drew strength from these stories. Joseph, in the Old Testament, was sold into slavery by his brothers and later served a prison sentence as the result of a malicious accusation. Peter was one of Jesus's twelve disciples, put to death in Rome.

Sprinkled through much of our conversation in the first interview was Rob's appropriation of religious language and scriptural references. His desire was to intimidate through his self-professed exemplary knowledge of things biblical. Coming from an Assemblies of God religious tradition, Rob felt fully empowered as a layperson to interpret the Bible without any guidance from those with ordination credentials. His father was a minister, and he grew up in a household that was strict and orderly, the kind of household he wished he could impose on his family. He lamented that this was not the case.

Before the 911 call and seeking help at STOP, the Mellors sought pastoral counsel. But Rob was not pleased with the advice they were given. He wanted the pastor to invoke church discipline and make their marital woes public—in front of the entire congregation. When the pastor would not comply with Rob's plan, they left the church. Rob exuded black-and-white thinking; for him, there were no shades of gray. He believed that as a couple, he and his wife were *unequally yoked,* a reference to the biblical notion that they did not share the same worldview or theological beliefs. *For instance, my wife calling the police, or getting the courts involved, or filing for divorce . . . it's so not part of what a Christian should ever consider even thinking about.*

Rob's use of the Bible to intimidate others was not successful at STOP. The facilitators were able to speak that language, too. This dismantled his power. Yet he criticized them for not being religious enough. But he credits the program and its staff for their humility, something of which he appeared to have a short supply. At one point, Rob thought about being a pastor himself, but he left Bible college after eighteen months of instruction, because he *didn't agree with the theology.*

Frequent disagreements and excessive rigidity featured prominently in Rob's life. The incident that brought him into contact with STOP involved a fight over his laptop, a struggle to ensure that his wife did not have access to it. He overpowered her, took the laptop, and left to go to a friend's house. She called the police, and he was stopped by them on the way home, and charged. Those charges were later dropped *based on insufficient evidence.*

Two years later, we were able to interview Rob again. By his own account, he had completed as many classes as he needed to in order to satisfy his wife. *I got here, went through, you know, was obedient, and did what I was told as far as what my wife wanted me to do. She loosened the reins to the point that I didn't have to come back. . . . I started a new strategy and was able to more or less bring things to an even keel, make it more peaceful at the house, and not set off triggers or make her go get really angry and upset. So since then, we have also done quite a bit of marriage counseling, and that's been off and on.* We asked Rob to comment on whether he feels the intervention had been successful. *Hmm, it's been with very little success, because only one person here has identified what she's doing as perhaps the problem, as opposed to just looking at me as the problem. So it goes on, we go to session after session, and I sometimes wonder if we are getting anyplace.*

Rob and Brenda were still together, and there were no further 911 calls. Rob left his teaching career after one year and returned to a sales job, for which he traveled across the United States. They continued to attend church, but Rob was not very satisfied with either the fellowship or the pastoral care they received. *There is no support there, but yes, I go.* The one thing that Rob mentioned as helpful was the couples class that he and Brenda attended together. From a criminal justice perspective, Rob and Brenda were living within the confines of the law. From a therapeutic standpoint, they were receiving help to increase the quality of their marriage and parenting. They had a network of people, including their church family, who offered some level of support.

Was Rob a changed man? There was little evidence that he had taken any ownership of his controlling behavior or his abusive acts. He appeared to be committed to the marriage, reinforced by a strong belief that divorce was wrong. They had a financially secure existence. He believed he had learned some strategies at STOP that enabled him to bring peace to the household. From a cynical perspective, he had learned what he was able to do within the confines and context of the law. For some men, that might give greater license for physically violent behavior. For Rob, however, it appeared to control how far he was willing to go. He did not want another 911 call. He wanted to live at home with his family. He appeared committed to doing what it took to make sure that his place in the home was secure.

The three stories we have just presented all involve men who had—at least initially—a strong desire to continue to be in relationships with the women they had abused. All of them were involved with the STOP program for an extended period of time, and although Rob did not graduate from the STOP program, he transferred, as it were, to the couples class and continued there. Only the young

Felipe seemed to take full responsibility for his violence, but his resolve was no match for his propensity to drink to excess. All three felt that their communities of faith were an important part of their lives, and all sought respite and care there, even if their expectations did not meet with the reality of what assistance was provided.

As a point of contrast, we now turn to two men who were lower-functioning as adults, with very difficult life circumstances. Their stories unfolded in slightly different ways.

DOMESTIC VIOLENCE COUPLED WITH
VERY DIFFICULT LIFE EXPERIENCES

Stu Wright, whose story we highlight in chapter 5, was a man with very modest dreams. At forty-two, he bought an old RV, and he and his girlfriend of four years were in the process of *cleaning it up*. He had a dog to which he was really attached. He credited his girlfriend, who was ten years younger, with helping him to stop drinking. For relaxation and fun, Stu and Betsy went *treasure hunting* at Goodwill or St. Vincent de Paul. *We shop and spend money. That's what we like to do.*

Stu was rough around the edges, without the ability to sugarcoat any aspect of himself. In our first interview, he described his new girlfriend as *a young wild thing* and their relationship as *we are going to make something of it. I am just not going to throw her out, it's not like that.* Early on, Stu recognized that he was *part of the problem.* He talked about the tools he had learned in group and how he was attempting to use those tools at home. *There are some tools that you can take home. I totally have used some of that . . . they have worked to my advantage, I think. . . . I am not perfect. . . . I don't want to go home and argue. The last thing I want to do is argue and fight, but it happens, a lot, it seems like, it sucks.*

By the fifth time we interviewed Stu, he had graduated from the program and still wanted to keep attending. He said that STOP taught him a lot about himself and his girlfriend. In fact, he was so convinced that the program worked that he gave out STOP cards at work. Stu was hoping that he could continue with the couples classes. He tried to explain to Betsy some of the things he learned in the STOP program, but this seemed difficult for him. *I can't really explain it to her. They can explain better. . . . We both have baggage. She has her own struggles.* Unlike some of the other men whose stories we recount earlier in this chapter, Stu just wanted to get by—have a roof over his head, stay out of prison, eat, stop fighting, and go to Goodwill on Saturdays. Whether he and Betsy would ever qualify to go to couples group, we were not able to assess; our research program ended, and we did not see Stu again.

Another man who was just getting by was Sam Greencorn. In his mid-twenties, he was still living at home with his brother and their parents in an old farmhouse the family owned in the country. His only means of support apart from his parents were food stamps that he received from the government. For a short while, he worked stocking shelves, but with a tremor in his hands, he found even this work a bit challenging. Sam had two preschool-age children who lived with his wife in an apartment she shared with her brother.

Sam did not have a problem with drugs or alcohol. He was painfully shy, and for most of his life, he was without friends or a support network beyond his immediate family. He mentioned that his wife was *actually my first true friend, I'd like to say, because everybody else always wanted something, and she's the first person who didn't ask me for anything.* This was his first and only serious relationship with a woman. They started talking to each other in a high school class, and very shortly thereafter, he moved out of his parents' house to be with her, helping her to escape from a very abusive mother. They spent the early part of their relationship camping out. His parents would not let her live at their house, and her mother's apartment was not an option.

Sam acknowledged his abusive behavior and credited the program for helping him to learn how to act differently. He went to group faithfully and completed it on schedule. We asked if there were reasons for this, and he credited the judge. *He didn't really say a lot to me, because I didn't really talk to him. He just asked me, guilty or innocent? And I said guilty. Then he said I had to go to county mental health for evaluation. I went back to the judge, and I remember he was giving someone else a lecture, sort of, because they weren't going to their groups like they were supposed to. I went, nah, I don't want to get a lecture, so I went to the group.*

When we saw Sam six months later, one year from when he began the program, he had graduated from STOP, was still living with his parents, was still looking for a job, and was still in contact with his wife and children, the oldest of whom had just started school. He noted that his parents said they could see a big change in his behavior, as evidenced by how well he played with his children when they were over for a visit. After a further six months, we learned that Sam had separated from his wife and sought legal assistance to maintain contact with his children, something for which he was very proud. *So I told her I wanted to separate, and she was, like, "Fine." She took the kids, and I had to get a lawyer to get the kids back. But I did everything legally this time.*

For Sam, this was evidence that STOP had an impact on him. He used the system to ensure that his rights were met, rather than resorting to his fists. He fulfilled all the orders of the court and continued to have contact with his children. He dreamed of one day having a job so that he could be off food stamps and live independently from his parents. From a therapeutic point of view, he attended classes even after he graduated from the program in an attempt to learn more skills related to parenting.

UNDERSTANDING HOPE

Men such as Stu and Sam had modest dreams. In cases like these, hope could be measured in very small indices. They wanted to stay out of trouble with the law and to live independent lives. Stu wanted to improve his relationship with Betsy, and Sam wanted to help his children overcome the difficulties he believed they would face at school. Both had accepted a degree of responsibility for the violence they had meted out, and both wanted never to go down that path again.

For men such as Rob and George, resentment and rigidity appeared to play key roles in their lives in the aftermath of abuse. Neither accepted full responsibility for the events surrounding the abuse, but both were willing to work together with their partners to carve out a brighter future. They were financially secure. They were living with their children. They had a broad context of friends and family who would walk alongside them.

Felipe appeared to have made a decision that what STOP required of him was just too much work the long run. As we followed him for several years, it seemed he was doing the work required to change, but then he gave up and went back to living dangerously, and his wife and daughter sought respite in a different part of the country.

These five stories, and the countless others like them described in these pages, help to put a real face on partners who abuse, the struggles and successes in the aftermath of their violence, and the road toward justice, accountability, and group intervention that follows.

At this point, we need to stop and take stock of some of the things we have learned through the lives of men such as George, Rob, Stu, Sam, and Felipe, whom we have interviewed on so many occasions during a period of many years. First, the misuse of drugs and alcohol thwart the healing journey toward changed thinking and changed behavior related to abuse. There is overwhelming evidence in our data that a central ingredient in stopping the violence and thinking and acting differently about abuse revolves around gaining control over one's abuse of substances. Second, some degree of hope is necessary for everyone involved in the journey of men toward changed thinking and behavior. This is as true for the men themselves as it is for the workers who walk alongside them. The work of change is grueling for the individuals and taxing for the workers. Hope for change is what motivates them to keep doing what is required. When men lose hope, they stop doing the work. When workers lose hope, they have less impact and are less likely to treat the men with respect and kindness. It becomes a vicious cycle. To be sure, the distance between hope and despair is short, especially for many of the men. It is often related to one unfavorable decision, especially one that affects their relationships with their children. We pick up threads related to the men's view of hope and the workers' view of hope later in this chapter.

Third, accepting responsibility for one's actions and the pain one has created is a major step on the road to justice, healing, and wholeness in the aftermath of domestic violence. Sometimes the development of empathy and the acceptance of responsibility grow together. But without an understanding of and a willingness to accept responsibility for one's abusive behavior, there is very little hope for changed thinking or a different way of acting in the future.

Fourth, men who are still married to the women they have violated appear to bring with them to the STOP program additional support for their changed thinking and changed behavior. It is as if the women themselves have great faith in the program, and that confidence seems to be a bonus for the men. For many years, we have argued, based on our research, that women of faith are very optimistic that if only their batterers would get help, they would be willing and able to change, their marriages would be restored, and peace would return to their homes. As a result, religious women in particular believe that abusive men—their abusive husbands—can change. For sure, this is a reflection, in part, of a religious worldview that considers conversion, repentance, and forgiveness as hallmarks of the walk of faith. Thus, highly committed religious women might speak more enthusiastically of the STOP program and support their partners more fully when they are engaged in the groups there.

Fifth, the coordinated community response to the abusive behavior is a very important piece of the puzzle involving accountability and change. There is a lot of evidence at STOP of a coordinated effort to respond to all family members—including the offenders—in the aftermath of violence at home. This comes to us from many sources, including the men themselves, the facilitators at the groups, the executive director of the agency, other therapeutic staff, personnel in the criminal justice system, including probation and parole, and the judiciary. We also heard this from victim advocates and some clergy members in the local area.

Finally, and perhaps more controversially, there is an added element that personal faith and involvement with a faith community bring to the coordinated community table and the work with men who have acted abusively. The language of faith is replete with notions of second chances, forgiveness, hope, love, insight, repentance, and renewal. More conservative or evangelical traditions talk about conversion directly, a turning away from the old life and embracing a new life fashioned in likeness to God. The language of the spirit, including the traditions, the words, the sacred texts, the music, and the fellowship of others of like faith, might offer someone who has acted abusively that extra incentive, or strength, to see tomorrow as a new day and a determination to make a new start. Certainly, twelve-step programs have harnessed this language in the hope of change.

MEN'S UNDERSTANDING OF THE JOURNEY TOWARD HOPE AND CHANGE

Here we attempt to understand from the men's point of view what the future might hold for them and what they hope will transpire in the next years of their lives. We asked all of the men we interviewed to talk about their hopes and dreams. This seemed to be relatively easy for them to do. Here are a few of the most common responses. We differentiate between broader issues of hope and the precise responses men gave to our inquiries about what they hoped to be able to tell us in six months' time, responses we have noted throughout earlier sections of the book.

1. Hope Is a Life without Dependence on Alcohol

A large number of men linked their personal notions of hope with a desire to live without abusing alcohol. For many men in our research, alcohol use and abuse were commingled with their violence. Curbing their drinking, then, was a necessary step on the road to their changed thinking and altered behavior. It was necessary, but alone, of course, it was not sufficient. With the passing of time, few men blamed their abusive behavior solely on their addictions. Those who were prone to do so and had resisted intervention attempts to help them think otherwise left the program. For the others, the STOP program helped them to take some responsibility for the violence they had meted out. And as they attempted to understand their controlling and abusive behavior, they were faced with a personal conclusion that it was linked to their desire to drink excessively and, for a smaller number, the continued pull to live (or want to live) dangerously, as they had done for a time in the past.

An example is Skip, whose story we feature in chapter 8. He reflected on how important it was now for him to get away from people who were drinking and doing drugs. He noted how his elderly father had wanted him to get away from that life for so many years. And he said with a tone of sadness, *I mean, I knew I was alcoholic for the longest time, but did I do anything? No!* He talked about his five years of sobriety and how he and his new wife (of eighteen months) encouraged each other in staying away from alcohol. While he did not blame the abuse on his alcoholism, he believed that it provided a context where other things spiraled out of control. And control was what he learned he was trying to achieve with his abuse.

When we ponder the story of Danny, highlighted in chapter 4, we see that it was his propensity to hang out with and derive enjoyment from the drinking and doping crowd—especially women who were drunk and high—that paved the way for his entrance right back into prison. His friend, whom we also interviewed, also made this observation. And it was this friend who told us on our fifth interview with him that Danny had been sent back to prison for an alcohol-related offense.

The link between alcohol and abuse is contested territory in the domestic violence literature. This is understandable. Many abusers believe that their violence is a result of excessive drinking. Many women who are victims of that violence excuse the abusive behavior and believe that it is a result of an addiction or periodic drunkenness on the part of the abusive partners. These are excuses and justifications, often used by both the men who are violent and the women who suffer from the violence. Domestic violence advocates have lobbied consistently for society to recognize that abuse in the family is about controlling, harmful behavior, not simply an example of what happens when men drink too much. Many studies look at the relationship between alcohol and violence. The majority of men in batterer intervention programs have alcohol problems (Stuart 2005). Usually, men with substance abuse problems have been required to seek treatment as a condition of probation or parole, and others have participated in self-help groups such as Alcoholics Anonymous or Narcotics Anonymous past the bounds of their court mandates. Often, the narratives of these men include attributions of responsibility to their addictions. Rather than denying their violence, they believe that their violent behavior stems from their substance abuse (Cartier, Farabee, and Prendergast 2006). Research has shown, however, that this link is complex and that while the alcohol and drugs serve as disinhibitors to normative behavior, they do not cause the violence (Willson et al. 2000; Rogers et al. 2003; Galvani 2004). Regardless of the fact that abusive behavior cannot be accounted for simply by looking at consumption of alcohol (many alcoholics are not abusive, and many abusive men do not drink to excess), nevertheless, for the men in our study, hope was definitely related to reduced alcohol consumption. It was a necessary part of their overall plan for changed thinking and changed behavior. And it was extremely difficult for them to change, both in the short run and over the longer haul.

2. Hope Comes from God Alone

Some of the men who (re)connected with God in prison continued to find great strength in believing that hope for their future was linked to the supernatural. Jay Primer is one such man. A heroin addict for many years, he turned his life around after several spiritual experiences.

He believed that *God gives me hope, and I know. I mean, I have got scriptures written on cardboard taped all over my house. I go to Goodwill and buy nothing but Christian reading material. . . . When I was in jail once, I started reading the Bible. I couldn't read anything else. . . . Christ has moved in my life and I guess made me see things from a whole different perspective.*

Jay was willing and able to learn many of the STOP lessons. *You know, putting your hands on someone is wrong. . . . I still have problems with it myself, dealing with people, not my wife, but dealing with people out there, you know, because of the way I was raised. Someone shoves you, you shove back. . . . I believe God sent me to this DHS place to test me.*

Jay's personal assessment was that many, if not most, of the experiences of life could be reduced to spiritual lessons, spiritual struggles, and spiritual successes. This was how Jay saw his struggles with the DHS and the workers there with whom he negotiated for a second chance with his child. It was a trial that he needed to endure. He clung to the notion of a God who tested one's strength and offered one more as one built up one's character. He did not see God as someone who punished him but rather as a God who called him to endure suffering and trials. And Jay believed that if he endured, he would win the prize of reunification with his child, a theme we develop more fully below. Hope, then, from this perspective, is a gift. One receives it. And it comes from God alone.

Other men drew great strength and hope from the upbeat message and music of large community-centered churches. The men could be rather anonymous at services, caught up in the excitement of the music and the friendliness of the crowd, and then choose to join, or not join, many of the special-interest groups held during the weekly routine of church life. Several men we interviewed went to a men-only Bible study; others were involved in supportive groups for people who were struggling with various emotional or relationship problems (such as divorce care groups).

3. Hope Is Linked to a Belief That One Will Reconnect with One's Children

Many, if not most, of the men with children, especially if those children were still young, wanted to reestablish connections. Sometimes the men talked as if the reconnected family unit would look like the Brady Bunch, a happy-go-lucky group of kids with two parents who seek one adventure after another, with sufficient money to own a large house and employ a housekeeper. Some men appeared to be in denial about how average families function; others clung to a notion based more on fantasy than reality. For some men whose family ties were severed as a result of time in prison, there was an often-held misguided belief that they would be able to establish warm, close relationships with their children at a time of the men's own choosing. In other words, the children were just waiting for them to call or send a present or take them on a holiday. For men who were under no-contact orders, for a matter of months or even a year, their notions were more realistic, grounded in more extensive parenting experiences from their past.

But there was no doubt that for many men, it was the hope of being reconnected with their children that kept them coming to group and doing the hard work required of them there. It was only when they believed they had jumped through the hurdles and yet still not won the prize of reconnection that despair began to set in, something we discuss later in this chapter.

One example of hope for reconnection with his children is an African American man we called Jake and whose story we discuss in chapters 2 and 7. Jake spoke about his time in prison as a *blessing in disguise*. From his perspective, it was *what I really needed at the time*. When we asked what he hoped for or dreamed of, he only talked about his son and his son's brother, a child he had raised since that boy was an infant. Six months later, when we spoke to Jake again, he was one step closer to getting his son back. He was having unsupervised visits three times a week. But the news on the other boy was not so hopeful. The court had decided that since Jake was a felon, despite the fact that the boy's biological father was in prison and had not been involved in raising him, Jake was not a good choice. So the boys would be split up, but there was a further court date yet to be scheduled to determine when that would occur. In the meantime, Jake had been in contact with the boy's father in prison, and together they had petitioned the court to keep the two children together. Hope kept Jake going, hope that they could all be reunited as a family of four. For the moment, though, it was just Jake and the children's mother. They both worked and attended church, and he had passed several courses recently at community college. In the meantime, he was waiting. Six months later, Jake did not respond to our request for a follow-up interview.

For many men in our research, the desire to reconnect with their children was strong motivation to come and do the work. They hoped for the day, they worked toward the day, but when it became clear that their dream was not going to be actualized in the way they thought, they gave up.

4. One Can Hope to Make a Difference in Someone's Life

Ben Chamois really used the language of hope in his conversations with us. *I have a lot of hope. I do, I do. I don't know how, but I do know that I will make a difference, somehow, even if it's one person, then I will be satisfied. Although my girlfriend seems to think the way everybody else does. I am never satisfied with just a little. I always want more and more and more. So I have a lot of hope. I see things happening daily that—good things—more good things than I do bad, and it's never been like that for me. I have feelings now that are genuine, you know. It's really hard to explain. I have a zest for life and a thirst, and when I wake up in the morning, I know it's just going to be a beautiful day, and it's going to be what I make of it. And hope, I think everybody's gotta have hope. I know I need hope.*

Several men talked about helping others with their anger, disappointments, or failed relationships. Stu gave out STOP cards at work. Several men talked about dispensing advice to their brothers or friends based on what they learned at STOP. Some mentioned that they now had a big tool kit for advice giving and that they felt motivated to share with others some of the strategies they believed were helping them to change. Greg White kept coming to group because he believed he could help other men. However, the vast majority of those we interviewed were interested primarily in their own lives and reconnecting with their children.

Wanting to make a difference in someone else's life is connected, no doubt, to the spiritual quest of many of the men. This was a message they must have heard from the chaplain in prison and in their communities of faith since their release. Living for God and living in community are twin pillars of congregational life. So it is not surprising that the men learned that if they could make a difference in even one person's life, they would have given back in small measure the second chance God had given them.

5. Hope Is Having Travel Restrictions Lifted

Several men in our study longed for the day when they could travel beyond the borders of the state in which they now lived and to which they were restricted until the conditions of their court orders were met. In his last interview with us, seventy-three-year-old Clifford White spoke enthusiastically of the special travel pass his parole officer was going to provide so that he could visit a cousin in another state. *I had to go pick up my travel permit from my parole lady, and I says, "Yeah, my cousin wants me to meet a lady, and this lady want to meet me; I don't know why." And she says, "Now, remember your domestic violence." I told her, I says, "Don't worry, I never want to go through this hell again!" . . . I like ladies, I always have. And I can't wait to maybe have a real emotional relationship . . . to be able to treat a lady real nice, go to dinner, maybe hold hands or something like that. I am looking forward to trying that again. If it don't work, it don't work.*

A younger man, Craig Winslow, wanted to move to a warmer climate with his new girlfriend. This was something we heard from several men—the desire to relocate to other states or other parts of the country when they were in new relationships. All of them were waiting for permission from the courts. As a result of their violence, their movements were curtailed. And they were anxious to regain the right to travel where and when they wished. Of course, for those who were felons, their travel restrictions might be permanent in some cases.

Freedom of movement, of course, had a deeper reality for those who had been incarcerated. In prison, their daily life was ordered, and they longed to be in control of what they did, what they ate, when they showered, and with whom they slept. For the men in our study, hope was also related to freedom to travel. They longed for the day when they would no longer have to ask permission of a parole or probation officer to go on a holiday.

The workers at STOP were givers of hope. So, too, are many faith leaders who know and speak the language of hope. At a 2013 conference on abuse at Gordon Conwell Theological Seminary in Massachusetts, it was very interesting to hear the president of the seminary, Dennis Hollinger, speak out against any form of domestic violence—including physical, emotional, verbal, and spiritual abuse—using both scriptures and contemporary social statistics. Other staff, such as the dean of students, a professor of psychology, and a professor of pastoral counseling, offered specific remarks revealing the degree to which they took seriously protocols and best practices concerning abuse. Seminary staff have to be concerned about two issues simultaneously: the training of their ministerial students as it relates to knowledge of abuse and best practices for responding, and support for any student faced with abuse in his or her present life circumstances or from the past. Thus, in this context specifically, knowledge and supportive services must go hand-in-hand. As we have learned from our research in the past twenty-five years, most religious leaders feel they lack the training to deal with issues of domestic violence. In fact, in one of our studies, involving more than seven hundred ministers, less than 10 percent felt well equipped to offer assistance to families affected by abuse, perpetrators and victims alike.

WHEN HOPE DISAPPEARS

The flip side of hope is despair. Many of the men we met in the course of our inter-views had experienced that flip side. They had lived it in the days after the abusive incident that brought them into contact with the criminal justice system. Some experienced it while incarcerated. For others, it came with the realization that what they were holding on to—their goal or dream—was not working out. What happens when hope fades or evaporates?

We begin to think about the concept of despair, or the disappearance of hope, through the eyes of one of the men we interviewed, Luke Rivers. Luke was a very personable young man in his mid-twenties. When we first met him, he was wearing a white baseball cap turned backward, brand-name clothing, and a big smile as he answered our questions. It appeared that Luke worked out at the gym and that he might use his size and strength to intimidate others. Yet he spoke with a soft voice, and his diction was punctuated by phrases such as *Hey, dude.*

Since his teen years, Luke had been a hustler. He said he was easily angered. He smiled when he thought someone agreed with him. What Luke did when someone didn't agree with him was recorded in the pages of his case file, the many charges and arrests and time behind bars. He was involved in the lives of many women. His outgo-ing personality and good looks, coupled with his manipulative, confident style, ensured that there were, and continued to be, an ample supply of girlfriends and acquaintances.

When we met Luke for the second time, he had two things on his mind: to get back into his daughter's life and to become part of the carpenters trade union. Those were dreams that he anticipated would become reality in the very near future.

By the time of our third interview with Luke, he had completed the fifty-two-week program at STOP and had been accepted as an apprentice in the union. He talked positively about a new girlfriend and the fact that he was approaching the end of his probation. From his point of view, things seemed very hopeful for his future, except for his current living arrangements. Those were not to his liking. Luke was back again with his parents, and his mother is was on crystal meth. His face became downcast, and he lowered his eyes. *My mother is on drugs really bad, but she's really bad, there's not much I can do about it at this point.*

Our interview focused on things that had changed in the way Luke saw and lived his own life. He smiled once again but admitted: *Honestly, I don't know if I use all the steps. I don't get mad at things anymore. They call me Smiley at work. Even in the pouring rain, I am the only guy out there smiling. I love my life. I like that, and they like me a lot. . . . Next time, I will tell you that I have a house.*

Luke had regular contact with his daughter, but he could not see her as much as he would like. And things there were rocky at times, especially since he had a new girlfriend. *Now that my daughter's mother found out that I have another girl, she won't let me take her. I almost exploded. I was crying. The old me would just have started breaking everything.*

The intervention at the STOP program attempted to assist men like Luke to see themselves and the world in new ways and to give them the tools that would help them behave differently from how they had in the past. This was what the executive director of STOP would say every so often: "We are helping you to walk the world in a different way."

We talked about ways in which Luke could reach out to others for assistance now that he had completed the STOP program. He went to the parenting classes, and his friends told him to hang in there. He had no pastor or priest. His mother was an addict. He tried to keep his personal life quiet at work. He was worried about what would happen when he went to court regarding joint custody of his daughter. *I want my daughter . . . [but] I am an offender. . . . I look pretty bad when I go to court, my history. Right now, it kinda feels like it's really hopeless. Honest, what I am hoping to do is not to touch my vacation pay, save it up, hoping that fifteen thousand dollars will help me to buy [back] my daughter.*

One year later, we saw Luke again. He had broken up with the girlfriend and tried to reunite with the mother of his daughter. She, too, had a severe crystal meth problem, and Luke finally decided to report her to the police as an unfit mother. He was still fighting for custody of his daughter, and the state had awarded foster care to Luke's mother, also, as we have seen, a drug addict. He was back in school at community college, and there seemed to be a constant supply of young women who wished to help him succeed at his studies. He was on the referral list for the union, but a downturn in the economy meant that there was not much work. He had no further problems with the police after he began the program at STOP several years ago. In a few more days, he would no longer need to check in with his probation officer and would be free to travel outside the state.

Was Luke a changed man? This was a very difficult question to answer. For sure, he was less violent than he used to be. But there was little evidence that he had altered his thinking or taken responsibility to walk the world in a different way. He was frustrated by the system and frustrated with his own mother and the mother of his child. He seemed to have many younger women to date, but his relationships did not last very long. We learned of several different girlfriends during the period of our research. He was beginning to understand that his criminal history would determine the custody arrangements for his child, and that made him feel a deep sense of despair. Just before we finalized our last interview with Luke, he turned to us and said, *Do you guys let one little simple assault charge control your life?* He had no idea that his question held, in large measure, the gravity of his own despair. This comment revealed how thwarted he was on the journey to accountability, justice, and wholeness. He failed to understand fully the longer-term consequences of the many charges for which he was convicted, and he was only beginning to see that the life of reckless abandon to which he was once committed still cast a long shadow over those he loved. Despite his efforts to retrain, save money, and give up living dangerously himself, he could not wriggle free of the web of drug abuse of his own mother or the mother of his child. As hope faded, Luke was sliding to despair. We could see it in his countenance and hear it in his words.

WHEN HOPE IS REGAINED

In direct contrast with Luke is another young man, Skater. We discuss Skater's story in chapter 8 on accountability. To recap briefly, he started doing crystal meth when he was thirteen, and by his mid-twenties, he had several children, all of whom had been in relative foster care (cared for by a family member, in this case the paternal grandmother) for prolonged periods of time. He had been in jail as a result of an

assault on his father, and since his teen years, he had been on some form of probation. When we first interviewed Skater, he refused to maintain eye contact, sniffled
constantly, and presented as someone unable to look after himself, let alone his
family. Two years later, he was a changed man. He was working for a fast-food restaurant, as was his wife, had two of his small children returned to their care, and
had fulfilled all the mandates of his criminal justice probation, including the STOP
program. He had changed dramatically. He said he was *living one day at a time and
praying to God that I get another day.*

What were some of the markers of his success? First and foremost, he was drug-
and alcohol-free at this point in time. *It was a domestic disturbance between me and my
dad, and alcohol was involved and different things, and to turn around and see it today,
he's my biggest supporter and everything else. So when I got my one year in NA, I got a
coin, and I gave it to him and told him he earned this as much as I did for putting up with
my crap all these years. I think he was going to cry, so he walked away. My dad is still one
of those kind of guys, you know, ex-military, so he kind of gave me a hug and walked away.*
Both Skater and his wife still attended NA and AA meetings occasionally, although
work and other commitments made it harder to go on a regular basis.

Second, we saw the level of family support for his change. It is important to
remember that it was his mother who had foster custody of two of his children. And
it was his father whom he assaulted, a crime for which Skater was sent to prison.
During his prison term and afterward while he was unemployed, it was his wife's job
at a fast-food restaurant that kept the family financially afloat.

Third, he credited the STOP program for helping him to see that there was a better way and offering him the skills and encouragement to start doing the work that
was required. Clearly, the content of the program was important—the STOP technique and other skills—but the process of coming seemed to have had the greatest
impact. *I think my biggest thing was being able to walk in here . . . it's uncomfortable
because it's all your fault, you're a bad person, you're this, and when I walked in here,
there was a very good sense of religion in here. There was a very good sense of, you know,
you can be healed, and you can be fixed from this, and it was open arms.*

How did those open arms manifest themselves? *They weren't . . . man haters, and
there are a lot of them out there, because my significant other went to another program
before she came over here, and she couldn't take it. She just couldn't take it. The whole
time, they were telling her I wouldn't change. . . . It's not dark and gloomy to walk into this
place, you know, you are not took back into the bottom recesses of society because of what
you done. And the feeling is just beautiful, you know.*

Fourth, there was broader community support. For Skater, this came in the
form of a faith community whose members believed that his life was important to
God and to them. One year after we met Skater, he was volunteering at the local
church, running one of the cameras for the televised service. He was transported
to and from the worship center by the foster parents of one of his children (not
by his mother, who was looking after two of his other children). Skater and his
wife felt supported by the congregation in their efforts to change their lives and
circumstances.

We asked Skater to name some of the hardest things for him at that point in his
life. *I still have some of the inner communication things that I need to work on. . . . It's
more people than situations. There have been people along the way, I count backwards
and STOP and do everything that I can. The training that I got here helped me to carry*

on, to deal with situations better. I go, OK, time to go back to the folders from STOP. Not much in the training I got here that hasn't gone with me.

When we interviewed Skater midway through the STOP program, he talked about being an *emotional wreck and a mess.* Of his wife, he said: *She wants, you know, she wants to take her own time on fixing herself, but she wants me to fix myself in a hurry.* Then he reflected: *We have had a lot of wreckage, and I have had a lot of wreckage in my past, and past deaths of friends and everything else, you know. I used drugs to cover up . . . Lost a couple of other daughters to the state. And I found myself, what was it, a couple of months ago, just waking up in the middle of the night and just started crying because it finally, you know, hit me, what all went on. . . . I didn't have to get loaded to hide it. . . . Every once in a while, there is a screaming and hollering fight. . . . This is not going to get us anywhere. . . . She is still attending STOP right now. . . . I realized what I learned with my tools and the things I have learned about, you know, communication, here and everything else. . . . I start realizing maybe she hasn't learned that here yet, and I just leave it alone and let her come around to it on her own.*

By his own count, he was continuing to do the work, to practice the things he learned in group, and now to let his wife practice the things she was learning in her group and what they have learned together in couples class and in the parenting class. There was a lot of learning to do, many personal and relationship issues to be resolved, and Skater was right, it couldn't all happen at once. For more than two years, as we followed his case, he continued the progression. From where he started to where he presented now represented tremendous growth.

The other hard struggle involved finances. *Money, definitely still. The past is still catching up with me. I have outstanding debts from the past because of the way I lived my life. Just trying to cap the past, to get things paid up and paid off.*

We asked where he would like to be in six months' time. *That I have quit smoking. I have goals this year. That I have been able to get my driver's license back and I could do some more with my family. That I can get my GED. Got to get that before my daughters beat me! I also want to go to college and am looking at my situation. This is not the life I really want. I would like to get a job where I am really comfortable, a good job, and have a roof over my head and something in the bank rather than living pay check to pay check. I want to know that the bills are paid and that there is a little in the account. We will see what God and life has to offer.*

There was reason for hope in the case of Skater. There was progress, real change. Considering where he started in his early days of coming to STOP (and our first interview) and where he was at the point of our last contact with him showed substantial change. To be sure, Skater and his wife had enormous challenges ahead of them, and they would both need to keep on doing the work, learning to parent, and upgrading their skills if they were to reach Skater's goal of a little money in the bank after the bills had been paid.

Only through some degree of hope can men and their families achieve markers of success. For Skater, small successes led to renewed hope. He had support both within his family and within the broader faith community of which he was a part. Some practical issues needed to change in order for hope to be sustained. In Skater's case, it was the return of two of his children and his employment at a fast-food restaurant that helped him to keep on doing the work. He was being rewarded in his journey to change his thinking and his behavior. But Skater's dreams were realistic and modest. He understood that his propensity to drink alcohol and use illegal drugs needed constant vigilance and that parenting was something he needed to treat as a priority in his life. With the support of his parents, his partner, and others in the community, he was staying on the road, one step at a time.

PROGRAM COMPLETION AS A MARKER OF SUCCESS

Successful completion of the fifty-two-week batterer intervention program was one important element, or marker, of success. It was necessary but certainly not sufficient. Of course, it was one of the ways the executive directors and group facilitators at STOP measured their impact. After we had been conducting fieldwork at STOP for several years, we were asked to present some of our findings to the men (and separately to the staff) in a group context. This was a great opportunity for us and an enormous challenge. To be honest, we were rather intimidated at the prospect, particularly knowing that men we had interviewed would be present and perhaps prepared to argue with us about our observations, our conclusions, or the broader subject of domestic violence. But something quite amazing happened. We learned afterward from the agency director that our research presentation was helpful to the men. It had a therapeutic impact for good, for those who were part of our research program and for new men who had begun the program long after we started data collection. As a result, on our next (and last) visit to STOP, we were asked to prepare another presentation for the men and for the staff. Several features of those two presentations are blended into the conclusions we offer below.

We explained to the men then, and we still believe now, that a large part of the good news of STOP was that large numbers of men kept coming week after week until they had clocked in fifty-two weeks. Looking at their stories, revealed to us through their interviews, we made seven observations about why some men were willing to engage with the program until they graduated from it, whether they were ordered to do so by a judge, an agency, or a partner, or they came voluntarily week after week.

1. Connecting with the Dynamics and Strategy of STOP

Some men were willing to connect with the dynamics of the STOP program very quickly. They liked the strategy of how things worked there. For others, it took a bit longer; of course, some were never able, or willing, to make that connection, and they stopped coming to STOP regardless of the consequences of their noncompliance. But being able to see a connection between one's life and the program's offerings was essential to continued attendance. This was as true for men mandated to attend as it was for those who were there without any court order. Skip's story, told in chapter 8, offers an excellent example of seeing the value of the program early and making a decision to do what it took to follow through and graduate from it. Some of the men, like Skip, had attended a few sessions at another program in town. In some ways, these men were the biggest proponents of what STOP had to offer. They had experienced the competition and were very grateful for the attitudes of the STOP facilitators and the way the program was delivered. They were consumers, and they appreciated the level of service they received, even though they wished they had never needed the program in the first place.

2. Connecting with Professionals in the Community Supportive of STOP

When we presented some of our research findings to the men at STOP, we used the story of Casiano, highlighted in chapter 2, as evidence of this point. He was one of several men we interviewed who had a rather large group of people offering him support in his efforts to keep drug- and alcohol- and violence-free and to chart a more positive course for his own life and those of his wife and children. He became a father at eighteen; his girlfriend had grown up with a drug-addicted mother and as a result had been part of the DHS system since she was very young. But the bright spot in his life was a bivocational pastor who was a carpenter, who hired him and gave him the first big break he had ever had, and who then held him accountable as he journeyed toward change, respectability, and financial solvency.

Where hope seemed to be most evident—not only in words spoken by the men but also in demonstrated behavior that was able to stand the test of time during our research project—was where there was a significant group of professionals and laypeople in the community who were supportive of the STOP program in the life of a man who was, or had been, enrolled in it. In chapter 8, we refer to this as part of the process of accountability. But for many men, it extended beyond those who might be what has been traditionally understood as "accountability partners." In Casiano's case, the bivocational minister was also his employer. Accountability for his behavior had economic and emotional rewards, and it ensured, in a way, the continued support of the congregation and the various practical ways its members helped Casiano and his partner maintain contact with their children.

3. Connecting with the Content of the Program

Not all men connected fully with the content of the program, but almost all of those we interviewed connected with some of it. Those who did not came to only a handful of classes. Kevin Grant, and a few others like him, resented it so much that he was not willing even to consider that anything might be useful or helpful within it. These men understood that there were consequences imposed by the criminal justice system if they did not follow through on court-ordered group attendance. But they were willing to pay the price of their noncompliance, being sent back to jail or to road crew.

The vast majority found help from some of the curriculum, especially the STOP technique and the idea of building a tool kit of strategies to enhance one's emotional well-being. Drew Barley, from chapter 2, connected fully and quickly with the content of the program and its goals. He spoke at length during one of our interviews of how the program taught him different ways of handling a situation. He was amazed at the concept that a negative situation could be turned into positive outcomes. This idea alone, he said, made a huge difference in how he saw things in his life, at work and at home.

4. Connecting with the Other Men in the Program

It is no secret that we can sometimes see in someone else's life what we cannot see— or refuse to see—in our own. That is why a group experience can be so powerful.

Men gained insight and support, not to mention knowledge, through listening to the life stories of others. We heard many of the men talk about first observing in others patterns that were occurring in their own lives. As they watched other men, especially those there for the first few times, they could reflect back on their own early days of group attendance. As they listened to the struggles of men as they checked in, they sometimes felt proud of how much they had added to their own tool belts, how they had learned to STOP before acting, and how they had used other techniques picked up through the weekly sessions. Class attendance was making a difference, and this was the proof.

One poignant example of this was Buddy, featured in chapter 7. When he first came to group, he did not believe he was an abusive person. Over time, he realized he had been. As he became more comfortable with the group setting and listened to the stories of the other men, he could see that things in his own life were not as dismal as he thought. Buddy came with the goal to reunite with his wife, but over time, he obtained something that he did not expect: personal growth. The changes he observed in himself were valuable enough to keep him coming to group, to keep him engaged and listening to the other men and to the content of the curriculum, and to keep him paying (as he did not have any insurance). He was not able to reunite with his wife, but he learned to accept her lack of interest in a continued relationship. As a result, he took a first step in gaining strength to become a new man in the aftermath of violent, controlling behavior and to establish some new goals for his future.

5. Connecting the Dots: Seeing the Impact of STOP Strategies

Pete, whose story we feature in chapters 3 and 4, is an excellent example of a man who began to connect the dots and see the impact in his own life of harnessing some of the strategies he was learning at STOP. He had been addicted to drugs and alcohol since his teen years, and he had been violent with many girlfriends. In fact, he had been arrested more than twenty times, and the incident for which he was ordered to attend STOP involved abuse of his elderly mother. While Pete was a long way from being a completely changed man, he was learning to begin to take responsibility for his actions and to see that taking some responsibility for his behavior meant that he could become a responsible adult. This gave him hope for the future, even as it reinforced his AA and NA mantra of "one day at a time."

Pete was also learning empathy for those he had treated so badly. This was a slow process. It was hard for him to see any point of view other than his own. He had spent his life blaming someone else—or something else, such as an addiction—for the harm he had inflicted on others. Many of the men talked about the hard work they were doing to assume responsibility for their actions—and then the rewards that sometimes followed. For Pete, it meant that his sisters were now agreeing to meet with him and celebrate part of the Christmas holiday together. This was an enormous first step in trying to make amends for the harm he had caused them and their (now-deceased) mother.

6. Connecting the Dots: Family Members
Who Support the Journey toward Change

There is little doubt that most men in the program had family members who felt that they should change their behavior. But some men had family members who were willing to walk alongside them as they changed and support them through the very difficult early days after their initial involvement with the criminal justice system. Bobby's story, featured in chapter 4, and the way his journey developed in the aftermath of the 911 call provide an example of this. By his own admission, Bobby had a problem with his temper, and both he and his wife had a drinking problem. His parents were very supportive of his efforts to change his life, and he lived with them in the aftermath of his short jail term, since the restraining order would not allow him to return home.

After his wife filed for divorce, Bobby was back in the house he'd owned before the marriage. His parents, siblings, and children all rallied around him, and his employer turned a blind eye to his few days of incarceration and missed employment. He accepted with gratefulness the generosity of his extended network, and he appeared to draw strength from their belief that he could do the work necessary to change his thinking and his behavior. We followed his story for several years and as he began a new relationship with a woman he met over the Internet. There were no further incidents with the police, and he completed the fifty-two-week program at STOP.

7. Connecting the Dots: Celebrating Small
Successes and Small Changes

Reinforcement for doing the hard work of changing how one thinks and acts is critical. This was very true for Luke, whose story is told earlier in this chapter. But many men offered us recent stories of how they would have responded to disappointment or frustration in the past and how they actually did respond to disappointment or frustration in the days or weeks before an interview. Luke said, *The old me would have just started breaking everything.* Felipe referred to how he would get very angry and then he said, *Now I am just warm.*

ELEMENTS THAT ARE NOT MARKERS OF SUCCESS

Some men did not complete the program. Others never really connected with the curriculum, the facilitators, or the other men. Still others gave up or stopped coming. We learned through our interviews, supplemented by direct observation of groups, that there were many factors associated with these situations. We discuss five of these below.

1. Refusal to Surrender the Belief That They Are the Real Victims

Many of the men in classes at STOP or in our research interviews talked at some point about being a victim of abuse themselves. They believed that they were the *real* victims, despite the fact that the criminal justice system or other people saw them as perpetrators. The men who spoke this way might have been referring to their child-hood homes and the abusive acts that occurred there. Less often, they were refer-ring to acts of bullying against them at school or on the streets. Even less often, they were referring to their wives or girlfriends and the altercations that eventually led to arrest and subsequent involvement with the law, the courts, and probation services. If this statement about personal victimization occurred while a man was in group, the facilitator listened to what he had to say, empathized appropriately, and then made it clear that he had also engaged in acts that had victimized others. In our interviews, a few men used the language of victimization to refer to some of their childhood expe-riences, but most did not, even if it might have been appropriate to do so.

But there were a couple of men who were adamant that they were the *real*, and only, victims in the circumstances and the altercations that brought them into con-tact with justice services and that it was completely unreasonable for them to be placed in a context where they needed to learn to curb and control their own abusive behavior. Kevin is one example. He dominated a focus group discussing his own victimization. The other men did not buy his story, and they grew rather agitated as the focus group progressed. In our personal interview, he manipulated the ques-tions to talk only about how he was being treated poorly by just about everyone, including neighbors, past and current girlfriends and their children, the police, and other workers in the criminal justice system.

Craig Winslow, featured in chapter 5, is another example. He was the young man who broke the phone as his girlfriend was making a 911 call and then had an altera-tion with the police after they arrived on the scene, which resulted in the need for immediate surgery for his own broken jaw. Craig blamed everyone but himself for his injuries and the pain he had caused so many, including his girlfriend and their daughter.

Both of these men were unwilling to see that they had caused harm to others. Their refusal to challenge that belief meant that they received very little from the STOP program's content, the facilitators, or the group experience. In six months, one man was back in prison, but we were able to follow the other over several inter-views. He received little from the group and eventually gave up hope that the separa-tion from his daughter would end.

2. Refusal to See Overlapping Features between One's Own Life and That of Others in Group

As we discuss in chapter 7, the group experience was very powerful for most of the men who attended STOP. They were exposed to the facilitators and the curriculum and learned to think and do things in a different way. But the interaction with the other men was very powerful, too. They could see parts of themselves in others: the controlling behavior, the excuses, the justification, the resentment, the conse-quences, and eventually the resolve to change and the progress. But there were some for whom this did not happen. The most obvious example of the failure to connect with others in group was Rob Mellor, whose story appears earlier in this chapter. Rob was the most explicitly religious man we interviewed, and he was convinced that he was unlike the other men in group, most of whom had been ordered to attend by the courts.

We met other men who had either been mandated by their wives to come to the STOP program or came voluntarily, but we did not meet anyone else like Rob who exhibited such disgust at being grouped with the other men at STOP. Whereas other nonmandated men could see how their own behavior could have led them into contact with the criminal justice system, Rob was unwilling to make any connections between his abusive acts and the acts of the other men. He continued to attend for a short period of time but then transferred within the agency to another program with which he was better able to connect.

3. Resignation to Circumstances and Relationships Being Beyond Any Capacity to Change

Surprisingly, most of the men we interviewed embraced the notion of change in their own lives and the lives of their family members. For them, the past did not dictate the future, although it obviously cast a rather long shadow. But a few men embraced pessimism. We interviewed Dwight on many occasions. In chapter 4, we highlight several features of his story. He drew strength and confidence from his ability to work in the woods and make money, and it appeared that he spent those resources as fast as, or faster than, he made them. He was also creative, and he sometimes spoke of his desire to do artistic work from his home to support himself, although given his proclivity to live wildly, this seemed rather unlikely. In time, Dwight became convinced that there was little hope for his long-term relationship with his girlfriend, that his work, which had once brought in money and meaning, was evaporating before his eyes as a result of a downturn in the economy, that the house he had built with his own talent and sweat might be taken from under his feet by the banks, and that his life was on an accelerated downward spiral.

Dwight continued to live dangerously, drinking and drugging off and on with his girlfriend, who embraced those choices herself. They would live apart when one or the other of them had a court-initiated no-contact order; each had called the police on several occasions, sometime for violence, sometimes for the removal of items when a no-contact order had been served. They had been together a long time but shared no children.

The last time we interviewed Dwight, he seemed resigned to the fact that for him, and for them, change would never come. Understood from this vantage point, tomorrow would bring more of the same, and despite his work ethic and his talents, the past had caught up with him and the future held no promise. He had given up; he had not stopped coming to group, but he did so on an irregular basis, once or twice a month.

4. Resistance to the Hard Work to Keep Clean, Sober and Abuse-Free

There was a lot of hard work ahead for most of the men if they were going to change the course of their lives and keep clean, sober, and abuse-free. As we saw above in the section on factors that kept them going, there must be positive reinforcement for their hard work, celebration of successes, and evidence of change. Those who wanted to be reunited with their children, return home to a partner after a no-contact order, or complete schooling and obtain a job that would enable them to live independent lives had markers that let them assess their own progress and see all the hard work as worth the effort. But this was not the case for everyone at the beginning and certainly not as time progressed.

Some men referred to this as *banging my head against a wall*, while others talked of depression or the burdens they were carrying. After many classes at STOP, some men assessed their own prospects and felt that the road to change was unlikely or too steep to climb. As one man said, *I'm not Buddha; I'm not Jesus, either. If somebody slaps me, I am going to slap them back, probably. Usually, they don't slap me, because I am a mean-looking guy.... It's against my religion to kill myself, but frankly, I just can't deal with that stuff anymore.*

5. Resentment toward Life and Frustration with the Program

Finally, some men felt that they were dealt a bad hand of cards. This was how they assessed their lives and their chances for success. Some felt that the deck was stacked against them and that others were out to get them. Yet others claimed that if it had not been for their father, or mother, or girlfriend, or the bully in elementary school, or the bully at work, things would have turned out differently. Such resentment toward life affected how these men saw the program. From this vantage point, nothing was going to work for them. They clung to the notion, why bother? Harboring this type of attitude, they were certainly unwilling to do the hard work of change. In fact, they were not even willing to come to group week after week. As a result, they quit rather early on and faced the consequences.

We turn now from a focus on the men and the STOP program to consider the broader therapeutic, and then criminal justice, context of which it is a part. We explore our interviews with agency staff and workers in other agencies (such as probation and parole services, the courts, and women's shelters). We also interject some of our observations from the courts.

THE THERAPEUTIC CONTEXT

During the five-year period in which we visited the STOP agency, we never once heard a facilitator, therapist, or staff member utter the word *despair*. They talked frequently about challenges, setbacks, obstacles, disappointments, hurt, and pain. They were not deluded. Their eyes were fixed firmly on the task at hand, and, like a race horse, they kept their eyes on the goal, in this case the goal of helping men take responsibility for their actions. They urged them to stop completely the violence, along with their excuses or justifications for it; to learn skills that would enable them to walk the world in a different way; to be better parents and partners; and to navigate successfully all the demands of the criminal justice system in the aftermath of their abusive acts.

While they did not talk about despair or hopelessness, the STOP workers often used the word *hope*. In a sense, they were hope givers, although they never referred to themselves in this way. But it is clear that the facilitators and the therapists individually and the agency we call STOP collectively were beacons of light shining in the darkness, attempting to help men navigate the rough waters of their violent acts to the safety of the harbor of peace. Of course, everyone—without exception—condemned the violence that had been meted out and refused to accept excuses or explanations for it. But they did this with kindness, respect, and deep care for the men. It needs to be said that staff members were motivated in large measure by their goal to provide peace and safety in homes, for women and for children, but in the men's groups, the primary consumers were the men. As we mention in chapter 8, this differentiated them, to some degree, from others who offered batterer intervention services. The difference, though, was in process, not goals or content.

Clearly, the agency and its workers were harnessing the language of change and imbuing it with religious or spiritual significance. A seasoned therapist who had been at STOP from its very early days put it this way: "What I often try to see happen is for them to have internal motivation to change, where a man says he wants to change, even if she never comes back. Many men will say, 'My behavior is bad' and 'I love my wife.' But I like to see men who say, 'I want to be a good human being.'"

In the minds of the therapists at STOP and in the work they did with the men and with their families, hope was always very close to the surface. It was what helped keep everyone motivated, the notion that tomorrow was a new day and that with a new day came the possibility of a new start. While many of the men talked about the AA mantra of "one day at a time," staff members did not. Rather, they talked about hope and change; sometimes they talked of healing or wholeness. It was interesting that talk of hope was usually commingled with change. In other words, it was hope in action. It was careful, but not careless, compassion. Hope and accountability went hand-in-hand.

Therapists were very quick to differentiate their notion of hope, grounded in skepticism and the reality of recidivism and setbacks, from the blind hope that they believed some pastors and other religious leaders, or even the men themselves, employed. A seasoned therapist at STOP spoke directly about the role of faith: "Faith makes a huge amount of difference." From his vantage point, the buy-in to the work of change was stronger, there was a greater commitment to the relationship, and there was a support structure beyond the agency and the workers that the men and the women, perhaps even the children, could call on if needed.

At STOP, couples counseling was not frowned on as it was in many sectors of the domestic violence community. However, like so many other things at STOP, there was a very rational and reasoned approach to understanding when and how couples counseling could be incorporated into the broader services offered to families in crisis, including those impacted by abuse. From the perspective of the same therapist, "As long as the partners feel safe and there is no damage going on, or anything that is harmful. . . . Oftentimes, though, it requires individual progress before they can get to do that."

We asked how a therapist could assess whether it was safe. "The safety piece comes through my evaluation. I won't take a couple on without an evaluation of the client and speaking to the female first individually before we begin. Then I bounce it off the executive director. Some situations I have been in, we have had two therapists, a male and a female, but sometimes in those situations, therapy can become tense. Then we stop."

What was not mentioned in this interview but happened frequently at the agency was that a man might graduate from the batterer intervention classes at the end of fifty-two completed weeks, and based on his interest and whether the executive director felt there was a "good fit," he and his partner might be invited to participate in a couples class. During our time of fieldwork, this program for couples was just developing, but the classes were becoming more popular each year, and many of the men referred to them in their follow-up interviews with us. By the last year of our research, there was a regular couples class. Without exception, the men preselected for them found them helpful. But, as we have shown, not all of the men who attended these classes remained in their relationships over the longer period of time that our research followed them.

There was a lot of talk at staff meetings and in the hallways related to the notion of caring for oneself, self-care for the therapist. Regularly, workers asked one another about time off, noted what they were eating or not eating, and reinforced time for holidays and other family events. It was clearly an environment where it was safe to say that one took time off to care for oneself and one's family. As we note in an earlier chapter, even though the executive director was an extremely busy woman with a very hectic and demanding schedule, she took frequent holidays and work-related respite times during which she read the literature and renewed her commitment to the work and strategies to perform it well. She modeled family living and spoke frequently of grandchildren; several times when we were at the agency, a teenage grandchild would be helping out in the office, cleaning or filing or photocopying something for the staff. The executive director's husband, a retired, very success-ful businessman, was often seen around the agency fixing computers or assessing repairs before a carpenter or electrician would be called.

All of this further reinforced the notion that the work at STOP was taken very seriously by everyone employed there and everyone who interned or volunteered at the agency. Since the work was so demanding, it held true that therapists and staff had to care for themselves—their bodies, minds, and emotions—to enable them to do what was required of them. A tired, worn-out group facilitator might get angry at a man. A tired, emotionally drained receptionist might fail to be friendly. The execu-tive director expected all staff members to be "on their game," noting that the men would test them and try their patience on a regular basis.

THE CRIMINAL JUSTICE CONTEXT

One of the judges in the area joked with us that he hoped not to see the men again—that was his measure of his own success and the success of the men he saw in his courtroom.

We spoke briefly with him about treatment and criminal justice intervention in the lives of men who act abusively. "I can't even say whether domestic violence treatment in general is effective, except we have very little recidivism." Is there any hope, we asked? "I like to think there is. I have seen cases where it seems to have worked. . . . The problem from where I sit is that I can only see so much—what's in my courtroom and what the windows show me. I spend a lot of time talking with people to try to find as much as possible from the defendant and from the victim—try to find out what is going on. On darker days, I think no. But on brighter days, I think yes, this guy has really started to see things properly."

Changing the behavior and the thinking of those who act abusively is an enormous undertaking. From a criminal justice perspective, recidivism is one of the key indices of change: do the men end up back in the system or not? Since many of the men cannot (by court order) or do not (because they are restricted by finances or responsibilities) leave the area, the window on the world of the abusive man offered by this judge is a critical piece of evidence in the longer-term value of the work of an agency such as STOP. Judges in other jurisdictions where we conducted interviews were slightly less optimistic, but they, too, were very supportive of any community-coordinated effort to reduce men's violence. One female judge mentioned that she often would say a few words personally to each man, with her court microphone turned off, that encouraged them to engage with the therapeutic process so that when they appeared before her next time, she would be able to see if there was progress. "I want them to think they are special and that I care. . . . Now I say whatever God means to you, do not neglect the spiritual dimension of your life. The power to accept help appears to come from the spiritual inside you." In a maternal tone, she told us she would admonish them to behave much as a grandmother might with a grandson who had found himself drinking too much and was about to go out on a Saturday night.

It would be easy to dismiss the impact of these personal statements, but we learned from the men we interviewed that what judges said to them played in their minds, over and over again. We note earlier in this chapter that the "lecture" the judge gave one man had an impact on another man: "I did not want to get that lecture, so I went to group consistently."

Probation and parole officers tell another part of the story—for it is their job to follow the cases assigned to them over the period of time deemed necessary by the court through the judge's orders. Some researchers believe that probation officers are the most critical link between the criminal justice system and batterer interventions (Healey, Smith, and O'Sullivan 1998).

In the United States, clients actually pay for their own parole and probation services as a standard term of probation. For example, in one Western state, clients on probation were required to pay what were called "supervision fees" of thirty-five dollars per month, plus fines, restitution, or other fees ordered by the court. Not surprisingly, many of the men resented this. For victims who were still in relationships with the men who meted out violence to them, it was one more personal cost of their abuse, one more hand dipping into the family's shared fiscal pie.

A female parole officer said, "I have had professional experience with that—with a minister who was supporting the male and telling him, 'Well, just get a handle on it,' . . . and that was a mess, because it took like a year before we finally were able to get him to enroll in a domestic violence counseling program, and he had to go back to court two or three times, and every time, he got his minister in there to support him, and he was a rough one. He ended up getting revoked."

The conversation turned back to the STOP program. All of the parole officers agreed that STOP was respected by the community. "They are recognized, they are at the table with community leaders," said an experienced parole officer. "They do a wonderful job of promoting themselves to the social service world, and they get a tremendous amount of respect in the law enforcement community," said another.

And she continued: "People out there see people making change in their lives. They encounter them under horrible circumstances, and a few years later, they encounter them when they are just working their butts off—they can't believe it's the same person."

In some ways, probation and parole staff members are offered the longitudinal view. They see the men time after time over an extended period. They see them when things are going well, and they see the dirty urine tests and the breaches of no-contact orders or other conditions of probation, and they are in contact with the intervention services and staff at agencies such as STOP. If they had a more reasonable caseload, they could follow up more effectively and more efficiently. But there is a level of coordination—even if it could be smoother and swifter—between the offices housing probation and the executive director of STOP. Finding the right words to talk about collaborative ventures and to name domestic violence in a way that encompasses all workers responding to those impacted by it is also critical (Nason-Clark and Holtmann 2013).

THE ROLE OF RELIGION

Hope is a central theme of the Christian tradition. Religious leaders, such as priests and pastors, are schooled in the language of hope and the belief that second chances are gifts from God. This is true for both Catholics and Protestants. The language of hope permeates Christendom. However, for those ministers who serve in an evangelical or conservative Protestant tradition, there is the additional belief in the process of conversion, which enables a believer to change course, to turn around, to redirect a sinful life toward a life dedicated to God and holy, and wholesome, purposes.

Many men who had a history of abusive behavior of which they were now ashamed and for which they felt remorse found comfort in the notion of a new start, supported by God and their religious traditions. Understood in this context, God became part of their new plan for living. Religious actions, such as going to church, offered encouragement to keep on doing the work of change. In other words, all of their hard work mattered; ultimately, it was important even to God.

Thus, there was the supportive network of a faith community, broadly speaking, and, for some men, the direct support of a pastor or a priest. However, for many, there was a commingling between their religious journeys and their experiences of family life. Religion mattered because it was important to people they cared for, their own families. And even though they had failed their families in the past, for some of the men, their renewed religious resolve met with strong support in their families.

CONCLUDING COMMENTS

Over five years ago, we set out to tell the story of men who batter and to offer snapshots of their journeys through childhood, early intimacy, living dangerously, being caught in the act, being charged and sentenced, doing time, being monitored, checking in and doing the work of a batterer intervention program, becoming accountable for the harm they had done, and learning to embrace changed attitudes and changed behavior. Throughout the book, we have recounted the stories of the men over time. We have told the stories of those who walked alongside them. We have observed courtrooms and group meetings. We have conducted hundreds of interviews and analyzed scores of case files. As a result, we have our own story to tell—of puzzlement, disappointment, encouragement, surprise, and challenge. Theirs is a story of human vulnerability and the long and arduous journey toward justice, accountability, and change. Ours is a story of two social scientists intent on trying to hear the voices of men who batter and to assess whether there is any reason to hold out hope that they will change. In the closing pages, we offer three research observations, followed by six concluding thoughts.

Research Observations

1. We did not set out to assess the impact of the work of STOP. Our goal was to understand men who batter and their journey toward justice, accountability, and change in the aftermath of domestic violence. But in the process of hearing their stories and following their lives for many years, we learned a good deal about STOP, its program and staff, and its coordination with the broader domestic violence community. We found no evidence that its work in the area of domestic violence was compromised by its faith-based nature but ample evidence that it offered a unique though sometimes controversial approach to men who had caused substantial harm to those they claimed to love.

2. We were prompted to begin the studies described in this book as a result of previous research that focused on the voices of religious victims/ survivors of domestic violence, the role of religious leaders and advocates in responding to them, and the broader issue of the interface between domestic violence and religion. When violence strikes religious families, some of the dynamics in its aftermath are influenced by the "faith factor." To isolate but one of these, many religious women cling to a notion that if only their batterers could find help, things would change in their own lives and within the family. We wanted to assess whether there was any research evidence to support this belief. Some men change a lot; most do not. Almost all of the men change some of their attitudes and some of their behaviors.

3. We are convinced that a coordinated community response to domestic violence is consistent with the published literature, small-scale and larger research initiatives to study the abuser and the abused, and professional best practices to respond in its aftermath. However, beyond the principles undergirding such an approach, its strategy must be community-specific, rooted in a particular place and time. It depends on the resources, people, problems, culture, and history of a given geographical location. We have attempted to document how this worked in one region of the United States at one point in time. While we believe that there are important principles at stake that can be replicated in other jurisdictions, any notion of a cookie-cutter approach must be resisted as naive and prone to failure.

Concluding Thoughts

1. *Harnessing hope.* We are convinced beyond a shadow of a doubt that hope—that vapor or mist that is impossible to define except by its presence and impact—is a central ingredient on the journey toward justice, accountability, healing, and wholeness for those whose lives have been impacted by domestic violence. While many talk of the need for survivors of domestic violence to have hope for themselves and their children, this is also true for those who have perpetrated the violence. As men who batter experience the impact of their abusive acts, through the full extent of the law and the services available to them in community-based contexts, they need to have hope that change is possible in their own lives and in the lives of those they have harmed. How hope is operationalized, the practices that encompass it, and the journey toward its fulfillment are part of the story of the coordinated community response to domestic violence. Hope means that tomorrow can be different—who one is today does not dictate who one is tomorrow. Additionally, hope offers workers in the criminal justice system, along with those who work in advocacy or intervention services, a light—however dim at times—at the end of the tunnel, revealing that their work matters and makes a difference. Harnessing hope involves creating supportive structures and encouraging individual agency. It is very hard work.

2. *Measuring success.* Measuring program success in the area of domestic violence is not as straightforward as one might think. For sure, the ultimate goal of any domestic violence program is the elimination of all forms of abusive behavior and the provision of best practices by all agencies and individuals responding to the needs of those whose lives have been impacted by it, abused and abusers alike. When success is measured in small indices that involve changed thinking and changed behavior in the lives of men who batter, there is overwhelming evidence that the STOP program is successful. When success is measured as accepting full responsibility for one's violent past and holding oneself accountable (and submitting to the accountability of others) for living a life free of violent, controlling behavior, the results are less encouraging.

3. *Identifying vulnerabilities.* Most of the men who participated in the batterer intervention program we call STOP grew up in circumstances that might be categorized as placing them at increased risk for later difficulties in life. The majority had at least one parent who abused alcohol or drugs. The majority regarded their childhoods as difficult or troubled, reporting that they faced a combination of economic, social, and emotional challenges. Many witnessed or experienced violence as children. As teens, most of the men drank to excess. It was not uncommon for the men to become involved with the criminal justice system before their eighteenth birthdays.

4. *Celebrating resiliency.* In the face of such enormous personal and family obstacles, the stories of the men we have studied reveal many examples of resiliency. Obtaining and keeping employment form one such area to highlight. The majority of the men we followed in the STOP program

were able to secure jobs in tight economic times, even after they spent time in prison. As children, many men had to learn early how to negotiate their way in the absence of stable parental figures and living arrangements that could be counted on to provide the necessities of food, shelter, and protection. Building on notions of resiliency, the STOP program and, at times, its criminal justice and advocacy partners were vigilant in attempting to see, and then celebrate, any efforts or experiences of the men to make progress in their attempts at changed attitudes and behavior in the aftermath of domestic violence.

5. *Choosing religious resources.* Not unlike the case with the American population at large, religion was found to be a resource for many men who participated in the STOP program. It offered them a language that could embody and embrace their "new start," practices that helped make sense of their daily routines and trials, and strength to face major life challenges. Many men reconnected with their religious traditions, practices, rituals, and sense of religious belonging while in prison. Most often, they spoke of this spiritual awakening or realignment as "connecting with God." Sometimes it was experienced as part of the prison system's faith-based community activities, through attendance at Bible studies, or in worship services. Often, it was experienced in solitude, as they thought about their lives in context, their dashed dreams, their addictions, their losses, and their failures. Many men became connected, or reconnected, to faith leaders and religious congregations after their abusive acts became public and were adjudicated through the criminal justice system. These religious resources were viewed and experienced as spiritual supplements. They were an additional element for the men that involved accountability structures and offered support in their quest to stay free from the influence of drugs and alcohol and strong in their resolve to end violence and other abusive behavior in their family relationships.

6. *Building bridges.* The dogged determination and skill of the executive director of STOP to build bridges with the men the agency worked with should not be underestimated. By word and by example, she treated the men who found their way to her programs—men who batter—with the utmost care, offering them a premium service and incorporating emerging research and best practices within the agency. Believing them to be the consumers the agency was serving, STOP saw its role in the wider coordinated community response to domestic violence as providing help for the men to live and act in a different way from how they had in the past. But building bridges also occurred between various programs at the agency and between the agency and the criminal justice, therapeutic, and advocacy workers in their geographic jurisdiction. Interestingly, building bridges with the religious leaders of the area proved to be one of STOP's biggest challenges.

METHODOLOGY APPENDICES

The research on which this book is based draws its data from three primary sources, supplemented by six additional research projects. All projects that involved data collection received individual Research Ethics Board approval at the University of New Brunswick.

PROJECT TITLE EXPLORING ISSUES OF JUSTICE, ACCOUNTABILITY, AND CHANGE AMONG RELIGIOUS MEN WHO BATTER THEIR WIVES

Funded by grants from the Louisville Institute for the Study of Protestantism and American Religion and several smaller research awards, this project sought to understand how men who were mandated (or volunteered) to attend a state-certified faith-based batterer intervention group in the state of Oregon talked about their involvement in the group, the factors that led to their participation, and ways in which their involvement in the program impacted their lives. Participants were recruited through the groups where the facilitator read our research invitation letter. Men who were interested in being part of the research left their contact information with the administrative assistant at the agency. More men volunteered than we were able to accommodate in the focus groups or interviews.

A total of fifty-five men were interviewed individually (for about an hour) at least once at the agency premises in Oregon. Follow-up interviews with these fifty-five men were held twice a year for four years and lasted between forty-five and ninety minutes each. Participation in the follow-up interviews varied (there was attrition as a result of death, reincarceration, relocation, and other factors). We spent between ten days and two weeks each time data were collected. Additionally, five focus groups (of between five and twenty men) were held; each focus group lasted between sixty and ninety minutes. Food was provided at all focus groups and interviews; men were given twenty-five dollars for participating in the data collection.

During each site visit, we observed several batterer intervention groups, attended staff meetings, and spoke regularly with staff members, group facilitators, and the executive director. We were granted access to the case files of men who agreed to participate in our research (interviews or focus groups). As we highlight the story of any individual man in the book, we make it clear how many times we had contact with him and over what period of time.

For the first interview with each of the men, we explained the research project (as per our protocols) and asked him to read carefully (or we volunteered to read to him, not wishing to single out any of the men who might be unable to read) the various consent forms for participation in our research. After these were signed, we read this preamble, followed by the questions below. Interviews lasted between 45 and 90 minutes.

Thank you so much for agreeing to participate in our research project entitled Men's Stories of Hope and Change. We are interested in learning more about whether faith makes any difference in the lives of men and women after the experience of abuse. As you may know, the program here at [STOP] is very unique, and we want to understand it more from your perspective and experience. Your story is important to us, and we are hoping, with your help, to be able to offer insight to other families facing similar circumstances in other places around the United States and beyond.

1. Please explain how you heard about [STOP] and began attending one of the programs.
2. From your experience, what does [STOP] have to offer to men who have acted abusively?
3. From your experience, how has [STOP] impacted on your life? On the lives of those you care about?
4. From your perspective, how has religious faith/spirituality impacted your life? Ever helped you transform? Ever given you false hope?
5. What advice would you give to a man who has acted abusively in the past but has never sought group intervention?
6. Is there anything else that would assist us in understanding the role of [STOP], or your faith community, in your life over the last few years?

At the close of the interview, we asked the men what they hoped to be able to tell us when we returned in six months' time. Then we asked if they had any questions for us.

Follow-up interviews began by asking the men to update us on their lives since our last interview.

FOCUS GROUPS/INTERVIEWS WITH CRIMINAL JUSTICE STAFF

Focus groups or individual interviews with criminal justice workers included the following questions, which we asked after the research consent forms had been signed.

Focus Group/Personal Interview Schedule

PROBATION/PAROLE OFFICERS
Personal experience with faith-based treatment providers:

1. Please explain how you initially became aware of the various faith-based treatment providers in the area.
2. How many of the staff or board members of these groups have you met?
3. Have you ever made a referral to a faith-based treatment provider? What prompted you to do so? How often do you make a referral to a faith-based treatment provider?
4. Are there certain men or families that you would be more likely to refer to a faith-based agency rather than another agency?

Knowledge of faith-based treatment providers and services:

1. In what ways would you consider [STOP] to be faith-based?
2. How does [STOP] differ in your mind from an agency that does not claim to be faith-based?
3. From your perspective, how does [STOP] intervene in the lives of men who batter?
4. From your perspective, what is the unique contribution of [STOP] to changing the abusive behavior of men?

Relationship between faith-based treatment providers and the criminal justice system:

1. From your perspective, what is/are the major challenge(s) that a faith-based agency [like STOP] faces in responding to the needs of men who batter in the family context?
2. From your perspective, are there any tension points in the relationship between a faith-based agency [like STOP] for families in crisis and your organization?
3. In what ways can a faith-based agency for families in crisis [like STOP] assist your organization?
4. How could the relationship between you, your organization, and [STOP] be strengthened?

Relationship between clients of faith-based treatment providers and the criminal justice system:

1. When you make a referral suggestion to a man in your caseload, do you offer services to his family?
2. What type of follow-up contact do you normally have with men who have entered a batterer intervention program? What have you learned through such contact?

3. Do you believe this type of intervention program is successful in changing the thinking and behavior of abusive men? Does faith make a difference in changing their attitudes or behavior? Does faith produce some obstacles to change?

4. Do you have any suggestions that might improve the program at [STOP] and the ultimate goal of ending violence in the family context?

5. Do you have any contact with other organizations (such as congregations or religious groups) that work with faith-based treatment providers and their clients? How might the various agencies that work with faith-based treatment providers enhance their relationship with each other?

Other:

1. Do you have any other additional comments or suggestions that would enable us to understand the work of faith-based treatment providers and your relationship with their mission and services?

Note: A slightly amended version of this interview schedule was used for interviewing judges and other criminal justice employees and staff members at the shelter and other domestic violence advocates.

Note: We also conducted two focus groups of clergy in the local area using a slightly different version of this interview schedule.

PROJECT TITLE: CELEBRATING THE GRADUATES—AN EXPLORATION INTO THE NATURE AND EXTENT OF CHANGE IN THE LIVES OF MEN WHO HAVE GRADUATED FROM A BATTERERS PROGRAM

Funded by grants from several organizations, this research examined the closed case files of more than one thousand men who had attended groups in a faith-based batterer intervention program in Seattle, Washington. Those files covered more than a ten-year period, from 1989 to 2001. The first group of files (n = 1,059) included all men who had been part of this state-certified program from the early days of its existence until 2002; a second group of files (n = 75), analyzed later, were closed between 2002 and 2005. The contents of the closed files include the client face sheet, the intake form, the letter of responsibility, the letter of empathy, the graduation checklist, and any police or medical reports provided by third parties involved in the case (e.g., probation reports, etc.). All identifying information such as the full names of clients, victims' names, and addresses and telephone numbers were blackened out before files were made available for research use. A total of 283 variables were available for analysis (using SPSS), but the level of missing data severely restricted the quantitative analysis. A smaller part of this research involved interviews with the executive director of the agency, members of its board of directors, staff, and group facilitators; also included were a small number of interviews with members of the criminal justice community in the Seattle region. A total of seventeen interviews were conducted.

PROJECT TITLE: A COORDINATED COMMUNITY
RESPONSE TO DOMESTIC VIOLENCE

Funded by the Lilly Endowment, after seed grants from several agencies and foundations, one part of this project that is related to batterer intervention programs involved interviews and informal contact with probation and parole officers, police, judges, therapists, group facilitators, and shelter staff in several regions across the United States (Eugene, OR; Columbia, MO; Charlotte, NC) and in the western Canadian city of Calgary, Alberta. Observations also occurred in several courtrooms. In Oregon, where we collected interview and focus group data from men who had acted abusively and were now part of groups in one specific faith-based agency (see the first project listed above), we had regular contact (for several years) with shelter staff, criminal justice workers, clergy, and therapists. While we had informal conversations and interactions with more than one hundred fifty workers in the domestic violence community, we conducted focus groups or formal interviews with forty-one.

SUPPLEMENTARY PROJECTS (COMPLETED ALONGSIDE
THE RESEARCH ABOVE OR AT AN EARLIER TIME)

Seminary Project

Data were collected at four seminaries from more than three hundred students to identify their training experiences and learning needs as they related to domestic violence. There was a noted gap between their classroom experiences and ministry demands on issues of abuse.

Transition House Workers and Clergy

This was a pilot project that examined tensions, contradictions, and collaboration between clergy and transition house workers in selected regions of eastern Canada, with a goal of identifying areas of cooperation and coordination. Twelve different geographic sites were chosen.

Pastors and Domestic Violence

This quantitative study involved a sample of 343 clergy (70 percent response rate) in Atlantic Canada. The data collection (seven-page questionnaire) covered clergy experience with woman and child abuse, work with those who act abusively, knowledge of family violence issues, and referral practices related to violence and abuse. Additional data collection occurred in later years among pastors in other selected ministry contexts (n = 225).

Pastoral Counseling in Cases of Domestic Violence

Building on the previous study, personal interviews were conducted with a sample of one hundred ministers in various locations in eastern Canada. This project focused specifically on the advice and support that clergy offer to families in crises. A further stage of this project involved twenty-five interviews with clergy in other Christian denominations outside the original sample.

Women Helping Women after Abuse

This project explored the unique and specific needs of church women who suffer abuse and the responses of women within the Christian church to those needs. It involved focus group interviews in thirty congregations, representing rural, urban, and small-town contexts. A total of 247 women participated in these focus groups.

Church Youth Groups

A small project involved ten church youth groups and their youth leaders. Data were collected on the help-seeking behavior of young men and women of faith and their leaders' response to those calls for help.

CHAPTER 1

1. Kroeger, Nason-Clark, and Fisher-Townsend 2008; Nason-Clark, Kroeger, and Fisher-Townsend 2011; Nason-Clark, Fisher-Townsend, and Fahlberg 2013.
2. This agency used the widely employed but sometimes contested Conflict Tactics Scale developed by Straus and colleagues at the University of New Hampshire.
3. Some possible questions about signs of change that we have heard victims/survivors offer in workshops or in our team work for the RAVE website include: "Has your partner completely stopped saying and doing things that frighten you?" "Can you express anger without being punished for it?" "Can your partner listen to your opinion and respect it, even when disagreeing with you?" "Does your partner argue without being abusive or having to be right?" "Has your partner stopped expecting you to do things that you may not want to do?" "Can you spend time with friends or family without being afraid that your partner will retaliate?" "Do you feel safe leaving the children with your partner?" "Does your partner listen to what you have to say?"
4. One study involved a master's thesis completed by Christy Terris (Hoyt) in the sociology department, University of New Brunswick (1996) under the supervision of Nancy Nason-Clark; the other was an honor's project completed by Amanda Henry while she was a research assistant for Nancy Nason-Clark.
5. UCR2 (United Nations Commission on Human Rights) consists of police-reported incident-based crime statistics based on data provided by 166 police agencies in nine provinces, representing 53 percent of the national volume of reported crime.

CHAPTER 3

1. O'Keefe 2005, 1. According to a 2003 special report of the Bureau of Justice Statistics on intimate partner violence, 7 percent of all murder victims in 1995 were young women killed by their boyfriends.
2. http://www.opdv.state.ny.us/professionals/advocacy/court/documents/mhsubstance-abuse.pdf.
3. http://www.usda.gov/da/shmd/aware.htmf.
4. http://www.nimh.nih.gov/statistics/1ANYANX_ADULT.shtml.
5. http://www.nimh.nih.gov/statistics/1MDD_ADULT.shtml.

CHAPTER 5

1. It is estimated that "over 300 courts in the United States have recognized the need for special attention to domestic violence cases by incorporating specialized processing and structure within existing judicial systems" (Gover and MacDonald 2003, 111).

CHAPTER 6

1. For the "ripple effect" in prison counseling, see www.the-ripple-effect.info/basics_abuser.php

Ad Hoc Federal-Provincial-Territorial Working Group Reviewing Spousal Abuse Policies and Legislation. 2003. Final Report: Prepared for the Federal-Provincial-Territorial Ministers Responsible for Justice. www.justice.gc.ca/eng/rp-pr/cj-jp/fv-vf/pol/index.html

Adams, D. 2003. Certified Batterer Intervention Programs: History, Philosophies, Techniques, Collaborations, Innovations and Challenges. Originally published in *Clinics in Family Practice* 5.1. Updated online: <www.futureswithoutviolence.org/userfiles/file/Children_and_Families/Certified Batterer Intervention Programs.pdf>

Ai, A.L. and C.L. Park. 2005. "Possibilities of the Positive Following Violence and Trauma: Informing the Coming Decade of Research." *Journal of Interpersonal Violence* 20.2: 242–250.

Aldarondo, E. 2012. "Evaluating the Efficacy of Interventions with Men Who Batter." *Family & Intimate Partner Violence Quarterly* 4.3: 247–66.

Amaro, H., L. E. Fried, H. Cabral, and B. Zuckerman. 1990. "Violence during Pregnancy and Substance Use." *American Journal of Public Health* 80.5: 575–80.

Ames, L. J., and K. T. Dunham. 2002. "Asymptotic Justice: Probation as a Criminal Justice Response to Intimate Partner Violence." *Violence against Women* 8.1: 6–34.

Ammerman, N. Tatom. 2014. *Sacred Stories, Spiritual Tribes: Finding Religion in Everyday Life*. New York: Oxford University Press.

Areán, J. C., and L. Davis. 2007. "Working with Fathers in Batterer Intervention Programs: Lessons from the Fathering after Violence Project." In *Parenting by Men Who Batter: New Directions for Assessment and Intervention*, edited by J. Edleson and O. Williams, 118–30. New York: Oxford University Press.

Areán, J. C., and N. Raines. 2013. "The Effects of Love on Children." In *Strengthening Families and Ending Abuse: Churches and Their Leaders Look to the Future*, edited by N. Nason-Clark, B. Fisher-Townsend, and V. Fahlberg, 27–39. Eugene, OR: Wipf and Stock.

Avery-Leaf, S., M. Cascardi, K. D. O'Leary, and A. Cano. 1997. "Efficacy of a Dating Violence Prevention Program on Attitudes Justifying Aggression." *Journal of Adolescent Health* 21: 11–17.

Bancroft, L. 2003. *Why Does He Do That? Inside the Minds of Angry and Controlling Men*. New York: Berkley.

Bandura, A. 1973. *Aggression: A Social Learning Analysis*. Oxford: Prentice-Hall.

Bauer, N. S., T. I. Herrenkohl, P. Lozano, F. P. Rivara, K. G. Hill, and J. D. Hawkins. 2006. "Childhood Bullying Involvement and Exposure to Intimate Partner Violence." *Pediatrics* 118.2: 235–42.

Beaman, L., and N. Nason-Clark. 1999. "Evangelical Women as Activists: Their Response to Violence against Women." In L. Beaman, *Shared Beliefs, Different Lives: Women's Identities in Evangelical Context*, 111–32. St. Louis, MO: Challice.

Beaman-Hall, L., and N. Nason-Clark. 1997. "Partners or Protagonists: Exploring the Relationship between the Transition House Movement and Conservative Churches." *Affilia: Journal of Women and Social Work* 12.2: 176–96.

Bembry, J. X. 2011. "Strengthening Fragile Families through Research and Practice." *Journal of Family Social Work* 14.1: 54–67.

Bender, C. 2003. *Heaven's Kitchen: Living Religion at God's Love We Deliver*. Chicago: University of Chicago Press.

Bennett, L., and M. Piet. 1999. "Standards for Batterer Intervention Programs: In Whose Interest?" *Violence against Women* 5.1: 6–24.

Bennett, L., and O. Williams. 2002. Controversies and Recent Studies of Batterer Intervention Program Effectiveness. http://www.vawnet.org/applied-research-papers/print-document.php?doc_id=373.

Berliner, L. 2003. "Introduction: Making Domestic Violence Victims Testify." *Journal of Interpersonal Violence* 18.6: 666–68.

Bilodeau, D. 1990. "L'Approche Féminist en Maison d'Hébergement: Quand la Pratique Enrichit la Théorie." Nouvelle Pratiques Sociales, 3(2):45–55.

Black, D. S., S. Sussman, and J. B. Unger. 2010. "A Further Look at the Intergenerational Transmission of Violence: Witnessing Interparental Violence in Emerging Adulthood." *Journal of Interpersonal Violence* 25.6: 1022–42.

Bograd, M. 1988. "Feminist Perspectives on Wife Abuse: An Introduction." In *Feminist Perspectives on Wife Abuse*, edited by K. Yllö and M. Bograd, 11–26. Newbury Park, CA: Sage.

———. 1999. "Strengthening Domestic Violence Theories: Intersections of Race, Class, Sexual Orientation, and Gender." *Journal of Marital and Family Therapy* 25: 275–89.

Braden, N. 1969. *The Psychology of Self-Esteem*. New York: Bantam.

Bradley, I. K. 2002. "Domestic Violence Courts: An Examination of DVI Courts in Ontario and the United States." *Crown NetLetter Collection of Criminal Law Articles* (CRWN/RP-013).

Brookoff, D., K. K. O'Brien, C. S. Cook, T. D. Thompson, and C. Williams. 2007. "Characteristics of Participants in Domestic Violence Cases." *Journal of the American Medical Association* 277: 1369–73.

Brown, J.C. and C.R. Bohn. 1989. "Introduction," in *Christianity, Patriarchy and Abuse: A Feminist Critique*, edited by J.C. Brown and C.R. Bohn, xiii–xv. Cleveland, OH: The Pilgrim Press.

Brown, T. 2000. *Charging and Prosecution Policies in Cases of Spousal Assault: A Synthesis of Research, Academic and Judicial Responses*. Ottawa: Department of Justice Canada.

Brown, T. G., A. Werk, T. Caplan, and P. Seraganian. 1999. "Violent Substance Abusers in Domestic Violence Treatment." *Violence and Victims* 14.2: 179–90.

Brownridge, D., and S. Halli. 2001. "Marital Status as Differentiating Factor in Canadian Women's Coping with Partner Violence." *Journal of Comparative Family Studies* 32.1: 117–25.

Buck, N. M., E. P. Leenaars, P. M. Emmelkamp, and H. J. Van Marle. 2012. "Explaining the Relationship between Insecure Attachment and Partner Abuse: The Role of Personality Characteristics." *Journal of Interpersonal Violence* 27.16: 3149–70.

Bureau of Justice Statistics, US. 2003. Intimate Partner Violence in the United States. http://bjs.gov/content/pub/pdf/ipvus.pdf.

Burgess-Proctor, A. 2003. "Evaluating the Efficacy of Protection Orders for Victims of Domestic Violence." *Women & Criminal Justice* 15.1: 33–52.

Butts, J. A. 2001. "Introduction: Problem-Solving Courts." *Law & Policy* 23: 121.

Buzawa, E. S., T. L. Austin, J. Bannon, and J. Jackson. 1992. "Role of Victim Preference in Determining Police Response to Victims of Domestic Violence." In *Domestic Violence: The Changing Criminal Justice Response*, edited by E. S. Buzawa and C. G. Buzawa, 255–69. Westport, CT: Auburn House.

Buzawa, E. S., and C. G. Buzawa. 2003. *Domestic Violence: The Criminal Justice Response.* Thousand Oaks, CA: Sage.

Cadge, W. 2013. *Paging God: Religion in the Halls of Medicine.* Chicago: University of Chicago Press.

Campbell, J. C., D. Webster, J. Koziol-McLain, C. Block, D. Campbell, M. A. Curry, F. Gary, N. Glass, J. McFarlane, C. Sachs, P. Sharps, Y. Ulrich, S. A. Wilt, J. Manganello, Xiao Xu, J. Schollenberger, V. Frye, and K. Laughon. 2003. "Risk Factors for Femicide in Abusive Relationships: Results from a Multisite Case Study." *American Journal of Public Health* 93: 1089–97.

Carlton, B. S., D. A. Goebert, R. H. Miyamoto, N. N. Andrade, E. S. Hishinuma, G. K. Makini Jr., N. Y. C. Yuen, C. Bell, L. D. Mccubbin, I. R. N. Else, and S. T. Nishimura. 2006. "Resilience, Family Adversity and Well-Being among Hawaiian and Non-Hawaiian Adolescents." *International Journal of Social Psychiatry* 52.4: 291–308.

Cartier, J., D. Farabee, and M. L. Prendergast. 2006. "Methamphetamine Use, Self-Reported Violent Crime, and Recidivism among Offenders in California Who Abuse Substances." *Journal of Interpersonal Violence* 21.4: 435–45.

Cassidy, M. A., and D. Trafimow. 2002. "The Influence of Patriarchal Ideology on Outcomes of Legal Decisions involving Woman Battering Cases: An Analysis of Five Historical Eras." *Social Science Journal* 39.2: 235–45.

Catalano, R. F., K. P. Haggerty, S. Oesterle, C. B. Fleming, and D. J. Hawkins. 2004. "The Importance of Bonding to School for Healthy Development: Findings from the Social Development Research Group." *Journal of School Health* 74.7: 252–61.

Cavanaugh, M. M., and R. J. Gelles. 2005. "The Utility of Male Domestic Violence Offender Typologies: New Directions for Research, Policy, and Practice." *Journal of Interpersonal Violence* 20.2: 155–66.

Center for Court Innovation; Labriola, M., S. Bradley, C. O'Sullivan, M. Rempel and S. Moore. 2009. "A National Portrait of Domestic Violence Courts." <www.courtinnovation.org/sites/default/files/national_portrait.ped>

Chalk, R., and P. A. King, eds. 1998. *Violence in Families: Assessing Prevention and Treatment Programs.* Washington, DC: National Academy Press.

Chen, P., and H. R. White. 2004. "Gender Differences in Adolescent and Young Adult Predictors of Later Intimate Partner Violence: A Prospective Study." *Violence against Women* 10.11: 1283–1301.

Clarke, R. L. 1986. *Pastoral Care of Battered Women.* Philadelphia: Westminster.

Cook, D., M. Burton, A. Robinson, and C. Vallely. 2004. *Evaluation of Specialist Domestic Violence Courts/Fast Track Systems.* London: Crown Prosecution Service.

Cook, K. J. 2006. "Doing Difference and Accountability in Restorative Justice Conferences." *Theoretical Criminology* 10.1: 107–24.

Coulter, M., and C. VandeWeerd. 2009. "Reducing Domestic Violence and Other Criminal Recidivism: Effectiveness of a Multilevel Batterers Intervention Program." *Violence & Victims* 24.2: 139–52.

Cowan, G., and R.D. Mills. 2004. "Personal Adequacy and Intimacy Predictors of Men's Hostility Toward Women." *Sex Roles* 51: 67–78.

Critical Components Project Team. 2008. *Keeping Women Safe: Eight Critical Components of an Effective Response to Domestic Violence.* Victoria: Government of British Columbia.

Crocker, D. 2005. "Regulating Intimacy: Judicial Discourse in Cases of Wife Assault (1970 to 2000)." *Violence against Women* 11.2: 197–226.

Cunradi, C. B., R. Caetano, and J. Schafer. 2002. "Socioeconomic Predictors of Intimate Partner Violence among White, Black, and Hispanic Couples in the United States." *Journal of Family Violence* 17.4: 377–89.

Dalton, B. 2001. "Batterer Characteristics and Treatment Completion." *Journal of Interpersonal Violence* 16.2: 1223–38.

Daly, J., T. Power, and E. W. Gondolf. 2001. "Predictors of Batterer Program Attendance." *Journal of Interpersonal Violence* 16.10: 971–91.

Davis, R. C., B. E. Smith, and L. B. Nickles. 1998. "The Deterrent Effect of Prosecuting Domestic Violence Misdemeanors." *Crime & Delinquency* 44.3: 434–42.

Davis, R. C., and B. G. Taylor. 1999. "Does Batterer Treatment Reduce Violence? A Synthesis of the Literature." *Women & Criminal Justice* 10.2: 69–93.

Dawson, M., and R. Dinovitzer. 2001. "Victim Cooperation and the Prosecution of Domestic Violence in a Specialized Court." *Justice Quarterly* 18.3: 593–622.

Day, A., D. Chung, P. O'Leary, and E. Carson. 2009. "Programs for Men Who Perpetrate Domestic Violence: An Examination of the Issues Underlying the Effectiveness of Intervention Programs." *Journal of Family Violence* 24.3: 203–12.

Delsol, C., and G. Margolin. 2004. "The Role of Family-of-Origin Violence in Men's Marital Violence Perpetration." *Clinical Psychology Review* 24.1: 99–122.

Delsol, C., G. Margolin, and R. S. John. 2003. "A Typology of Maritally Violent Men and Correlates of Violence in a Community Sample." *Journal of Marriage and Family* 65.3: 635–51.

DeMaris, A. 1989. "Attrition in Batterers' Counseling: The Role of Social and Demographic Factors." *Social Service Review* 63: 142–54.

Denham, D., and J. Gillespie. 1999. *Two Steps Forward . . . One Step Back: An Overview of Canadian Initiatives and Resources to End Woman Abuse 1989–1997.* Ottawa: National Clearinghouse on Family Violence, Health Canada.

DeRuyter, D. 2002. "The Virtue of Taking Responsibility." *Educational Philosophy and Theory* 34.1: 25–55.

Dignan, J., A. Atkinson, H. Atkinson, M. Howes, J. Johnstone, G. Robinson, J. Shapland, and A. Sorsby. 2007. "Staging Restorative Justice Encounters against a Criminal Justice Backdrop: A Dramaturgical Analysis." *Criminology and Criminal Justice* 7.1: 5–32.

Dobash, R. E., and R. P. Dobash. 2000. "Evaluating Criminal Justice Interventions for Domestic Violence." *Crime & Delinquency* 46.2: 252–70.

Dobash, R.E., Dobash, R.P., Cavanagh, K., and R. Lewis. 2000. *Changing Violent Men.* Thousand Oaks, CA: Sage.

———. 2002. "Domestic Violence: A Sociological Approach." In *Encyclopedia of Social and Behavioural Sciences*, Vol. 20, edited by N. J. Smelser and P. B. Baltes, 3830–34. Oxford: Pergamon.

Dobash, R. P., and R. E. Dobash. 1979. *Violence against Wives: A Case against the Patriarchy*. New York: Free Press.

Donnellan, M.B., K. Trzeniewski, R. Robins, T. Moffitt and A. Caspi. 2005. "Low Self-Esteem is Related to Aggression, Anti-Social Behavior and Deliquency." *Psychological Science* 16(4): 328–335.

Dutton, D. 1998. *The Abusive Personality*. New York: Guilford.

Dworkin, A. 1981. *Pornography: Men Possessing Women*. New York: Putnam.

Easton, C. J., A. H. Weinberger, and T. P. George. 2007. "Age Onset of Smoking among Alcohol Dependent Men Attending Substance Abuse Treatment after a Domestic Violence Arrest." *Addictive Behaviors* 32.10: 2020–31.

Edleson, J. L., A. L. Ellerton, E. A. Seagren, S. L. Kirchberg, and S. O. Schmidt. 2007. "Assessing Child Exposure to Adult Domestic Violence." *Children and Youth Services Review* 29.7: 961–71.

Edleson, J. L., and O. Williams. 2007. *Parenting by Men Who Batter: New Directions for Assessment and Interventions*. New York: Oxford University Press.

Ehrensaft, M., P. Cohen, J. Brown, E. Smailes, H. Chen, and J. G. Johnson. 2003. "Intergenerational Transmission of Partner Violence: A 20-Year Prospective Study." *Journal of Consulting & Clinical Psychology* 71.4: 741–54.

Eisenstein, Z. 1984. *Feminism and Sexuality Equality: Crisis in Liberal America*. New York: Monthly Review.

Ellsberg, M., L. Heise, R. Pena, S. Agurto, and A. Winkvist. 2001. "Researching Domestic Violence against Women: Methodological and Ethical Considerations." *Studies in Family Planning* 32.1: 1–16.

Epstein, D. 1999. "Effective Intervention in Domestic Violence Cases: Rethinking the Roles of Prosecutors, Judges, and the Court System." *Yale Journal of Law and Feminism* 11.3: 3–50.

Epstein, D., M. E. Bell, and L. A. Goodman. 2003. "Transforming Aggressive Prosecution Policies: Prioritizing Victims' Long Term Safety in the Prosecution of Domestic Violence Cases." *Journal of Gender, Social Policy & the Law* 11.2: 465–98.

Erez, E., and J. Belknap. 1998. "In Their Own Words: Battered Women's Assessments of the Criminal Justice Processing System's Responses." *Violence and Victims* 13: 251–68.

Fals-Stewart, W. 2003. "The Occurrence of Partner Physical Aggression on Days of Alcohol Consumption." *Journal of Consulting and Clinical Psychology* 71.2: 41–52.

Faulkner, K. K., R. Cogan, M. Nolder, and G. Shooter. 1991. "Characteristics of Men and Women Completing Cognitive/Behavioral Spouse Abuse Treatment." *Journal of Family Violence* 6.3: 243–54.

Feder, L., and D. R. Forde. 2003. "The Broward Experiment." In *Batterer Intervention Programs: Where Do We Go from Here?* 5–13. Washington, DC: National Institute of Justice.

Finn, M. A., B. S. Blackwell, L. J. Stalans, S. Studdard, and L. Dugan. 2004. "Dual Arrest Decisions in Domestic Violence Cases: The Influence of Departmental Policies." *Crime & Delinquency* 50.4: 565–89.

Finn, P., and S. Colson. 1998. "Civil Protection Orders: Legislation, Current Court Practice, and Enforcement." In *Legal Interventions in Family Violence: Research*

Findings and Policy Implications, edited by National Institute of Justice, 43–47. Washington, DC: US Department of Justice.

Fiorenza, E. S., and S. M. Copeland, eds. 1994. *Violence against Women*. London: SCM.

Fisher-Townsend, B., N. Nason-Clark, L. Ruff, and N. Murphy. 2008. "I Am Not Violent: Men's Experience in Group." In *Beyond Abuse in the Christian Home: Raising Voices for Change*, edited by C. Clark Kroeger, N. Nason-Clark, and B. Fisher-Townsend, 78–99. Eugene, OR: Wipf and Stock.

Fortune, M. 1991. *Violence in the Family: A Workshop Curriculum for Clergy and Other Helpers*. Cleveland, OH: Pilgrim.

Funk, R. 2006. *Reaching Men: Strategies for Preventing Sexist Attitudes, Behavior and Violence*. St. Paul, MN: Jist.

Galvani, S. 2004. "Responsible Disinhibition: Alcohol, Men and Violence to Women." *Addiction Research & Theory* 12.4: 357–71.

Garner, J., and C. Maxwell. 2000. "What Are the Lessons of the Police Arrest Studies." *Journal of Aggression, Maltreatment & Trauma* 4.1: 83–114.

Gerlock, A. A. 2001. "A Profile of Who Completes and Who Drops Out of Batterers' Rehabilitation." *Issues in Mental Health Nursing* 22: 379–420.

Gilchrist, E., and J. Blissett. 2002. "Magistrates' Attitudes to Domestic Violence and Sentencing Options." *Howard Journal of Criminal Justice* 41.4: 348–63.

Goldenberg, S. 1997. *Thinking Sociologically*. Toronto: Oxford University Press.

Goldman, M. 2012. *The Soul Rush: Esalen and the Rise of Spiritual Privilege*. New York: New York University Press.

Gondolf, E. W. 1995. "Alcohol Abuse, Wife Assault, and Power Needs." *Social Service Review* (June): 274–84.

———. 2000. "A 30-Month Follow-Up of Court-Referred Batterers in Four Cities." *International Journal of Offender Therapy and Comparative Criminology* 44.1: 111–28.

———. 2002. *Batterer Intervention Systems: Issues, Outcomes and Recommendations*. Thousand Oaks, CA: Sage.

———. 2004. "Evaluating Batterer Counseling Programs: A Difficult Task Showing Some Effect and Implications." *Aggression and Violent Behavior* 9.6: 605–31.

Gondolf, E. W., D. A. Heckert, and C. M. Kimmel. 2002. "Nonphysical Abuse among Batterer Program Participants." *Journal of Family Violence* 17.4: 293–314.

Gover, A. R. 2004. "Risky Lifestyles and Dating Violence: A Theoretical Test of Violent Victimization." *Journal of Criminal Justice* 32.2: 171–80.

Gover, A. R., and J. M. MacDonald. 2003. "Combating Domestic Violence: Findings from an Evaluation of a Local Domestic Violence Court." *Criminology and Public Policy* 3.1: 109–32.

Greenfield, T. K. 1998. "Evaluating Competing Models of Alcohol-Related Harm." *Alcoholism* 22: 52–62.

Hagstroem, T. 1991. *Young People's Lifestyles—The Demands of Working Life. A Review of Research*. Arbete and Haelsa, Solna: Arbetsmiljoeintitutet.

Halsey, P. 1984. *Abuse in the Family: Breaking the Church's Silence*. New York: Office of Ministries with Women in Crisis, General Board of Global Ministries, United Methodist Church.

Hamel, J. 2012. "'But She's Violent, Too!' Holding Domestic Violence Offenders Accountable within a Systemic Approach to Batterer Intervention." *Journal of Aggression, Conflict & Peace Research* 4.3: 124–35.

Hanna, C. 1996. "No Right to Choose: Mandated Victim Participation in Domestic Violence Prosecutions." *Harvard Law Review* 109: 1850–1909.

Hanson, R. K., O. Cadsky, A. Harris, and C. Lalonde. 1996. "Correlates of Battering among 997 Men: Family History, Adjustment and Attitudinal Differences." *Violence and Victims* 12.3: 191–208.

Hanson, R. K., and S. Wallace-Capretta. 2000. *A Multi-site Study of Treatment for Abusive Men 2000–05.* Ottawa: Solicitor General Canada.

Hartman, J. L., and J. Belknap. 2003. "Beyond the Gatekeepers: Court Professionals' Self-Reported Attitudes about and Experiences with Misdemeanor Domestic Violence Cases." *Criminal Justice and Behavior* 30.3: 349–73.

Healey, K., C. Smith, and C. O'Sullivan. 1998. *Batterer Intervention: Program Approaches and Criminal Justice Strategies.* Washington, DC: Issues and Practices in Criminal Justice.

Heath, D. B. 1998. "Cultural Variations among Drinking Patterns." In *Drinking Patterns and Their Consequences,* edited by M. Grant and J. Litvak, 103–28. Washington, DC: Taylor & Francis.

Heckert, D. A., and E. Gondolf. 2000. "Predictors of Underreporting of Male Violence by Batterer Program Participants and Their Partners." *Journal of Family Violence* 15.4: 423–43.

Helling, J.A. (n.d.) "Specialized Criminal Domestic Violence Courts." Battered Women's Justice Project. Minneapolis, MN. <www.bwjp.org/files/bwjp/articles/Specialized_Criminal_DV_Courts_part1.pdf>

Henning, K., and R. Holdford. 2006. "Minimization, Denial, and Victim Blaming by Batterers: How Much Does the Truth Matter?" *Criminal Justice and Behavior* 32: 110–30.

Herrenkohl, T. I., R. Kosterman, W. A. Mason, and J. D. Hawkins. 2007. "Youth Violence Trajectories and Proximal Characteristics of Intimate Partner Violence." *Violence and Victims* 22.3: 259–74.

Hirschel, D., and E. S. Buzawa. 2002. "Understanding the Context of Dual Arrest with Directions for Future Research." *Violence against Women* 8.12: 1449–73.

———. 2013. "The Impact of Offenders Leaving the Scene on Police Decision to Arrest in Cases of Intimate Partner Violence." *Violence against Women* 19: 1079–1103.

Hirschel, D., and I. W. Hutchison. 2001. "The Relative Effects of Offense, Offender and Victim Variables on the Decision to Prosecute Domestic Violence Cases." *Violence against Women* 7.1: 46–59.

Hirschi, T. 1969. *Causes of Delinquency.* Berkeley: University of California Press.

Högnäs, R. S., and M. J. Carlson. 2010. "Intergenerational Relationships and Union Stability in Fragile Families." *Journal of Marriage and Family* 72.5: 1220–33.

Holt, S., H. Buckley, and S. Whelan. 2008. "The Impact of Exposure to Domestic Violence on Children and Young People: A Review of the Literature." *Child Abuse and Neglect* 32.8: 797–810.

Holtzworth–Munroe, A., and G. L. Stuart. 1994. "Typologies of Male Batterers: Three Subtypes and the Differences among Them." *Psychological Bulletin* 116: 476–97.

Hope for Healing. 2005 www.hopeforhealing.org/.

Horton, A., and J. Williamson, eds. 1988. *Abuse and Religion: When Praying Isn't Enough.* New York: Heath.

Hoyle, C., and A. Sanders. 2000. "Police Response to Domestic Violence: From Victim Choice to Victim Empowerment." *British Journal of Criminology* 40.1: 14–36.

Humphreys, C., L. Regan, D. River, and R. K. Thiara. 2005. "Domestic Violence and Substance Use: Tackling Complexity." *British Journal of Social Work* 35: 1303–20.

Hutchison, I. W., and D. Hirschel. 1998. "Abused Women: Help-Seeking Strategies and Police Utilization." *Violence against Women* 4.4: 436–56.

Jacobs, J. 2010. *Memorializing the Holocaust: Gender, Genocide and Collective Memory.* New York: I. B. Tauris.

Jacobson, N., and J. Gottman. 1998. *When Men Batter Women: New Insights into Ending Abusive Relationships.* New York: Simon & Schuster.

James, S. E., J. Johnson, and C. Raghavan. 2004. "'I Couldn't Go Anywhere': Contextualizing Violence and Drug Abuse: A Social Network Study." *Violence against Women* 10.9: 991–1014.

Jenkins, A. 1990. *Invitations to Responsibility: The Therapeutic Engagement of Men Who Are Violent and Abusive.* Adelaide, Australia: Dulwich Center.

Jennings, J. L., and C. M. Murphy. 2000. "Male–Male Dimensions of Male–Female Battering: A New Look at Domestic Violence." *Psychology of Men and Masculinity* 1: 21–29.

Jessor, S. and R. Jessor. 1977. *Problem Behavior and Psychological Development: A Longitudinal Study of Youth.* New York, NY: Academic Press.

Johnson, J. M., Y. Lunn, and J. Stein. 2003. "Victim Protection Orders and the Stake in Conformity Thesis." *Journal of Family Violence* 18.6: 317–23.

Jordan, C. E. 2004. "Intimate Partner Violence and the Justice System: An Examination of the Interface." *Journal of Interpersonal Violence* 9.12: 1412–34.

Jory, B., D. Anderson, and C. Greer. 1997. "Intimate Justice: Confronting Issues of Accountability, Respect, and Freedom in Treatment for Abuse and Violence." *Journal of Marital and Family Therapy* 23.4: 399–419.

Kantor, G., and M. A. Straus. 1989. "Substance Abuse as a Precipitant of Wife Abuse Victimizations." *American Journal of Drug and Alcohol Abuse* 15: 173–89.

Kaplan, H., and C. H. Lin. 2005. "Deviant Identity, Negative Self-Feelings, and Decreases in Deviant Behavior: The Moderating Influence of Conventional Social Bonding." *Psychology, Crime and Law* 11.3: 289–303.

Katz, J. 2006. *The Macho Paradox: Why Some Men Hurt Women and How All Men Can Help.* Naperville, IL: Sourcebooks.

Kelley, B. T., T. P. Thornberry, and C. A. Smith. 1997. *In the Wake of Childhood Maltreatment.* Washington, DC: National Institute of Justice. www.ncjrs.gov/pdffiles1/165257.pdf.

Kerley, K., X. Xu, B. Sirisunyaluck, and J. Alley. 2010. "Exposure to Family Violence in Childhood and Intimate Partner Perpetration or Victimization in Adulthood: Exploring Intergenerational Transmission in Urban Thailand." *Journal of Family Violence* 25.3: 337–47.

Klein, A.R. and A. Crowe. 2007. "Findings from an Outcome Examination of Rhode Island's Domestic Violence Probation Program: Do Specialized Supervision Programs of Batterers Reduce Reabuse?" *Violence against Women* 14: 226–46.

Kroeger, C. Clark, and N. Nason-Clark. 2001. *No Place for Abuse: Biblical and Practical Resources to Counteract Domestic Violence.* Downers Grove, IL: InterVarsity.

———. 2010. *No Place for Abuse: Biblical and Practical Resources to Counteract Domestic Violence,* 2nd ed. Downers Grove, IL: InterVarsity.

Kroeger, C. Clark, N. Nason-Clark, and B. Fisher-Townsend, eds. 2008. *Beyond Abuse in the Christian Home: Raising Voices for Change.* Eugene, OR: Wipf and Stock.

Kulkarni, S. J., H. Bell, and D. McDaniel Rhodes. 2012. "Back to Basics: Essential Qualities of Services for Survivors of Intimate Partner Violence." *Violence against Women* 18: 85–101.

Larson, D. B., and S. S. Larson. 2003. "Spirituality's Potential Relevance to Physical and Emotional Health: A Brief Review of Quantitative Research." *Journal of Psychology and Theology* 31.1: 37–51.

Laub, J. H., and R. J. Sampson. 1993. "Turning Points in the Life Course: Why Change Matters to the Study of Crime." *Criminology* 31.3: 301–25.

Lentz, S. A. 1999. "Revisiting the Rule of Thumb: An Overview of the History of Wife Abuse." *Women and Criminal Justice* 10.2: 9–27.

Liz Claiborne Inc./Teen Research Unlimited. 2007. Study on Teen Dating Abuse. http://www.loveisnotabuse.com.

Loue, S. 2001. *Intimate Partner Violence: Societal, Medical, Legal and Individual Responses.* New York: Kluwer Academic/Plenum.

Loue, S., and K. J. Maschke. 2001. *Intimate Partner Violence: Societal, Medical, Legal and Individual Responses.* New York: Kluwer Academic/Plenum.

Lundy, M., and S. F. Grossman. 2005. "The Mental Health and Service Needs of Young Children Exposed to Domestic Violence: Supportive Data." *Families in Society* 86.1:17–29.

MacKinnon, C. 1989. *Toward a Feminist Theory of the State.* Cambridge, MA: Harvard University Press.

Mankowski, E. S., J. Haaken, and C. S. Silvergleid. 2002. "Collateral Damage: An Analysis of the Achievements and Unintended Consequences of Batterer Intervention Programs and Discourse." *Journal of Family Violence* 17.2: 167–84.

Martin, S.L., L. Mackie, L. Kupper, P. Buescher and K. Moracco. 2001. "Physical Abuse of Women Before, During and After Pregnancy." *Journal of American Medical Association* 285.12: 1581–1584.

Masten, A. S. 1999. "Resilience Comes of Age: Reflections on the Past and Outlook for the Next Generation of Research." In *Resilience and Development: Positive Life Adaptations*, edited by M. D. Glantz, J. Johnson, and L. Huffman, 282–96. New York: Plenum.

———. 2001. "Ordinary Magic: Resilience Processes in Development." *American Psychologist* 56.3: 227–38.

Maxwell, C., J. Garner, and J. Fagan. 2002. "The Preventive Effects of Arrest on Intimate Partner Violence: Research, Policy, Theory." *Criminology and Public Policy* 2.1: 51–95.

McCloskey, L. A., and J. Stuewig. 2001. "The Quality of Peer Relationships among Children Exposed to Family Violence." *Development and Psychopathology* 13.1: 83–96.

McFarlane, J., P. Wilson, D. Lemmey, and A. Malecha. 2000. "Women Filing Assault Charges on an Intimate Partner: Criminal Justice Outcome and Future Violence Experienced." *Violence against Women* 6.4: 396–408.

McGuire, M. B. 1988. *Ritual Healing in Suburban America.* New Brunswick, NJ: Rutgers University Press.

———. 2008. *Lived Religion: Faith and Practice in Everyday Life.* New York: Oxford University Press.

McMullin, S. and N. Nason-Clark. 2013. "Preparing Seminaries for Collaborative Work" in Strengthening Families and Ending Abuse: Churches and their Leaders Look to the Future, edited by N. Nason-Clark, B. Fisher-Townsend and V. Fahlberg, 40–64. Eugene, OR: Wipf and Stock.

Mederos, F., D. Gamache, and E. Pence. 1999. Domestic Violence and Probation. www.vaw.umn.edu/BWJP/probationV.htm.

Mejia, X. E. 2005. "Gender Matters: Working with Adult Male Survivors of Trauma." *Journal of Counseling & Development* 83: 29–40.

Michalski, J. H. 2004. "Making Sociological Sense out of Trends in Intimate Partner Violence—The Social Structure of Violence against Women." *Violence against Women* 10.6: 652–75.

Migliaccio, T. A. 2002. "Abused Husbands: A Narrative Analysis." *Journal of Family Issues* 23.1: 26–52.

Mirchandani, R. 2005. "What's So Special about Specialized Courts? The State and Social Change in Salt Lake City's Domestic Violence Court." *Law & Society Review* 39.2: 379–418.

Mulford, C., and P. Giordano. 2008. Teen Dating Violence: A Closer Look at Adolescent Romantic Relationships. www.nij.gov/journals/261/teen-dating-violence.htm.

Nansel, T. R., M. D. Overpeck, and D. L. Haynie. 2003. "Relationships between Bullying and Violence among US Youth." *Archives of Pediatrics & Adolescent Medicine* 157.4: 348–53.

Nason-Clark, N. 1995. "Conservative Protestants and Violence against Women: Exploring the Rhetoric and the Response." In *Sex, Lies and Sanctity: Deviance and Religion in Contemporary America,* edited by M. J. Neitz and M. Goldman, 109–30. Bingley, UK: Emerald Group.

———. 1997. *The Battered Wife: How Christians Confront Family Violence.* Louisville, KY: Westminster/John Knox.

———. 1998a. "Canadian Evangelical Church Women and Responses to Family Violence." In *Religion in a Changing World: Comparative Studies in Sociology,* edited by M. Cousineau, 57–65. Westport, CT: Greenwood.

———. 1998b. "The Evangelical Family Is Sacred . . . but Is It Safe?" In *Healing the Hurting: Giving Hope and Help to Abused Women,* edited by C. Clark Kroeger and James R. Beck, 109–25. Grand Rapids, MI: Baker.

———. 2000. "Making the Sacred Safe: Woman Abuse and Communities of Faith." *Sociology of Religion* 61.4: 349–68.

———. 2001. "Woman Abuse and Faith Communities: Religion, Violence, and the Provision of Social Welfare." In *Religion and Social Policy,* edited by P. Nesbitt, 128–45. Walnut Creek, CA: Rowman & Littlefield.

———. 2005. "Linking Research and Social Action: Violence, Religion and the Family: A Case for Public Sociology." *Review of Religious Research* 46.3: 221–34.

———. 2008. "When Terror Strikes the Christian Home." In *Beyond Abuse in the Christian Home: Raising Voices for Change,* edited by C. Clark Kroeger, N. Nason-Clark, and B. Fisher-Townsend, 167–83. Eugene, OR: Wipf and Stock.

———. 2014. "Talking about Domestic Violence and Communities of Faith in the Public Sphere: Celebrations and Challenges." In *Religion in the Public Sphere,* edited by S. Lefebvre and L. Beaman, 149–170. Toronto, ON: University of Toronto Press.

Nason-Clark, N., and C. Clark Kroeger. 2004. *Refuge from Abuse: Hope and Healing for Abused Christian Women.* Downers Grove, IL: InterVarsity.

Nason-Clark, N., C. Clark Kroeger, and B. Fisher-Townsend, eds. 2011. *Responding to Abuse in Christian Homes.* Eugene, OR: Wipf and Stock.

Nason-Clark, N., and B. Fisher-Townsend. 2005. "Chapter 10: Gender." In *Handbook on Sociology of Religion and Social Institutions,* edited by H. R. Ebaugh, 207–23. New York: Springer.

Nason-Clark, N., B. Fisher-Townsend, and V. Fahlberg, eds. 2013. *Strengthening Families and Ending Abuse: Churches and Their Leaders Look to the Future.* Eugene, OR: Wipf and Stock.

Nason-Clark, N., B. Fisher-Townsend, S. McMullin, and C. Holtmann. 2013. "Life Stories of Religious Men Who Act Abusively: Elements of the Coordinated Community Response." In *Strengthening Families and Ending Abuse: Churches and*

Their Leaders Look to the Future, edited by N. Nason-Clark, B. Fisher-Townsend, and V. Fahlberg, 40–64. Eugene, OR: Wipf and Stock.

Nason-Clark, N. and C. Holtmann. 2013. "Thinking about Cooperation and Collaboration Between Diverse Religious and Secular Community Responses to Domestic Violence." In *Varieties of Religious Establishment*, edited by L. Beaman and W. F. Sullivan, 187–200. Farnham, Surrey (UK): Ashgate.

Nason-Clark, N., S. McMullin, V. Fahlberg, and D. Schaefer. 2011. "Referrals between Clergy and Community-Based Resources: Challenges and Opportunities." In *Responding to Abuse in Christian Homes*, edited by N. Nason-Clark, C. Clark Kroeger, and B. Fisher-Townsend, 215–30. Eugene, OR: Wipf and Stock.

Nason-Clark, N., N. Murphy, B. Fisher-Townsend, and L. Ruff. 2003. "An Overview of the Characteristics or the Clients at a Faith-Based Batterers' Intervention Program." *Journal of Religion and Abuse* 5.4: 51–72.

NCIPC. 2005. Intimate Partner Violence: Fact Sheet. Centers for Disease Control and Prevention. www.cdc.gov/violenceprevention/nisvs/index.html.

National Criminal Justice Reference Service. 1984. Inmate Road Crew Survey. https://www.ncjrs.gov/App/publications/abstract.aspx?ID=99778.

National Institute of Justice, US. 2008. Domestic Violence Cases: What Research Shows about Arrest and Dual Arrest Rates. http://nij.gov/nij/publications/dv-dual-arrest-222679/introduction/arrest-laws.htm.

Neilson, L. 2009. *Domestic Violence and Family Law in Canada: A Handbook for Judges*. Ottawa: National Judicial Institute.

Neitz, M. J. 2000. "Queering the Dragonfest: Changing Sexualities in a Post-Patriarchal Religion." *Sociology of Religion* 61.4: 369–92.

Newmark, L., M. Rempel, K. Diffily, and K. M. Kane. 2001. *Specialized Felony Domestic Violence Courts: Lessons on Implementation and Impacts from the Kings County Experience*. Washington, DC: Urban Institute, Justice Policy Center.

O'Keefe, M. 2005. In Brief: Teen Dating Violence: A Review of Risk Factors and Prevention Efforts. http://www.vawnet.org/applied-research-papers/print-document.php?doc_id=409

Olweus, D. 1993. *Bullying at School: What We Know and What We Can Do*. Malden, MA: Blackwell.

Orsi, R. A. 1996. *Thank You, St. Jude*. New Haven, CT: Yale University Press.

Owens, J. 2011. "Notes from the Shelter," In *Responding to Abuse in Christian Homes*, edited by N. Nason-Clark, C. Clark Kroeger, and B. Fisher-Townsend, 147–57. Eugene, OR: Wipf and Stock.

Panchanadeswaran, S., L. Ting, J. Burke, P. O'Campo, K. McDonnell, and A. C. Gielen. 2010. "Profiling Abusive Men Based on Women's Self-Reports: Findings from a Sample of Urban Low-Income Minority Women." *Violence against Women* 16.3: 313–27.

Papadakaki, M., G. Tzamalouka, S. Chatzifotiou, J. Chliaoutakis. 2009. "Seeking for Risk of Intimate Partner Violence (IPV) in a Greek National Sample: The Role of Self-Esteem," *Journal of Interpersonal Violence* 24.5: 732–50.

Payne, A. A. 2009. "Girls, Boys and Schools: Gender Differences in the Relationships between School-Related Factors and Student Deviance." *Criminology* 47.4: 1167–1200.

Payne, A. A., D. C. Gottfredson, and G. D. Gottfredson. 2003. "Schools as Communities: The Relationships among Communal School Organization, Student Bonding, and School Disorder." *Criminology* 41.3: 749–77.

Pence, E. L., and M. Paymar. 1986. *Power and Control: Tactics of Men Who Batter.* Duluth: Minnesota Program Development.

Post, L. A., J. Klevens, C. Maxwell, G. Shelley, and E. Ingram. 2010. "An Examination of Whether Coordinated Community Responses Affect Intimate Partner Violence." *Journal of Interpersonal Violence* 25.1: 75–93.

Prairie Research Associates. 1994. *Manitoba Spouse Abuse Tracking Project: Final Report.* Ottawa: Department of Justice.

Ptacek, J. 1996. "The Tactics and Strategies of Men Who Batter. Testimony from Women Seeking Restraining Orders." In *Violence Between Intimate Partners: Patterns, Causes and Effects* edited by A.P. Cardacelli, 106–123. Boston, MA: Allyn and Bacon.

Rebovich, D. J. 1996. "Prosecution Response to Domestic Violence: Results of a Survey of Large Jursidictions." In *Do Arrests and Restraining Orders Work?* edited by E. S. Buzawa and C. G. Buzawa, 176–91. Thousand Oaks, CA: Sage.

Renzetti, C. 2011. "Toward a Better Understanding of Lesbian Battering." In *Shifting the Center: Understanding Contemporary Families,* edited by S. J. Ferguson, 454–66. New York: McGraw-Hill.

Rogers, B., G. Mcgee, A. Vann, N. Thompson, and O. J. Williams. 2003. "Substance Abuse and Domestic Violence: Stories of Practitioners That Address the Co-occurrence among Battered Women." *Violence against Women* 9.5: 590–98.

Ronel, N., and H. Claridge. 2003. "The Powerlessness of Control: A Unifying Model for the Treatment of Male Battering and Substance Addiction." *Journal of Social Work Practice in the Addictions* 3.1: 57–76.

Rosenbaum, A., and P. A. Leisring. 2003. "Beyond Power and Control: Towards an Understanding of Partner Abusive Men." *Journal of Comparative Family Studies* 34.1: 7–22.

Safford, M.C. and M. Warr. 1993. "A Reconceptualization of General and Specific Deterrence." *Journal of Research in Crime and Deliquency* 30.2: 123–135.

Salvaggio, F. 2002. "K-Court: The Feminist Pursuit of an Interdisciplinary Approach to Domestic Violence." *Appeal: Review of Current Law and Law Reform* 8: 6–17.

Saunders, D. G., and R. M. Hamill. 2003. *Violence against Women: Synthesis of Research on Offender Interventions.* Washington, DC: National Institute of Justice.

Schechter, S. 1982. *Women and Male Violence: The Visions and Struggles of the Battered Women's Movement.* Boston: SouthEnd.

Scott, K. L. 2004. "Predictors of Change among Male Batterers: Application of Theories and Review of Empirical Findings." *Trauma, Violence, & Abuse* 5.3: 260–84.

Sevcik, I., M. Rothery, N. Nason-Clark, and R. Pynn. Forthcoming. *Secular and Sacral Communities: Working Together to Address Intimate Partner Violence.* Edmonton: University of Alberta Press.

Sheehy, E. A. 1999. "Legal Responses to Violence against Women in Canada." *Canadian Woman Studies* 19.1/2: 62–73.

Sherman, L., and R. A. Berk. 1984. "The Specific Deterrent Effects of Arrest for Domestic Assault." *American Sociological Review* 49: 261–72.

Sherman, L., J. Schmidt, and D. Rogan. 1992. *Policing Domestic Violence: Experiments and Dilemmas.* New York: Free Press.

Sherman, L. and D. Smith. 1992. "Crime, Punishment and Stake in Conformity: Legal and Informal Control of Domestic Violence," *American Sociological Review* 37: 680–690.

Simmons, C. A., M. Farrer, K. Frazer, and M. J. Thompson. 2011. "From the Voices of Women: Facilitating Survivor Access to IPV Services." *Violence against Women* 17.10: 1226–43.

Simpson, S. S., L. A. Bouffard, J. Garner, and L. Hickman. 2006. "The Influence of Legal Reform on the Probability of Arrest in Domestic Violence Cases." *Justice Quarterly* 23.3: 297–316.

Sloan, F., A. Platt, L. Chepke, and C. Blevins. 2013. "Deterring Domestic Violence: Do Criminal Sanctions Reduce Repeat Offenses?" *Journal of Risk & Uncertainty* 46.1: 51–80.

Smith, A. 2000. "It's My Decision Isn't It? A Research Note on Battered Women's Perceptions of Mandatory Intervention Laws." *Violence against Women* 6.12: 1384–402.

Sokoloff, N. J., and I. Dupont. 2005. "Domestic Violence at the Intersections of Race, Class, and Gender." *Violence against Women* 11.1: 38–64.

Spickard, J., S. Landres, and M. McGuire. 2002. *Personal Knowledge and Beyond: Reshaping the Ethnography of Religion.* New York: New York University Press.

Statistics Canada. 2005. *Family Violence in Canada: A Statistical Profile.* Ottawa: Canadian Centre for Justice Statistics.

———. 2009a. *Incident-Based Uniform Crime Reporting Survey.* Ottawa: Canadian Centre for Justice Statistics.

———. 2009b. "Self-reported Violent Delinquency and the Influence of School, Neighbourhood and Student Characteristics." Ottawa: Canadian Centre for Justice Statistics, Catalogue no. 85-561-M, no. 17. http://www.statcan.gc.ca/pub/85-561-m/85-561-m2009017-eng.pdf.

———. 2010. "Children and Youth." Canadian Centre for Justice Statistics Profile Series. http://www5.statcan.gc.ca/bsolc/olc-cel/olc-cel?lang=eng&catno=85F0033M.

Stephens, B. J., and P. G. Sinden. 2000. "Victims' Voices: Domestic Assault Victims' Perceptions of Police Demeanor." *Journal of Interpersonal Violence* 15.5: 534–47.

Stith, S. M., K. H. Rosen, K. A. Middleton, A. L. Busch, K. Lundenberg, and R. P. Carlton. 2000. "The Intergenerational Transmission of Spouse Abuse: A Meta-Analysis." *Journal of Marriage and Family* 62.3: 640–55.

Straus, M. A., R. J. Gelles, and S. K. Steinmetz. 1980. *Behind Closed Doors: Violence in American Families.* New Brunswick, NJ: Transaction.

Straus, M. A., and G. K. Kantor. 1994. "Corporal Punishment of Adolescents by Parents: A Risk Factor in the Epidemiology of Depression, Suicide, Alcohol Abuse, Child Abuse, and Wife Beating." *Adolescence* 29: 543–61.

Stuart, G. L. 2005. "Improving Violence Intervention Outcomes by Integrating Alcohol Treatment." *Journal of Interpersonal Violence* 20.4: 388–93.

Sullivan, W. Fallers. 2009. *Prison Religion: Faith-Based Reform and the Constitution.* Princeton, NJ: Princeton University Press.

Sykes, G. M., and D. Matza. 1957. "Techniques of Neutralization: A Theory of Delinquency." *American Sociological Review* 22: 644–70.

Teague, R., P. Mazerolle, M. Legosz, and J. Sanderson. 2008. "Linking Childhood Exposure to Physical Abuse and Adult Offending: Examining Mediating Factors and Gendered Relationships. *Justice Quarterly* 25.2: 313–48.

TeenDVMonth.org. 2013. http://www.teendvmonth.org/about-teendvmonth.

Thistlewaite, A., J. Wooldredge, and D. Gibbs. 1998. "Severity of Dispositions and Domestic Violence Recidivism." *Crime & Delinquency* 44.3: 388–98.

Tiet, Q., and D. Huizinga. 2002. "Dimensions of the Construct of Resilience and Adaptation among Inner-City Youth." *Journal of Adolescent Research* 17.3: 260–76.

Tiet, Q., D. Huizinga, and H. Byrnes. 2010. "Predictors of Resilience among Inner City Youths." *Journal of Child and Family Studies* 19.3: 360–78.

Tiet, Q., H. R. Bird, M. Davies, C. Hoven, P. Cohen, P. Jensen and S. Goodman 1998. "Adverse Life Events and Resilience." *Journal of the American Academy of Child and Adolescent Psychiatry* 37.11: 1191–1200.

Tilley, D. S., and M. Brackley. 2005. "Men Who Batter Intimate Partners: A Grounded Theory Study of the Development of Male Violence in Intimate Partner Relationships." *Issues in Mental Health Nursing* 26: 281–97.

Timmins, L., ed. 1995. *Listening to the Thunder: Advocates Talk about the Battered Women's Movement.* Vancouver, BC: Women's Research Center.

Todahl, J., D. Linville, A. Tuttle Shamblin, and D. Ball. 2012. "Client Narratives about Experiences with a Multicouple Treatment Program for Intimate Partner Violence." *Journal of Marital and Family Therapy* 38.s1: 150–67.

Tolman, R. M., and L. W. Bennett. 1990. "A Review of Quantitative Research on Men Who Batter." *Journal of Interpersonal Violence* 5.1: 87–118.

Tsai, B. 2000. "The Trend toward Specialized Domestic Violence Courts: Improvements on an Effective Innovation." *Fordham Law Review* 68.4: 1285–1327.

Tzamalouka, G. S., S. K. Parlalis, P. Soultatou, M. Papadakaki, and J. E. Chliaoutakis. 2007. "Applying the Concept of Lifestyle in Association with Aggression and Violence in Greek Cohabitating Couples." *Journal of Aggressive Behavior* 33: 73–85.

Uekert, B. K. 2003. "The Value of Coordinated Community Responses." *Criminology and Public Policy* 133: 133–36.

Ursel, J., L. Tutty, and J. LeMaistre. 2008. *What's Law Got to Do with It? The Law, Specialized Courts and Domestic Violence in Canada.* Toronto: Cormorant.

Vallely, C., A. Robinson, M. Burton, J. Tregidga. 2005. Evaluation of Domestic Violence Pilot Sites at Caerphilly (Gwent) and Croydon 2004/05, Final Report. http://www.cps.gov.uk/publications/docs/eval_dv_pilots_04-05.pdf.

Van de Veen, S. L. 2004. "Some Canadian Problem Solving Court Processes." Excerpt. *Canadian Bar Review* 3.1.

Ventura, L. and G. Davis. 2005. "Domestic Violence: Court Case Conviction and Recidivism." *Violence against Women* 11.2: 255–277.

Vest, J. R., T. K. Catlin, J. J. Chen, and R. C. Brownson. 2002. "Multistate Analysis of Factors Associated with Intimate Partner Violence." *American Journal of Preventive Medicine* 22.3: 156–64.

Violence against Women Online Resources. 2010. Offline as of this writing, but see http://www.ovw.usdoj.gov.

Vittes, K. A., D. W. Webster, S. Frattarole, B. Claire, and G. J. Wintemute. 2013. "Removing Guns from Batterers: Findings from a Pilot Survey of Domestic Violence Restraining Order Recipients." *Violence against Women* 19.5: 602–16.

Voisin, D., and J. Hong. 2012. "A Meditational Model Linking Witnessing Intimate Partner Violence and Bullying Behaviors and Victimization among Youth." *Educational Psychology Review* 24.4: 479–98.

Weaver, A. J. 1993. "Psychological Trauma: What Clergy Need to Know." *Pastoral Psychology* 41: 385–408.

Wei, E., R. Loeber, and M. Stouthamer-Loeber. 2002. "How Many Offspring Born to Teenage Fathers Are Produced by Repeat Serious Delinquents." *Criminal Behavior and Mental Health* 12: 83–98.

Weiss, J. A., J. MacMullin, R. Waechter, and C. Wekerle. 2011. "Child Maltreatment, Adolescent Attachment Style, and Dating Violence: Considerations in Youths with Borderline-to-Mild Intellectual Disability." *International Journal of Mental Health and Addiction* 9.5: 555–76.

Whipple, V. 1987. "Counseling Battered Women from Fundamentalist Churches." *Journal for Marital and Family Therapy* 13.3: 251–58.

Wiesner, M., and M. Windle. 2004. "Assessing Covariates of Adolescent Delinquency Trajectories: A Latent Growth Mixture Modeling Approach." *Journal of Youth & Adolescence* 33.5: 431–42.

Williams, K. R. 2005. "Arrest and Intimate Partner Violence: Toward a More Complete Application of Deterrence Theory." *Aggression & Violent Behavior* 10.6: 660–79.

Willson, P., J. McFarlane, A. Malecha, K. Watson, D. Lemmey, P. Schultz, J. Gist, and N. Fredland. 2000. "Severity of Violence against Women by Intimate Partners and Associated Use of Alcohol and/or Illicit Drugs by the Perpetrator." *Journal of Interpersonal Violence* 15.9: 996–1008.

Wilson, J.Q. 1997. *Moral Judgment: Does the Abuse Excuse Threaten our Legal System?* New York: Harper.

Woldoff, R. A., and M. G. Cina. 2007. "Regular Work, Underground Jobs, and Hustling: An Examination of Paternal Work and Father Involvement." *Fathering: A Journal of Theory, Research, & Practice about Men as Fathers* 5.3: 153–73.

Wolf, M. E., U. Ly, M. A. Hobart, and M. A. Kernic. 2003. "Barriers to Seeking Police Help for Intimate Partner Violence." *Journal of Family Violence* 18.2: 121–29.

Wood, J. T. 2004. "Monsters and Victims: Male Felons' Accounts of Intimate Partner Violence." *Journal of Social and Personal Relationships* 21.5: 555–76.

Wooldredge, J. D. 1998. "Inmate Lifestyles and Opportunities for Victimization." *Journal of Research in Crime and Delinquency* 35.4: 480–502.

Worden, A. P., and B. E. Carlson. 2005. "Attitudes and Beliefs about Domestic Violence: Results of a Public Opinion Survey." *Journal of Interpersonal Violence* 20.10: 1219–43.

World Health Organization. 2002. http://www.who.int/topics/violence/en/.

Wright, J. P., and F. T. Cullen. 2004. "Employment, Peers, and Life-Course Transitions." *Justice Quarterly* 21.4: 183–205.

Yarbrough, D. N., and P. W. Blanton. 2000. "Socio-demographic Indicators of Intervention Program Completion with the Male Court-Referred Perpetrator of Partner Abuse." *Journal of Criminal Justice* 28.6: 517–26.

Yllö, K. 1988. "Political and Methodological Debates in Wife Abuse Research." In *Feminist Perspectives on Wife Abuse*, edited by K. Yllö and M. Bograd, 28–50. Newbury Park, CA: Sage.

———. 2005. "Through a Feminist Lens: Gender, Diversity and Violence: Extending the Feminist Framework." In *Current Controversies on Family Violence*, edited by D. Loseke, R. Gelles, and M. Cavanaugh, 19–34. Thousand Oaks, CA: Sage.

SUBJECT AND PARTICIPANT INDEX